Baby Blues® Scrapbook No.6

Night of the Living Dad

Baby Blues® Scrapbook No. 6

Night of the Living Dad

By Rick Kirkman & Jerry Scott

Andrews and McMeel
A Universal Press Syndicate Company
Kansas City

For information write Andrews and McMeel, a Universal Press Syndicate Company, 4520 Main Street, Kansas City, Missouri 64111.

ISBN: 0-8362-1310-6

Library of Congress Catalog Card Number: 95-80754

00 01 BAH 10 9 8 7 6

Other Baby Blues Scrapbooks from Andrews and McMeel

Guess Who Didn't Take a Nap?

I Thought Labor Ended When the Baby Was Born

We Are Experiencing Parental Difficulties ... Please Stand By

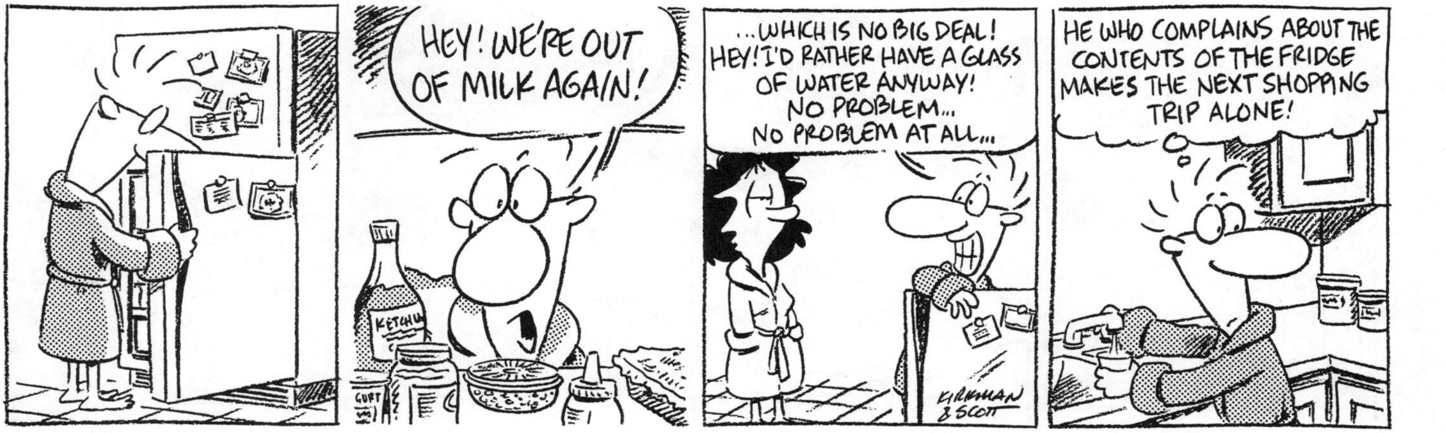
HEY! WE'RE OUT OF MILK AGAIN!
...WHICH IS NO BIG DEAL! HEY! I'D RATHER HAVE A GLASS OF WATER ANYWAY! NO PROBLEM... NO PROBLEM AT ALL...
KETCHUP
KIRKMAN & SCOTT
HE WHO COMPLAINS ABOUT THE CONTENTS OF THE FRIDGE MAKES THE NEXT SHOPPING TRIP ALONE!

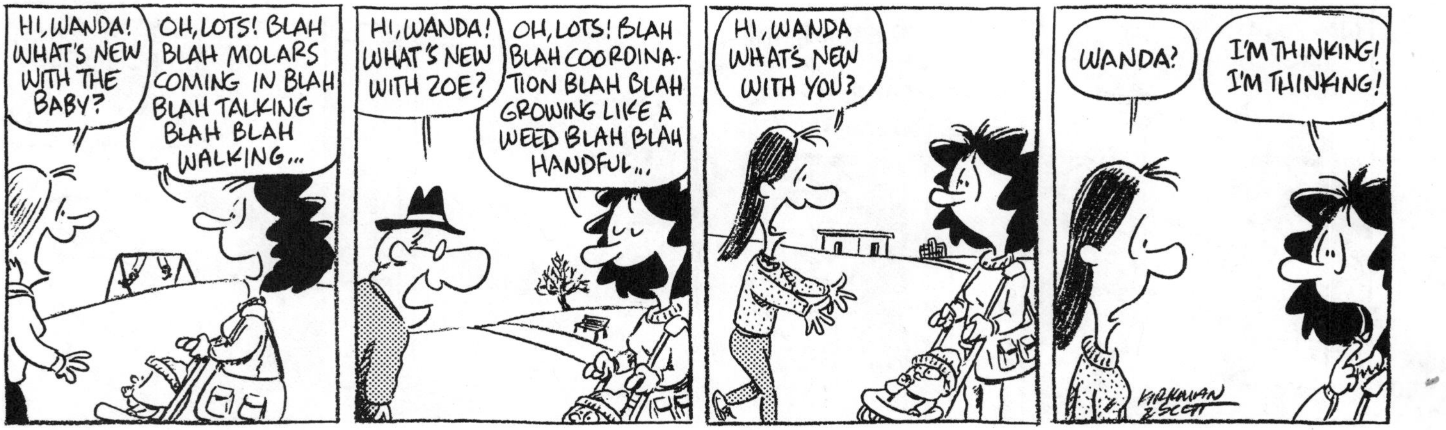
HI, WANDA! WHAT'S NEW WITH THE BABY?
OH, LOTS! BLAH BLAH MOLARS COMING IN BLAH BLAH TALKING BLAH BLAH WALKING...
HI, WANDA! WHAT'S NEW WITH ZOE?
OH, LOTS! BLAH BLAH COORDINATION BLAH BLAH GROWING LIKE A WEED BLAH BLAH HANDFUL...
HI, WANDA WHAT'S NEW WITH YOU?
WANDA?
I'M THINKING! I'M THINKING!
KIRKMAN & SCOTT

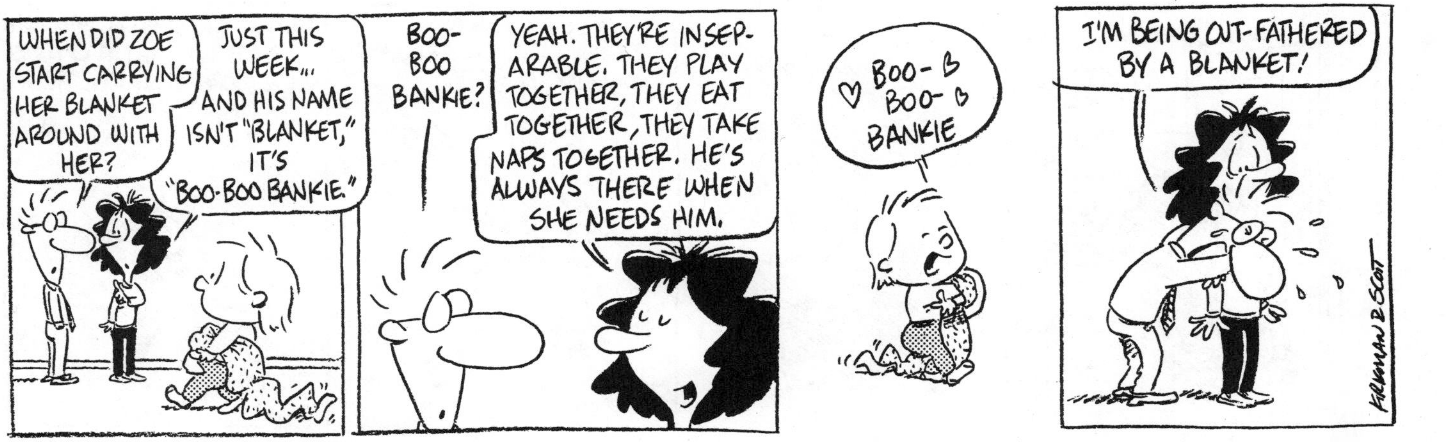
WHEN DID ZOE START CARRYING HER BLANKET AROUND WITH HER?
JUST THIS WEEK... AND HIS NAME ISN'T "BLANKET," IT'S "BOO-BOO BANKIE."
BOO-BOO BANKIE?
YEAH. THEY'RE INSEPARABLE. THEY PLAY TOGETHER, THEY EAT TOGETHER, THEY TAKE NAPS TOGETHER. HE'S ALWAYS THERE WHEN SHE NEEDS HIM.
♡ BOO-♡ BOO-♡ BANKIE
I'M BEING OUT-FATHERED BY A BLANKET!
KIRKMAN & SCOTT

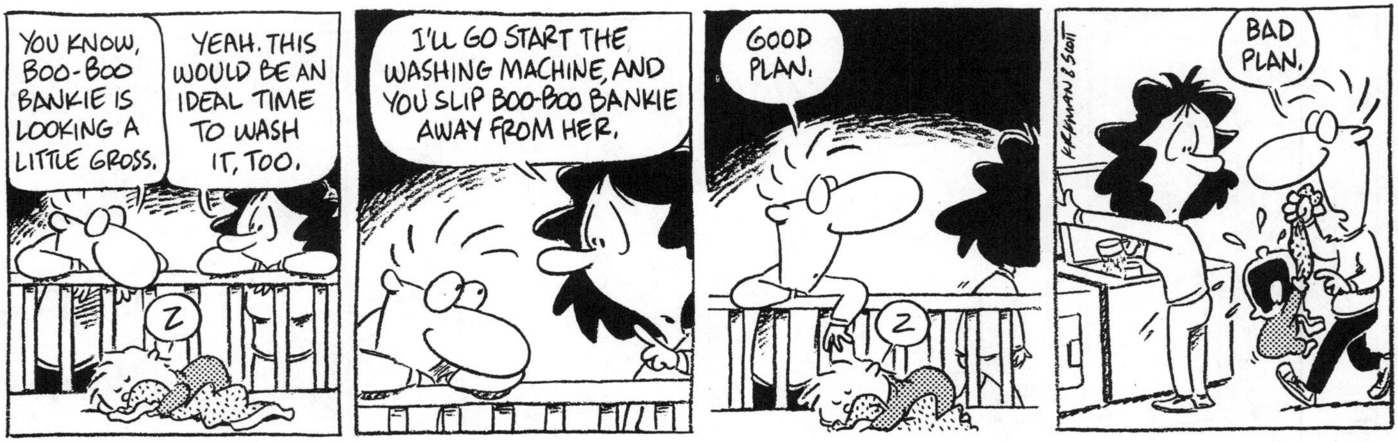
YOU KNOW, BOO-BOO BANKIE IS LOOKING A LITTLE GROSS.
YEAH. THIS WOULD BE AN IDEAL TIME TO WASH IT, TOO.
Z
I'LL GO START THE WASHING MACHINE, AND YOU SLIP BOO-BOO BANKIE AWAY FROM HER.
GOOD PLAN.
Z
BAD PLAN.

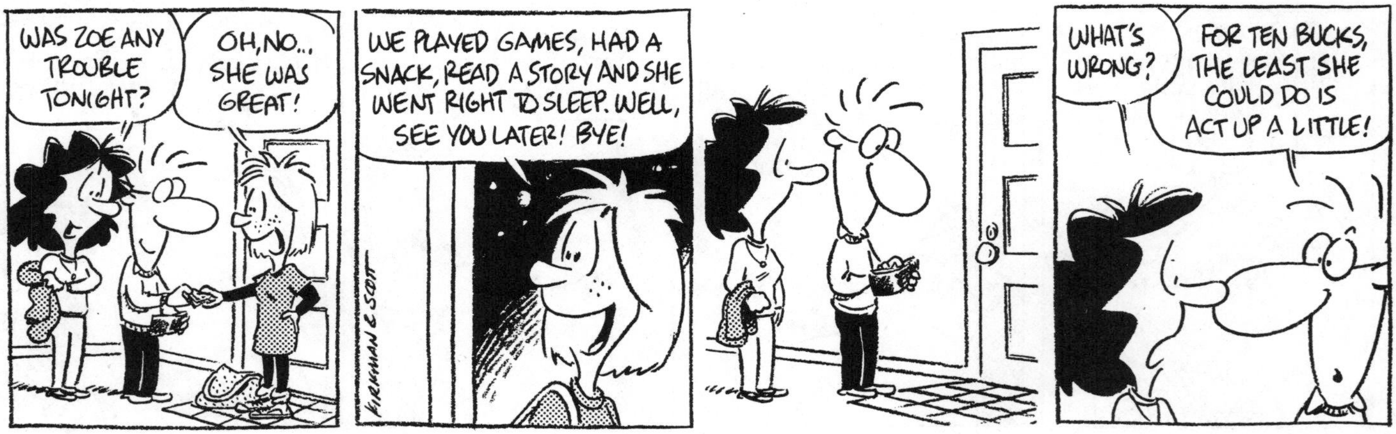
WAS ZOE ANY TROUBLE TONIGHT?
OH, NO... SHE WAS GREAT!
WE PLAYED GAMES, HAD A SNACK, READ A STORY AND SHE WENT RIGHT TO SLEEP. WELL, SEE YOU LATER! BYE!
WHAT'S WRONG?
FOR TEN BUCKS, THE LEAST SHE COULD DO IS ACT UP A LITTLE!

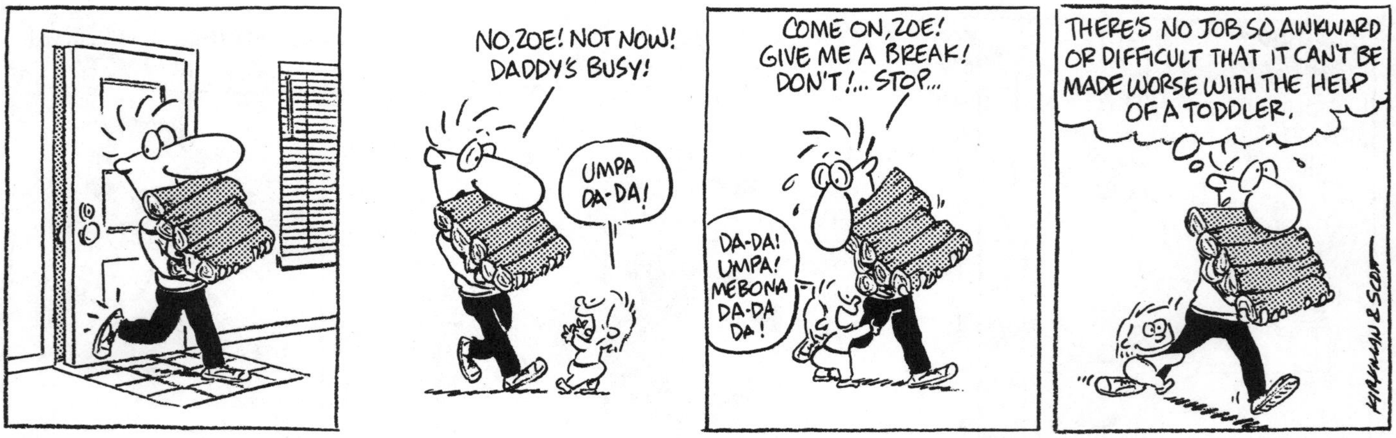
NO, ZOE! NOT NOW! DADDY'S BUSY!
UMPA DA-DA!
COME ON, ZOE! GIVE ME A BREAK! DON'T!... STOP...
DA-DA! UMPA! MEBONA DA-DA DA!
THERE'S NO JOB SO AWKWARD OR DIFFICULT THAT IT CAN'T BE MADE WORSE WITH THE HELP OF A TODDLER.

BABY BLUES®

BY RICK KIRKMAN / JERRY SCOTT

Panel 1: "CAMERA LOADED AND LENS CAP REMOVED?" / "LOADED AND LENS CAP REMOVED!"

Panel 2: "SUBJECT COMBED AND IN POSITION?" / "SUBJECT COMBED AND IN POSITION!"

Panel 3: "FOCUSED?" / "FOCUSED!" / "OKAY... GO!"

Panel 4: SWIP!

Panel 5: SHOOT! / FLASH CLICK!

Panel 7: "THAT WAS REALLY CUTE... I'LL TELL MOM ZOE LOVED THE DRESS," / "THESE AREN'T JUST BABY PHOTOS...THEY'RE EVIDENCE."

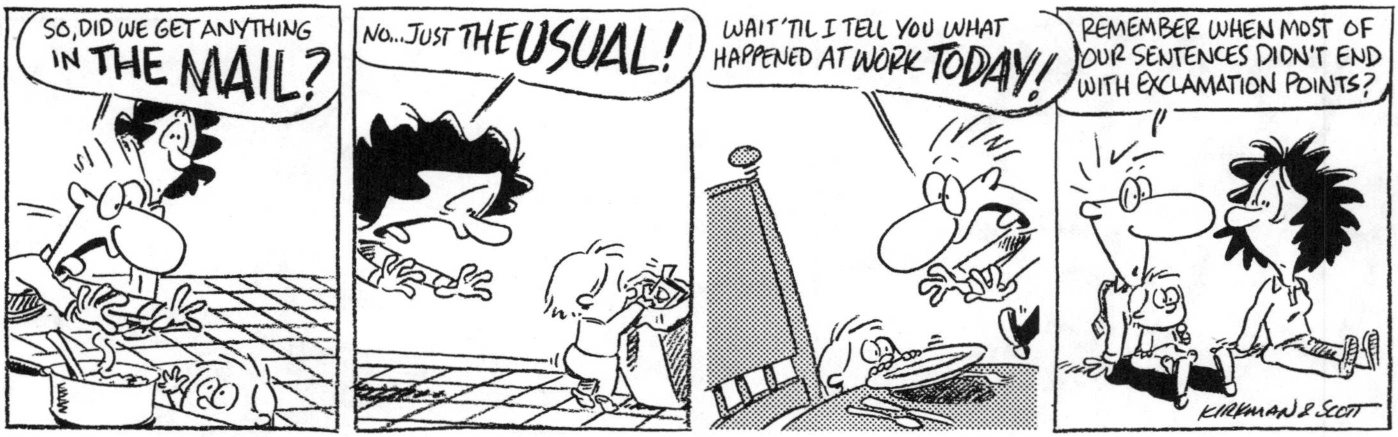
SO, DID WE GET ANYTHING IN THE MAIL?
NO... JUST THE USUAL!
WAIT 'TIL I TELL YOU WHAT HAPPENED AT WORK TODAY!
REMEMBER WHEN MOST OF OUR SENTENCES DIDN'T END WITH EXCLAMATION POINTS?
KIRKMAN & SCOTT

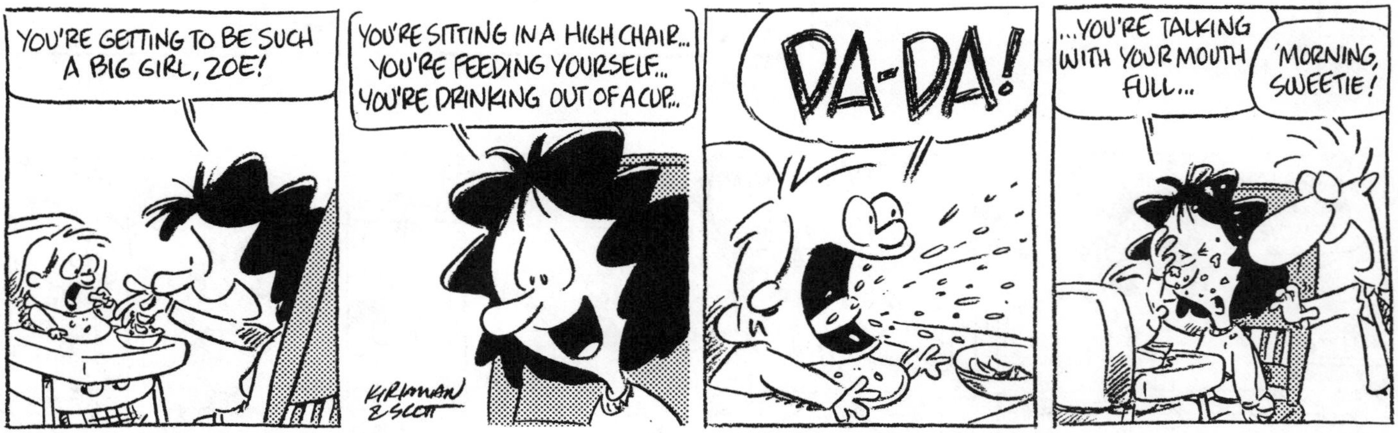
YOU'RE GETTING TO BE SUCH A BIG GIRL, ZOE!
YOU'RE SITTING IN A HIGH CHAIR... YOU'RE FEEDING YOURSELF... YOU'RE DRINKING OUT OF A CUP...
KIRKMAN & SCOTT
DA-DA!
...YOU'RE TALKING WITH YOUR MOUTH FULL...
'MORNING, SWEETIE!

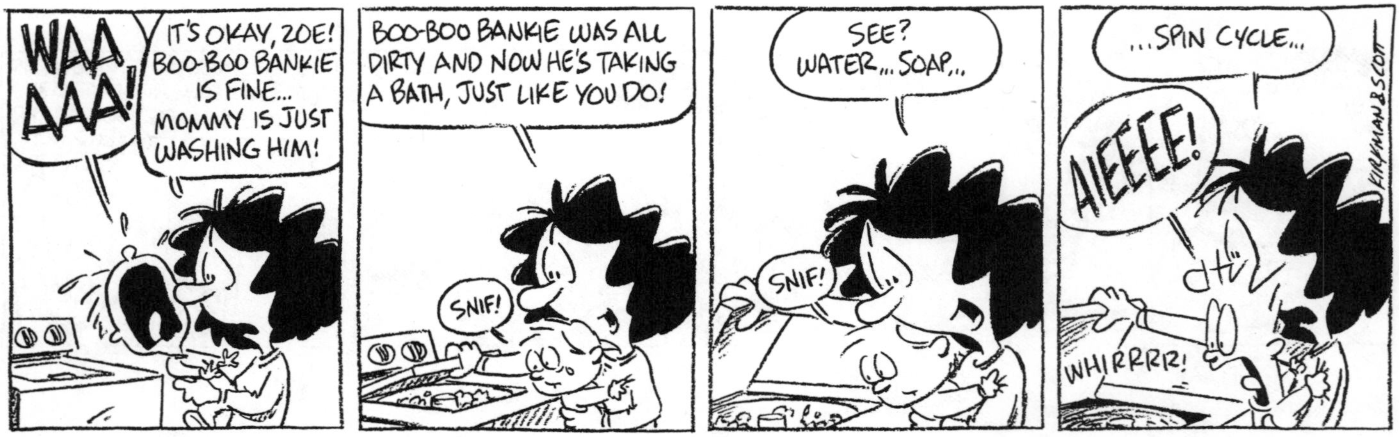
WAA AAA!
IT'S OKAY, ZOE! BOO-BOO BANKIE IS FINE... MOMMY IS JUST WASHING HIM!
BOO-BOO BANKIE WAS ALL DIRTY AND NOW HE'S TAKING A BATH, JUST LIKE YOU DO!
SNIF!
SEE? WATER... SOAP...
SNIF!
...SPIN CYCLE...
AIEEEE!
WHIRRRR!
KIRKMAN & SCOTT

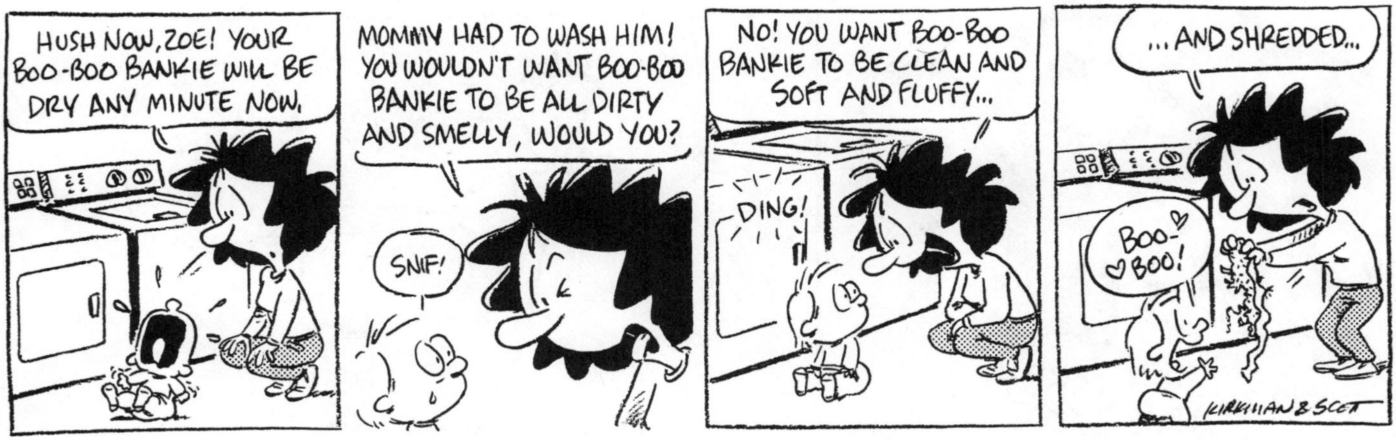
HUSH NOW, ZOE! YOUR BOO-BOO BANKIE WILL BE DRY ANY MINUTE NOW.
MOMMY HAD TO WASH HIM! YOU WOULDN'T WANT BOO-BOO BANKIE TO BE ALL DIRTY AND SMELLY, WOULD YOU?
SNIF!
NO! YOU WANT BOO-BOO BANKIE TO BE CLEAN AND SOFT AND FLUFFY...
DING!
...AND SHREDDED...
BOO-BOO!
KIRKMAN & SCOTT

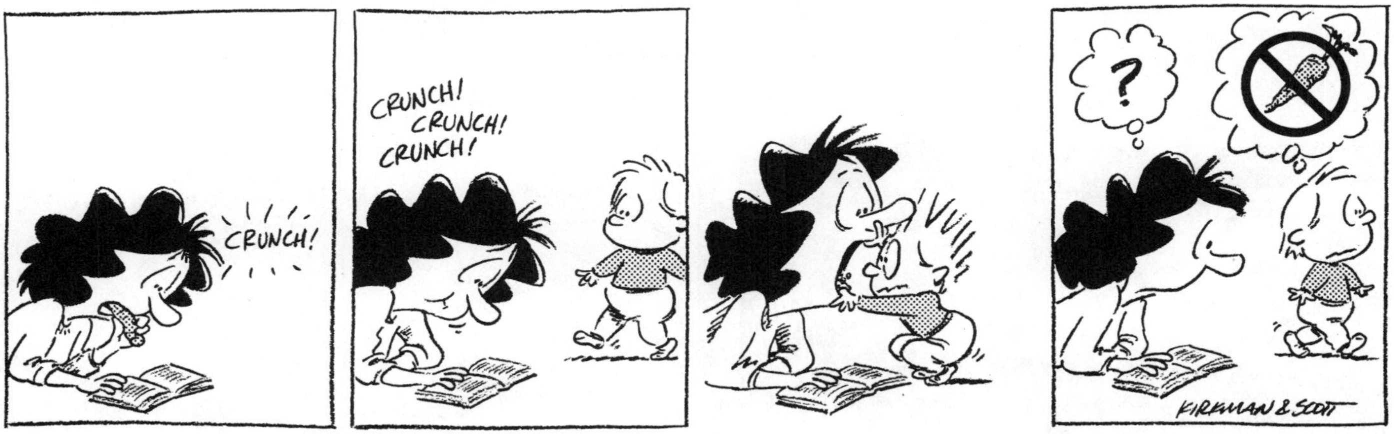
CRUNCH!
CRUNCH! CRUNCH! CRUNCH!
?
KIRKMAN & SCOTT

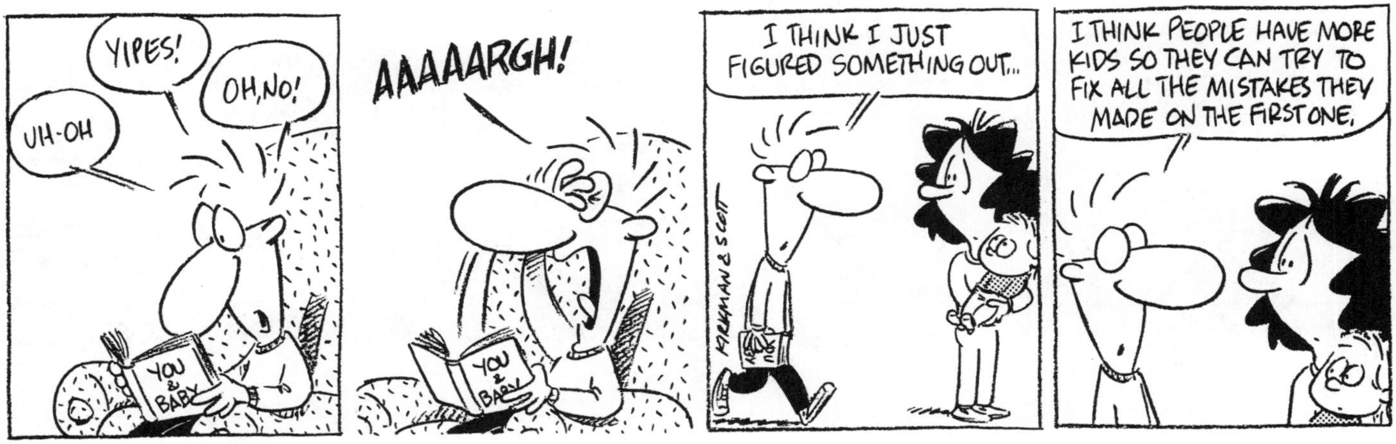
UH-OH
YIPES!
OH, NO!
YOU & BABY
AAAAARGH!
YOU & BABY
I THINK I JUST FIGURED SOMETHING OUT...
KIRKMAN & SCOTT
I THINK PEOPLE HAVE MORE KIDS SO THEY CAN TRY TO FIX ALL THE MISTAKES THEY MADE ON THE FIRST ONE.

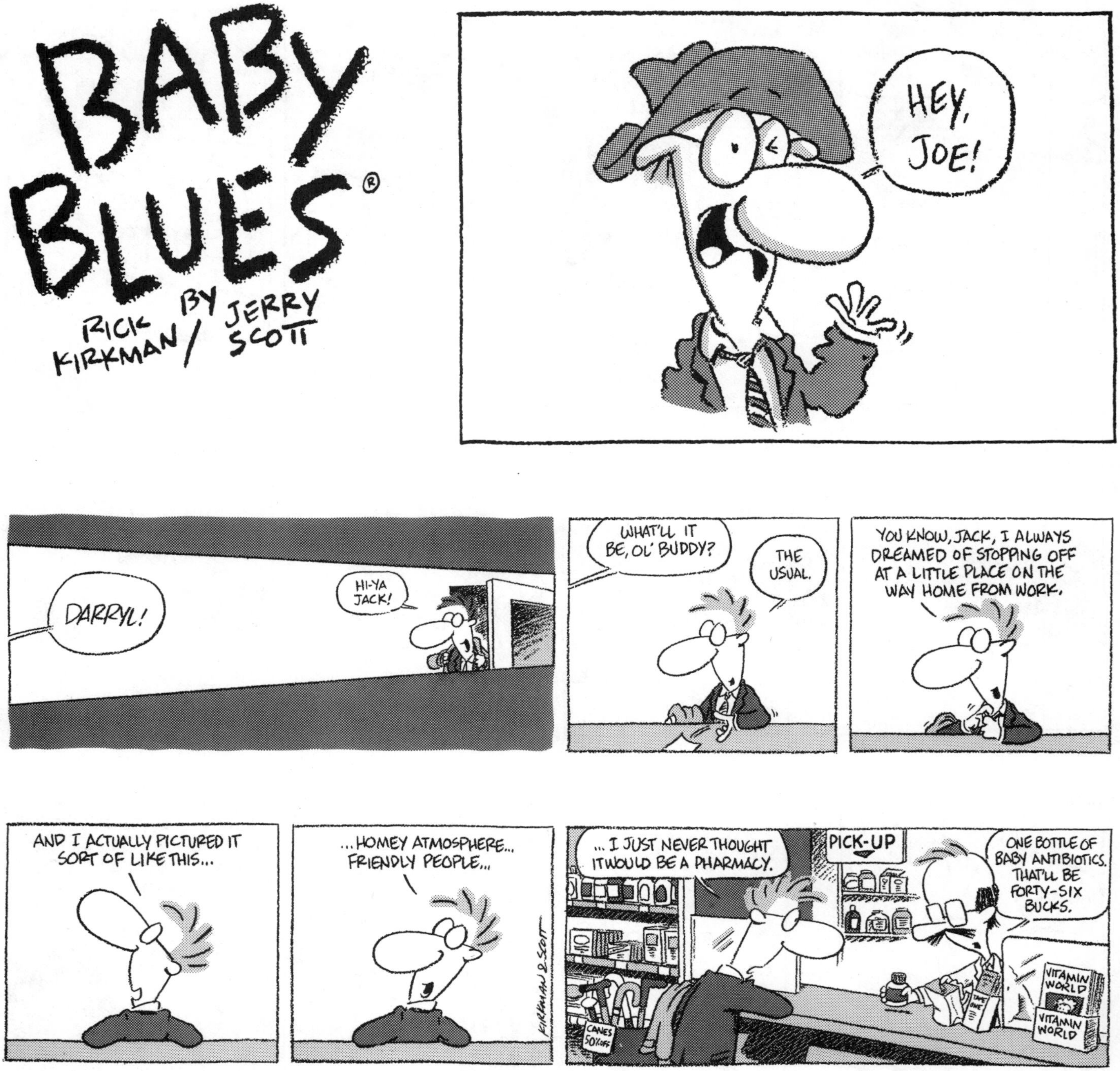
BABY BLUES®
BY RICK KIRKMAN / JERRY SCOTT
HEY, JOE!
DARRYL!
HI-YA JACK!
WHAT'LL IT BE, OL' BUDDY?
THE USUAL.
YOU KNOW, JACK, I ALWAYS DREAMED OF STOPPING OFF AT A LITTLE PLACE ON THE WAY HOME FROM WORK.
AND I ACTUALLY PICTURED IT SORT OF LIKE THIS...
...HOMEY ATMOSPHERE... FRIENDLY PEOPLE...
KIRKMAN & SCOTT
...I JUST NEVER THOUGHT IT WOULD BE A PHARMACY.
PICK-UP
ONE BOTTLE OF BABY ANTIBIOTICS. THAT'LL BE FORTY-SIX BUCKS.
CANES 50% OFF
VITAMIN WORLD
VITAMIN WORLD

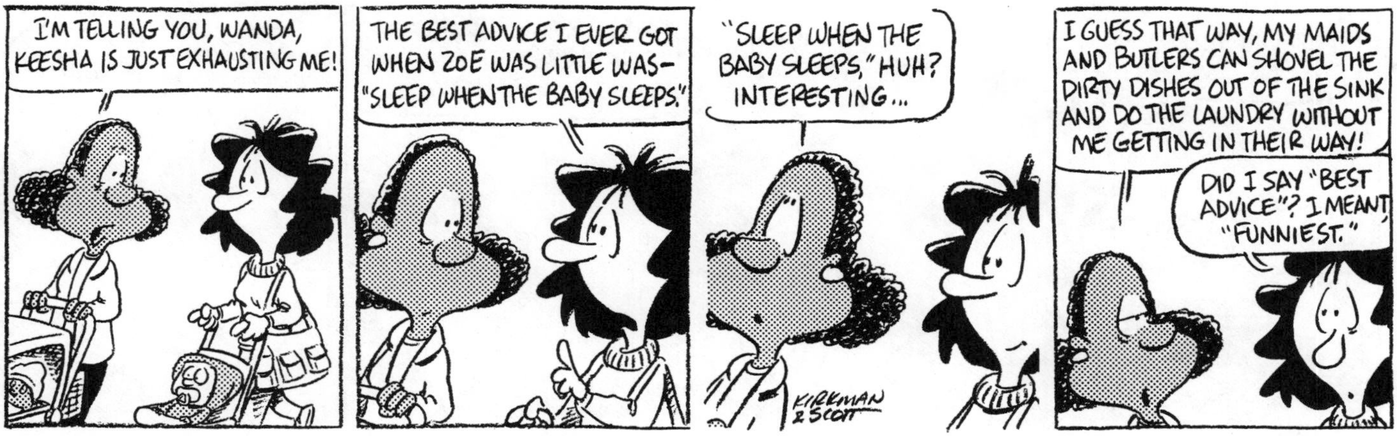
I'M TELLING YOU, WANDA, KEESHA IS JUST EXHAUSTING ME!
THE BEST ADVICE I EVER GOT WHEN ZOE WAS LITTLE WAS- "SLEEP WHEN THE BABY SLEEPS."
"SLEEP WHEN THE BABY SLEEPS," HUH? INTERESTING...
KIRKMAN & SCOTT
I GUESS THAT WAY, MY MAIDS AND BUTLERS CAN SHOVEL THE DIRTY DISHES OUT OF THE SINK AND DO THE LAUNDRY WITHOUT ME GETTING IN THEIR WAY!
DID I SAY "BEST ADVICE"? I MEANT "FUNNIEST."

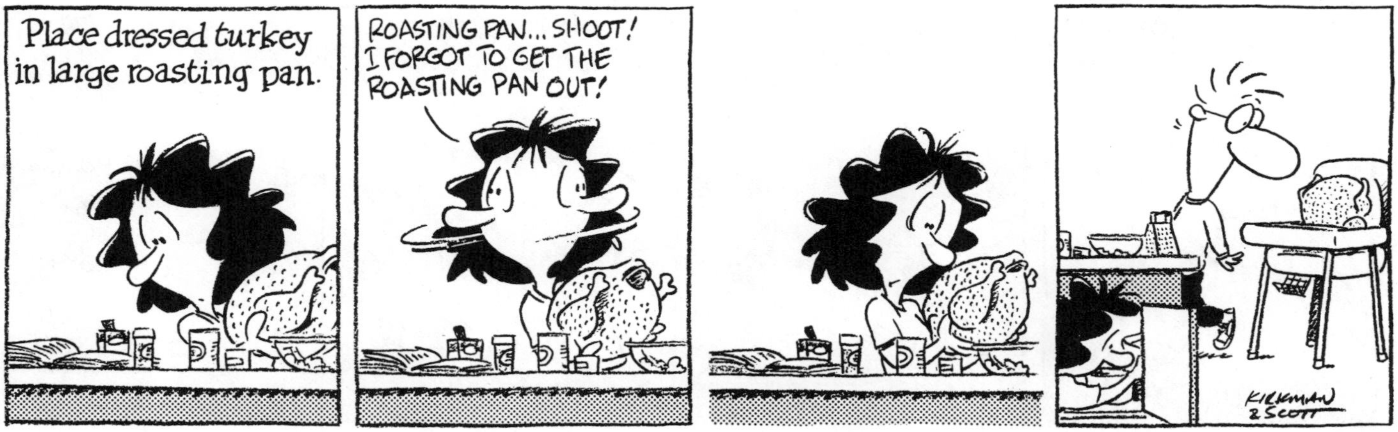
Place dressed turkey in large roasting pan.
ROASTING PAN... SHOOT! I FORGOT TO GET THE ROASTING PAN OUT!
KIRKMAN & SCOTT

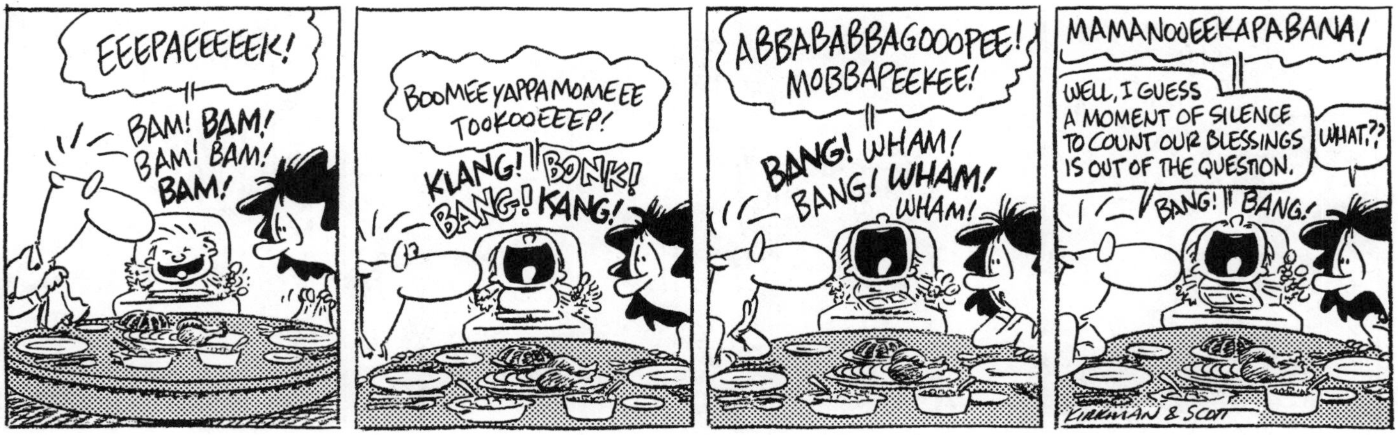
EEEPAEEEEEK!
BAM! BAM! BAM! BAM! BAM!
BOOMEEYAPPAMOMEEE TOOKOOEEEP!
KLANG! BONK! BANG! KANG!
ABBABABBAGOOOPEE! MOBBAPEEKEE!
BANG! WHAM! BANG! WHAM! WHAM!
MAMANOOEEKAPABANA!
WELL, I GUESS A MOMENT OF SILENCE TO COUNT OUR BLESSINGS IS OUT OF THE QUESTION.
WHAT??
BANG! BANG!
KIRKMAN & SCOTT

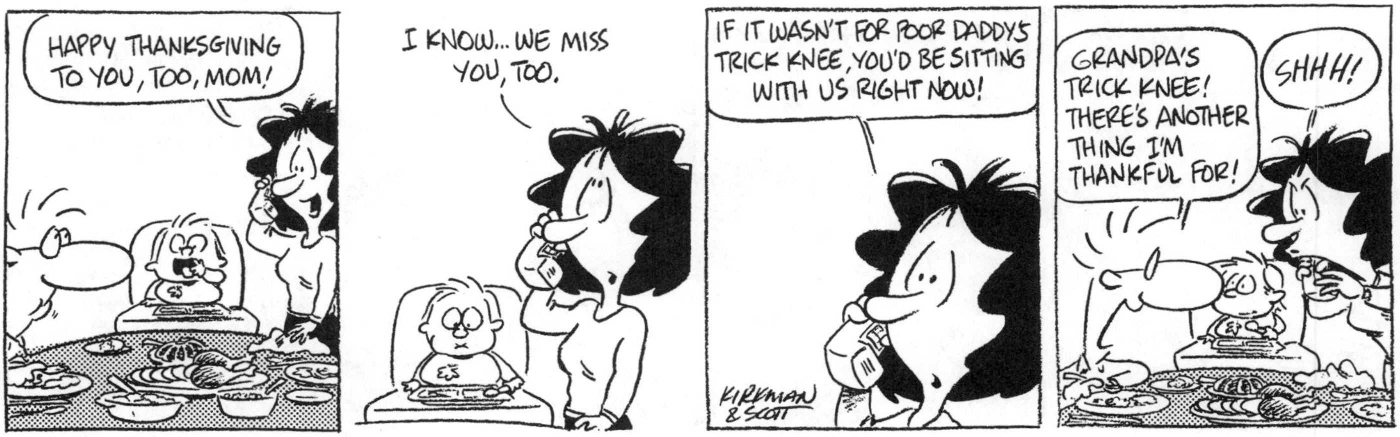
HAPPY THANKSGIVING TO YOU, TOO, MOM!
I KNOW... WE MISS YOU, TOO.
IF IT WASN'T FOR POOR DADDY'S TRICK KNEE, YOU'D BE SITTING WITH US RIGHT NOW!
KIRKMAN & SCOTT
GRANDPA'S TRICK KNEE! THERE'S ANOTHER THING I'M THANKFUL FOR!
SHHH!

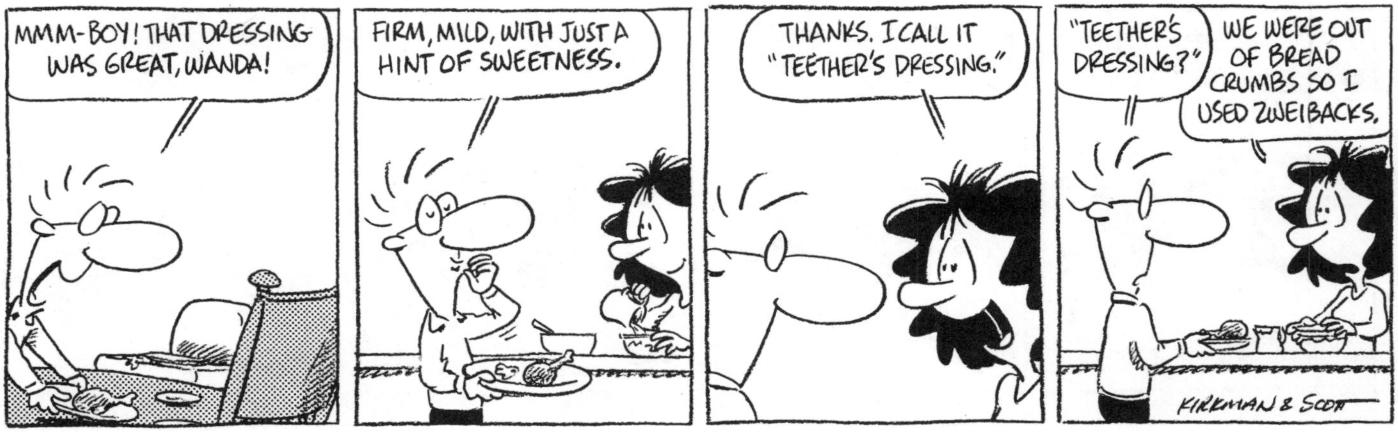
MMM-BOY! THAT DRESSING WAS GREAT, WANDA!
FIRM, MILD, WITH JUST A HINT OF SWEETNESS.
THANKS. I CALL IT "TEETHER'S DRESSING."
"TEETHER'S DRESSING?"
WE WERE OUT OF BREAD CRUMBS SO I USED ZWEIBACKS.
KIRKMAN & SCOTT

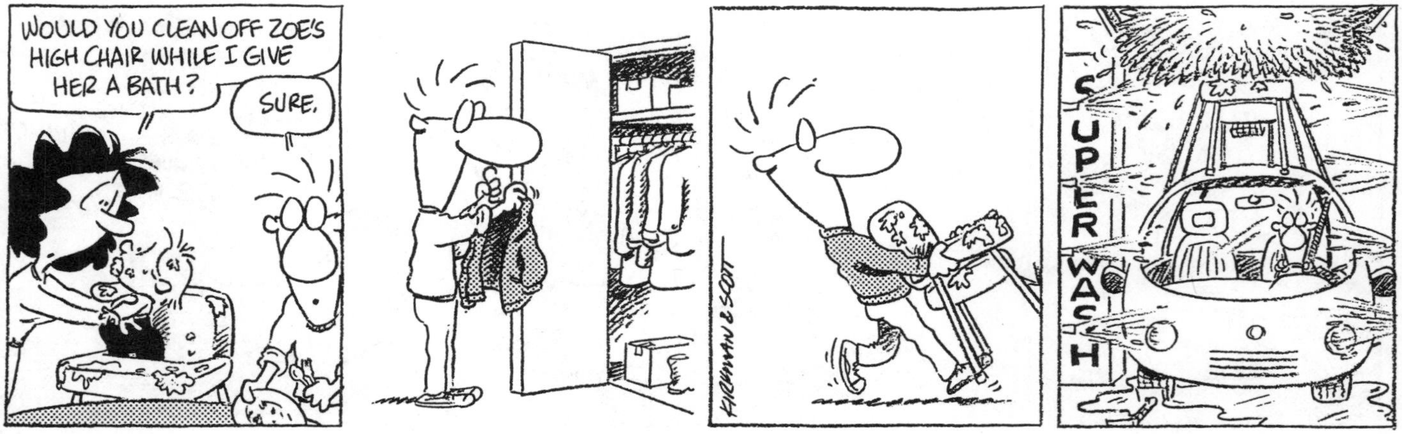
WOULD YOU CLEAN OFF ZOE'S HIGH CHAIR WHILE I GIVE HER A BATH?
SURE.
KIRKMAN & SCOTT
SUPER WASH

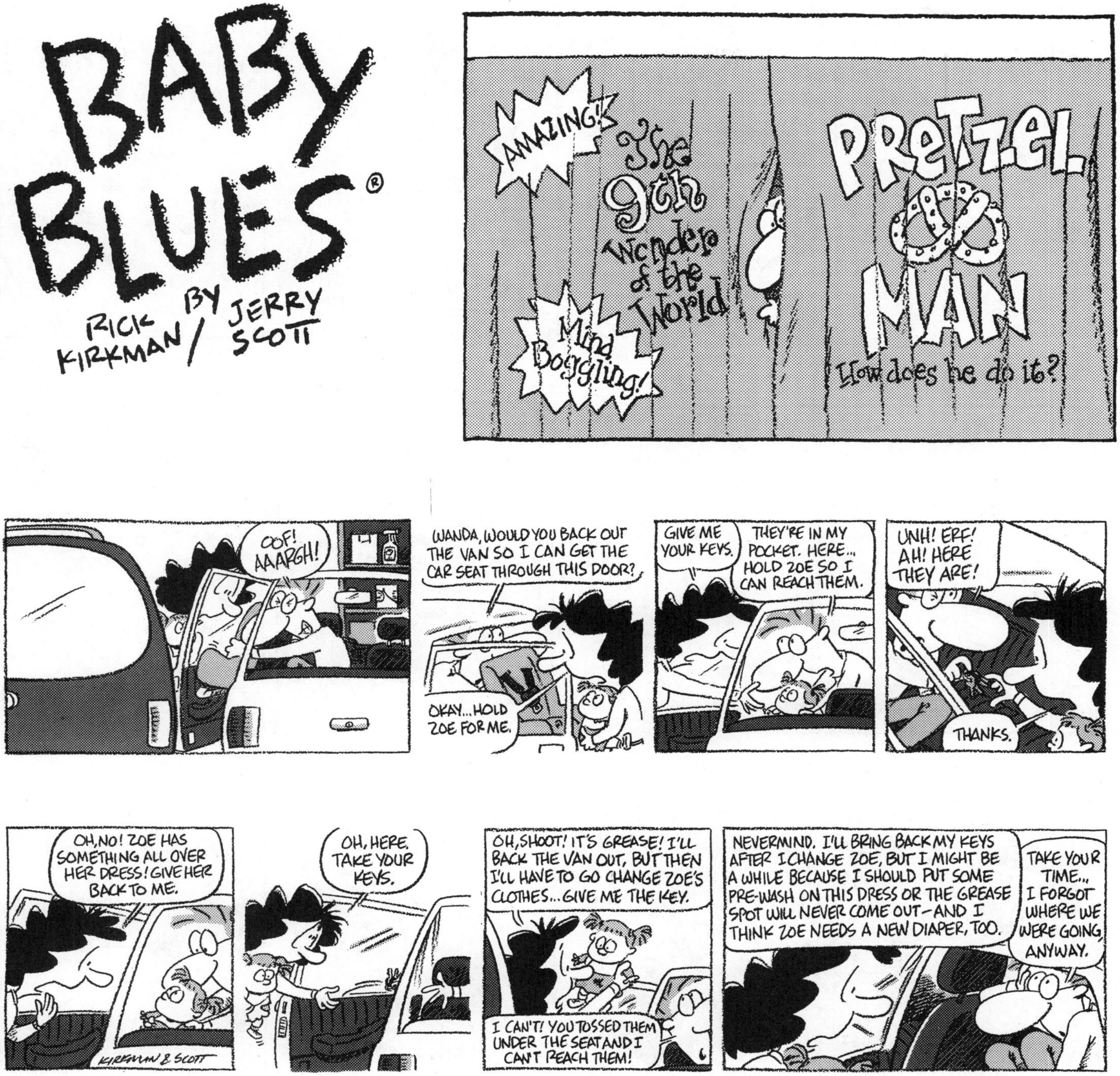
BABY BLUES®
BY RICK KIRKMAN / JERRY SCOTT
AMAZING!
The 9th Wonder of the World
Mind Boggling!
PRETZEL MAN
How does he do it?
OOF! AAARGH!
WANDA, WOULD YOU BACK OUT THE VAN SO I CAN GET THE CAR SEAT THROUGH THIS DOOR?
OKAY... HOLD ZOE FOR ME.
GIVE ME YOUR KEYS.
THEY'RE IN MY POCKET. HERE... HOLD ZOE SO I CAN REACH THEM.
UNH! ERF! AH! HERE THEY ARE!
THANKS.
OH, NO! ZOE HAS SOMETHING ALL OVER HER DRESS! GIVE HER BACK TO ME.
KIRKMAN & SCOTT
OH, HERE. TAKE YOUR KEYS.
OH, SHOOT! IT'S GREASE! I'LL BACK THE VAN OUT, BUT THEN I'LL HAVE TO GO CHANGE ZOE'S CLOTHES... GIVE ME THE KEY.
I CAN'T! YOU TOSSED THEM UNDER THE SEAT AND I CAN'T REACH THEM!
NEVERMIND. I'LL BRING BACK MY KEYS AFTER I CHANGE ZOE, BUT I MIGHT BE A WHILE BECAUSE I SHOULD PUT SOME PRE-WASH ON THIS DRESS OR THE GREASE SPOT WILL NEVER COME OUT-AND I THINK ZOE NEEDS A NEW DIAPER, TOO.
TAKE YOUR TIME... I FORGOT WHERE WE WERE GOING, ANYWAY.

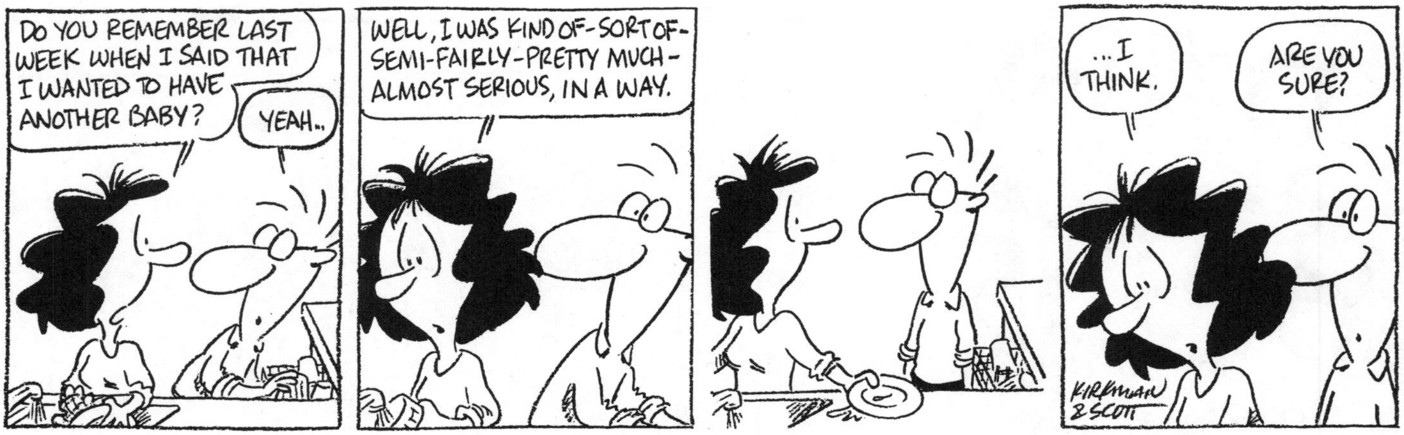
DO YOU REMEMBER LAST WEEK WHEN I SAID THAT I WANTED TO HAVE ANOTHER BABY?
YEAH..
WELL, I WAS KIND OF-SORT OF-SEMI-FAIRLY-PRETTY MUCH-ALMOST SERIOUS, IN A WAY.
...I THINK.
ARE YOU SURE?
KIRKMAN & SCOTT

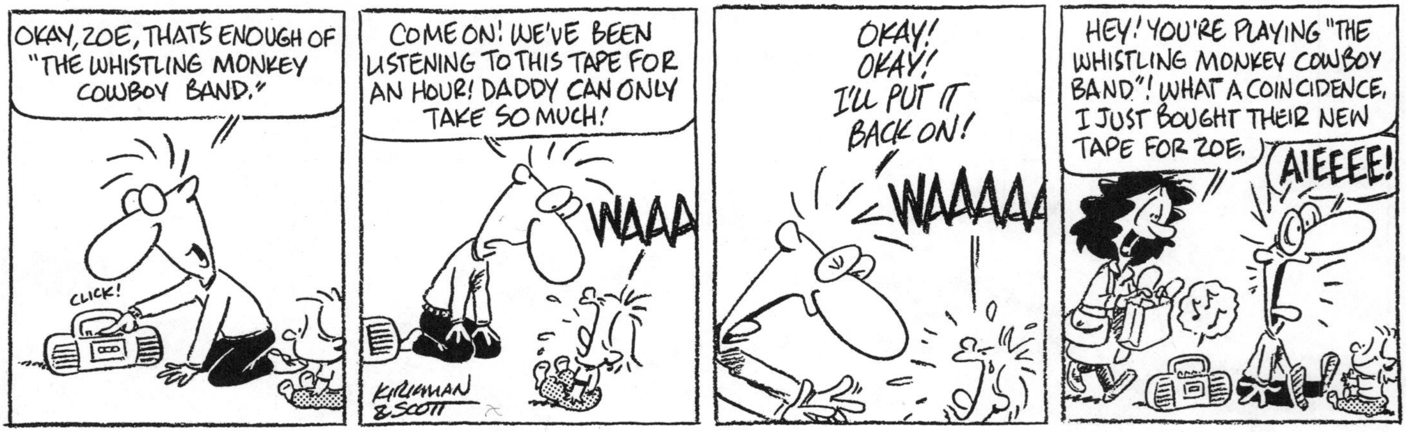
OKAY, ZOE, THAT'S ENOUGH OF "THE WHISTLING MONKEY COWBOY BAND."
CLICK!
COME ON! WE'VE BEEN LISTENING TO THIS TAPE FOR AN HOUR! DADDY CAN ONLY TAKE SO MUCH!
WAAA
KIRKMAN & SCOTT
OKAY! OKAY! I'LL PUT IT BACK ON!
WAAAAA
HEY! YOU'RE PLAYING "THE WHISTLING MONKEY COWBOY BAND"! WHAT A COINCIDENCE. I JUST BOUGHT THEIR NEW TAPE FOR ZOE.
AIEEEE!

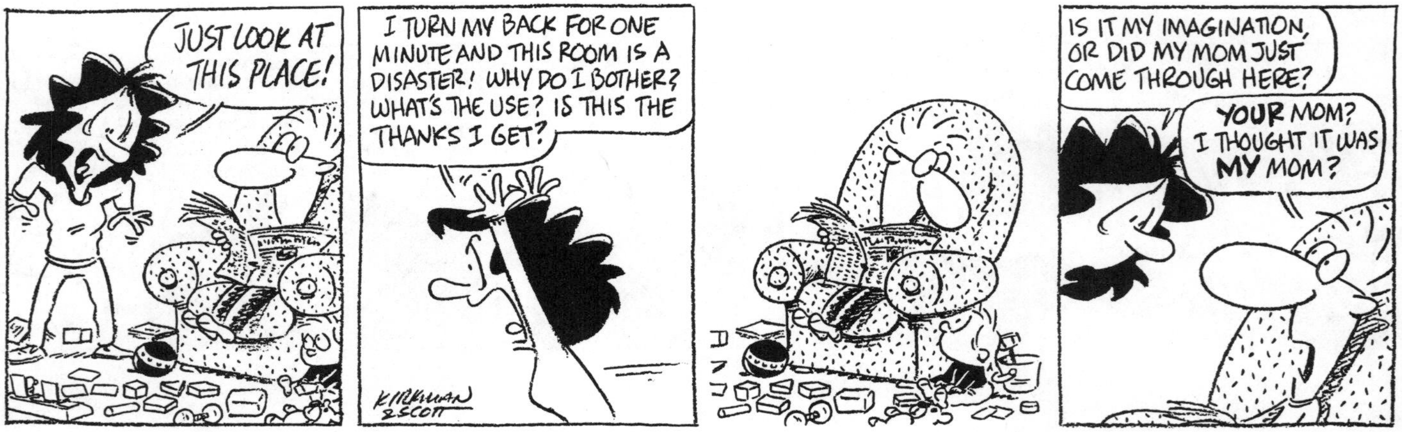
JUST LOOK AT THIS PLACE!
I TURN MY BACK FOR ONE MINUTE AND THIS ROOM IS A DISASTER! WHY DO I BOTHER? WHAT'S THE USE? IS THIS THE THANKS I GET?
KIRKMAN & SCOTT
IS IT MY IMAGINATION, OR DID MY MOM JUST COME THROUGH HERE?
YOUR MOM? I THOUGHT IT WAS MY MOM?

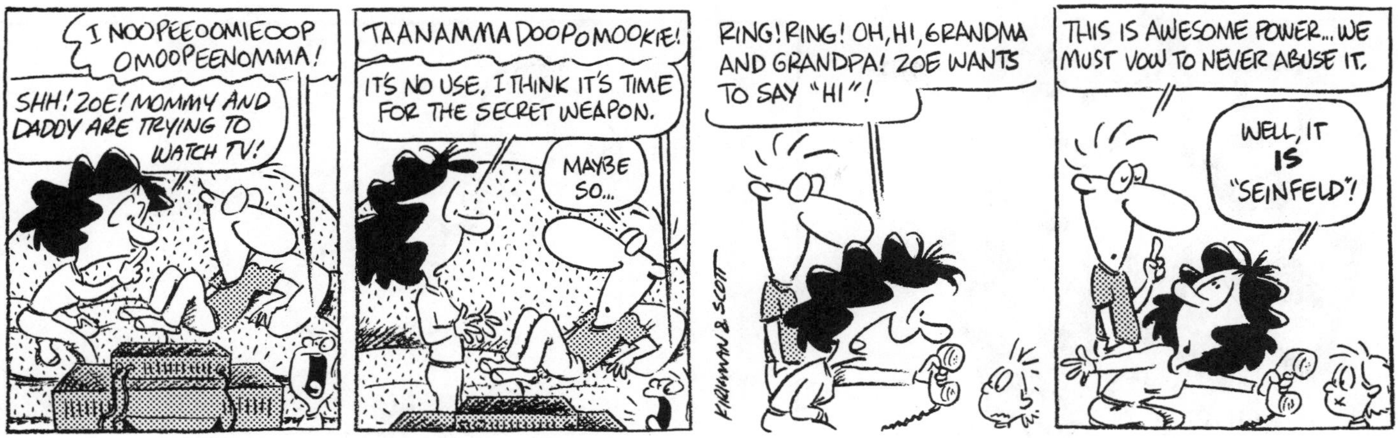
I NOOPEEOOMIEOOP OMOOPEENOMMA!
SHH! ZOE! MOMMY AND DADDY ARE TRYING TO WATCH TV!
TAANAMMADOOPOMOOKIE!
IT'S NO USE. I THINK IT'S TIME FOR THE SECRET WEAPON.
MAYBE SO...
RING! RING! OH, HI, GRANDMA AND GRANDPA! ZOE WANTS TO SAY "HI"!
KIRKMAN & SCOTT
THIS IS AWESOME POWER... WE MUST VOW TO NEVER ABUSE IT.
WELL, IT **IS** "SEINFELD"!

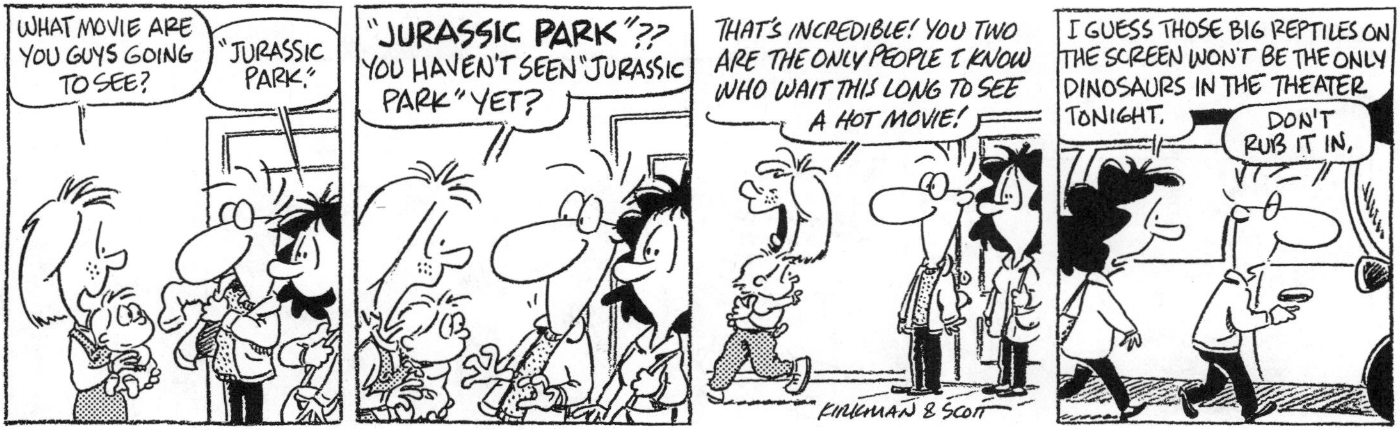
WHAT MOVIE ARE YOU GUYS GOING TO SEE?
"JURASSIC PARK."
"**JURASSIC PARK**"?? YOU HAVEN'T SEEN "JURASSIC PARK" YET?
THAT'S INCREDIBLE! YOU TWO ARE THE ONLY PEOPLE I KNOW WHO WAIT THIS LONG TO SEE A HOT MOVIE!
KIRKMAN & SCOTT
I GUESS THOSE BIG REPTILES ON THE SCREEN WON'T BE THE ONLY DINOSAURS IN THE THEATER TONIGHT.
DON'T RUB IT IN.

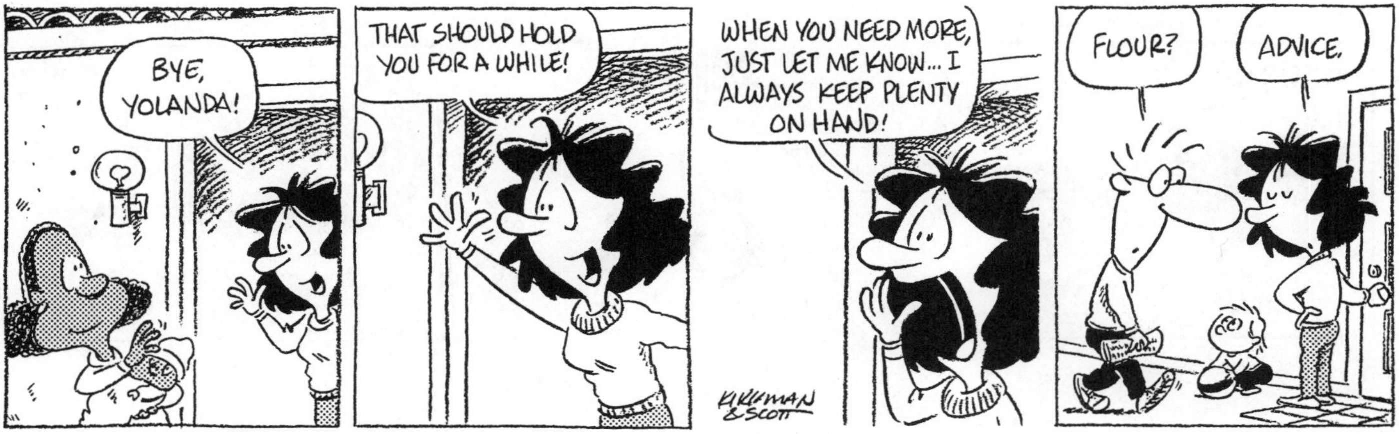
BYE, YOLANDA!
THAT SHOULD HOLD YOU FOR A WHILE!
WHEN YOU NEED MORE, JUST LET ME KNOW... I ALWAYS KEEP PLENTY ON HAND!
KIRKMAN & SCOTT
FLOUR?
ADVICE.

BABY BLUES®

BY RICK KIRKMAN / JERRY SCOTT

GRRRRR! HERE COMES THE BIG BAD BEAR!

EEEE!

DARRYL, MAYBE THAT'S NOT SUCH A GOOD IDEA... I DON'T WANT ZOE GROWING UP TO BE AFRAID OF ANIMALS

OH.

AAARRG! HERE COMES THE BIG MEAN MONSTER!

EEEEE!

NIGHTMARES. SCARY MONSTERS BREED NIGHTMARES.

RIGHT.

OOOOOOH! HERE COMES THE BIG BOOGIE MAN!

EEEEEE!

DISTRUST OF OTHER PEOPLE. CAUTION WITH STRANGERS IS FINE, BUT I WOULDN'T WANT IT TO DEVELOP INTO AN UNHEALTHY FEAR OF MEN IN GENERAL.

GOTCHA.

ROOAAR! HERE COMES THE GOVERNMENT BUREAUCRAT!

I CAN LIVE WITH THAT.

EEEEEE!

KIRKMAN & SCOTT

18

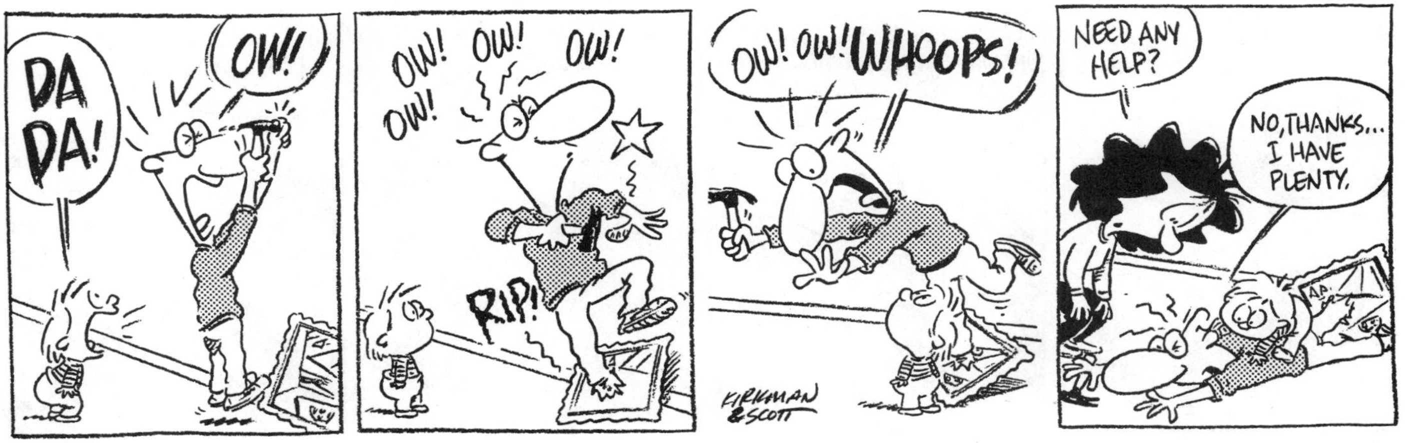
DA DA!
OW!
OW! OW! OW! OW!
RIP!
OW! OW! WHOOPS!
KIRKMAN & SCOTT
NEED ANY HELP?
NO, THANKS... I HAVE PLENTY.

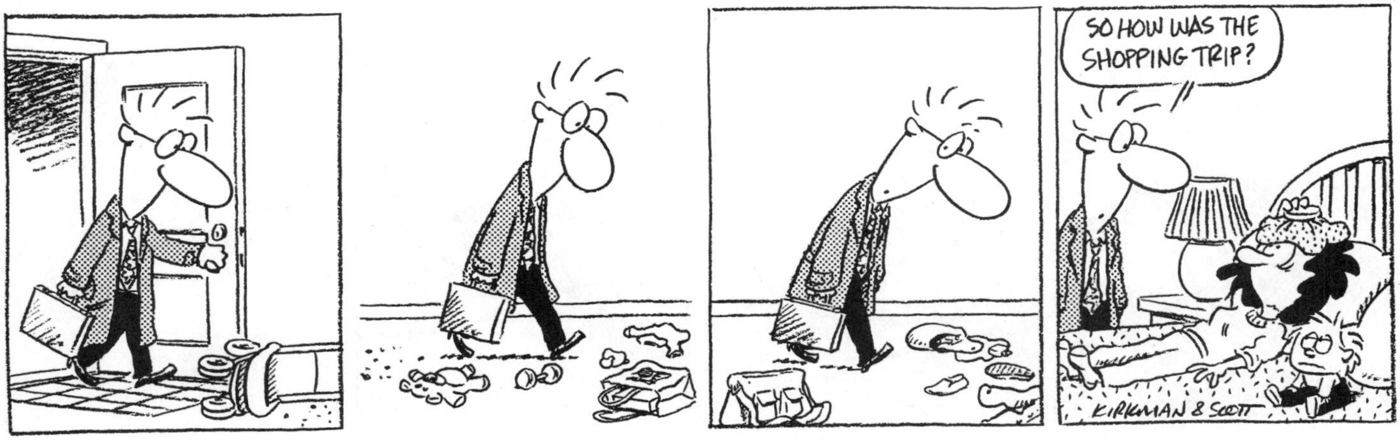
SO HOW WAS THE SHOPPING TRIP?
KIRKMAN & SCOTT

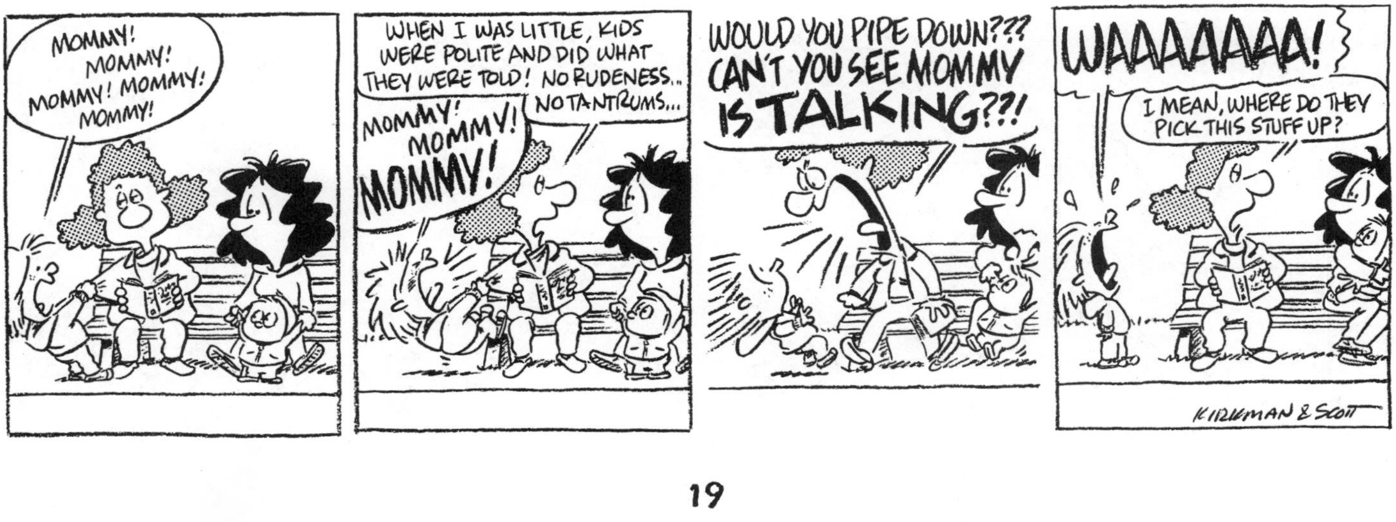
MOMMY! MOMMY! MOMMY! MOMMY! MOMMY!
WHEN I WAS LITTLE, KIDS WERE POLITE AND DID WHAT THEY WERE TOLD! NO RUDENESS...
NO TANTRUMS...
MOMMY! MOMMY! MOMMY!
WOULD YOU PIPE DOWN??? CAN'T YOU SEE MOMMY IS TALKING??!
WAAAAAAA!
I MEAN, WHERE DO THEY PICK THIS STUFF UP?
KIRKMAN & SCOTT

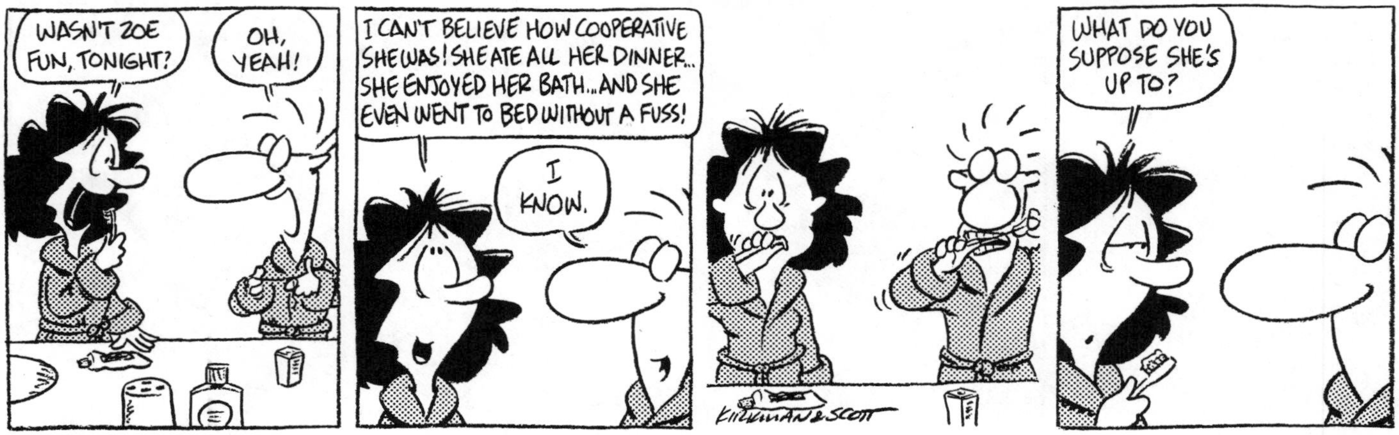
WASN'T ZOE FUN, TONIGHT?
OH, YEAH!
I CAN'T BELIEVE HOW COOPERATIVE SHE WAS! SHE ATE ALL HER DINNER... SHE ENJOYED HER BATH... AND SHE EVEN WENT TO BED WITHOUT A FUSS!
I KNOW.
KIRKMAN & SCOTT
WHAT DO YOU SUPPOSE SHE'S UP TO?

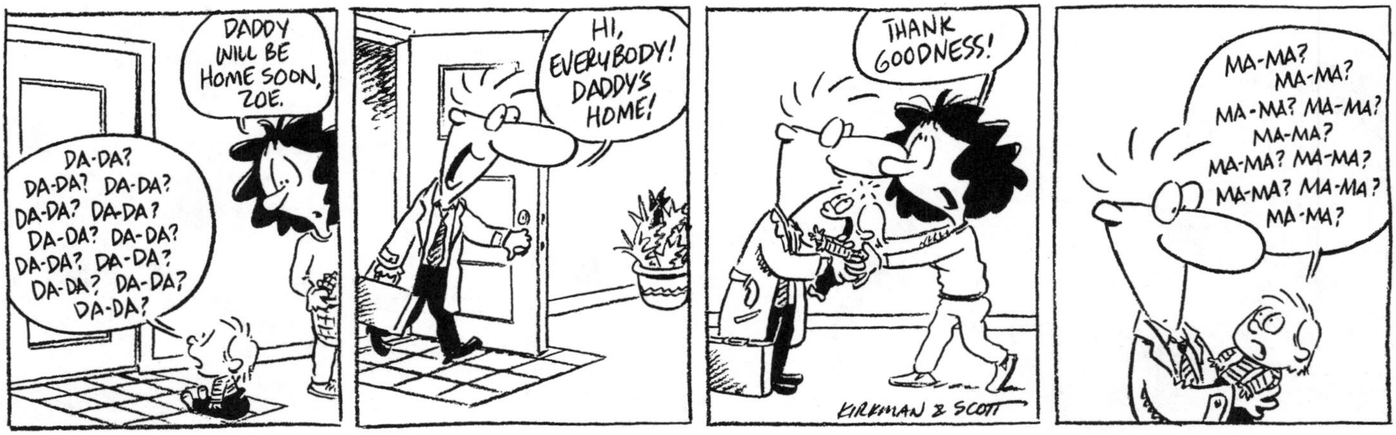
DADDY WILL BE HOME SOON, ZOE.
DA-DA? DA-DA? DA-DA? DA-DA? DA-DA? DA-DA? DA-DA? DA-DA? DA-DA? DA-DA? DA-DA? DA-DA?
HI, EVERYBODY! DADDY'S HOME!
THANK GOODNESS!
KIRKMAN & SCOTT
MA-MA? MA-MA? MA-MA? MA-MA? MA-MA? MA-MA? MA-MA? MA-MA? MA-MA? MA-MA?

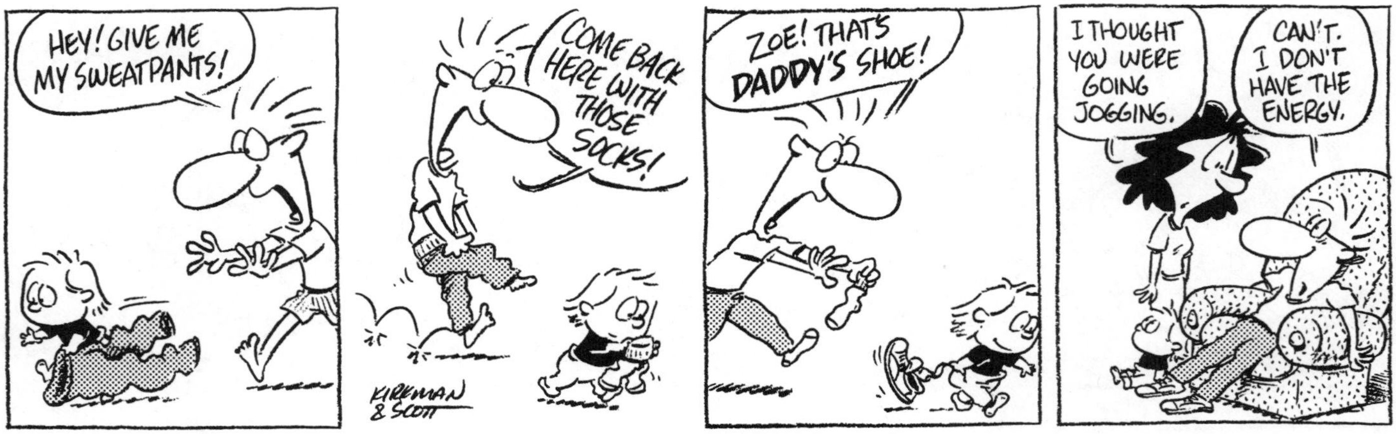
HEY! GIVE ME MY SWEATPANTS!
COME BACK HERE WITH THOSE SOCKS!
KIRKMAN & SCOTT
ZOE! THAT'S DADDY'S SHOE!
I THOUGHT YOU WERE GOING JOGGING.
CAN'T. I DON'T HAVE THE ENERGY.

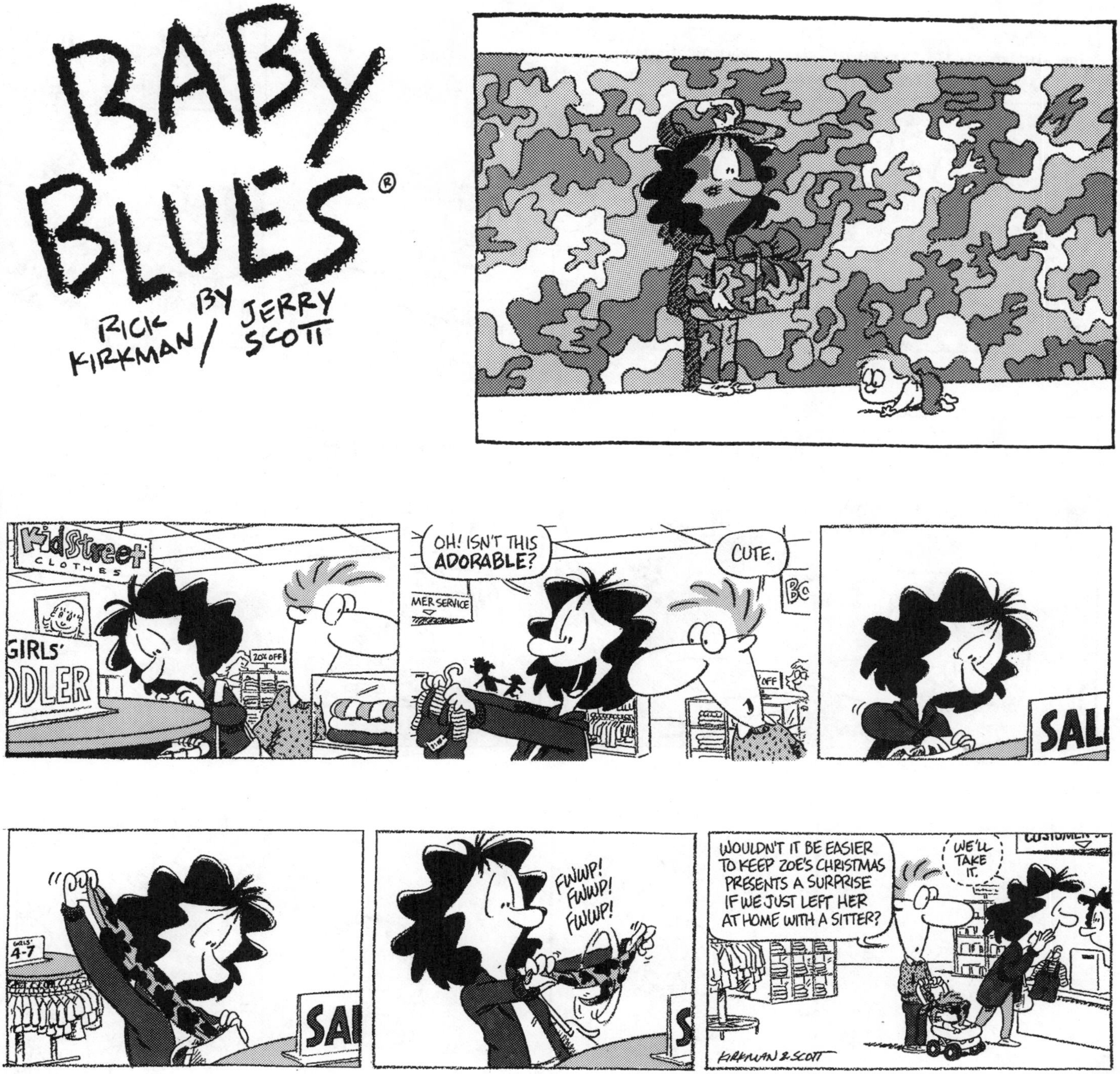
BABY BLUES®
BY RICK KIRKMAN / JERRY SCOTT
KidStreet CLOTHES
GIRLS'
DDLER
20% OFF
OH! ISN'T THIS **ADORABLE**?
CUTE.
MER SERVICE
SAL
GIRLS' 4-7
SAL
FWWP! FWWP! FWWP!
WOULDN'T IT BE EASIER TO KEEP ZOE'S CHRISTMAS PRESENTS A SURPRISE IF WE JUST LEFT HER AT HOME WITH A SITTER?
WE'LL TAKE IT.
KIRKMAN & SCOTT

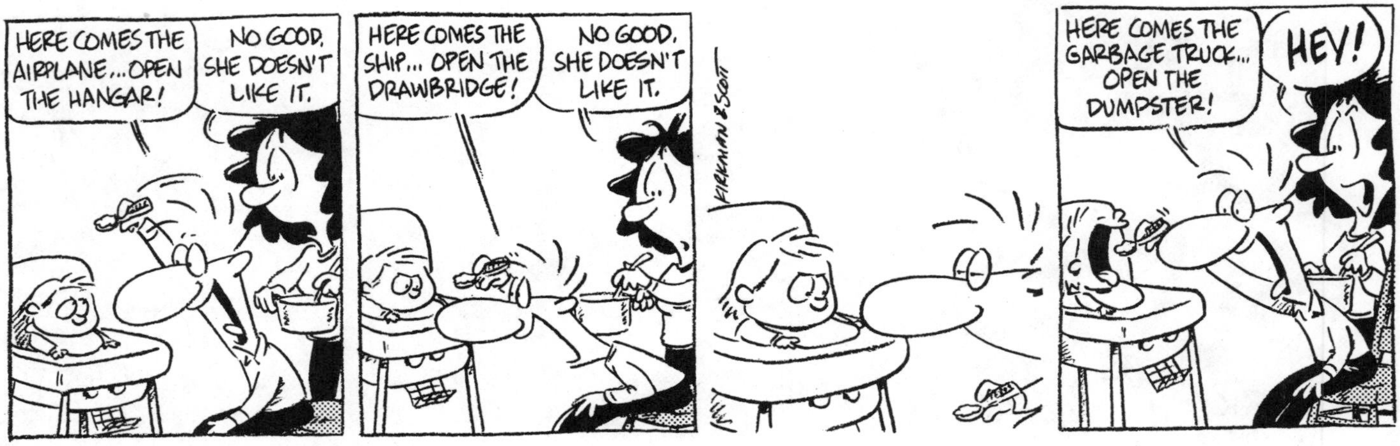
HERE COMES THE AIRPLANE... OPEN THE HANGAR!
NO GOOD. SHE DOESN'T LIKE IT.
HERE COMES THE SHIP... OPEN THE DRAWBRIDGE!
NO GOOD. SHE DOESN'T LIKE IT.
KIRKMAN & SCOTT
HERE COMES THE GARBAGE TRUCK... OPEN THE DUMPSTER!
HEY!

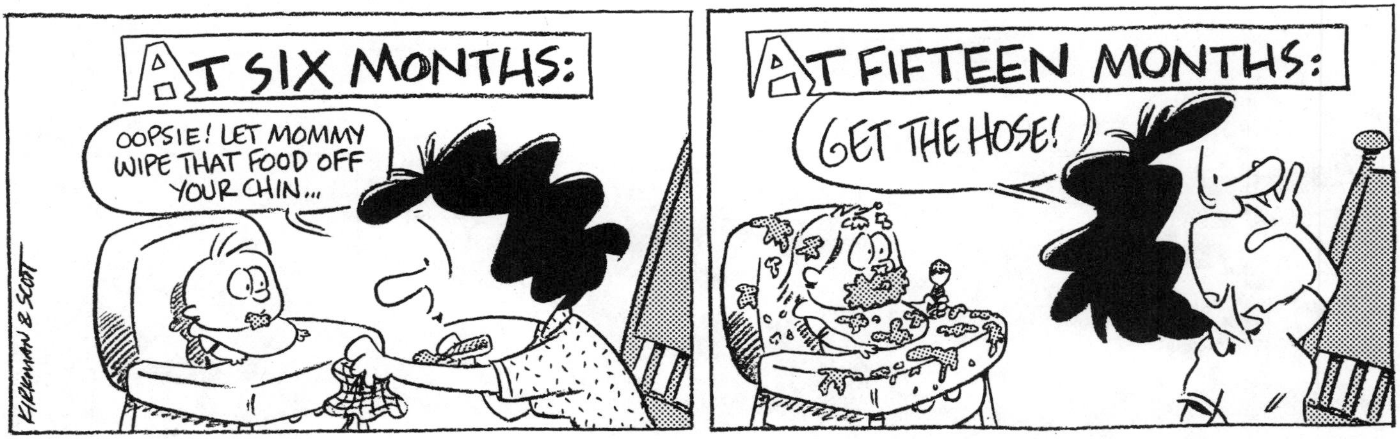
AT SIX MONTHS:
OOPSIE! LET MOMMY WIPE THAT FOOD OFF YOUR CHIN...
KIRKMAN & SCOTT
AT FIFTEEN MONTHS:
GET THE HOSE!

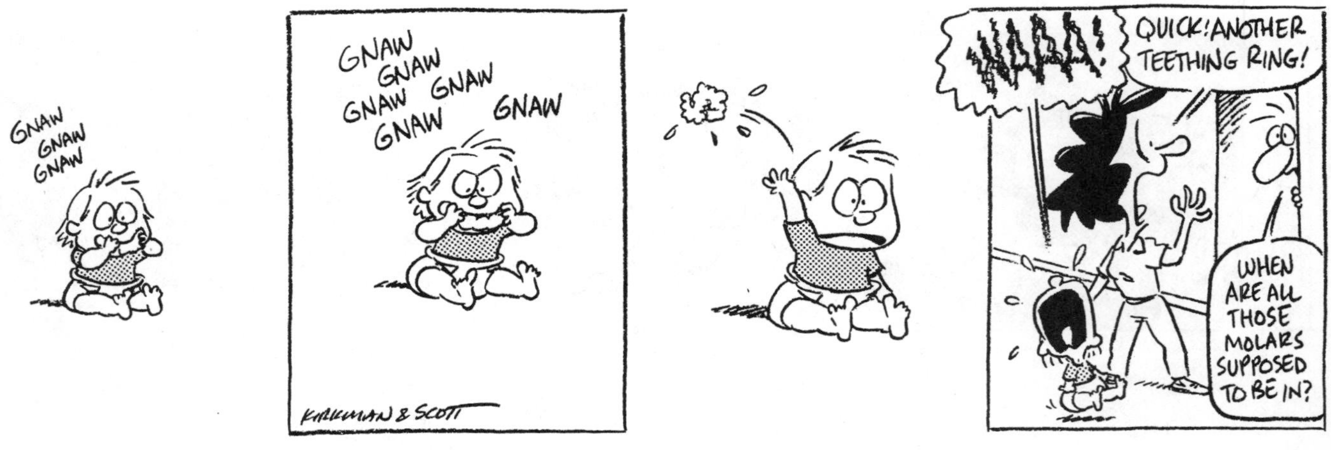
GNAW GNAW GNAW
GNAW GNAW GNAW GNAW GNAW GNAW
KIRKMAN & SCOTT
WAAA!
QUICK! ANOTHER TEETHING RING!
WHEN ARE ALL THOSE MOLARS SUPPOSED TO BE IN?

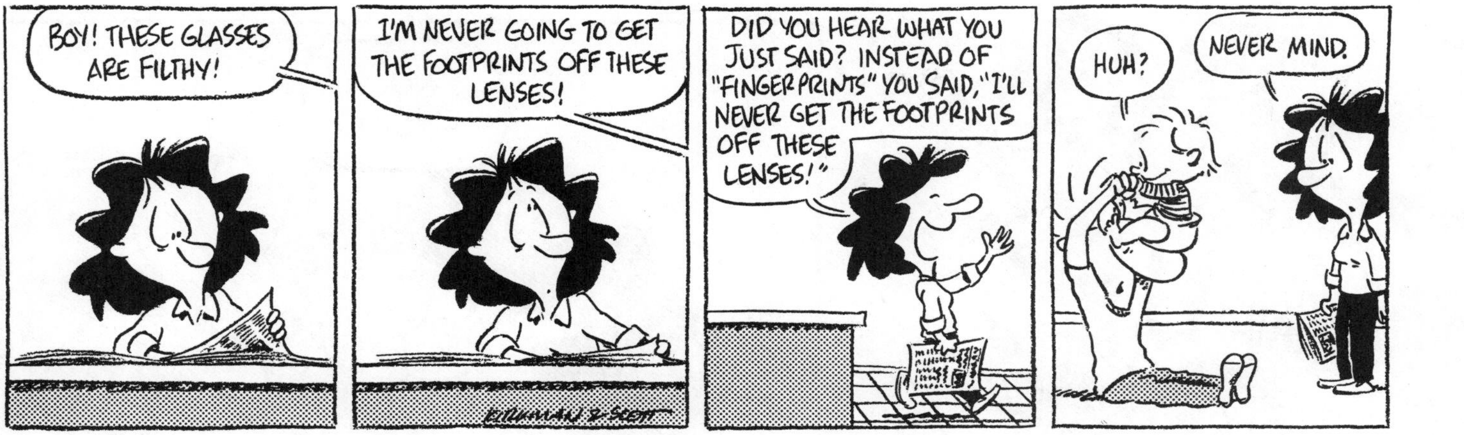
BOY! THESE GLASSES ARE FILTHY!
I'M NEVER GOING TO GET THE FOOTPRINTS OFF THESE LENSES!
KIRKMAN & SCOTT
DID YOU HEAR WHAT YOU JUST SAID? INSTEAD OF "FINGERPRINTS" YOU SAID, "I'LL NEVER GET THE FOOTPRINTS OFF THESE LENSES!"
HUH?
NEVER MIND.

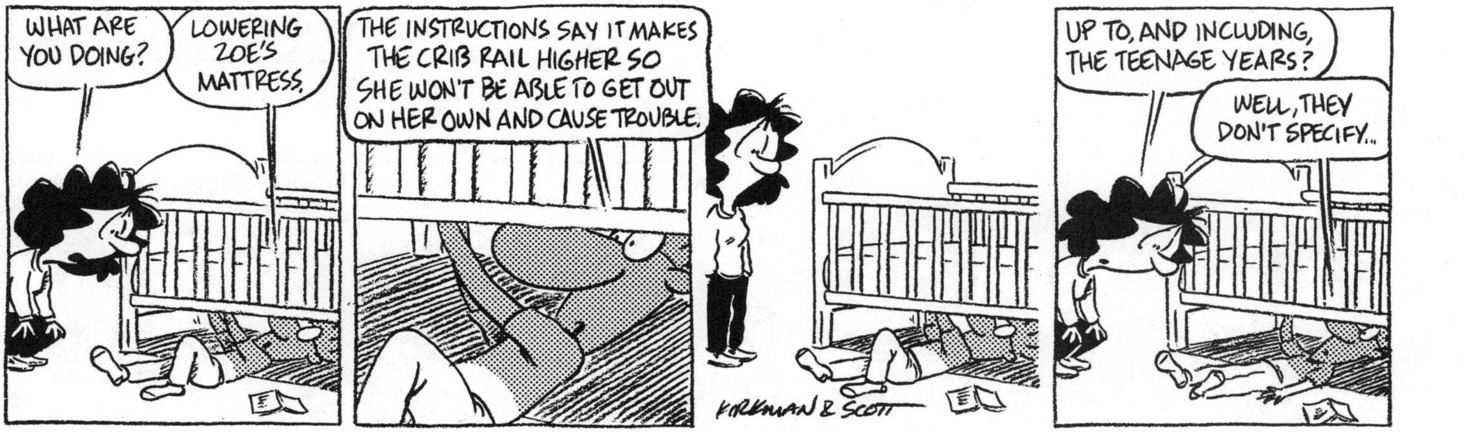
WHAT ARE YOU DOING?
LOWERING ZOE'S MATTRESS.
THE INSTRUCTIONS SAY IT MAKES THE CRIB RAIL HIGHER SO SHE WON'T BE ABLE TO GET OUT ON HER OWN AND CAUSE TROUBLE.
KIRKMAN & SCOTT
UP TO, AND INCLUDING, THE TEENAGE YEARS?
WELL, THEY DON'T SPECIFY...

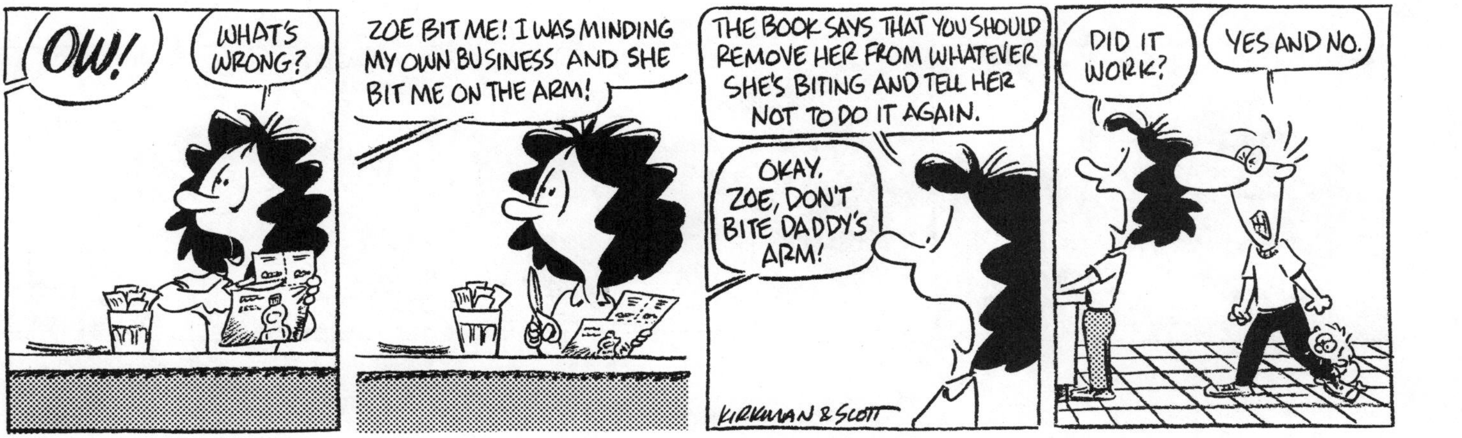
OW!
WHAT'S WRONG?
ZOE BIT ME! I WAS MINDING MY OWN BUSINESS AND SHE BIT ME ON THE ARM!
THE BOOK SAYS THAT YOU SHOULD REMOVE HER FROM WHATEVER SHE'S BITING AND TELL HER NOT TO DO IT AGAIN.
OKAY. ZOE, DON'T BITE DADDY'S ARM!
KIRKMAN & SCOTT
DID IT WORK?
YES AND NO.

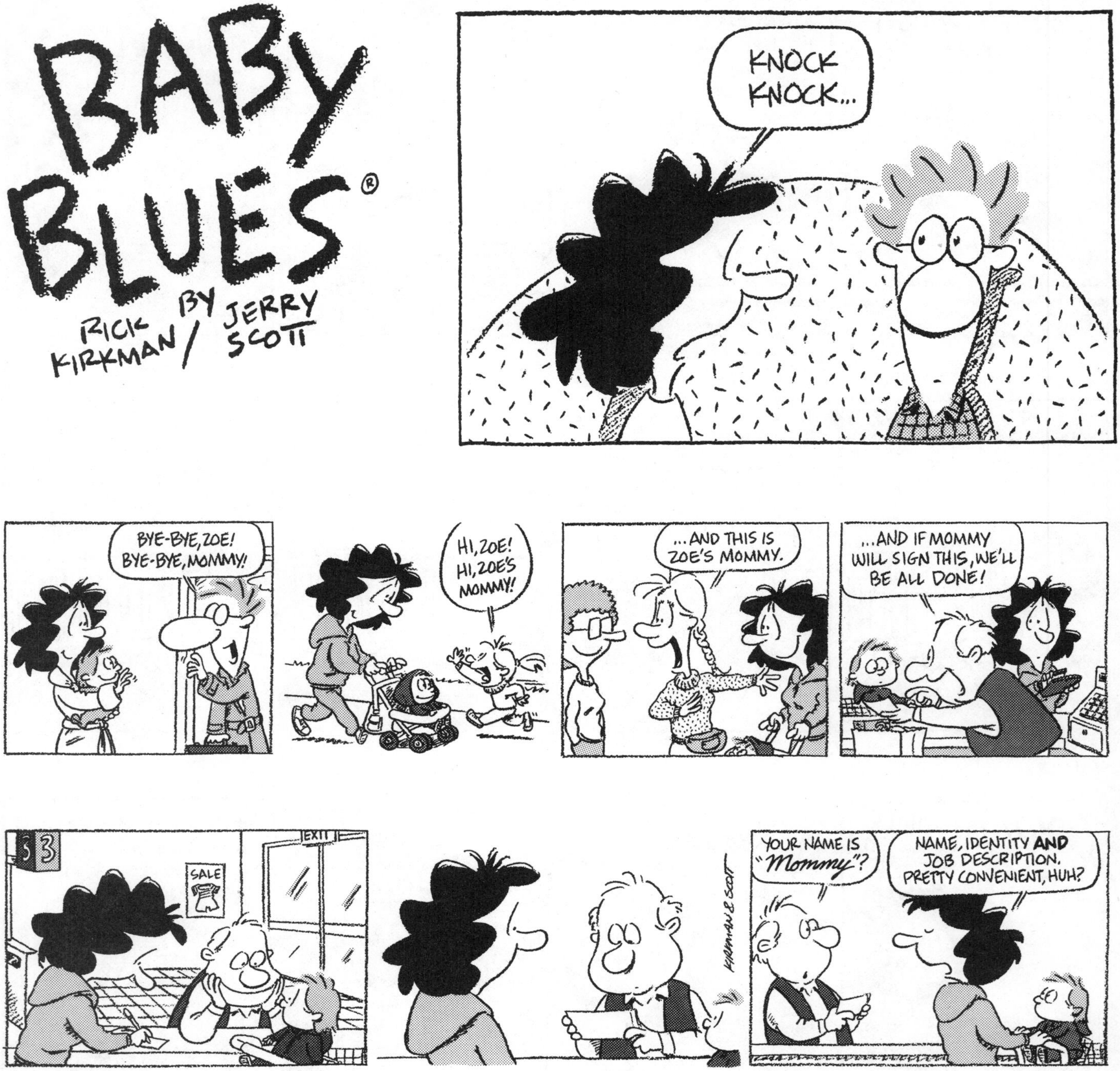
BABY BLUES®
BY RICK KIRKMAN / JERRY SCOTT
KNOCK KNOCK...
BYE-BYE, ZOE! BYE-BYE, MOMMY!
HI, ZOE! HI, ZOE'S MOMMY!
...AND THIS IS ZOE'S MOMMY.
...AND IF MOMMY WILL SIGN THIS, WE'LL BE ALL DONE!
SALE
EXIT
KIRKMAN & SCOTT
YOUR NAME IS "Mommy"?
NAME, IDENTITY **AND** JOB DESCRIPTION. PRETTY CONVENIENT, HUH?

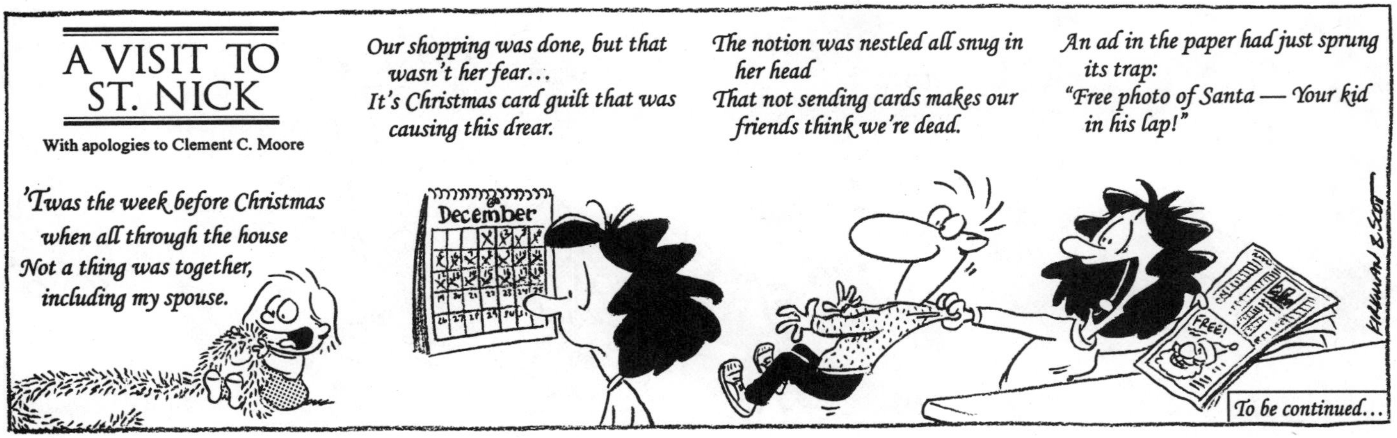
A VISIT TO ST. NICK
With apologies to Clement C. Moore
'Twas the week before Christmas when all through the house Not a thing was together, including my spouse.
Our shopping was done, but that wasn't her fear... It's Christmas card guilt that was causing this drear.
December
The notion was nestled all snug in her head That not sending cards makes our friends think we're dead.
An ad in the paper had just sprung its trap: "Free photo of Santa — Your kid in his lap!"
FREE!
To be continued...

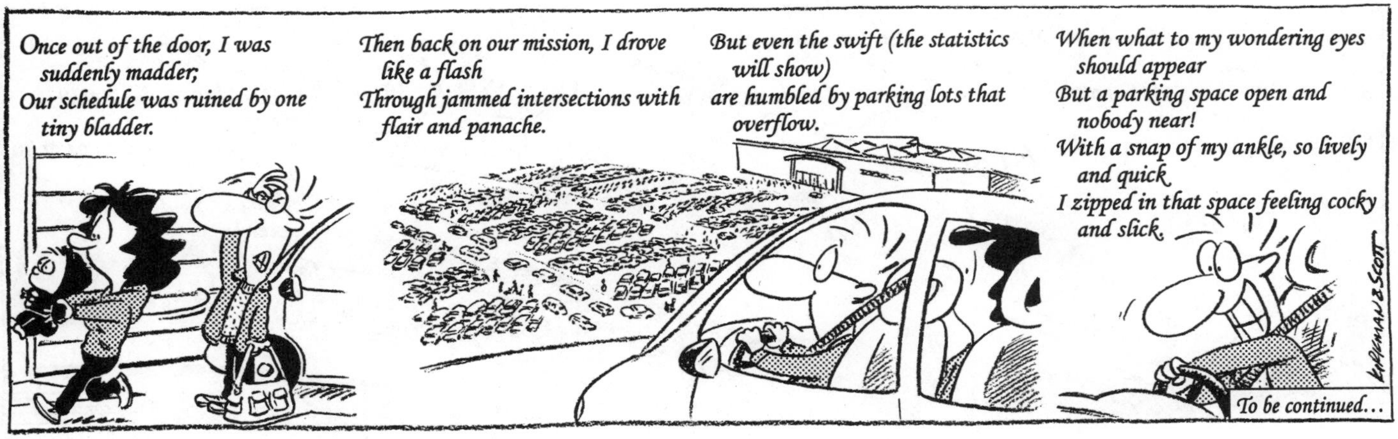
Once out of the door, I was suddenly madder; Our schedule was ruined by one tiny bladder.
Then back on our mission, I drove like a flash Through jammed intersections with flair and panache.
But even the swift (the statistics will show) are humbled by parking lots that overflow.
When what to my wondering eyes should appear But a parking space open and nobody near! With a snap of my ankle, so lively and quick I zipped in that space feeling cocky and slick.
To be continued...

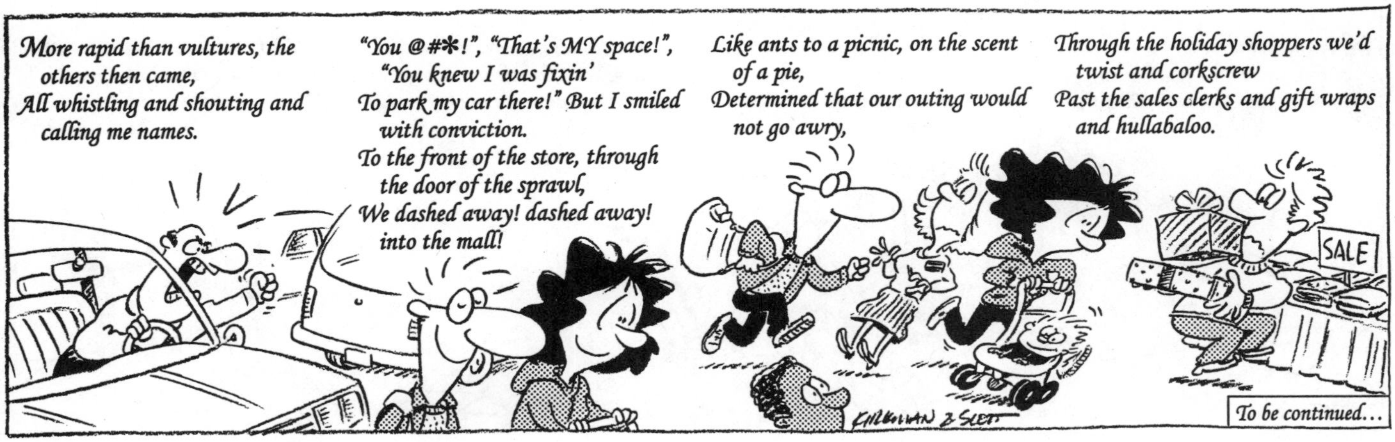
More rapid than vultures, the others then came, All whistling and shouting and calling me names.
"You @#*!", "That's MY space!", "You knew I was fixin' To park my car there!" But I smiled with conviction. To the front of the store, through the door of the sprawl, We dashed away! dashed away! into the mall!
Like ants to a picnic, on the scent of a pie, Determined that our outing would not go awry,
Through the holiday shoppers we'd twist and corkscrew Past the sales clerks and gift wraps and hullabaloo.
SALE
To be continued...

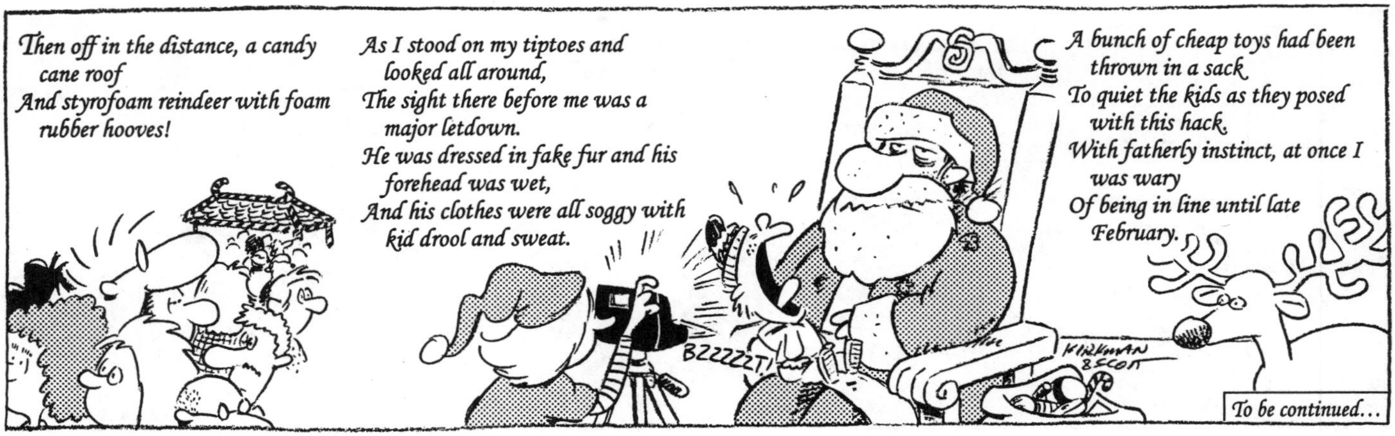
Then off in the distance, a candy cane roof
And styrofoam reindeer with foam rubber hooves!
As I stood on my tiptoes and looked all around,
The sight there before me was a major letdown.
He was dressed in fake fur and his forehead was wet,
And his clothes were all soggy with kid drool and sweat.
BZZZZZT!
A bunch of cheap toys had been thrown in a sack
To quiet the kids as they posed with this hack.
With fatherly instinct, at once I was wary
Of being in line until late February.
KIRKMAN & SCOTT
To be continued...

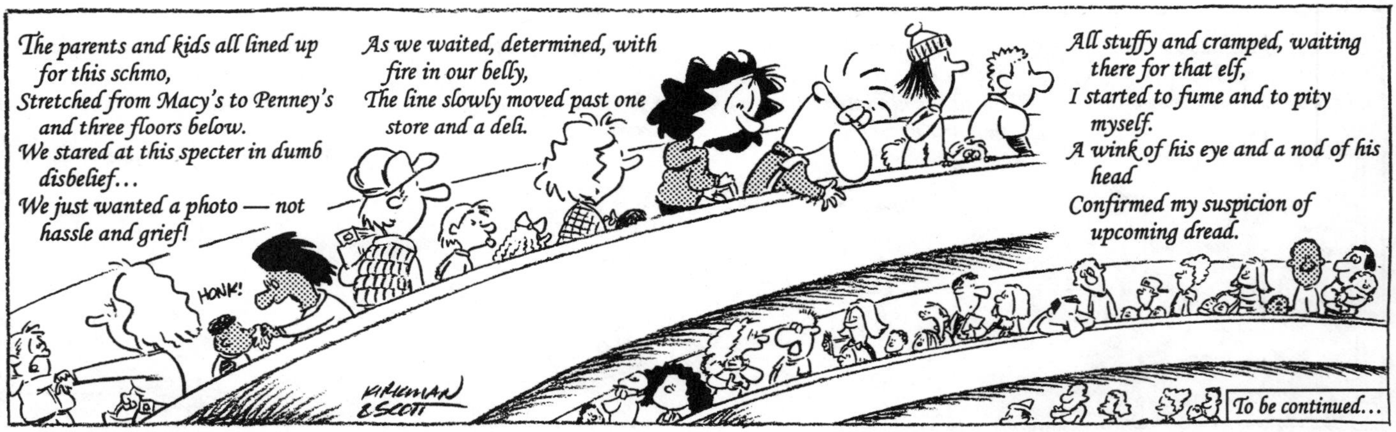
The parents and kids all lined up for this schmo,
Stretched from Macy's to Penney's and three floors below.
We stared at this specter in dumb disbelief...
We just wanted a photo — not hassle and grief!
As we waited, determined, with fire in our belly,
The line slowly moved past one store and a deli.
All stuffy and cramped, waiting there for that elf,
I started to fume and to pity myself.
A wink of his eye and a nod of his head
Confirmed my suspicion of upcoming dread.
HONK!
KIRKMAN & SCOTT
To be continued...

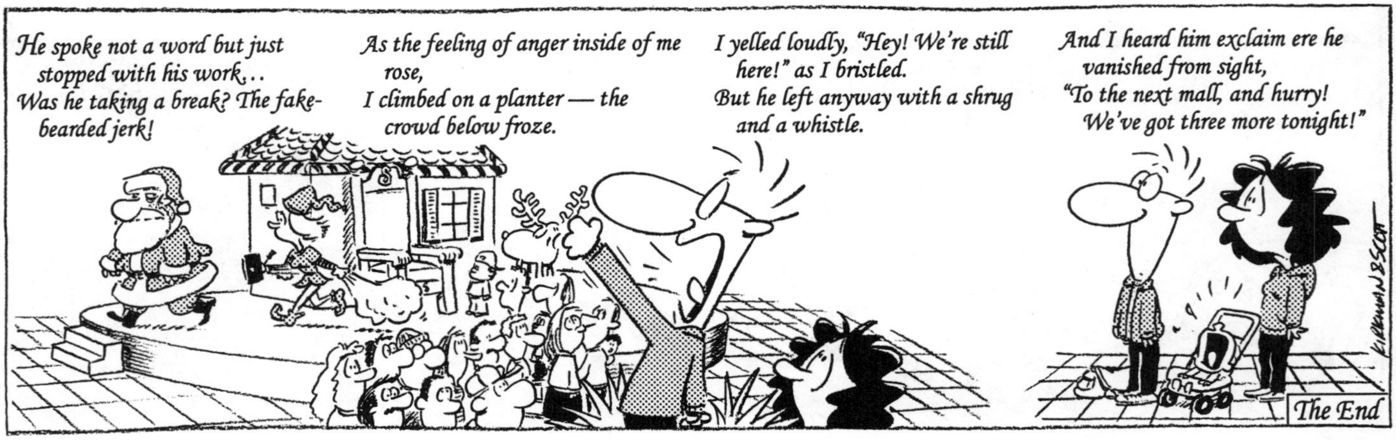
He spoke not a word but just stopped with his work...
Was he taking a break? The fake-bearded jerk!
As the feeling of anger inside of me rose,
I climbed on a planter — the crowd below froze.
I yelled loudly, "Hey! We're still here!" as I bristled.
But he left anyway with a shrug and a whistle.
And I heard him exclaim ere he vanished from sight,
"To the next mall, and hurry! We've got three more tonight!"
KIRKMAN & SCOTT
The End

BABY BLUES®

BY RICK KIRKMAN / JERRY SCOTT

Dad: HEY, ZOE! LET'S TRY OUT YOUR NEW HIGH-DENSITY FOAM, CHILD-SAFE BLOCKS IN BRIGHT VIBRANT COLORS THAT STIMULATE ACTIVE MINDS!

Zoe: NOT NOW, HUH?

Dad: OKAY, LET'S PLAY WITH YOUR NEW COUNT-O-MATIC EARLY MATH TRAINER INSTEAD!

Dad: ...OR NOT.

Dad: WELL, THEN YOU AND DADDY AT LEAST HAVE TO TAKE A SPIN IN YOUR NEW WHISTLING MONKEY COWBOY BAND PRETEND TOUR BUS OR PLAY A ROUND OR TWO OF YOUR NEW HAPPY HIPPO GAME, RIGHT?

Dad: SIGH! OKAY... YOU WIN.

Zoe: EEEE! WHEEE! WHACK! THACK-A-WACK! EEEWEEBEE!

Wanda: ZOE SURE SOUNDS HAPPY. WHAT'S SHE PLAYING WITH?

Dad: TWO EMPTY TOILET PAPER ROLLS AND A WOODEN SPOON.

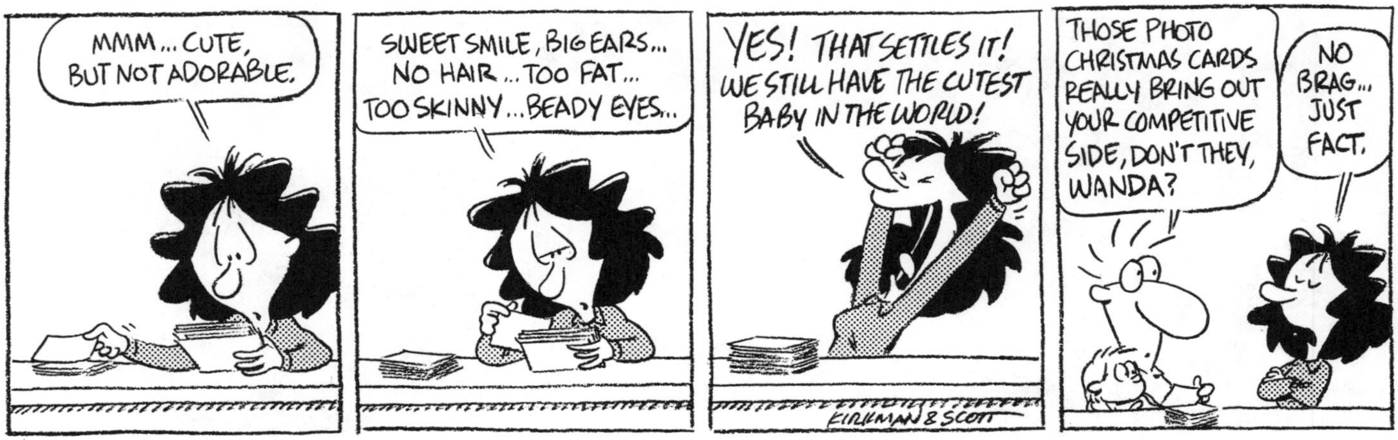
MMM... CUTE, BUT NOT ADORABLE.
SWEET SMILE, BIG EARS... NO HAIR... TOO FAT... TOO SKINNY... BEADY EYES...
YES! THAT SETTLES IT! WE STILL HAVE THE CUTEST BABY IN THE WORLD!
KIRKMAN & SCOTT
THOSE PHOTO CHRISTMAS CARDS REALLY BRING OUT YOUR COMPETITIVE SIDE, DON'T THEY, WANDA?
NO BRAG... JUST FACT.

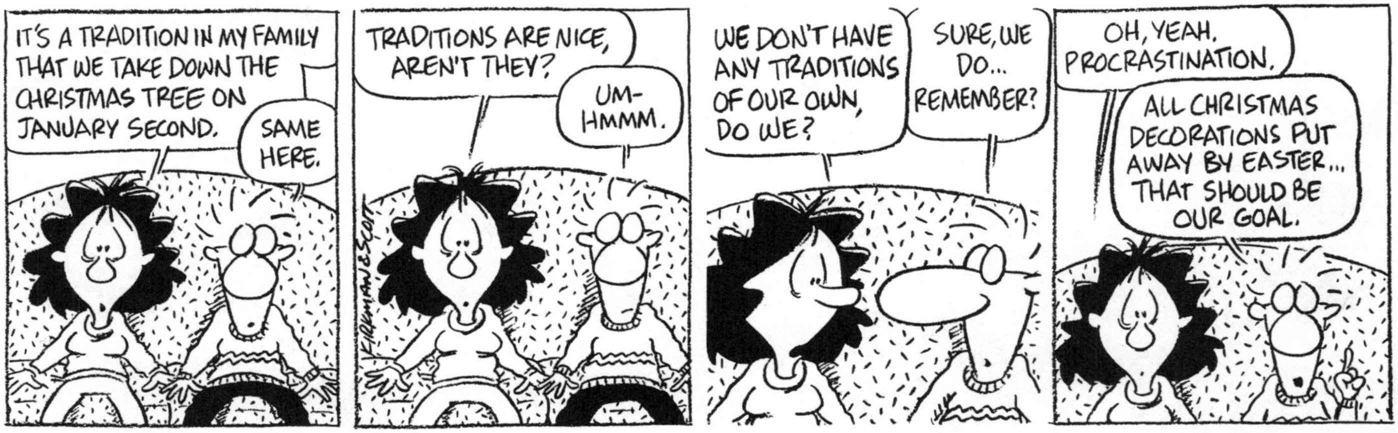
IT'S A TRADITION IN MY FAMILY THAT WE TAKE DOWN THE CHRISTMAS TREE ON JANUARY SECOND.
SAME HERE.
KIRKMAN & SCOTT
TRADITIONS ARE NICE, AREN'T THEY?
UM-HMMM.
WE DON'T HAVE ANY TRADITIONS OF OUR OWN, DO WE?
SURE, WE DO... REMEMBER?
OH, YEAH. PROCRASTINATION.
ALL CHRISTMAS DECORATIONS PUT AWAY BY EASTER... THAT SHOULD BE OUR GOAL.

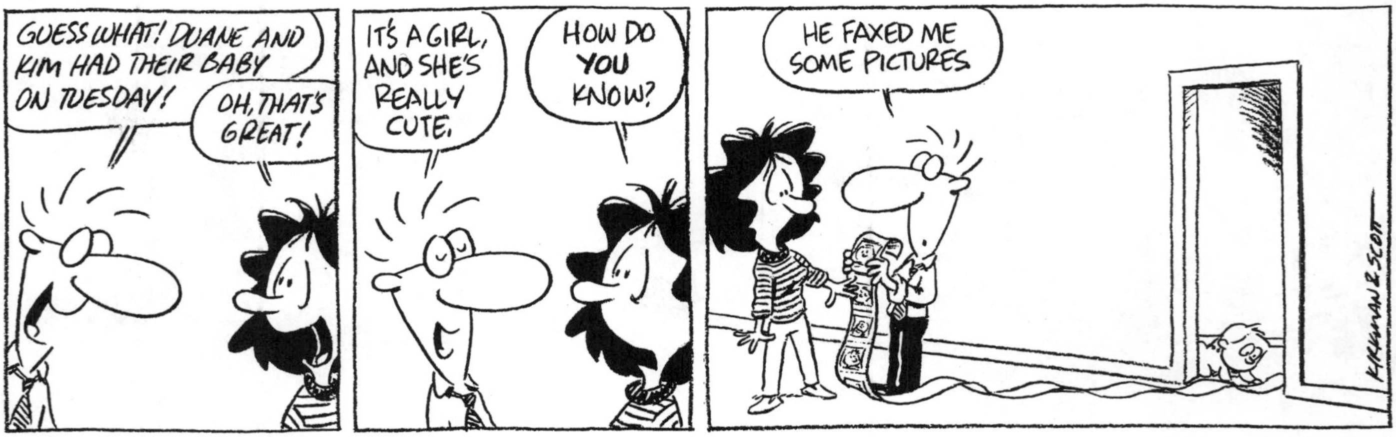
GUESS WHAT! DUANE AND KIM HAD THEIR BABY ON TUESDAY!
OH, THAT'S GREAT!
IT'S A GIRL, AND SHE'S REALLY CUTE.
HOW DO **YOU** KNOW?
HE FAXED ME SOME PICTURES.
KIRKMAN & SCOTT

LOOK AT THESE.

THERE WE ARE GETTING READY TO GO TO THE HOSPITAL...

AND THERE WE ARE GETTING READY TO COME HOME.

GIRL!

CONGRATULATIONS!

TALK ABOUT YOUR BAPTISM BY FIRE.

WHERE'S THE BABY?

WHATCHA DOING?

JUST LOOKING AT SOME PICTURES.

LOOK... HERE WE ARE JUST AFTER WE BROUGHT ZOE HOME FROM THE HOSPITAL...

...AND THERE I AM FEEDING HER...THERE YOU ARE HOLDING HER...THERE WE ARE CHANGING HER...FEEDING HER...HOLDING HER...CHANGING HER...FEEDING HER...BURPING HER...THIS ALBUM IS JUST JAMMED WITH UNFORGETABLE MOMENTS.

YEAH.

WE TOOK A LOT OF PHOTOS THAT DAY, DIDN'T WE?

ZOE VOL. I

KIRKMAN & SCOTT

OH, LOOK! HERE'S THE PICTURE I TOOK THE DAY ZOE'S UMBILICAL CORD CAME OFF.

PHOTOS

YEP.

PHOTOS

KIRKMAN & SCOTT

PHOTOS

YOU LOOK GOOD WHEN YOU'RE UNCONSCIOUS.

HEY, I WAS JUST A LITTLE SQUEAMISH BACK THEN, OKAY?

PHOTOS

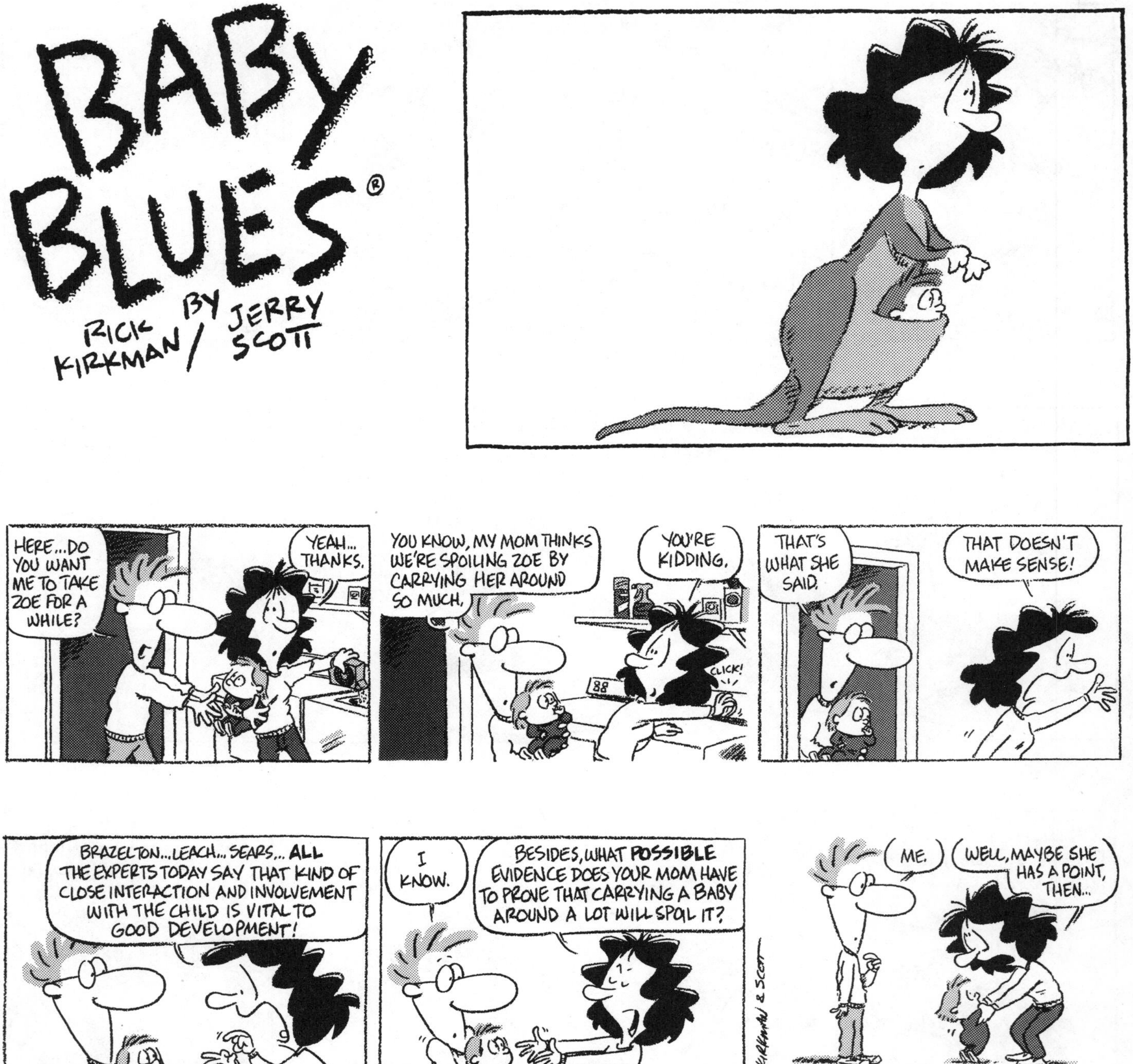
BABY BLUES®
BY RICK KIRKMAN / JERRY SCOTT
HERE...DO YOU WANT ME TO TAKE ZOE FOR A WHILE?
YEAH... THANKS.
YOU KNOW, MY MOM THINKS WE'RE SPOILING ZOE BY CARRYING HER AROUND SO MUCH.
YOU'RE KIDDING.
CLICK!
THAT'S WHAT SHE SAID.
THAT DOESN'T MAKE SENSE!
BRAZELTON...LEACH...SEARS... **ALL** THE EXPERTS TODAY SAY THAT KIND OF CLOSE INTERACTION AND INVOLVEMENT WITH THE CHILD IS VITAL TO GOOD DEVELOPMENT!
I KNOW.
BESIDES, WHAT **POSSIBLE** EVIDENCE DOES YOUR MOM HAVE TO PROVE THAT CARRYING A BABY AROUND A LOT WILL SPOIL IT?
KIRKMAN & SCOTT
ME.
WELL, MAYBE SHE HAS A POINT, THEN...

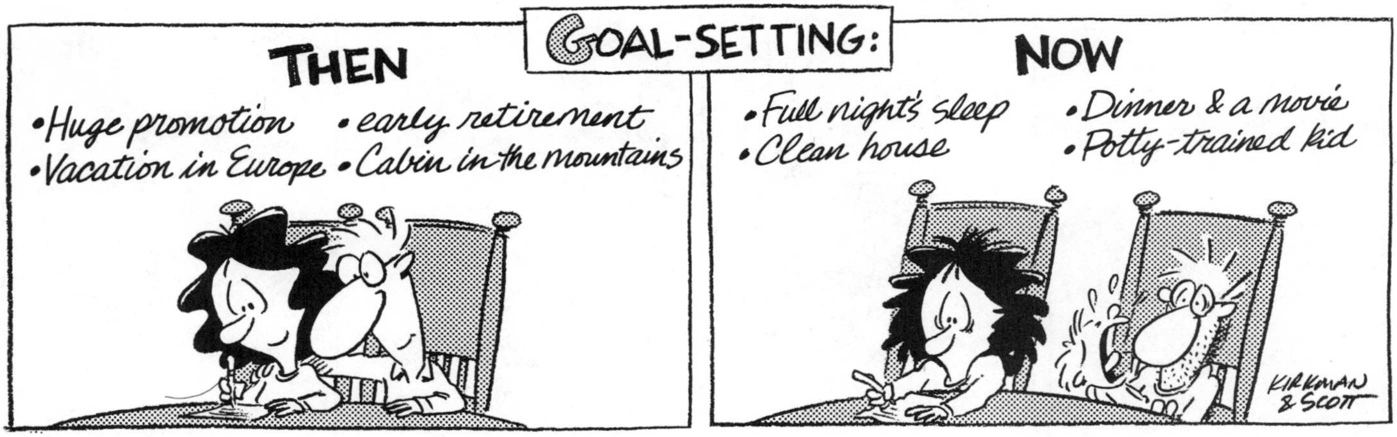
GOAL-SETTING:
THEN
•Huge promotion •early retirement
•Vacation in Europe •Cabin in the mountains
NOW
•Full night's sleep •Dinner & a movie
•Clean house •Potty-trained kid
KIRKMAN & SCOTT

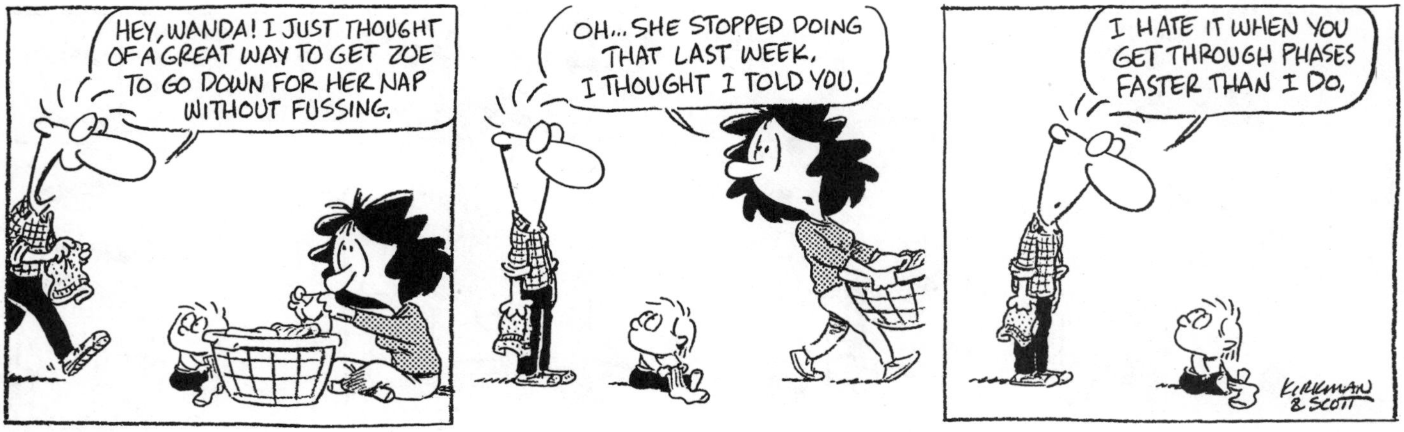
HEY, WANDA! I JUST THOUGHT OF A GREAT WAY TO GET ZOE TO GO DOWN FOR HER NAP WITHOUT FUSSING.
OH... SHE STOPPED DOING THAT LAST WEEK. I THOUGHT I TOLD YOU.
I HATE IT WHEN YOU GET THROUGH PHASES FASTER THAN I DO.
KIRKMAN & SCOTT

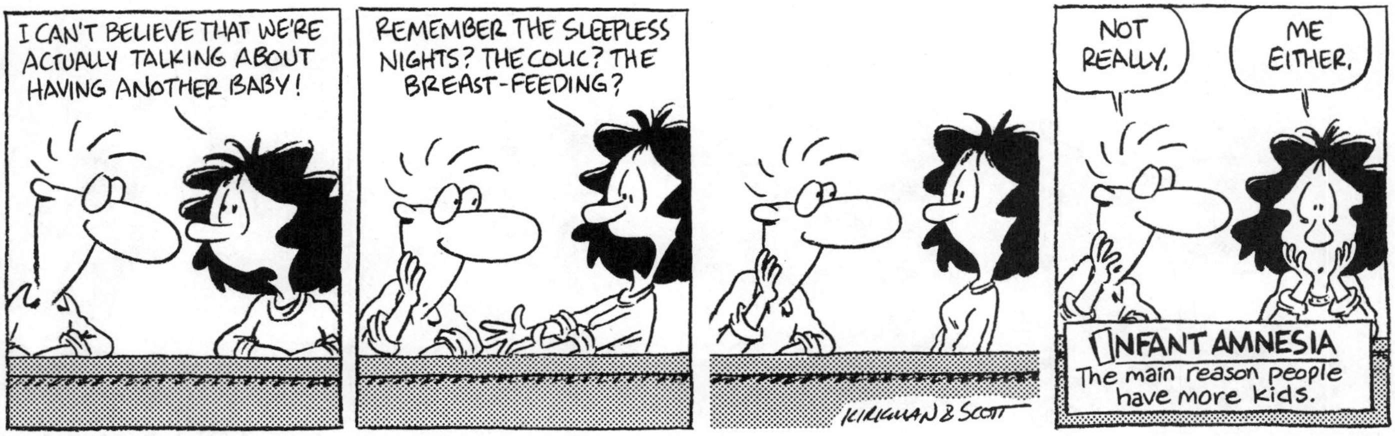
I CAN'T BELIEVE THAT WE'RE ACTUALLY TALKING ABOUT HAVING ANOTHER BABY!
REMEMBER THE SLEEPLESS NIGHTS? THE COLIC? THE BREAST-FEEDING?
KIRKMAN & SCOTT
NOT REALLY.
ME EITHER.
INFANT AMNESIA
The main reason people have more kids.

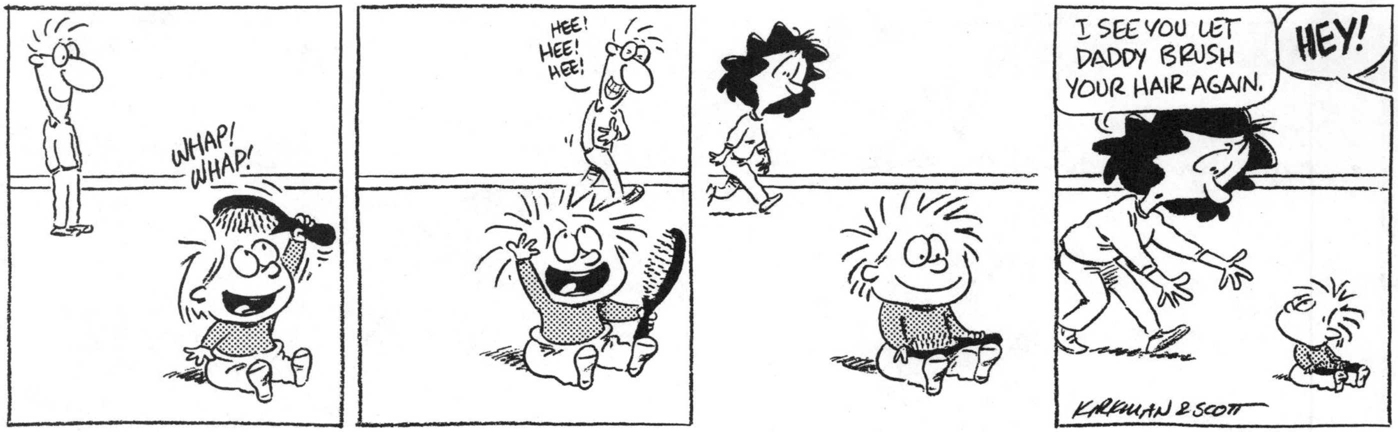
WHAP! WHAP!
HEE! HEE! HEE!
I SEE YOU LET DADDY BRUSH YOUR HAIR AGAIN.
HEY!
KIRKMAN & SCOTT

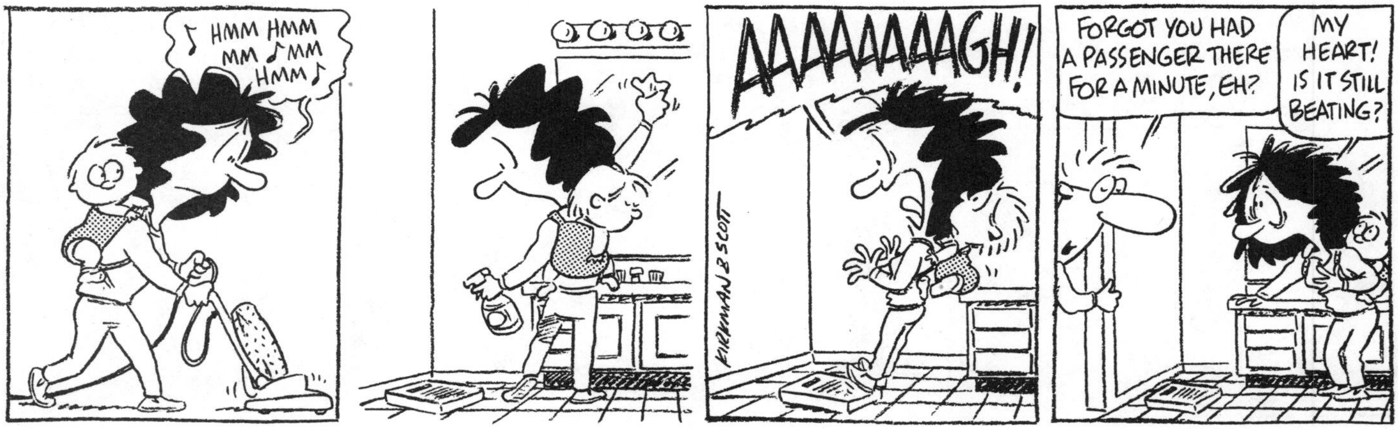
♪ HMM HMM MM ♪ MM HMM ♪
AAAAAAAAAGH!
KIRKMAN & SCOTT
FORGOT YOU HAD A PASSENGER THERE FOR A MINUTE, EH?
MY HEART! IS IT STILL BEATING?

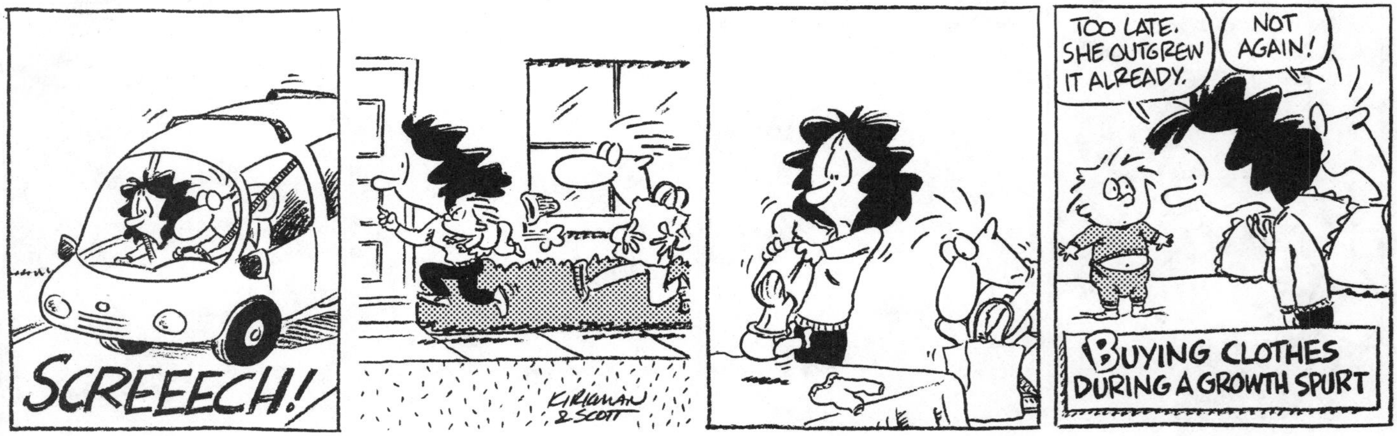
SCREEECH!
KIRKMAN & SCOTT
TOO LATE. SHE OUTGREW IT ALREADY.
NOT AGAIN!
BUYING CLOTHES DURING A GROWTH SPURT

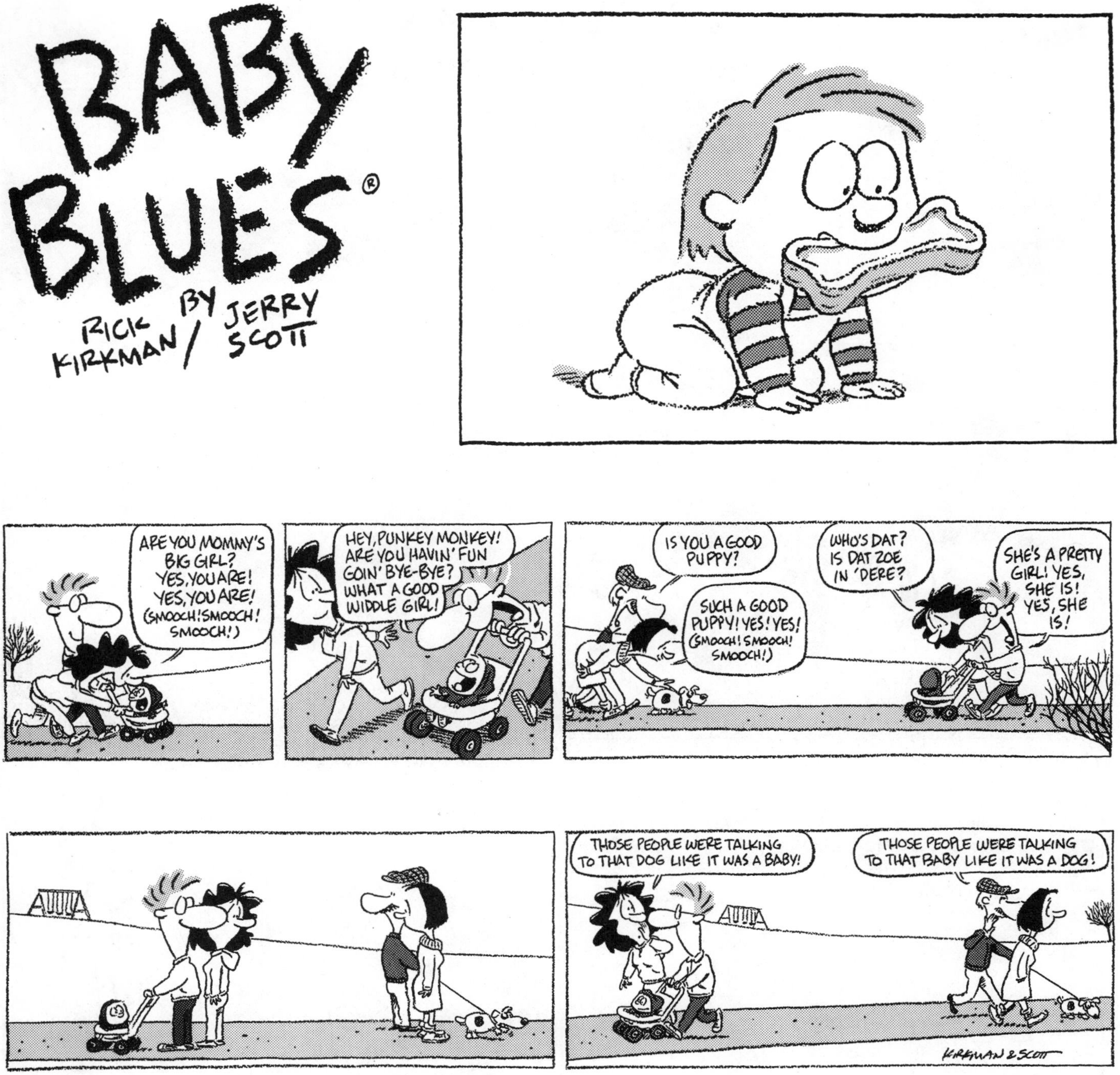
BABY BLUES®
BY RICK KIRKMAN / JERRY SCOTT
ARE YOU MOMMY'S BIG GIRL? YES, YOU ARE! YES, YOU ARE! (SMOOCH! SMOOCH! SMOOCH!)
HEY, PUNKEY MONKEY! ARE YOU HAVIN' FUN GOIN' BYE-BYE? WHAT A GOOD WIDDLE GIRL!
IS YOU A GOOD PUPPY?
SUCH A GOOD PUPPY! YES! YES! (SMOOCH! SMOOCH! SMOOCH!)
WHO'S DAT? IS DAT ZOE IN 'DERE?
SHE'S A PRETTY GIRL! YES, SHE IS! YES, SHE IS!
THOSE PEOPLE WERE TALKING TO THAT DOG LIKE IT WAS A BABY!
THOSE PEOPLE WERE TALKING TO THAT BABY LIKE IT WAS A DOG!
KIRKMAN & SCOTT

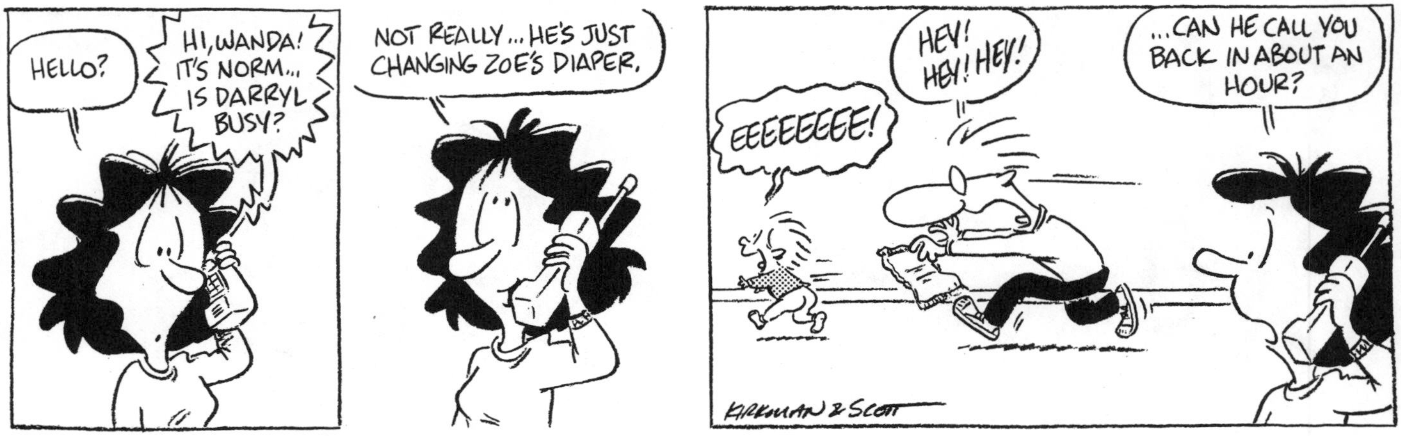
HELLO?
HI, WANDA! IT'S NORM... IS DARRYL BUSY?
NOT REALLY... HE'S JUST CHANGING ZOE'S DIAPER.
EEEEEEEE!
HEY! HEY! HEY!
...CAN HE CALL YOU BACK IN ABOUT AN HOUR?
KIRKMAN & SCOTT

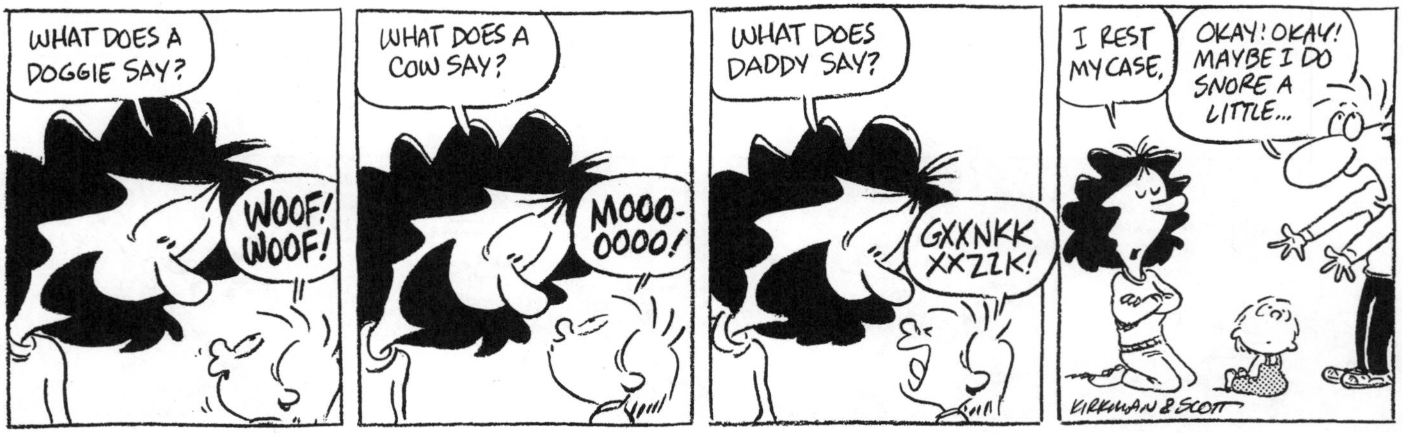
WHAT DOES A DOGGIE SAY?
WOOF! WOOF!
WHAT DOES A COW SAY?
MOOO-OOOO!
WHAT DOES DADDY SAY?
GXXNKK XXZZK!
I REST MY CASE.
OKAY! OKAY! MAYBE I DO SNORE A LITTLE...
KIRKMAN & SCOTT

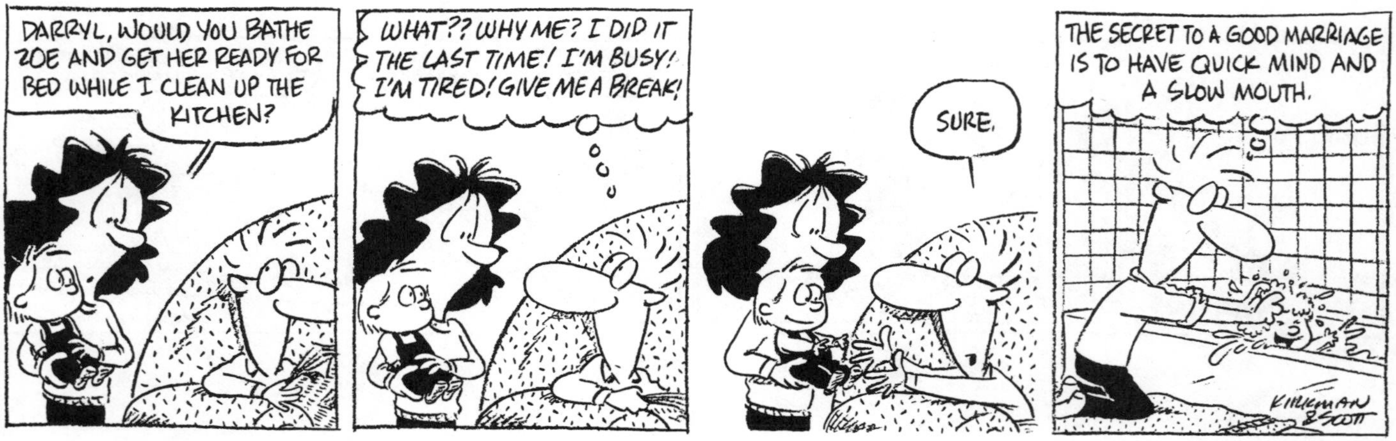
DARRYL, WOULD YOU BATHE ZOE AND GET HER READY FOR BED WHILE I CLEAN UP THE KITCHEN?
WHAT?? WHY ME? I DID IT THE LAST TIME! I'M BUSY! I'M TIRED! GIVE ME A BREAK!
SURE.
THE SECRET TO A GOOD MARRIAGE IS TO HAVE QUICK MIND AND A SLOW MOUTH.
KIRKMAN & SCOTT

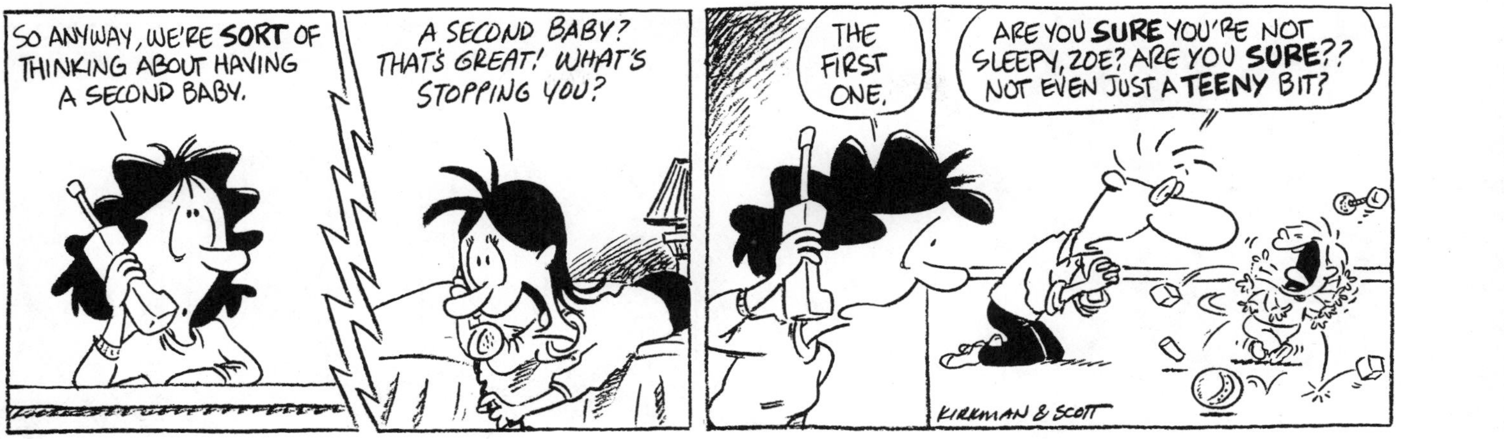
SO ANYWAY, WE'RE **SORT** OF THINKING ABOUT HAVING A SECOND BABY.
A SECOND BABY? THAT'S GREAT! WHAT'S STOPPING YOU?
THE FIRST ONE.
ARE YOU **SURE** YOU'RE NOT SLEEPY, ZOE? ARE YOU **SURE**?? NOT EVEN JUST A **TEENY** BIT?
KIRKMAN & SCOTT

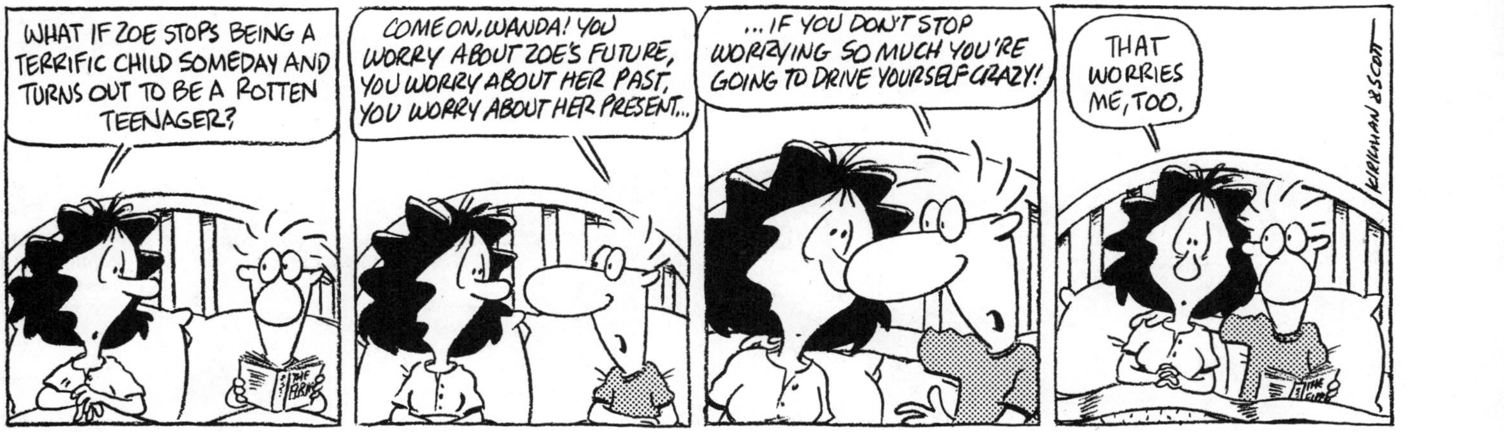
WHAT IF ZOE STOPS BEING A TERRIFIC CHILD SOMEDAY AND TURNS OUT TO BE A ROTTEN TEENAGER?
COME ON, WANDA! YOU WORRY ABOUT ZOE'S FUTURE, YOU WORRY ABOUT HER PAST, YOU WORRY ABOUT HER PRESENT...
...IF YOU DON'T STOP WORRYING SO MUCH YOU'RE GOING TO DRIVE YOURSELF CRAZY!
THAT WORRIES ME, TOO.
KIRKMAN & SCOTT

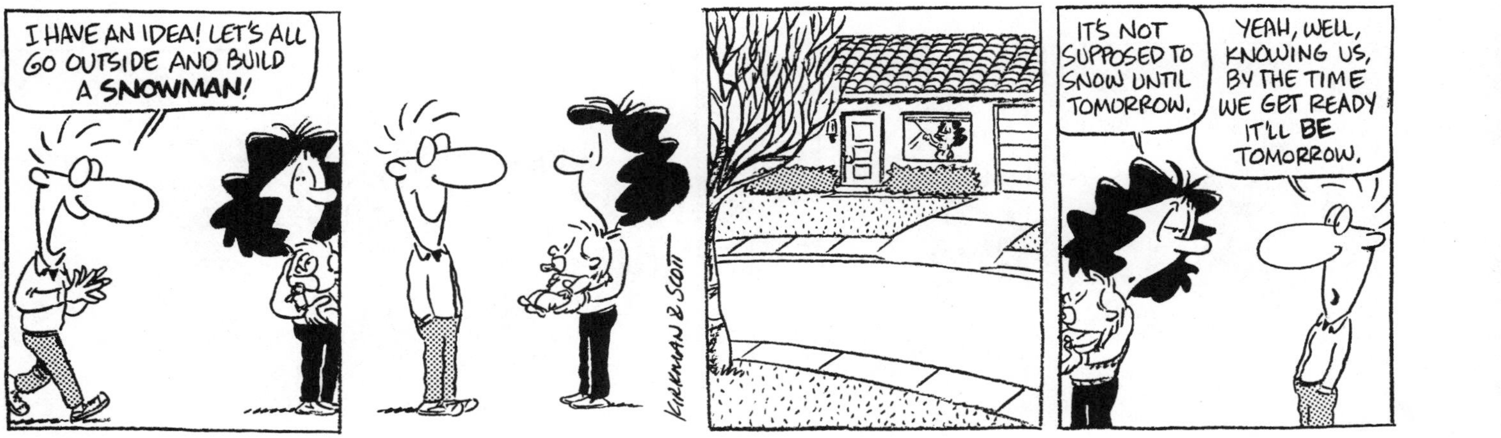
I HAVE AN IDEA! LET'S ALL GO OUTSIDE AND BUILD A **SNOWMAN**!
KIRKMAN & SCOTT
IT'S NOT SUPPOSED TO SNOW UNTIL TOMORROW.
YEAH, WELL, KNOWING US, BY THE TIME WE GET READY IT'LL **BE** TOMORROW.

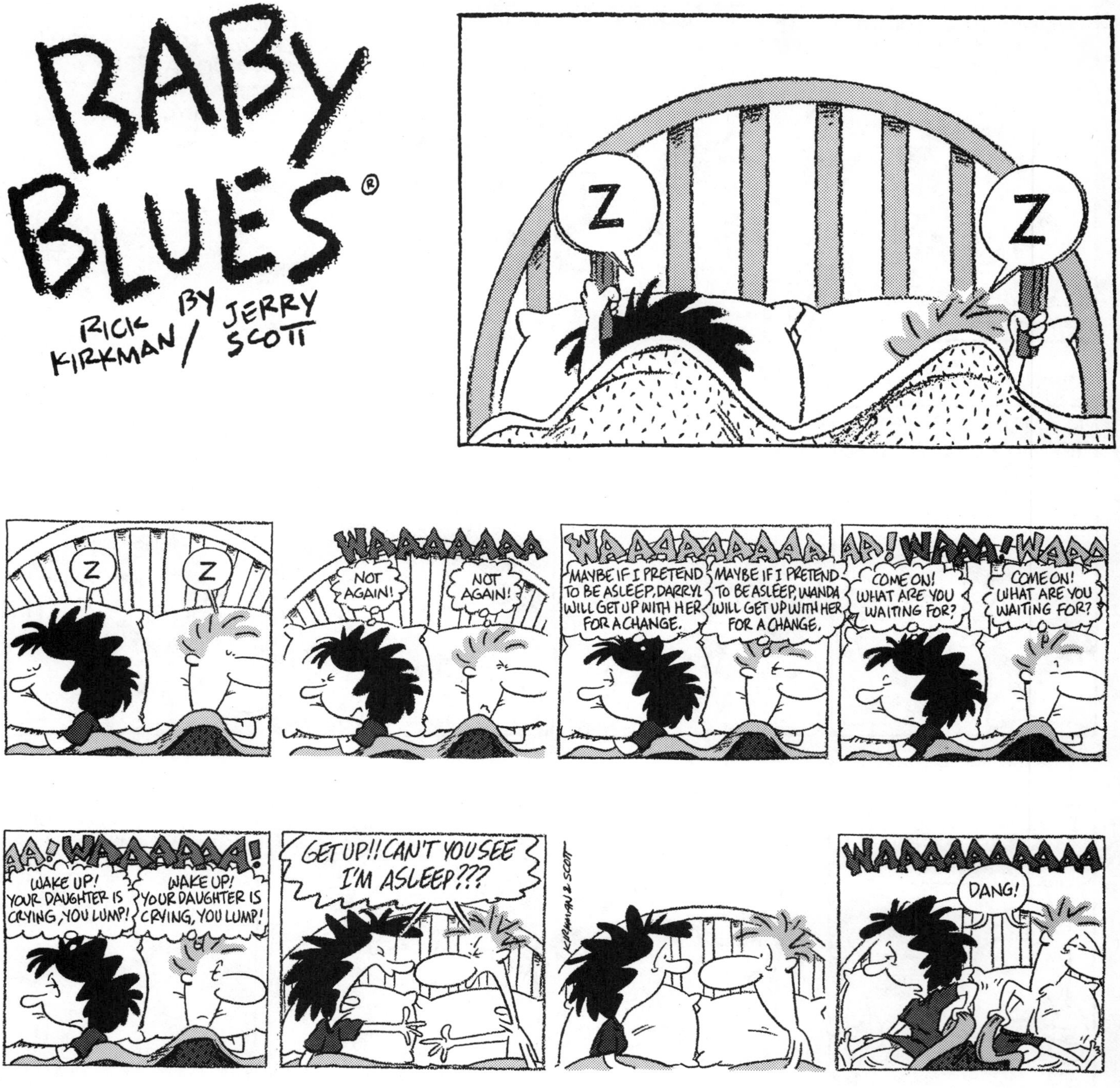

BABY BLUES®
BY RICK KIRKMAN / JERRY SCOTT
Z
Z
Z
Z
WAAAAAAAA
NOT AGAIN!
NOT AGAIN!
WAAAAAAAAAAAAA!
MAYBE IF I PRETEND TO BE ASLEEP, DARRYL WILL GET UP WITH HER FOR A CHANGE.
MAYBE IF I PRETEND TO BE ASLEEP, WANDA WILL GET UP WITH HER FOR A CHANGE.
WAAA! WAAA
COME ON! WHAT ARE YOU WAITING FOR?
COME ON! WHAT ARE YOU WAITING FOR?
AA! WAAAAAA!
WAKE UP! YOUR DAUGHTER IS CRYING, YOU LUMP!
WAKE UP! YOUR DAUGHTER IS CRYING, YOU LUMP!
GET UP!! CAN'T YOU SEE I'M ASLEEP???
KIRKMAN & SCOTT
WAAAAAAAAAA
DANG!

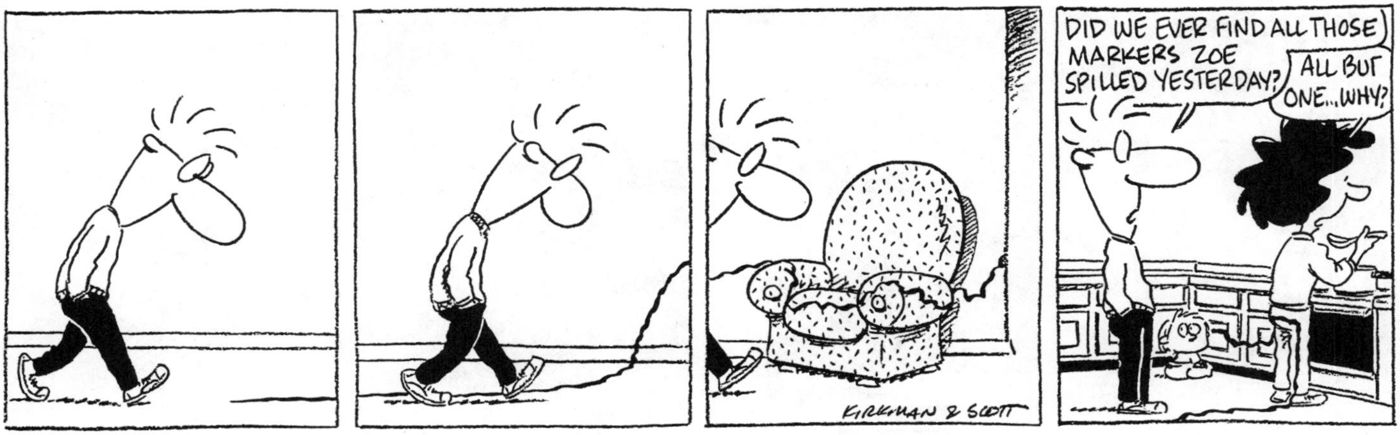
DID WE EVER FIND ALL THOSE MARKERS ZOE SPILLED YESTERDAY?
ALL BUT ONE... WHY?
KIRKMAN & SCOTT

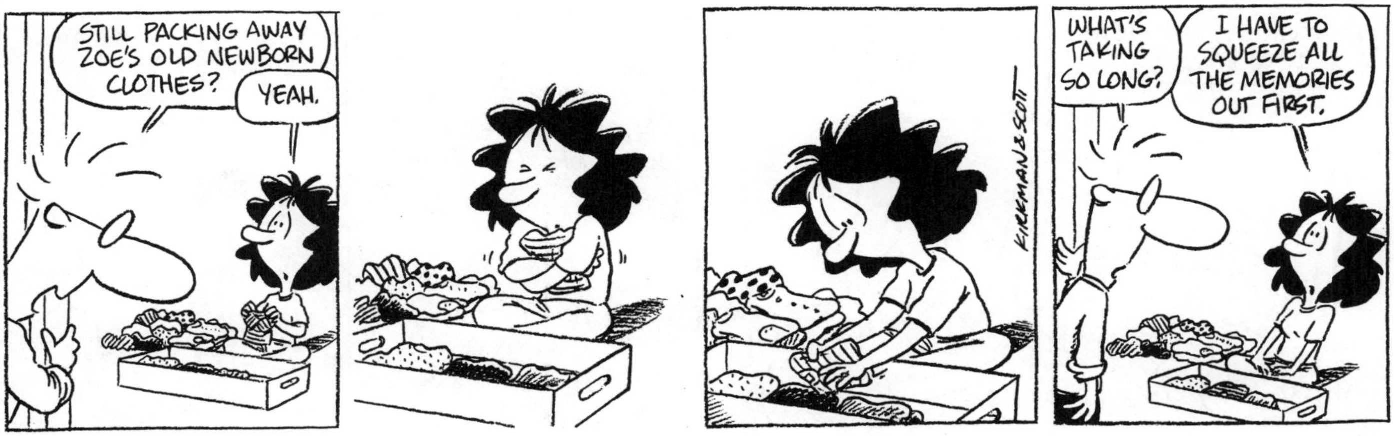
STILL PACKING AWAY ZOE'S OLD NEWBORN CLOTHES?
YEAH.
KIRKMAN & SCOTT
WHAT'S TAKING SO LONG?
I HAVE TO SQUEEZE ALL THE MEMORIES OUT FIRST.

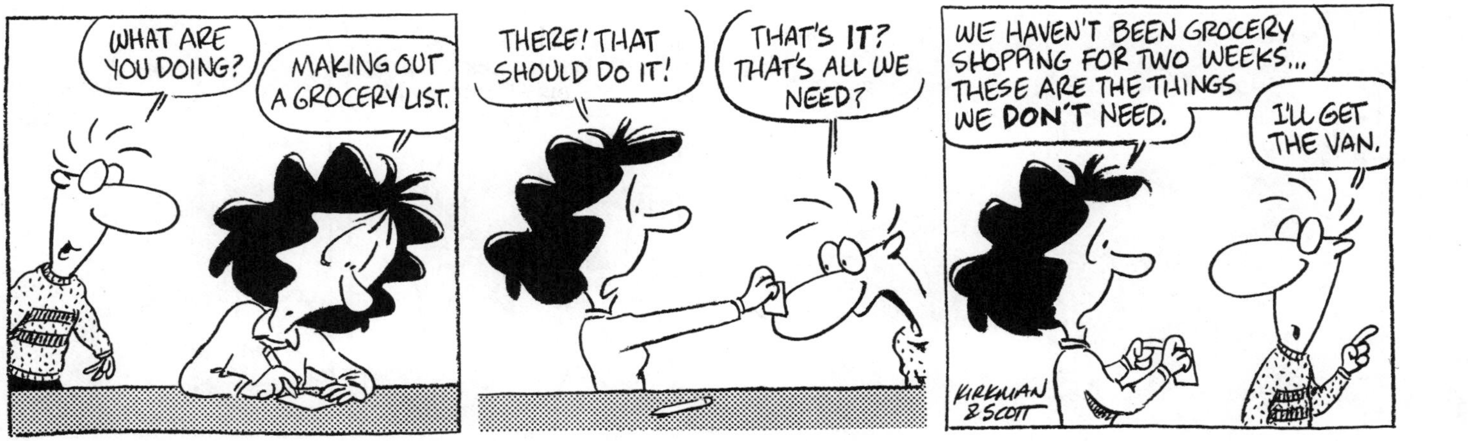
WHAT ARE YOU DOING?
MAKING OUT A GROCERY LIST.
THERE! THAT SHOULD DO IT!
THAT'S IT? THAT'S ALL WE NEED?
WE HAVEN'T BEEN GROCERY SHOPPING FOR TWO WEEKS... THESE ARE THE THINGS WE DON'T NEED.
I'LL GET THE VAN.
KIRKMAN & SCOTT

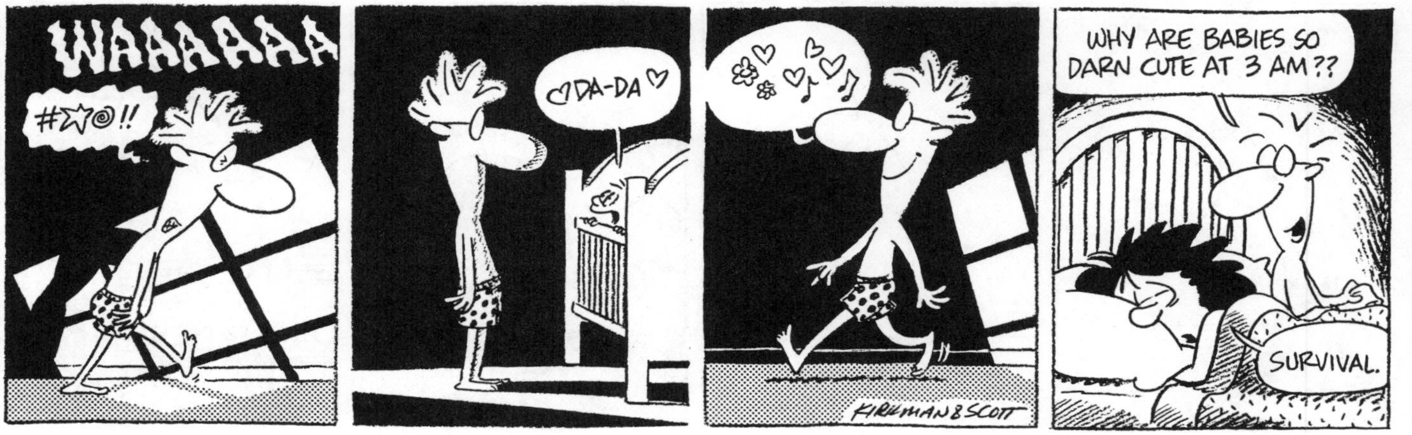
WAAAAAA
#☆◎!!
DA-DA
WHY ARE BABIES SO DARN CUTE AT 3 AM??
SURVIVAL.
KIRKMAN & SCOTT

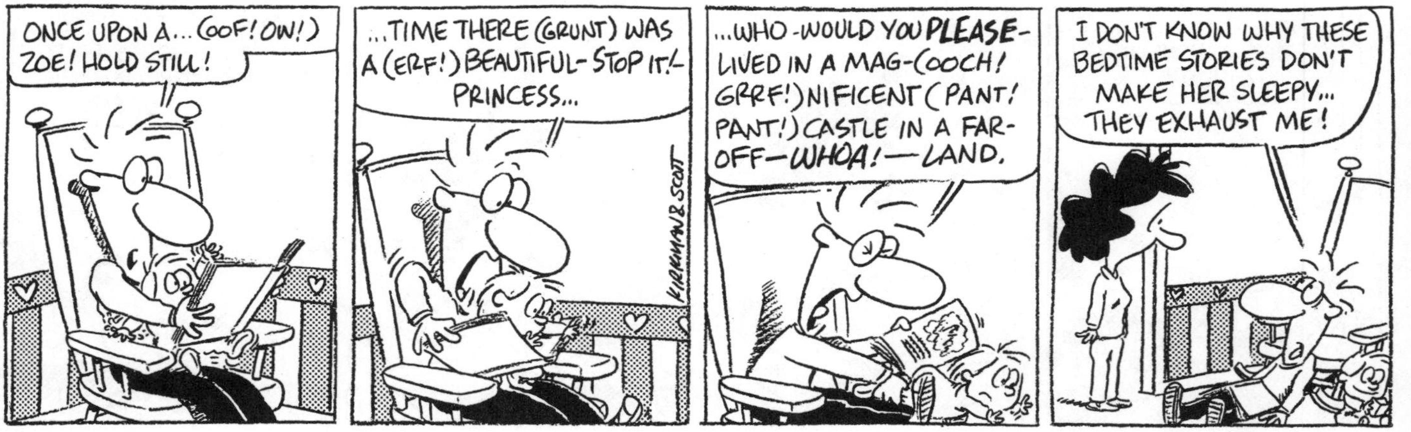
ONCE UPON A... (OOF! OW!) ZOE! HOLD STILL!
...TIME THERE (GRUNT) WAS A (ERF!) BEAUTIFUL- STOP IT!- PRINCESS...
KIRKMAN & SCOTT
...WHO-WOULD YOU PLEASE- LIVED IN A MAG-(OOCH! GRRF!) NIFICENT (PANT! PANT!) CASTLE IN A FAR-OFF—WHOA!—LAND.
I DON'T KNOW WHY THESE BEDTIME STORIES DON'T MAKE HER SLEEPY... THEY EXHAUST ME!

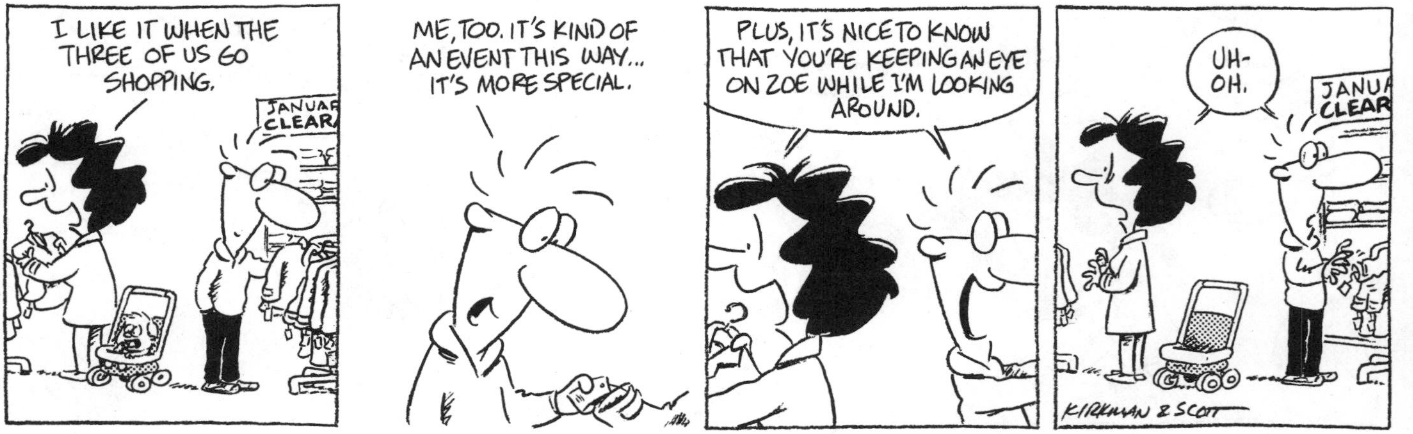
I LIKE IT WHEN THE THREE OF US GO SHOPPING.
ME, TOO. IT'S KIND OF AN EVENT THIS WAY... IT'S MORE SPECIAL.
PLUS, IT'S NICE TO KNOW THAT YOU'RE KEEPING AN EYE ON ZOE WHILE I'M LOOKING AROUND.
UH-OH.
KIRKMAN & SCOTT

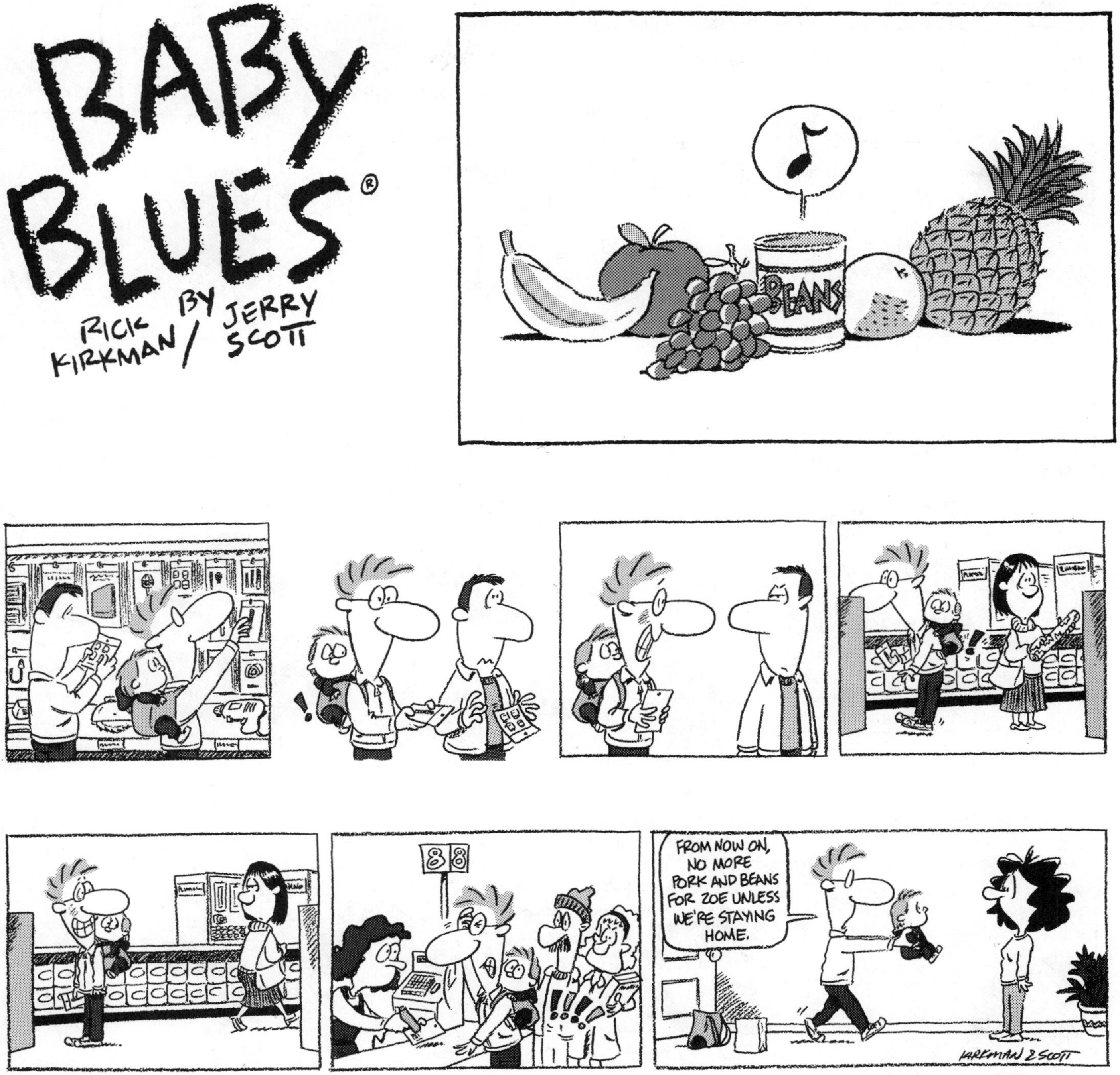
BABY BLUES®
BY RICK KIRKMAN / JERRY SCOTT
BEANS
88
FROM NOW ON, NO MORE PORK AND BEANS FOR ZOE UNLESS WE'RE STAYING HOME.
KIRKMAN & SCOTT

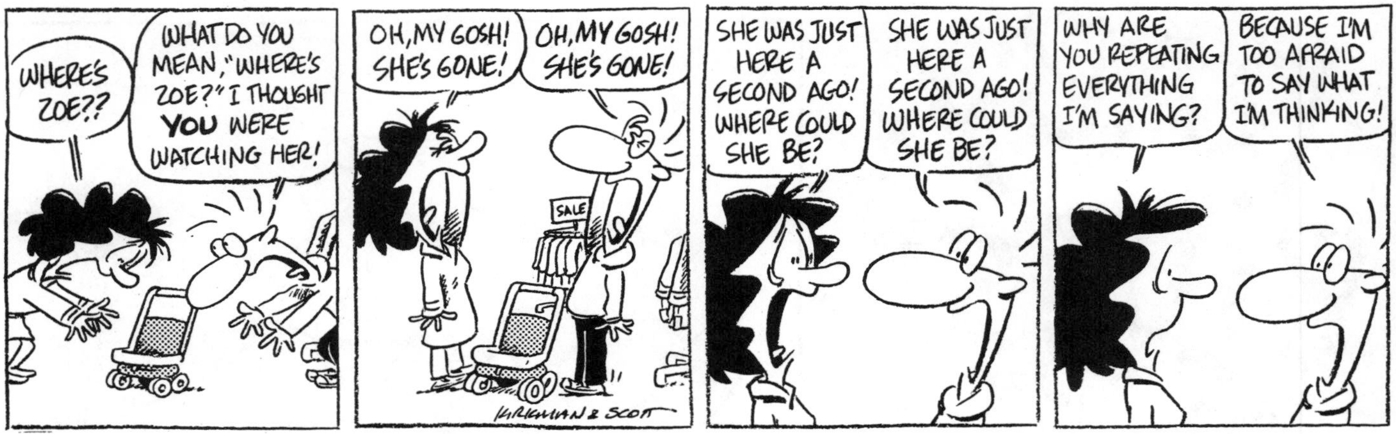
WHERE'S ZOE??
WHAT DO YOU MEAN, "WHERE'S ZOE?" I THOUGHT **YOU** WERE WATCHING HER!
OH, MY GOSH! SHE'S GONE!
OH, **MY** GOSH! SHE'S GONE!
SALE
KIRKMAN & SCOTT
SHE WAS JUST HERE A SECOND AGO! WHERE COULD SHE BE?
SHE WAS JUST HERE A SECOND AGO! WHERE COULD SHE BE?
WHY ARE YOU REPEATING EVERYTHING I'M SAYING?
BECAUSE I'M TOO AFRAID TO SAY WHAT I'M THINKING!

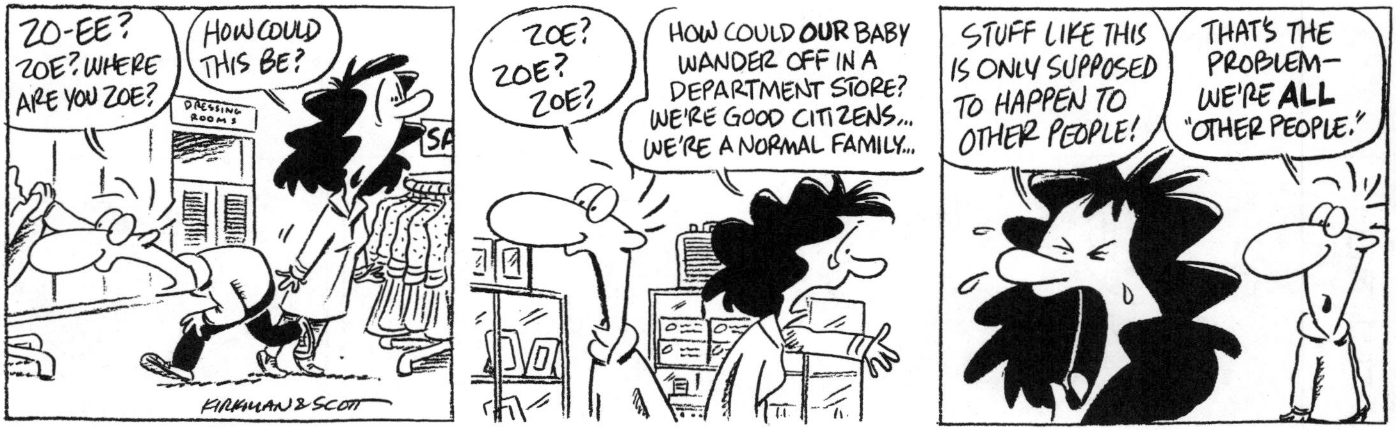
ZO-EE? ZOE? WHERE ARE YOU ZOE?
HOW COULD THIS BE?
DRESSING ROOMS
KIRKMAN & SCOTT
ZOE? ZOE? ZOE?
HOW COULD **OUR** BABY WANDER OFF IN A DEPARTMENT STORE? WE'RE GOOD CITIZENS... WE'RE A NORMAL FAMILY...
STUFF LIKE THIS IS ONLY SUPPOSED TO HAPPEN TO OTHER PEOPLE!
THAT'S THE PROBLEM— WE'RE **ALL** "OTHER PEOPLE."

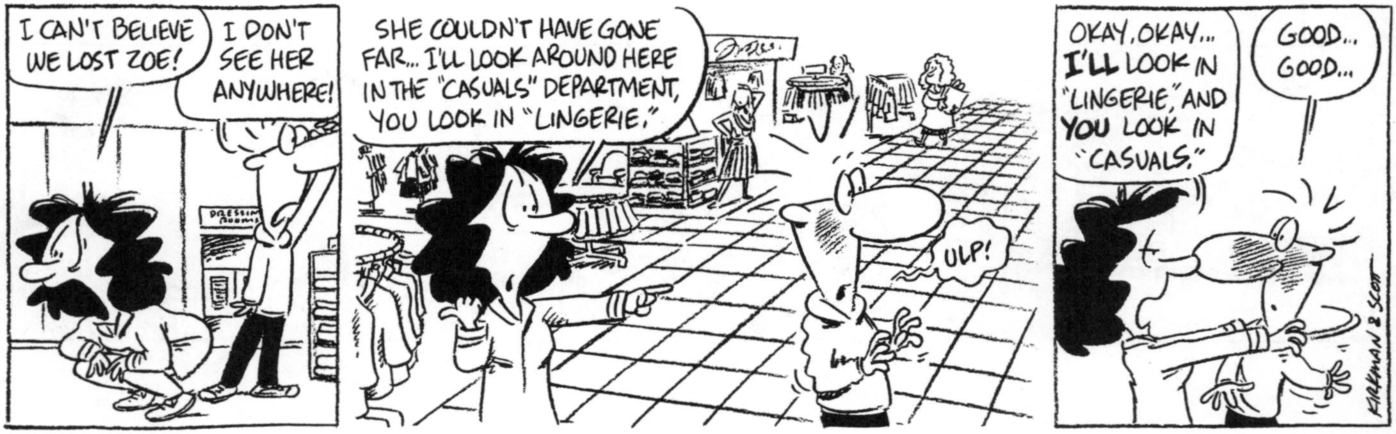
I CAN'T BELIEVE WE LOST ZOE!
I DON'T SEE HER ANYWHERE!
DRESSING ROOMS
SHE COULDN'T HAVE GONE FAR... I'LL LOOK AROUND HERE IN THE "CASUALS" DEPARTMENT, YOU LOOK IN "LINGERIE."
ULP!
OKAY, OKAY... **I'LL** LOOK IN "LINGERIE," AND **YOU** LOOK IN "CASUALS."
GOOD... GOOD...
KIRKMAN & SCOTT

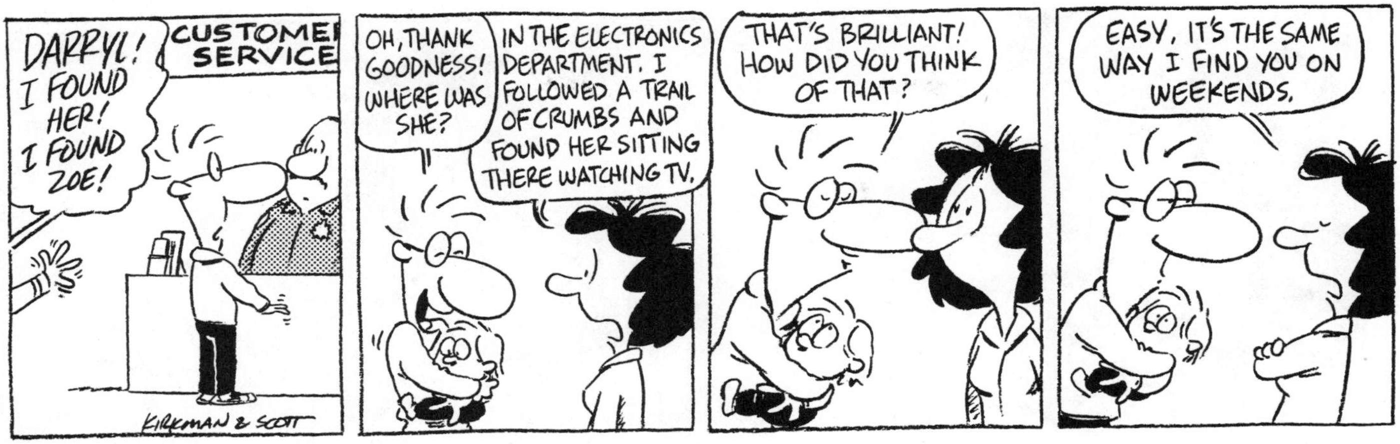
DARRYL! I FOUND HER! I FOUND ZOE!
CUSTOMER SERVICE
KIRKMAN & SCOTT
OH, THANK GOODNESS! WHERE WAS SHE?
IN THE ELECTRONICS DEPARTMENT. I FOLLOWED A TRAIL OF CRUMBS AND FOUND HER SITTING THERE WATCHING TV.
THAT'S BRILLIANT! HOW DID YOU THINK OF THAT?
EASY. IT'S THE SAME WAY I FIND YOU ON WEEKENDS.

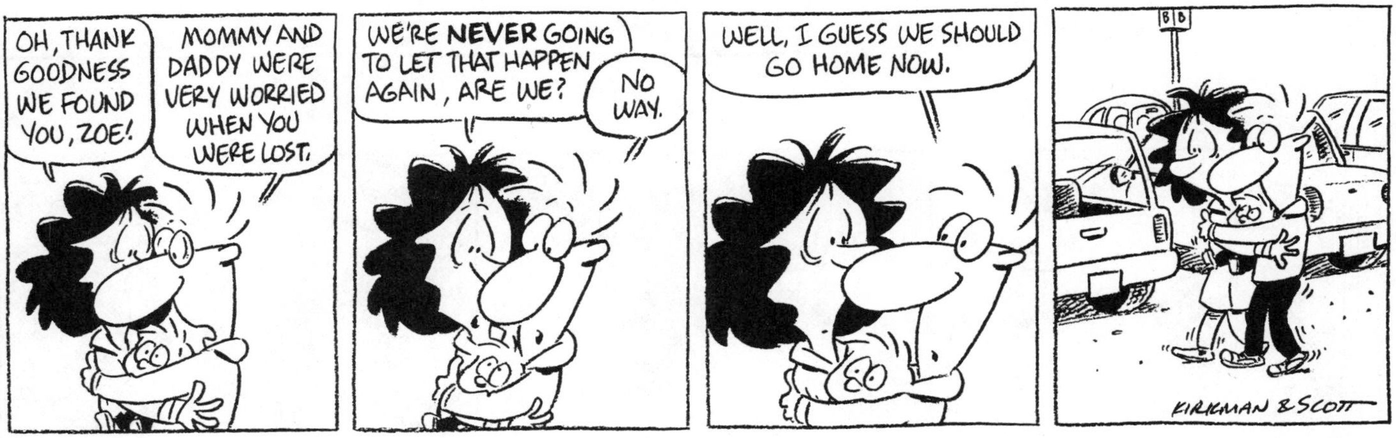
OH, THANK GOODNESS WE FOUND YOU, ZOE!
MOMMY AND DADDY WERE VERY WORRIED WHEN YOU WERE LOST.
WE'RE **NEVER** GOING TO LET THAT HAPPEN AGAIN, ARE WE?
NO WAY.
WELL, I GUESS WE SHOULD GO HOME NOW.
KIRKMAN & SCOTT

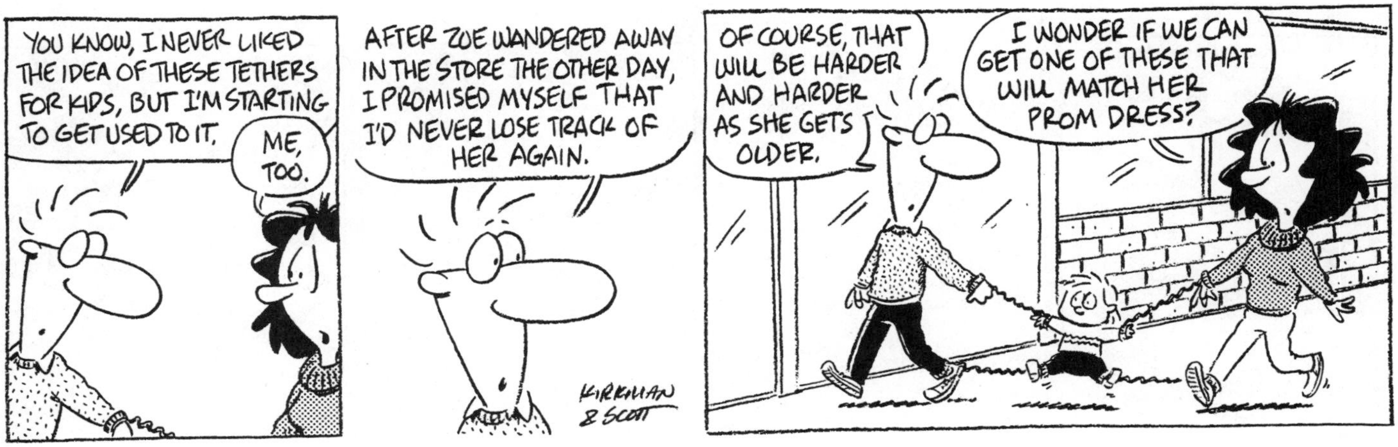
YOU KNOW, I NEVER LIKED THE IDEA OF THESE TETHERS FOR KIDS, BUT I'M STARTING TO GET USED TO IT.
ME, TOO.
AFTER ZOE WANDERED AWAY IN THE STORE THE OTHER DAY, I PROMISED MYSELF THAT I'D NEVER LOSE TRACK OF HER AGAIN.
KIRKMAN & SCOTT
OF COURSE, THAT WILL BE HARDER AND HARDER AS SHE GETS OLDER.
I WONDER IF WE CAN GET ONE OF THESE THAT WILL MATCH HER PROM DRESS?

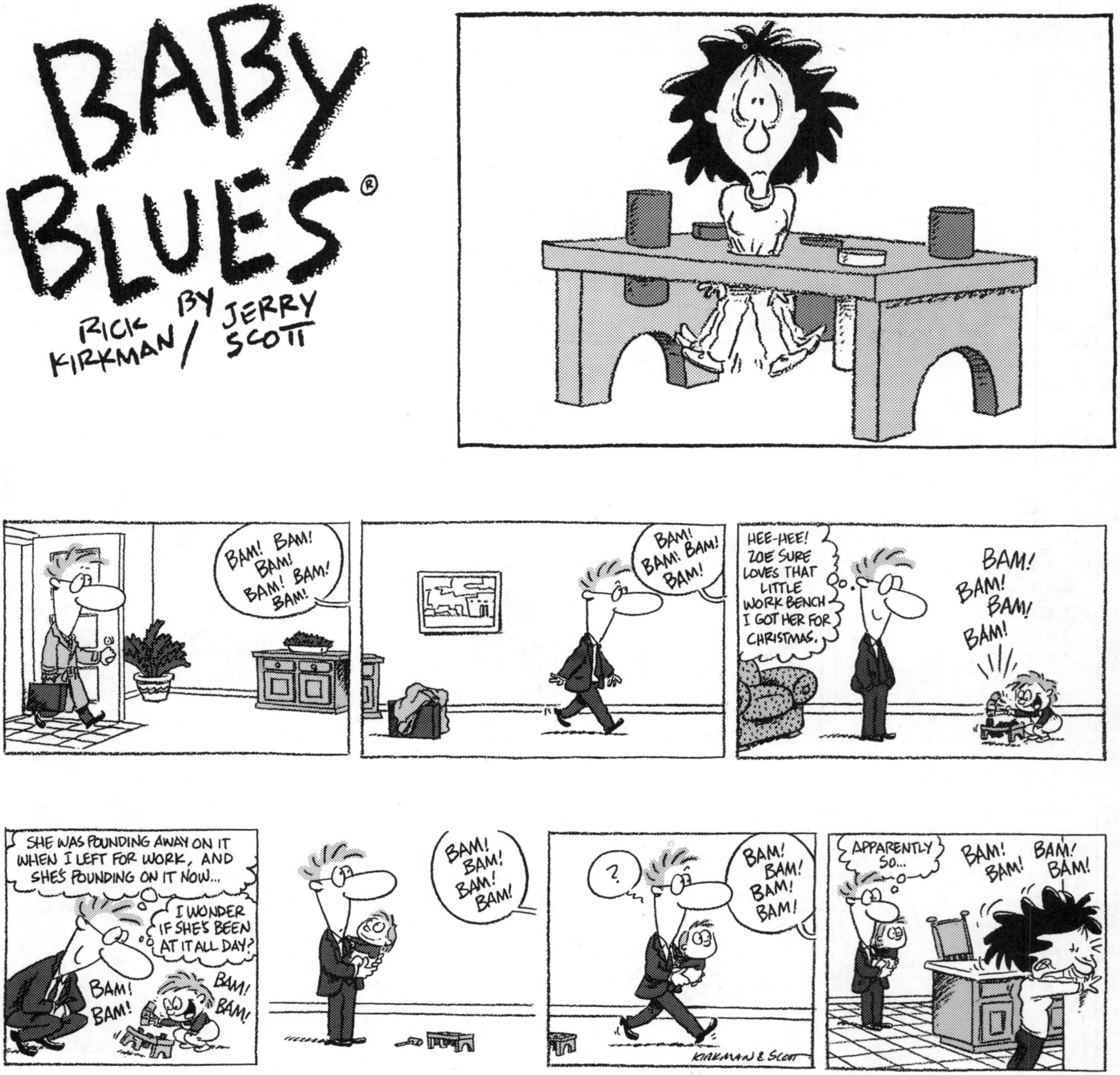

BABY BLUES®
BY RICK KIRKMAN / JERRY SCOTT
BAM! BAM! BAM! BAM! BAM! BAM!
BAM! BAM! BAM! BAM!
HEE-HEE! ZOE SURE LOVES THAT LITTLE WORK BENCH I GOT HER FOR CHRISTMAS.
BAM! BAM! BAM! BAM!
SHE WAS POUNDING AWAY ON IT WHEN I LEFT FOR WORK, AND SHE'S POUNDING ON IT NOW...
I WONDER IF SHE'S BEEN AT IT ALL DAY?
BAM! BAM!
BAM! BAM!
BAM! BAM! BAM! BAM!
?
BAM! BAM! BAM! BAM!
KIRKMAN & SCOTT
APPARENTLY SO...
BAM! BAM!
BAM! BAM!

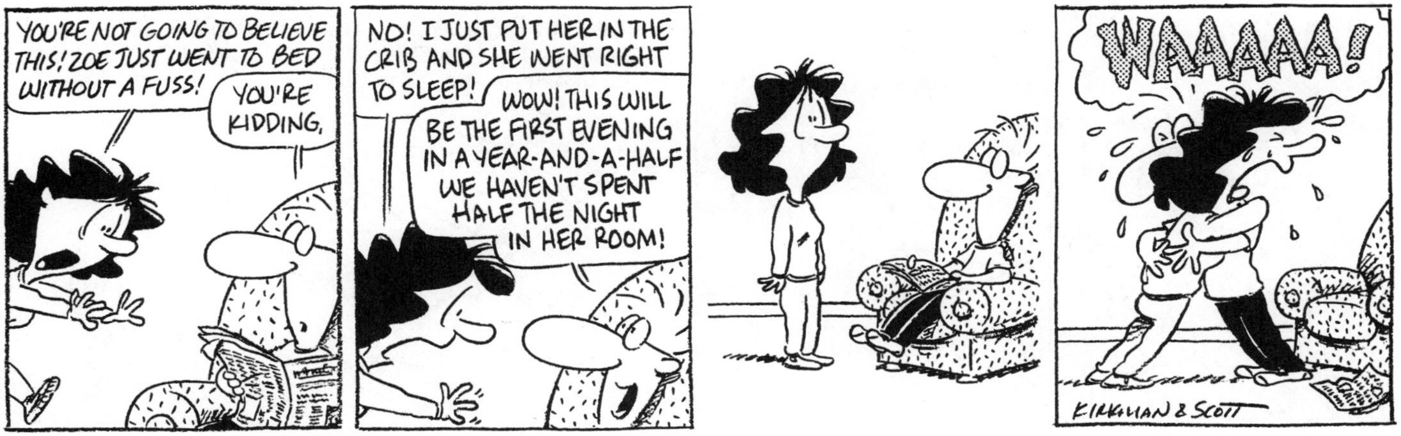
YOU'RE NOT GOING TO BELIEVE THIS! ZOE JUST WENT TO BED WITHOUT A FUSS!
YOU'RE KIDDING.
NO! I JUST PUT HER IN THE CRIB AND SHE WENT RIGHT TO SLEEP!
WOW! THIS WILL BE THE FIRST EVENING IN A YEAR-AND-A-HALF WE HAVEN'T SPENT HALF THE NIGHT IN HER ROOM!
WAAAAAA!
KIRKMAN & SCOTT

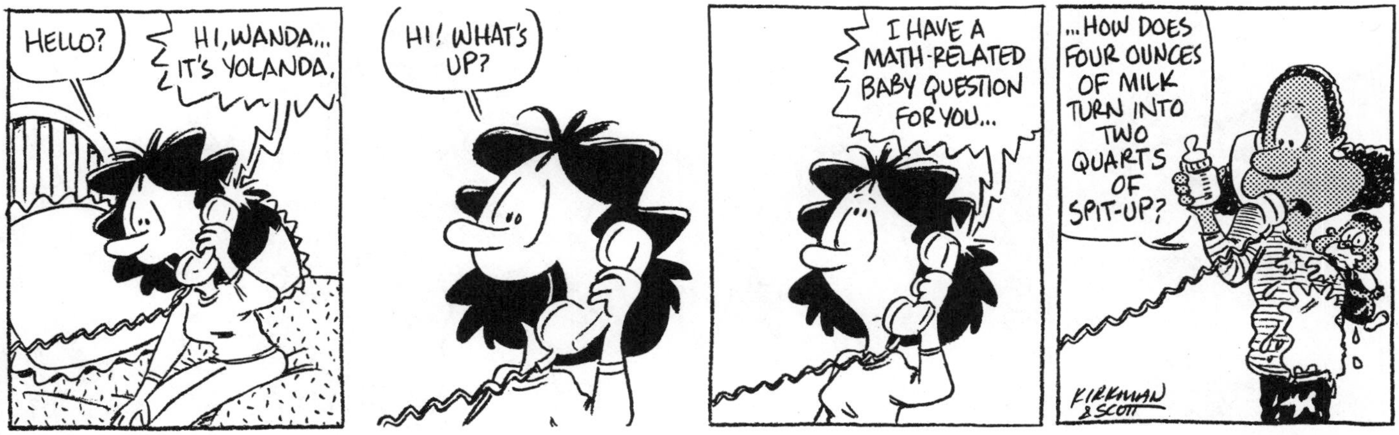
HELLO?
HI, WANDA... IT'S YOLANDA.
HI! WHAT'S UP?
I HAVE A MATH-RELATED BABY QUESTION FOR YOU...
...HOW DOES FOUR OUNCES OF MILK TURN INTO TWO QUARTS OF SPIT-UP?
KIRKMAN & SCOTT

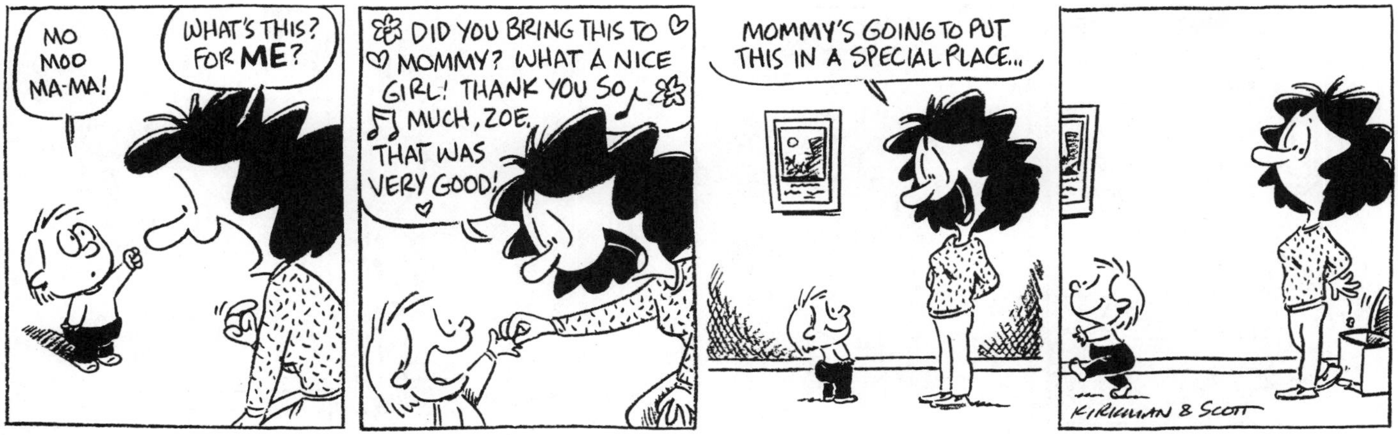
MO MOO MA-MA!
WHAT'S THIS? FOR **ME**?
DID YOU BRING THIS TO MOMMY? WHAT A NICE GIRL! THANK YOU SO MUCH, ZOE. THAT WAS VERY GOOD!
MOMMY'S GOING TO PUT THIS IN A SPECIAL PLACE...
KIRKMAN & SCOTT

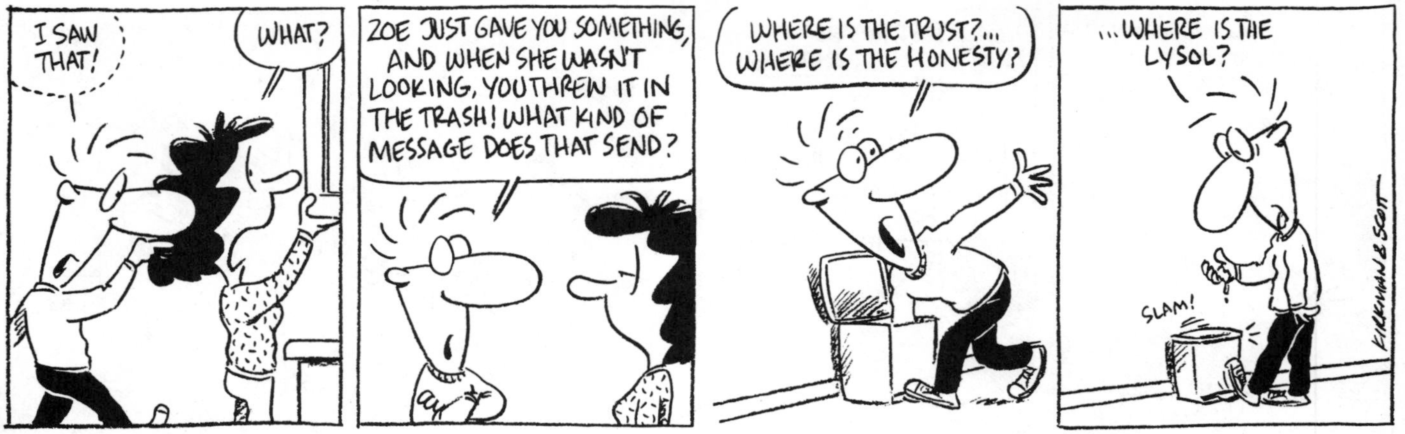
I SAW THAT!
WHAT?
ZOE JUST GAVE YOU SOMETHING, AND WHEN SHE WASN'T LOOKING, YOU THREW IT IN THE TRASH! WHAT KIND OF MESSAGE DOES THAT SEND?
WHERE IS THE TRUST?... WHERE IS THE HONESTY?
...WHERE IS THE LYSOL?
SLAM!
KIRKMAN & SCOTT

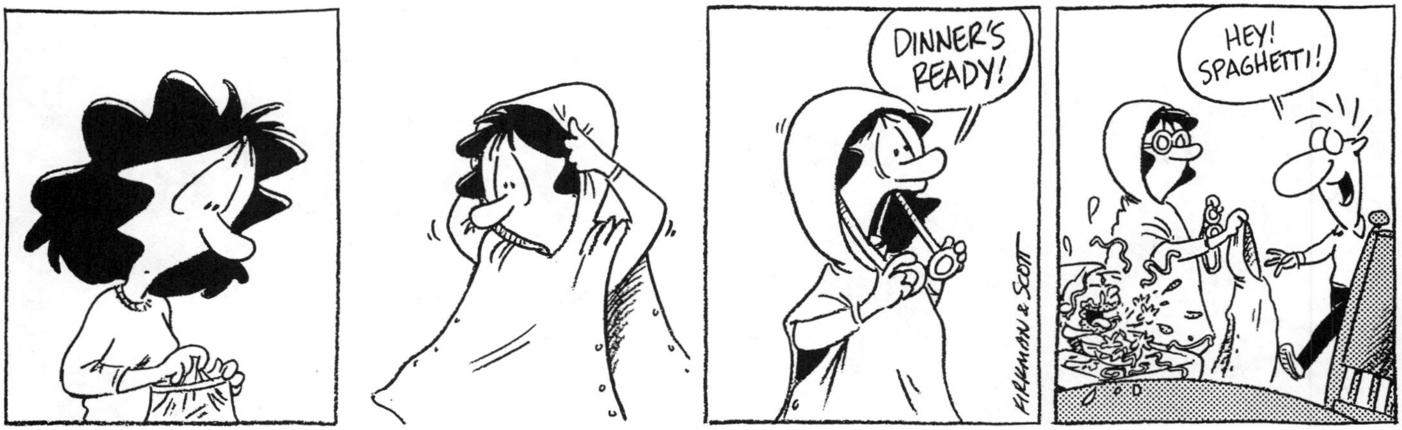
DINNER'S READY!
KIRKMAN & SCOTT
HEY! SPAGHETTI!

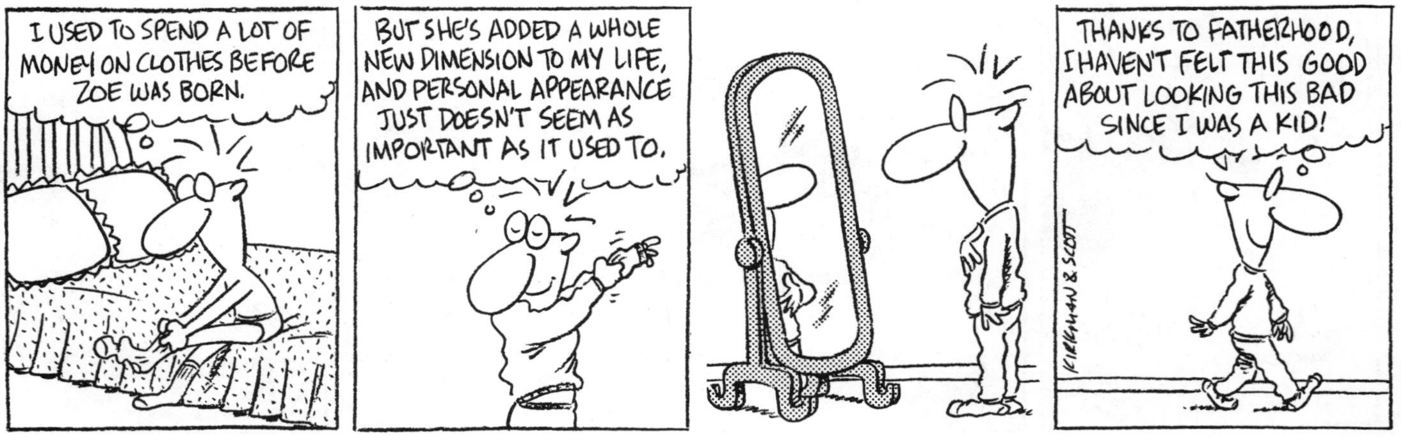
I USED TO SPEND A LOT OF MONEY ON CLOTHES BEFORE ZOE WAS BORN.
BUT SHE'S ADDED A WHOLE NEW DIMENSION TO MY LIFE, AND PERSONAL APPEARANCE JUST DOESN'T SEEM AS IMPORTANT AS IT USED TO.
KIRKMAN & SCOTT
THANKS TO FATHERHOOD, I HAVEN'T FELT THIS GOOD ABOUT LOOKING THIS BAD SINCE I WAS A KID!

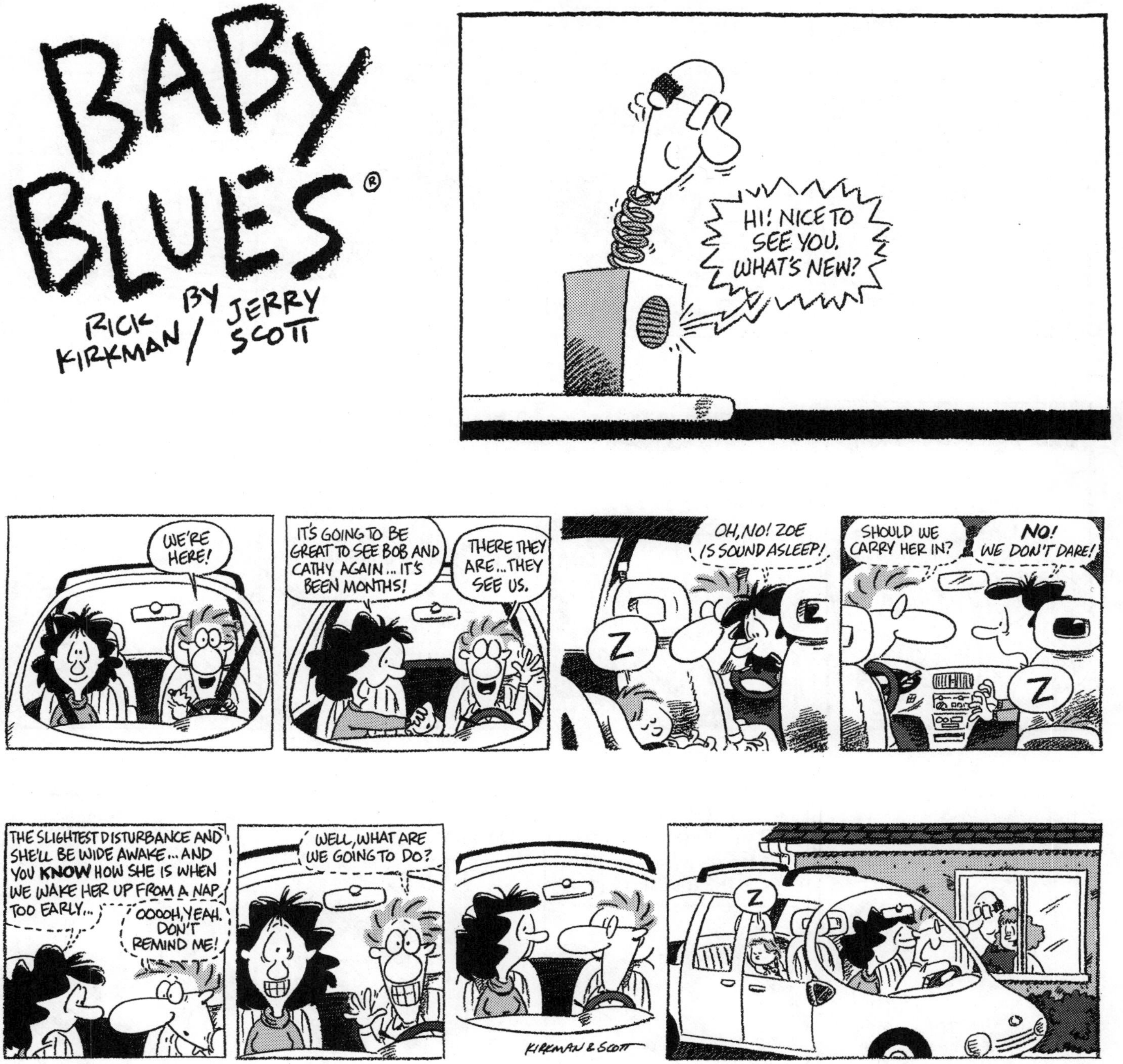
BABY BLUES®
BY RICK KIRKMAN / JERRY SCOTT
HI! NICE TO SEE YOU. WHAT'S NEW?
WE'RE HERE!
IT'S GOING TO BE GREAT TO SEE BOB AND CATHY AGAIN... IT'S BEEN MONTHS!
THERE THEY ARE... THEY SEE US.
OH, NO! ZOE IS SOUND ASLEEP!
Z
SHOULD WE CARRY HER IN?
NO! WE DON'T DARE!
Z
THE SLIGHTEST DISTURBANCE AND SHE'LL BE WIDE AWAKE... AND YOU KNOW HOW SHE IS WHEN WE WAKE HER UP FROM A NAP TOO EARLY...
OOOOH, YEAH. DON'T REMIND ME!
WELL, WHAT ARE WE GOING TO DO?
KIRKMAN & SCOTT
Z

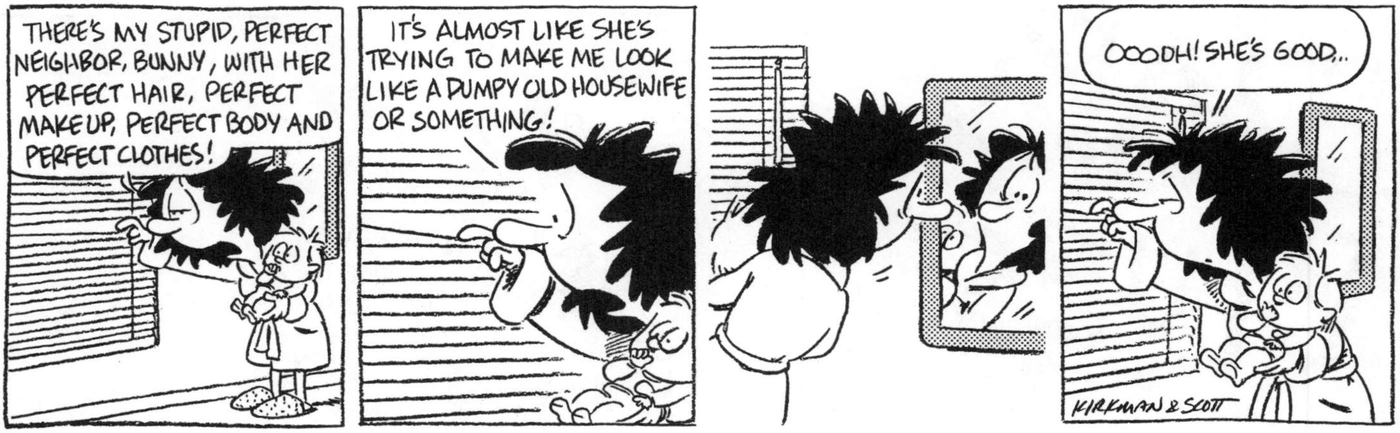
THERE'S MY STUPID, PERFECT NEIGHBOR, BUNNY, WITH HER PERFECT HAIR, PERFECT MAKEUP, PERFECT BODY AND PERFECT CLOTHES!
IT'S ALMOST LIKE SHE'S TRYING TO MAKE ME LOOK LIKE A DUMPY OLD HOUSEWIFE OR SOMETHING!
OOOOH! SHE'S GOOD...
KIRKMAN & SCOTT

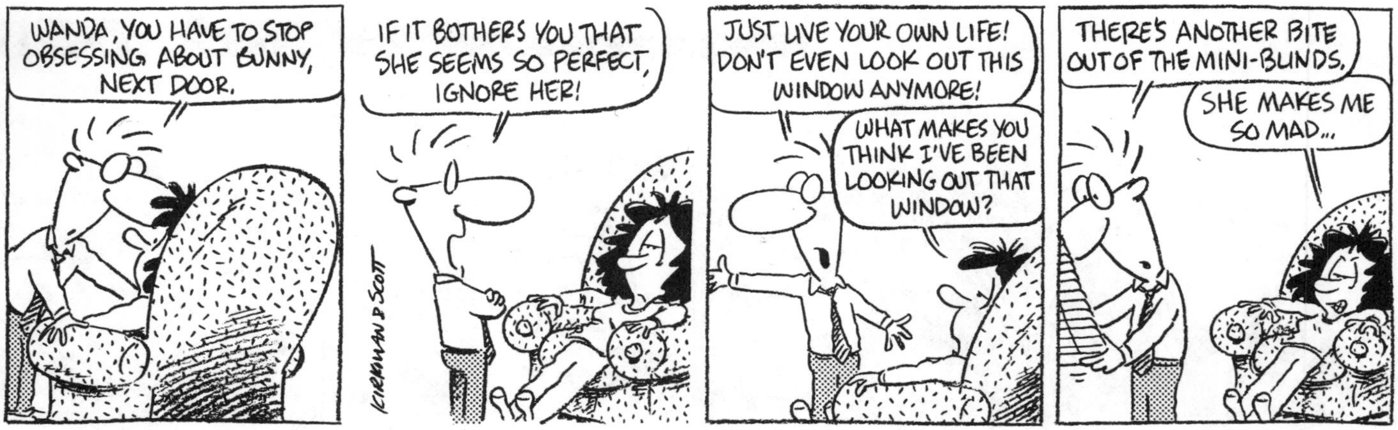
WANDA, YOU HAVE TO STOP OBSESSING ABOUT BUNNY, NEXT DOOR.
IF IT BOTHERS YOU THAT SHE SEEMS SO PERFECT, IGNORE HER!
KIRKMAN & SCOTT
JUST LIVE YOUR OWN LIFE! DON'T EVEN LOOK OUT THIS WINDOW ANYMORE!
WHAT MAKES YOU THINK I'VE BEEN LOOKING OUT THAT WINDOW?
THERE'S ANOTHER BITE OUT OF THE MINI-BLINDS.
SHE MAKES ME SO MAD...

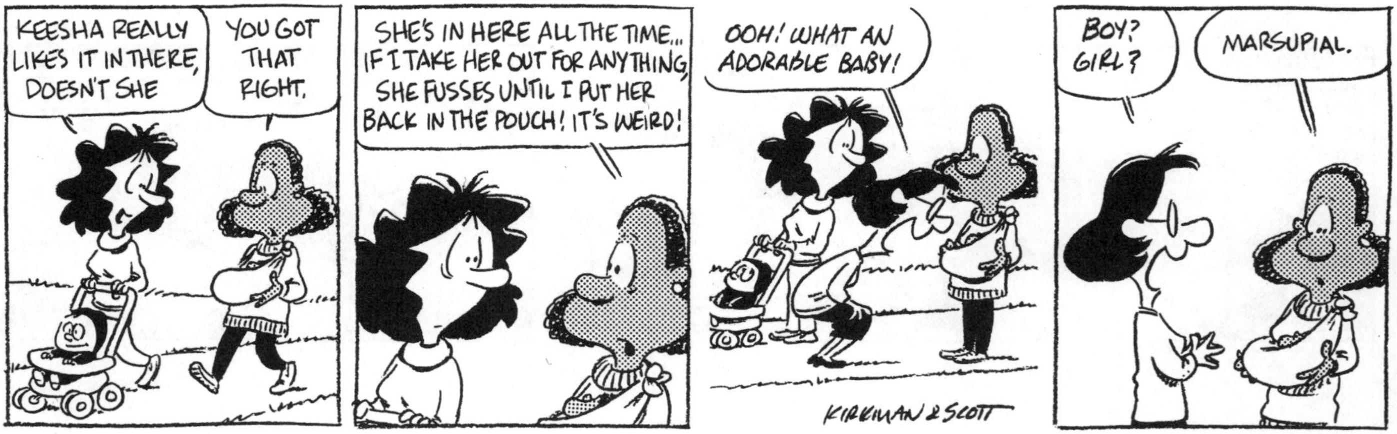
KEESHA REALLY LIKES IT IN THERE, DOESN'T SHE
YOU GOT THAT RIGHT.
SHE'S IN HERE ALL THE TIME... IF I TAKE HER OUT FOR ANYTHING, SHE FUSSES UNTIL I PUT HER BACK IN THE POUCH! IT'S WEIRD!
OOH! WHAT AN ADORABLE BABY!
KIRKMAN & SCOTT
BOY? GIRL?
MARSUPIAL.

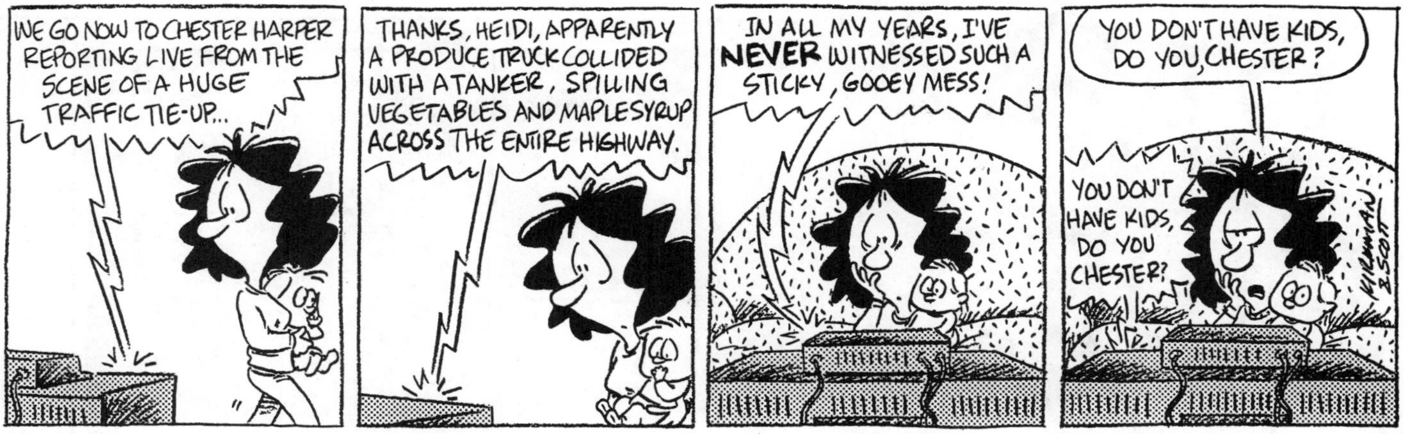
WE GO NOW TO CHESTER HARPER REPORTING LIVE FROM THE SCENE OF A HUGE TRAFFIC TIE-UP...
THANKS, HEIDI, APPARENTLY A PRODUCE TRUCK COLLIDED WITH A TANKER, SPILLING VEGETABLES AND MAPLE SYRUP ACROSS THE ENTIRE HIGHWAY.
IN ALL MY YEARS, I'VE **NEVER** WITNESSED SUCH A STICKY, GOOEY MESS!
YOU DON'T HAVE KIDS, DO YOU, CHESTER?
YOU DON'T HAVE KIDS, DO YOU CHESTER?
KIRKMAN & SCOTT

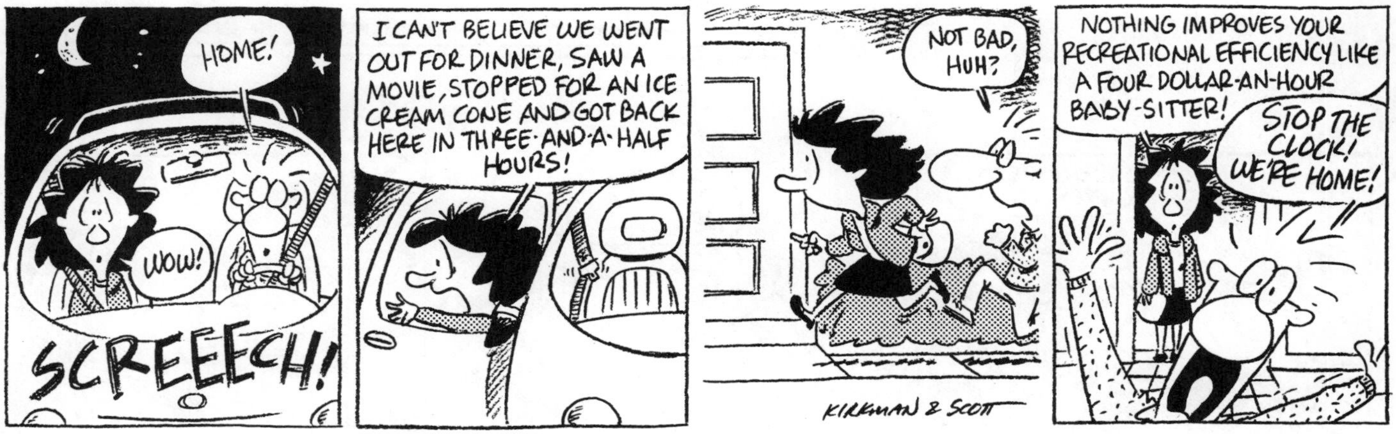
HOME!
WOW!
SCREEECH!
I CAN'T BELIEVE WE WENT OUT FOR DINNER, SAW A MOVIE, STOPPED FOR AN ICE CREAM CONE AND GOT BACK HERE IN THREE-AND-A-HALF HOURS!
NOT BAD, HUH?
KIRKMAN & SCOTT
NOTHING IMPROVES YOUR RECREATIONAL EFFICIENCY LIKE A FOUR DOLLAR-AN-HOUR BABY-SITTER!
STOP THE CLOCK! WE'RE HOME!

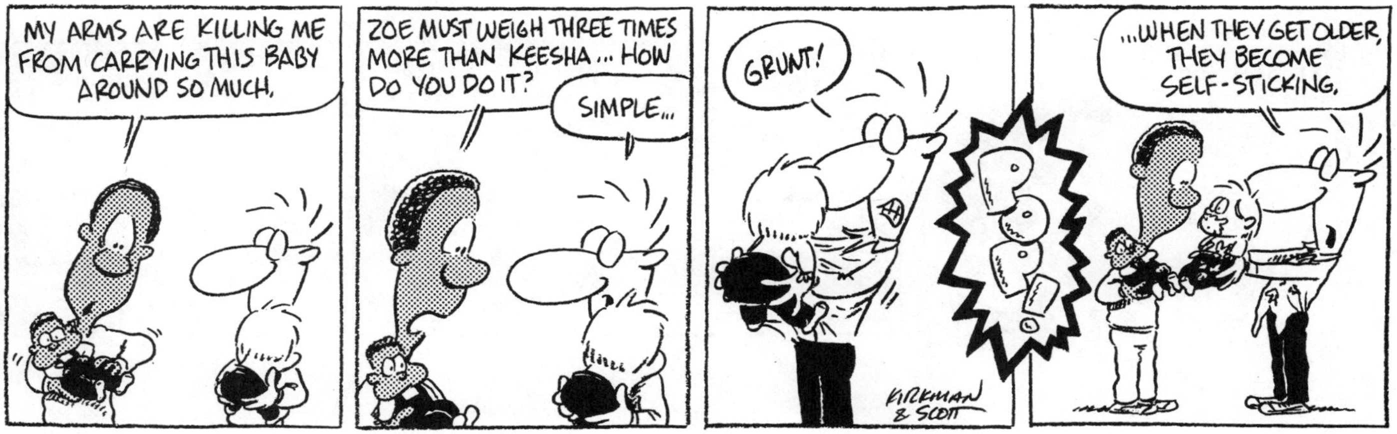
MY ARMS ARE KILLING ME FROM CARRYING THIS BABY AROUND SO MUCH.
ZOE MUST WEIGH THREE TIMES MORE THAN KEESHA... HOW DO YOU DO IT?
SIMPLE...
GRUNT!
POP!
KIRKMAN & SCOTT
...WHEN THEY GET OLDER, THEY BECOME SELF-STICKING.

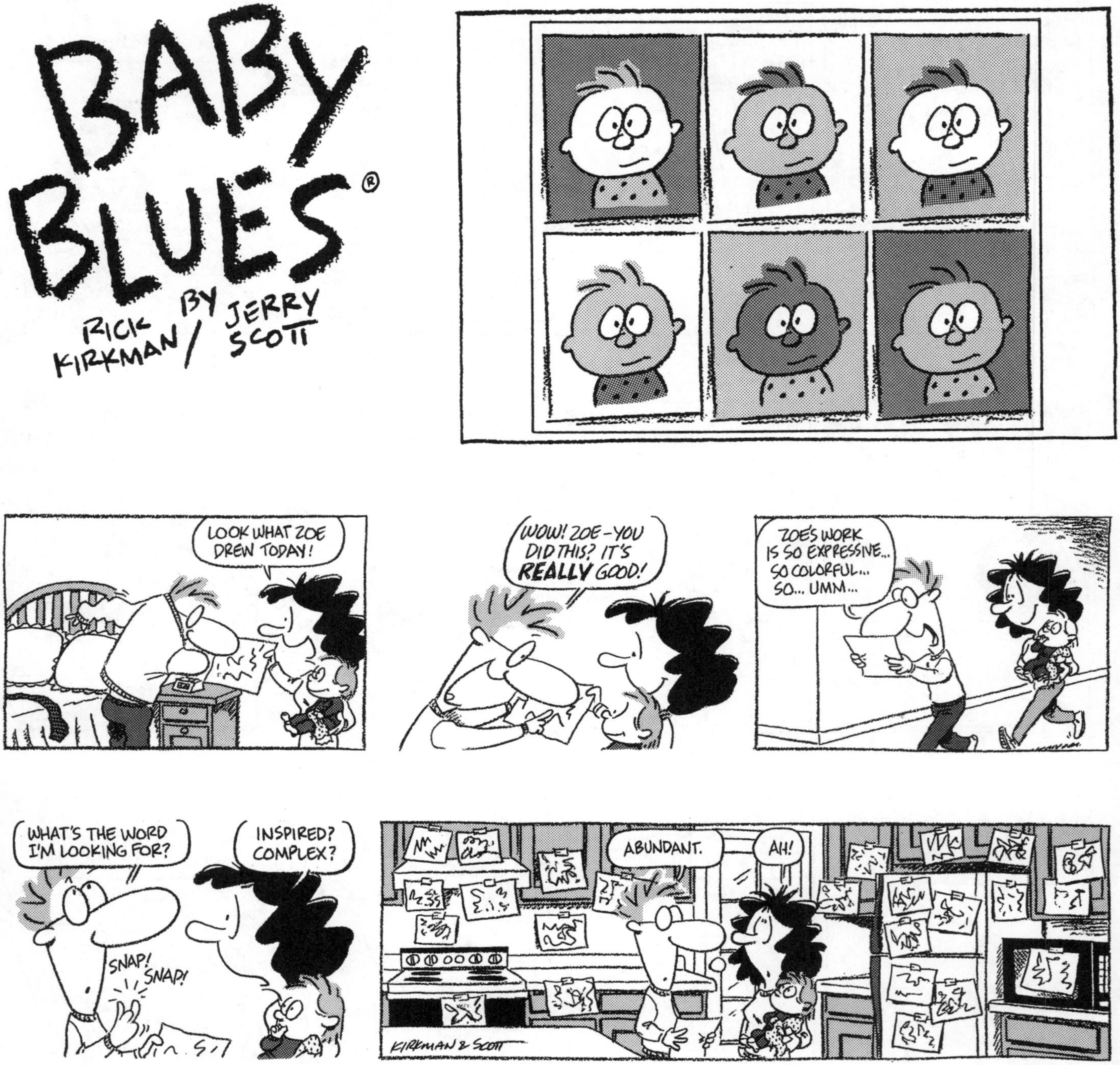
BABY BLUES®
BY RICK KIRKMAN / JERRY SCOTT
LOOK WHAT ZOE DREW TODAY!
WOW! ZOE - YOU DID THIS? IT'S REALLY GOOD!
ZOE'S WORK IS SO EXPRESSIVE... SO COLORFUL... SO... UMM...
WHAT'S THE WORD I'M LOOKING FOR?
SNAP! SNAP!
INSPIRED? COMPLEX?
ABUNDANT.
AH!
KIRKMAN & SCOTT

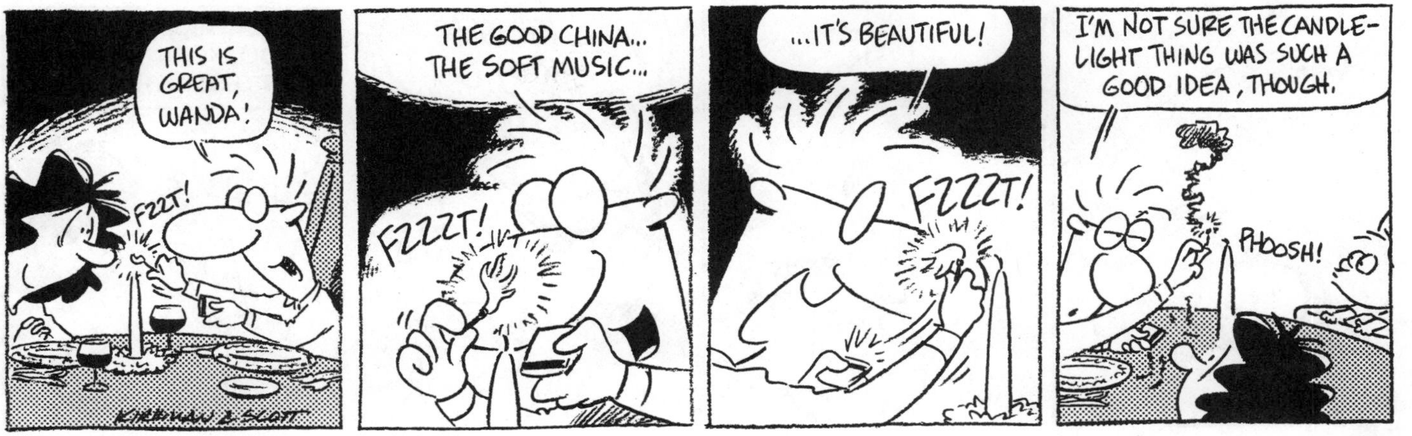
THIS IS GREAT, WANDA!
FZZT!
THE GOOD CHINA... THE SOFT MUSIC...
FZZZT!
...IT'S BEAUTIFUL!
FZZZT!
I'M NOT SURE THE CANDLE-LIGHT THING WAS SUCH A GOOD IDEA, THOUGH.
PHOOSH!
KIRKMAN & SCOTT

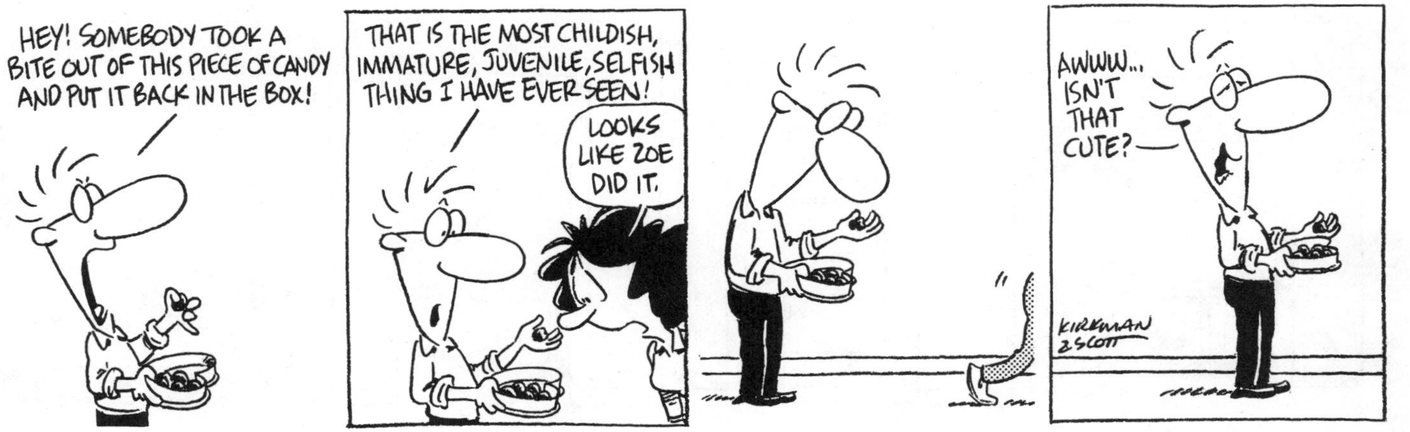
HEY! SOMEBODY TOOK A BITE OUT OF THIS PIECE OF CANDY AND PUT IT BACK IN THE BOX!
THAT IS THE MOST CHILDISH, IMMATURE, JUVENILE, SELFISH THING I HAVE EVER SEEN!
LOOKS LIKE ZOE DID IT.
AWWW... ISN'T THAT CUTE?
KIRKMAN & SCOTT

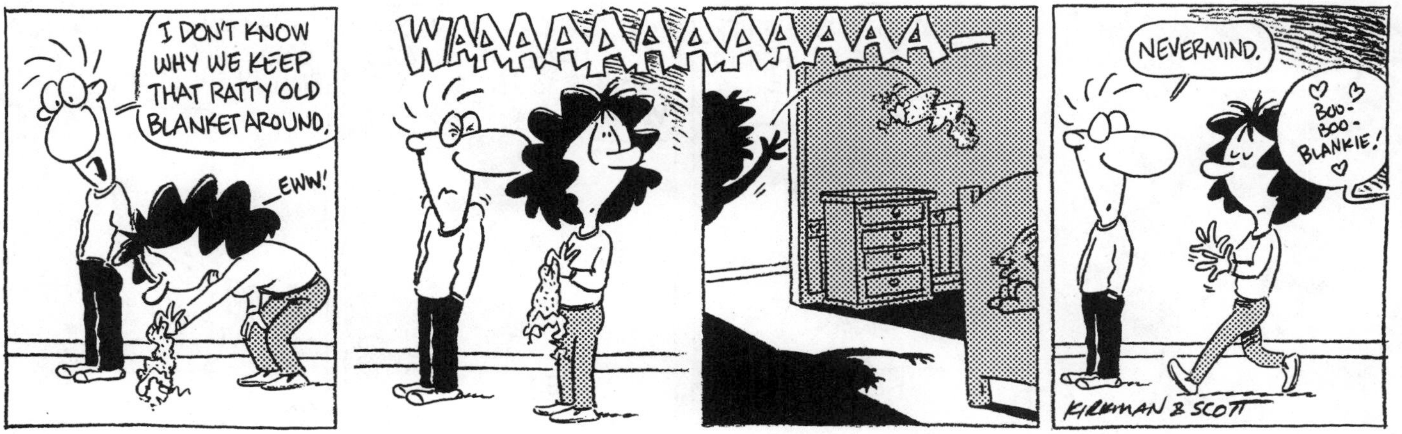
I DON'T KNOW WHY WE KEEP THAT RATTY OLD BLANKET AROUND.
EWW!
WAAAAAAAAAAAA-
NEVERMIND.
BOO-BOO-BLANKIE!
KIRKMAN & SCOTT

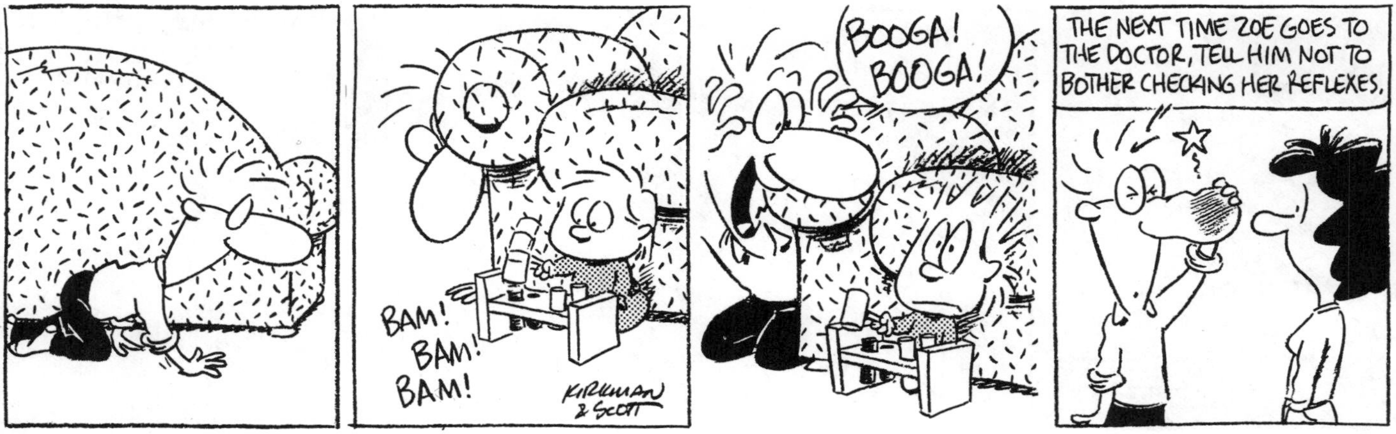
BAM! BAM! BAM!
KIRKMAN & SCOTT
BOOGA! BOOGA!
THE NEXT TIME ZOE GOES TO THE DOCTOR, TELL HIM NOT TO BOTHER CHECKING HER REFLEXES.

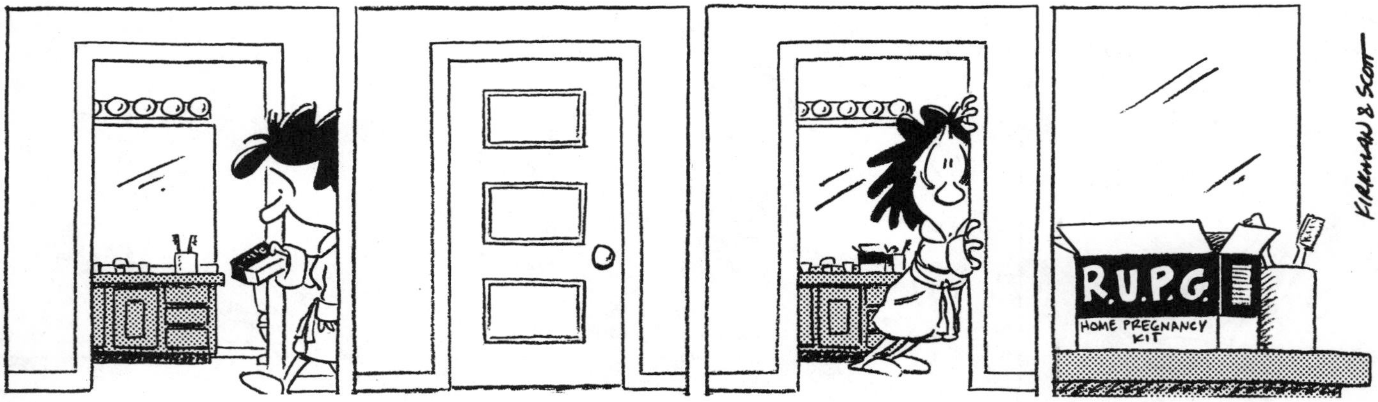
R.U.P.G.
HOME PREGNANCY KIT
KIRKMAN & SCOTT

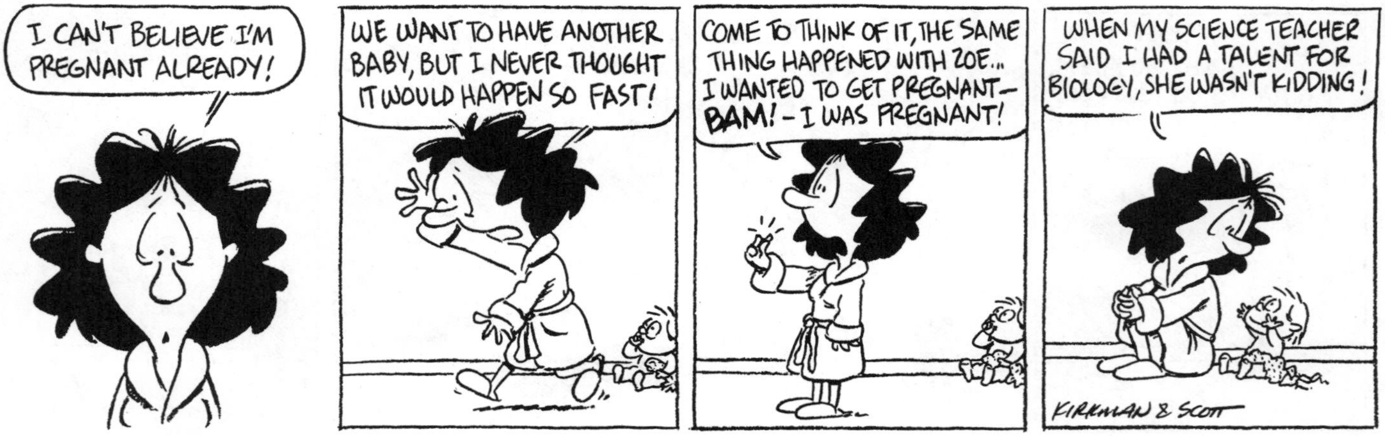
I CAN'T BELIEVE I'M PREGNANT ALREADY!
WE WANT TO HAVE ANOTHER BABY, BUT I NEVER THOUGHT IT WOULD HAPPEN SO FAST!
COME TO THINK OF IT, THE SAME THING HAPPENED WITH ZOE... I WANTED TO GET PREGNANT— **BAM!** — I WAS PREGNANT!
WHEN MY SCIENCE TEACHER SAID I HAD A TALENT FOR BIOLOGY, SHE WASN'T KIDDING!
KIRKMAN & SCOTT

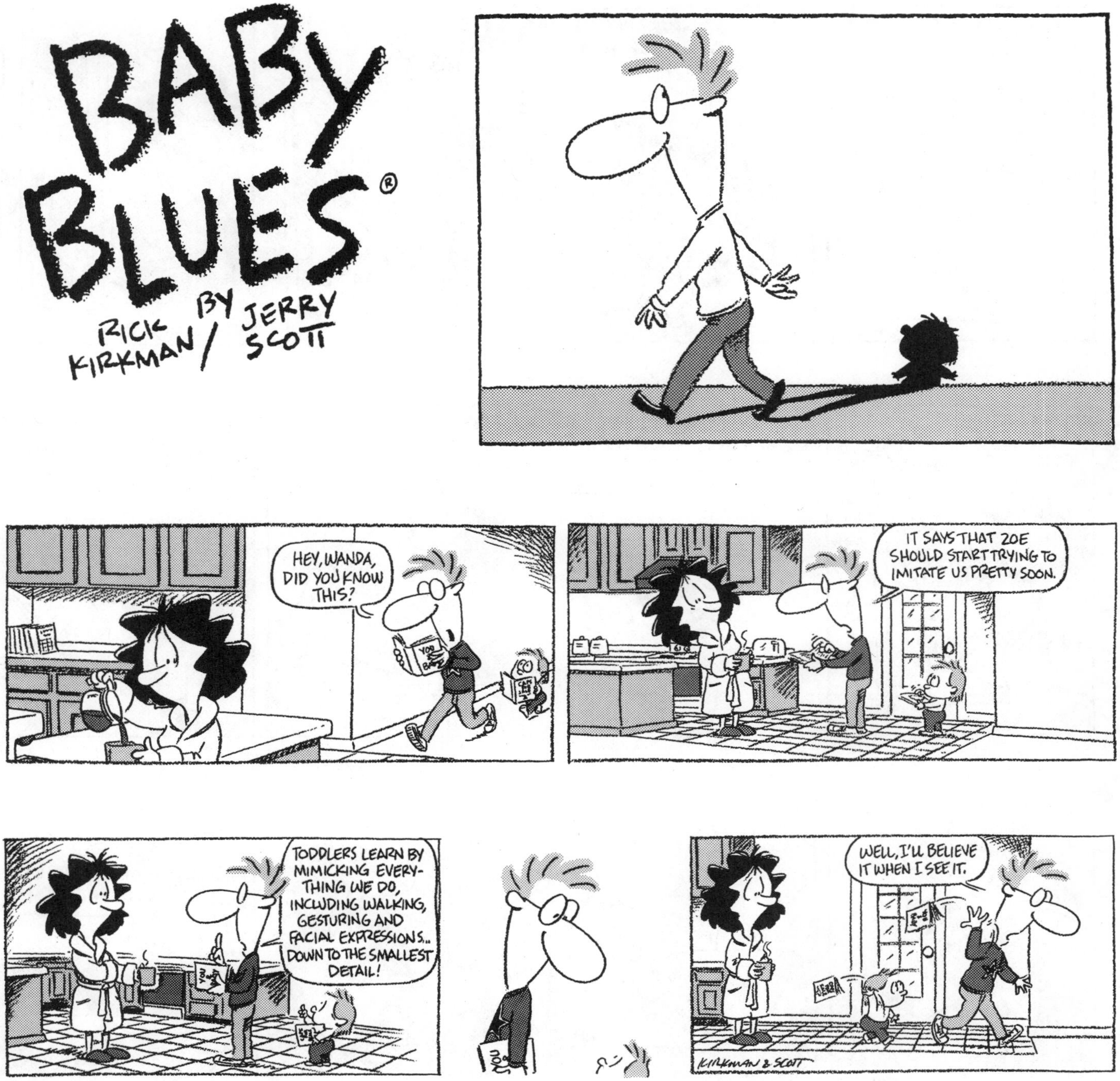

BABY BLUES®
BY RICK KIRKMAN / JERRY SCOTT
HEY, WANDA, DID YOU KNOW THIS?
IT SAYS THAT ZOE SHOULD START TRYING TO IMITATE US PRETTY SOON.
TODDLERS LEARN BY MIMICKING EVERYTHING WE DO, INCLUDING WALKING, GESTURING AND FACIAL EXPRESSIONS... DOWN TO THE SMALLEST DETAIL!
WELL, I'LL BELIEVE IT WHEN I SEE IT.
KIRKMAN & SCOTT

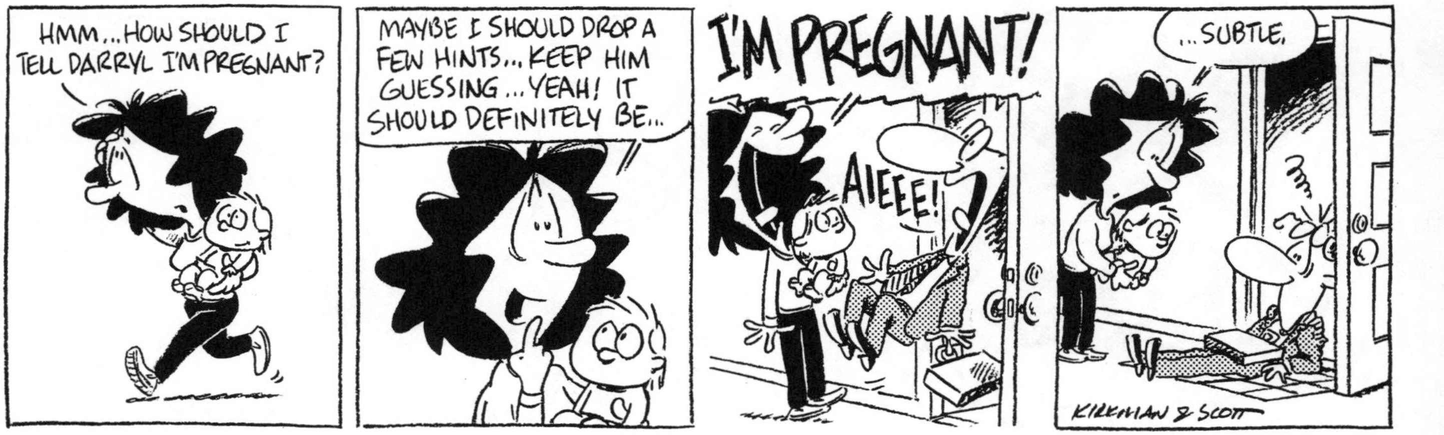
HMM... HOW SHOULD I TELL DARRYL I'M PREGNANT?
MAYBE I SHOULD DROP A FEW HINTS... KEEP HIM GUESSING... YEAH! IT SHOULD DEFINITELY BE...
I'M PREGNANT!
AIEEEE!
...SUBTLE.
KIRKMAN & SCOTT

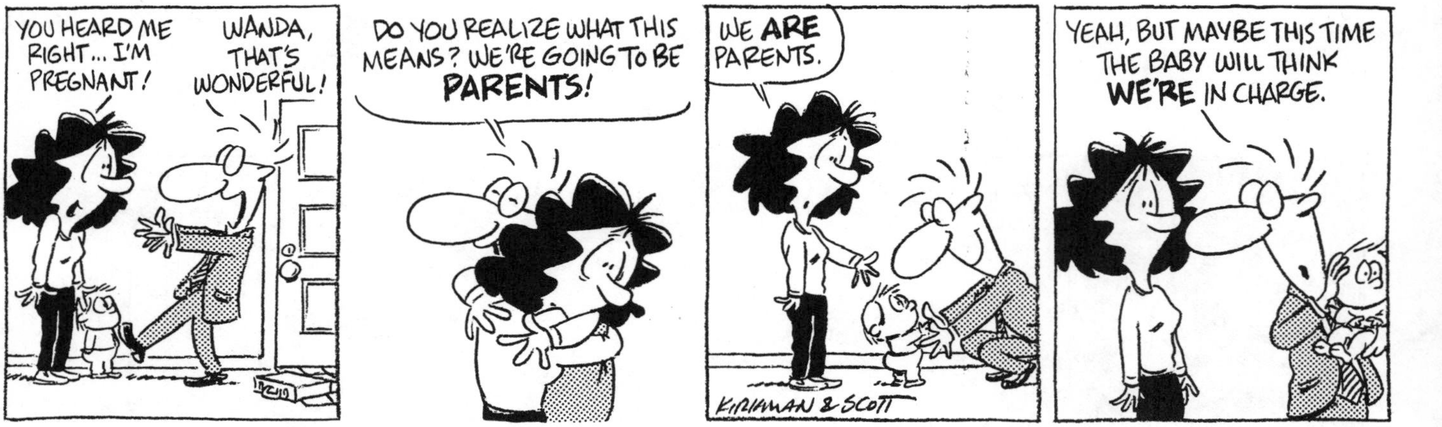
YOU HEARD ME RIGHT... I'M PREGNANT!
WANDA, THAT'S WONDERFUL!
DO YOU REALIZE WHAT THIS MEANS? WE'RE GOING TO BE **PARENTS**!
WE **ARE** PARENTS.
KIRKMAN & SCOTT
YEAH, BUT MAYBE THIS TIME THE BABY WILL THINK **WE'RE** IN CHARGE.

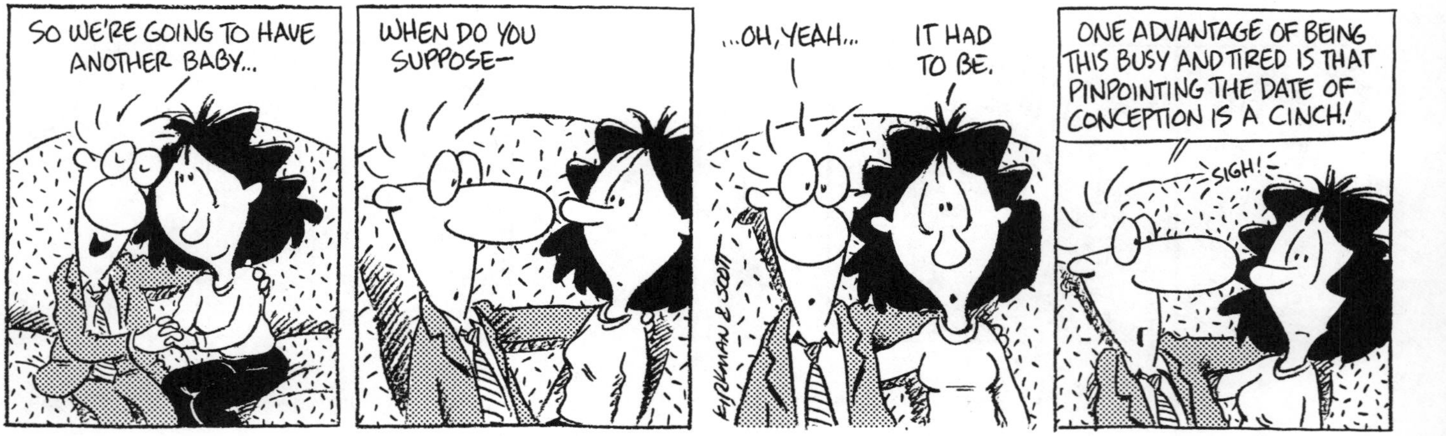
SO WE'RE GOING TO HAVE ANOTHER BABY...
WHEN DO YOU SUPPOSE—
...OH, YEAH...
IT HAD TO BE.
KIRKMAN & SCOTT
ONE ADVANTAGE OF BEING THIS BUSY AND TIRED IS THAT PINPOINTING THE DATE OF CONCEPTION IS A CINCH!
SIGH!

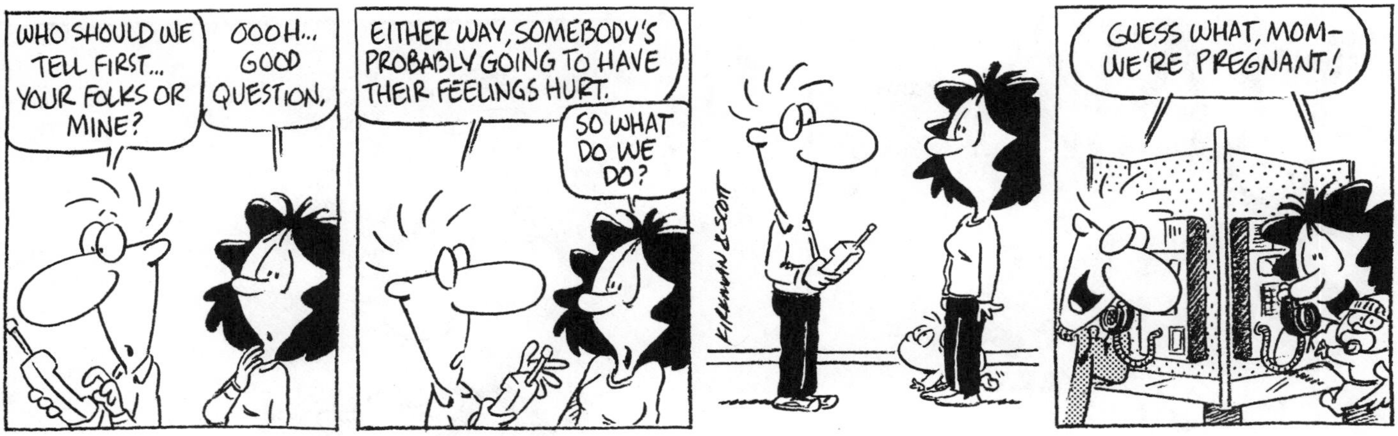
WHO SHOULD WE TELL FIRST... YOUR FOLKS OR MINE?
OOOH... GOOD QUESTION.
EITHER WAY, SOMEBODY'S PROBABLY GOING TO HAVE THEIR FEELINGS HURT.
SO WHAT DO WE DO?
KIRKMAN & SCOTT
GUESS WHAT, MOM- WE'RE PREGNANT!

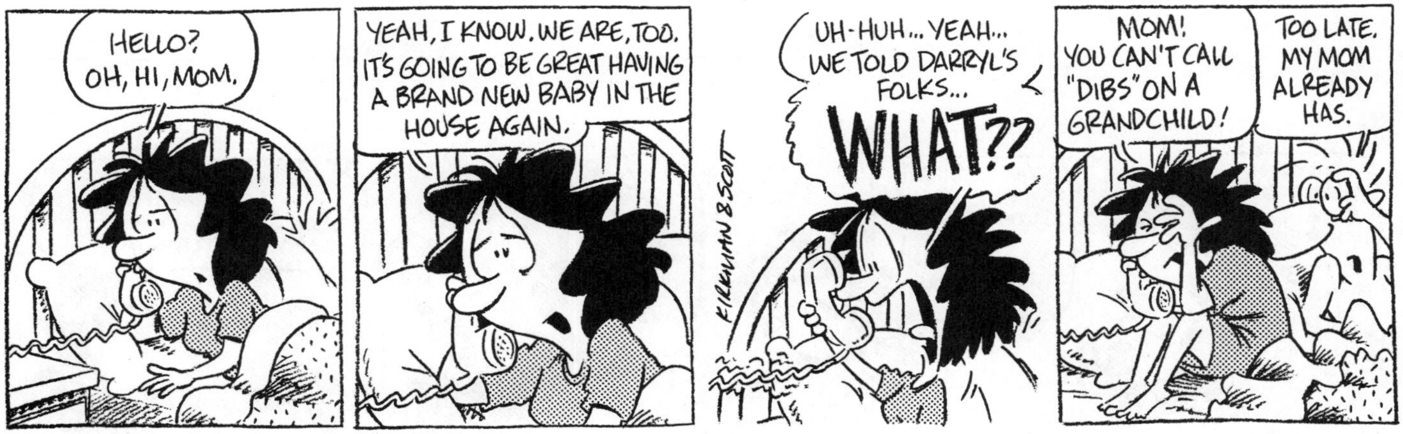
HELLO? OH, HI, MOM.
YEAH, I KNOW. WE ARE, TOO. IT'S GOING TO BE GREAT HAVING A BRAND NEW BABY IN THE HOUSE AGAIN.
KIRKMAN & SCOTT
UH-HUH... YEAH... WE TOLD DARRYL'S FOLKS...
WHAT??
MOM! YOU CAN'T CALL "DIBS" ON A GRANDCHILD!
TOO LATE. MY MOM ALREADY HAS.

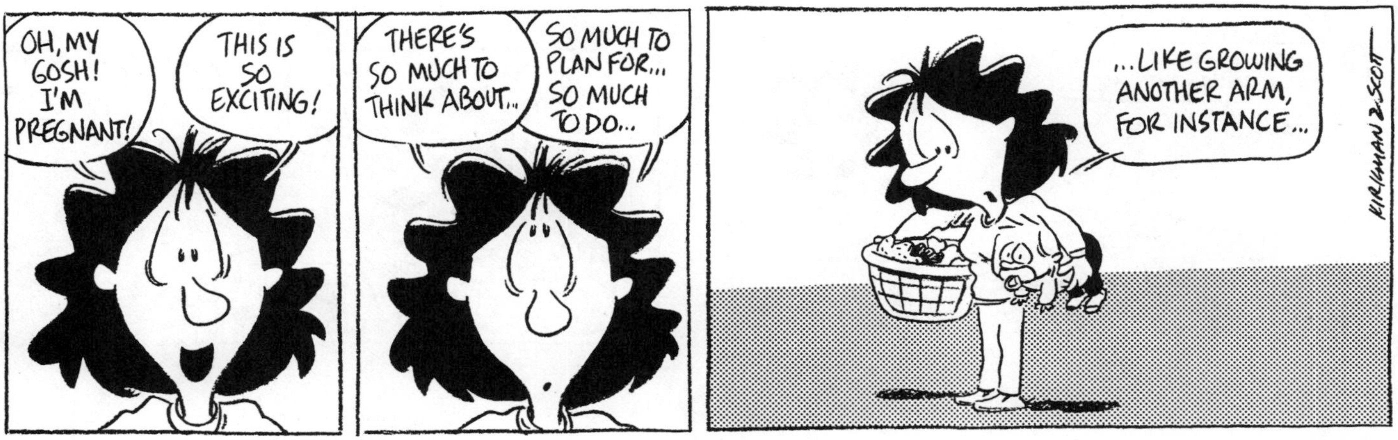
OH, MY GOSH! I'M PREGNANT!
THIS IS SO EXCITING!
THERE'S SO MUCH TO THINK ABOUT...
SO MUCH TO PLAN FOR... SO MUCH TO DO...
...LIKE GROWING ANOTHER ARM, FOR INSTANCE...
KIRKMAN & SCOTT

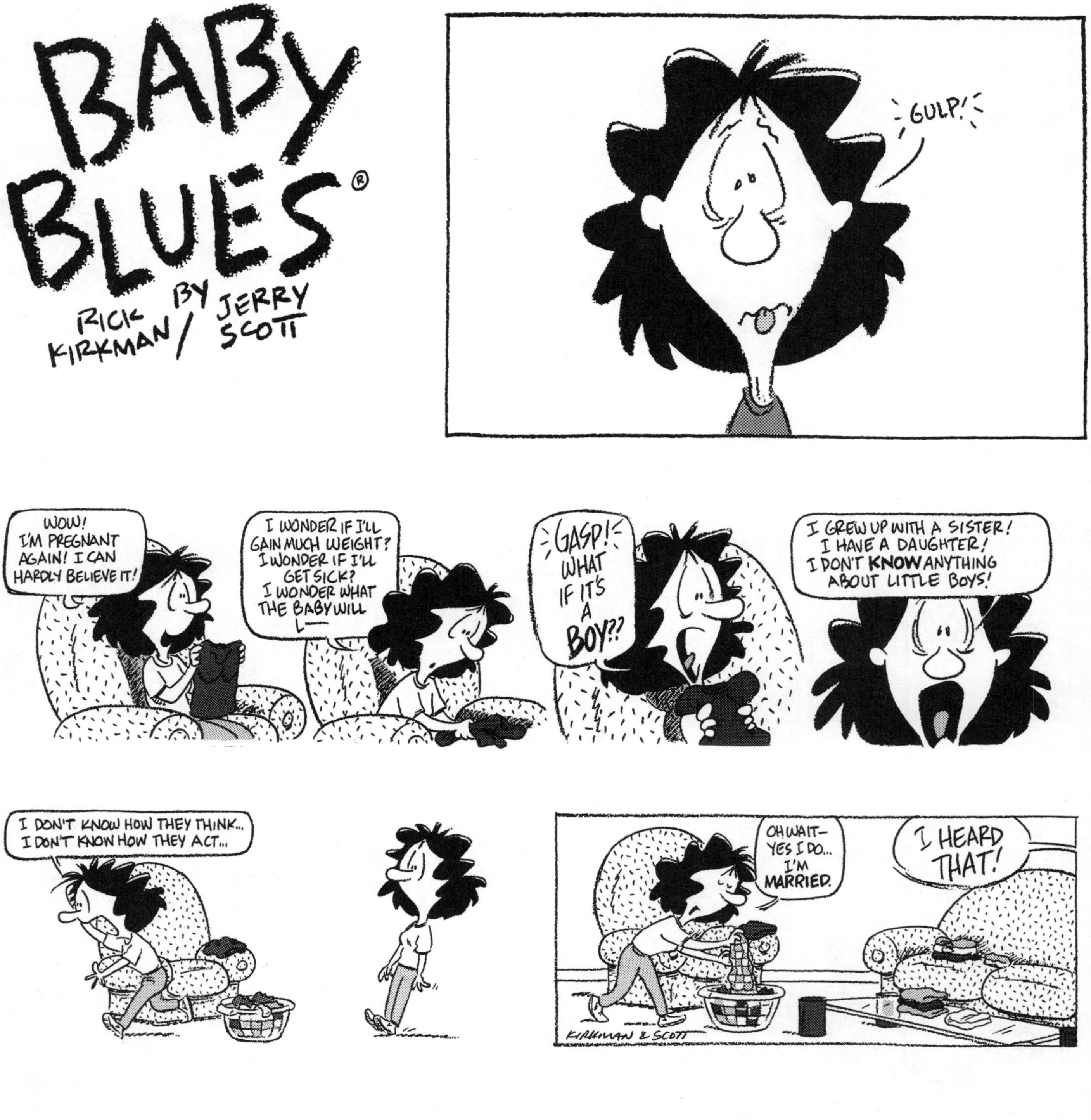
BABY BLUES®
BY RICK KIRKMAN / JERRY SCOTT
GULP!
WOW! I'M PREGNANT AGAIN! I CAN HARDLY BELIEVE IT!
I WONDER IF I'LL GAIN MUCH WEIGHT? I WONDER IF I'LL GET SICK? I WONDER WHAT THE BABY WILL L—
GASP! WHAT IF IT'S A BOY??
I GREW UP WITH A SISTER! I HAVE A DAUGHTER! I DON'T **KNOW** ANYTHING ABOUT LITTLE BOYS!
I DON'T KNOW HOW THEY THINK... I DON'T KNOW HOW THEY ACT...
OH WAIT— YES I DO... I'M **MARRIED**.
I HEARD THAT!
KIRKMAN & SCOTT

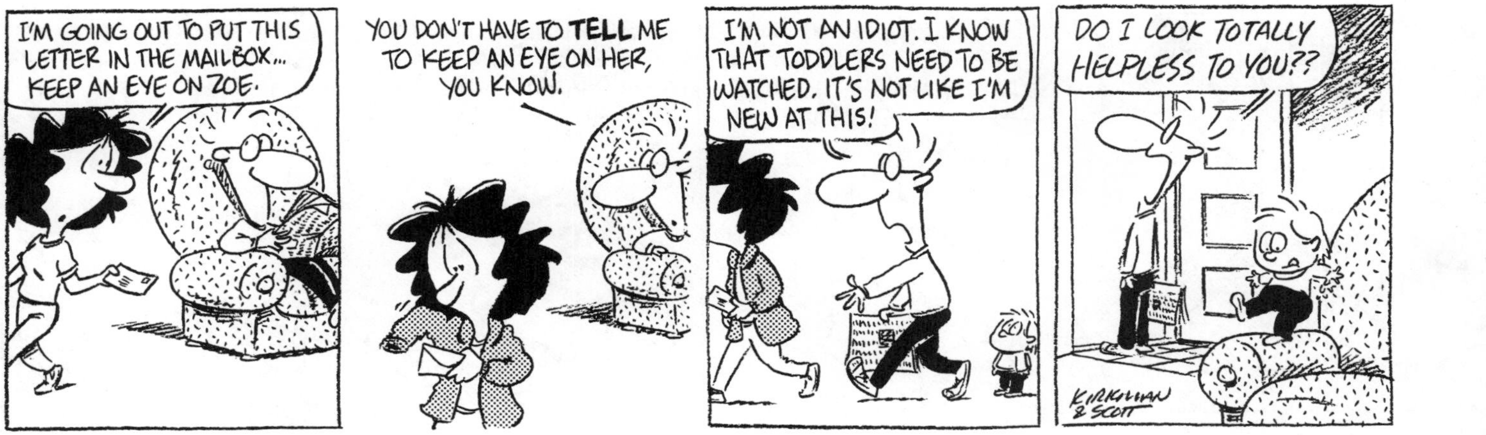
I'M GOING OUT TO PUT THIS LETTER IN THE MAILBOX... KEEP AN EYE ON ZOE.
YOU DON'T HAVE TO **TELL** ME TO KEEP AN EYE ON HER, YOU KNOW.
I'M NOT AN IDIOT. I KNOW THAT TODDLERS NEED TO BE WATCHED. IT'S NOT LIKE I'M NEW AT THIS!
DO I LOOK TOTALLY HELPLESS TO YOU??
KIRKMAN & SCOTT

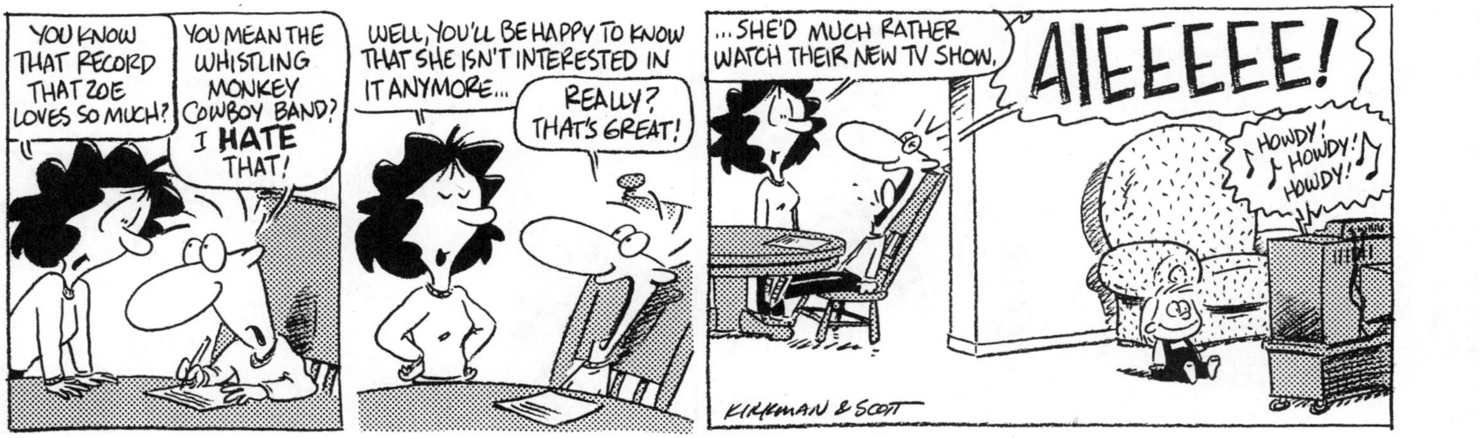
YOU KNOW THAT RECORD THAT ZOE LOVES SO MUCH?
YOU MEAN THE WHISTLING MONKEY COWBOY BAND? I **HATE** THAT!
WELL, YOU'LL BE HAPPY TO KNOW THAT SHE ISN'T INTERESTED IN IT ANYMORE...
REALLY? THAT'S GREAT!
...SHE'D MUCH RATHER WATCH THEIR NEW TV SHOW.
AIEEEEEE!
HOWDY! HOWDY! HOWDY!
KIRKMAN & SCOTT

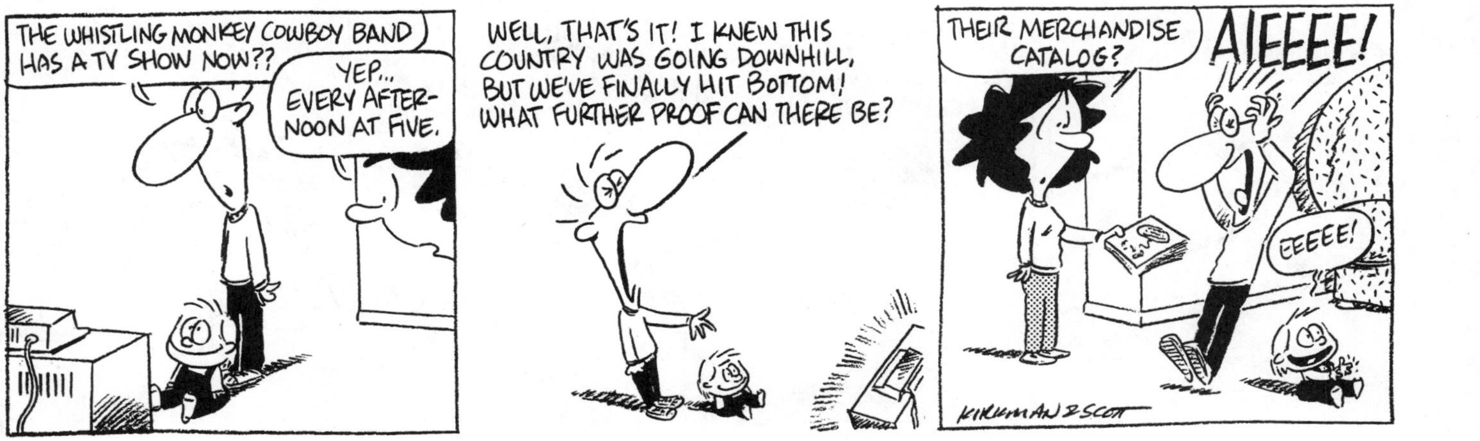
THE WHISTLING MONKEY COWBOY BAND HAS A TV SHOW NOW??
YEP... EVERY AFTER-NOON AT FIVE.
WELL, THAT'S IT! I KNEW THIS COUNTRY WAS GOING DOWNHILL, BUT WE'VE FINALLY HIT BOTTOM! WHAT FURTHER PROOF CAN THERE BE?
THEIR MERCHANDISE CATALOG?
AIEEEE!
EEEEE!
KIRKMAN & SCOTT

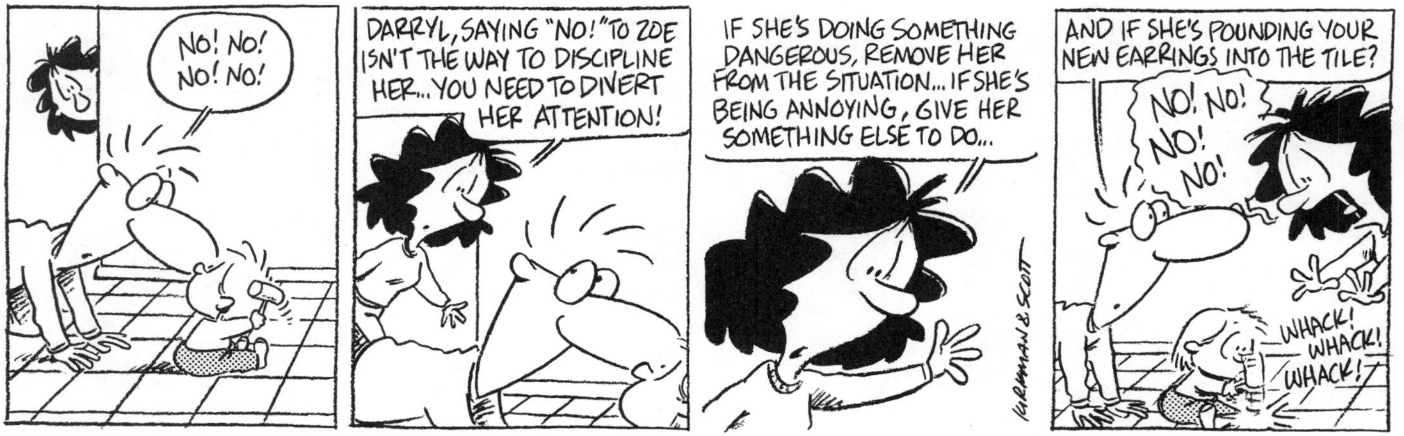
NO! NO!
NO! NO!
DARRYL, SAYING "NO!" TO ZOE ISN'T THE WAY TO DISCIPLINE HER... YOU NEED TO DIVERT HER ATTENTION!
IF SHE'S DOING SOMETHING DANGEROUS, REMOVE HER FROM THE SITUATION... IF SHE'S BEING ANNOYING, GIVE HER SOMETHING ELSE TO DO...
KIRKMAN & SCOTT
AND IF SHE'S POUNDING YOUR NEW EARRINGS INTO THE TILE?
NO! NO! NO! NO!
WHACK! WHACK! WHACK!

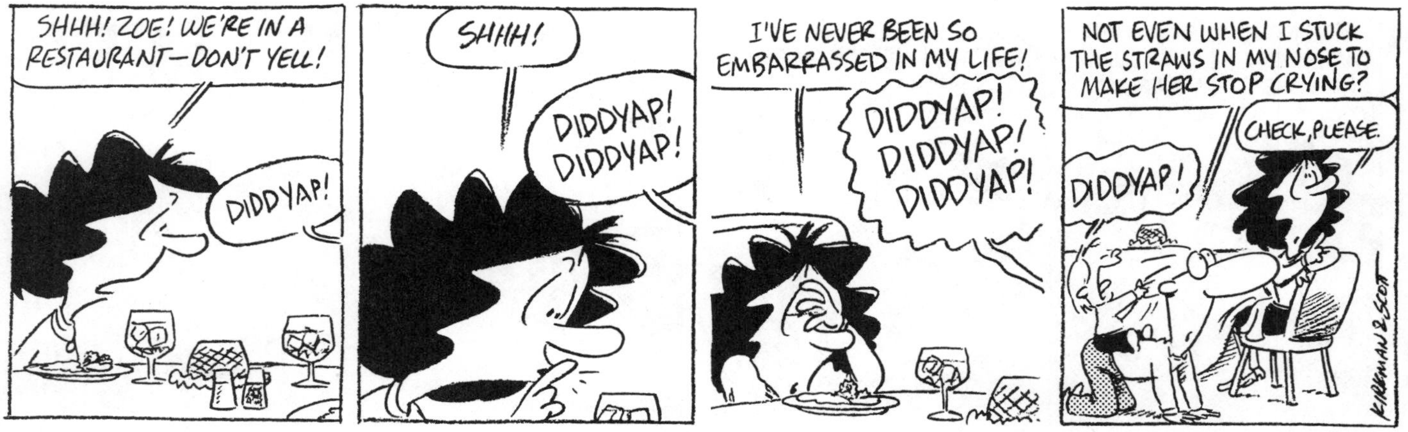
SHHH! ZOE! WE'RE IN A RESTAURANT—DON'T YELL!
DIDDYAP!
SHHH!
DIDDYAP! DIDDYAP!
I'VE NEVER BEEN SO EMBARRASSED IN MY LIFE!
DIDDYAP! DIDDYAP! DIDDYAP!
NOT EVEN WHEN I STUCK THE STRAWS IN MY NOSE TO MAKE HER STOP CRYING?
CHECK, PLEASE.
DIDDYAP!
KIRKMAN & SCOTT

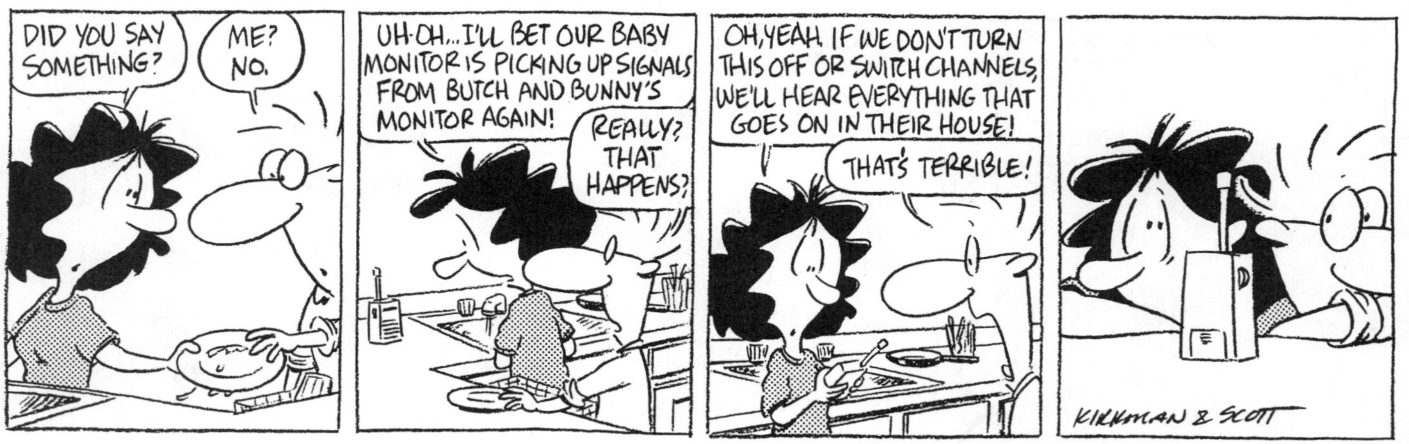
DID YOU SAY SOMETHING?
ME? NO.
UH-OH... I'LL BET OUR BABY MONITOR IS PICKING UP SIGNALS FROM BUTCH AND BUNNY'S MONITOR AGAIN!
REALLY? THAT HAPPENS?
OH, YEAH. IF WE DON'T TURN THIS OFF OR SWITCH CHANNELS, WE'LL HEAR EVERYTHING THAT GOES ON IN THEIR HOUSE!
THAT'S TERRIBLE!
KIRKMAN & SCOTT

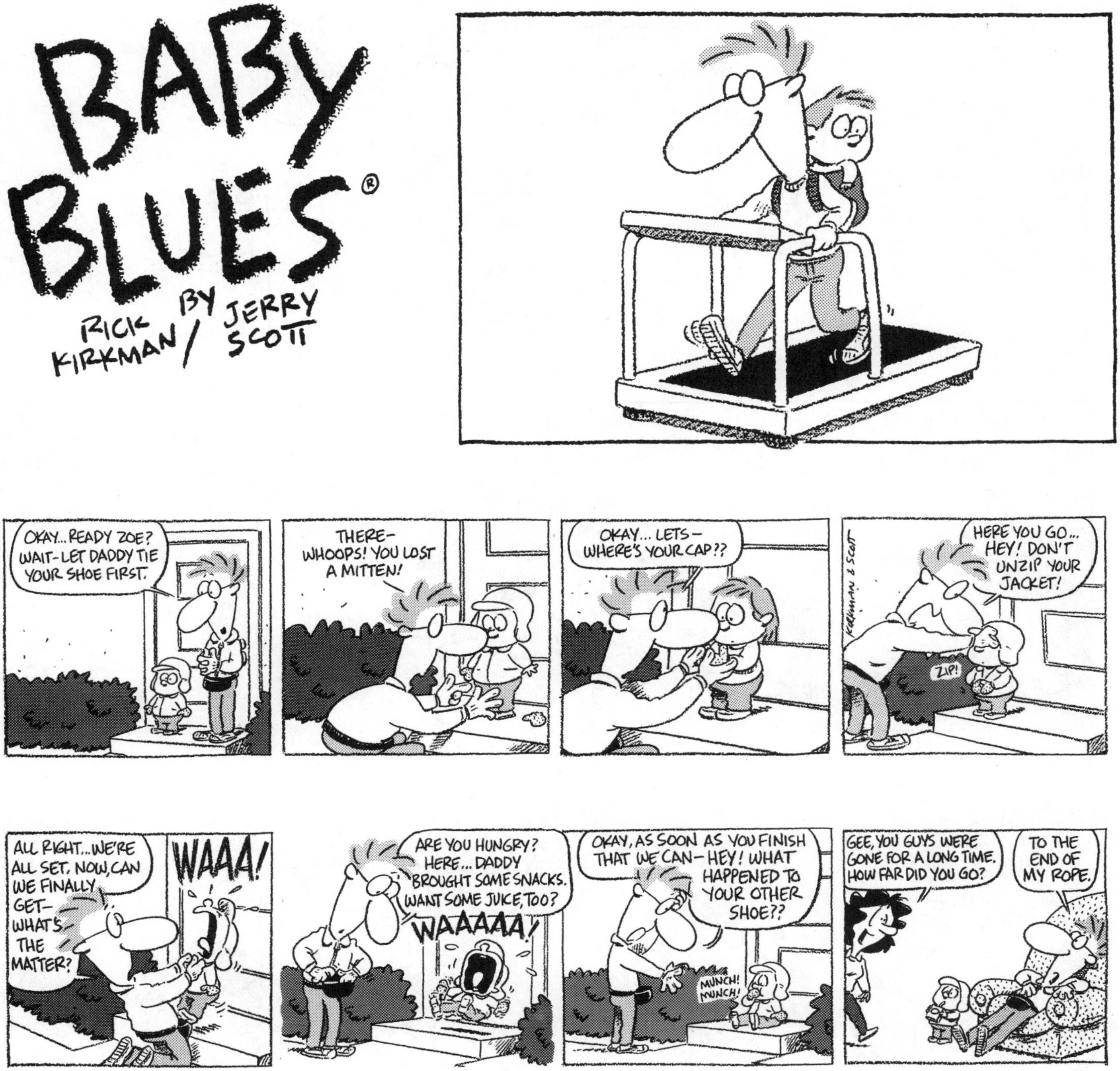
BABY BLUES®
BY RICK KIRKMAN / JERRY SCOTT
OKAY... READY ZOE? WAIT- LET DADDY TIE YOUR SHOE FIRST.
THERE- WHOOPS! YOU LOST A MITTEN!
OKAY... LETS- WHERE'S YOUR CAP??
KIRKMAN & SCOTT
HERE YOU GO... HEY! DON'T UNZIP YOUR JACKET!
ZIP!
ALL RIGHT... WE'RE ALL SET. NOW, CAN WE FINALLY GET- WHAT'S THE MATTER?
WAAA!
ARE YOU HUNGRY? HERE... DADDY BROUGHT SOME SNACKS. WANT SOME JUICE, TOO?
WAAAAA!
OKAY, AS SOON AS YOU FINISH THAT WE CAN- HEY! WHAT HAPPENED TO YOUR OTHER SHOE??
MUNCH! MUNCH!
GEE, YOU GUYS WERE GONE FOR A LONG TIME. HOW FAR DID YOU GO?
TO THE END OF MY ROPE.

Panel 1: I CAN'T BELIEVE WE'RE DOING THIS!

Panel 2: JUST BECAUSE OUR BABY MONITOR PICKS UP BUTCH AND BUNNY'S MONITOR DOESN'T GIVE US THE RIGHT TO EAVESDROP ON THEM!

Panel 3: IT'S NOT RIGHT! IT'S NOT HONEST!

THEY JUST SAID SOMETHING ABOUT YOU.

Panel 4: ...IT'S NOT LOUD ENOUGH.

KIRKMAN & SCOTT

Panel 5: IT'S INCREDIBLE. WE CAN HEAR EVERYTHING GOING ON IN BUTCH AND BUNNY'S HOUSE!

THAT'S WHAT HAPPENS WHEN THESE BABY MONITOR SIGNALS GET CROSSED.

Panel 6: DID YOU HEAR THAT? BUNNY JUST SAID OUR LAWN IS AN EYESORE!

OF ALL THE NERVE! THERE'S NOTHING SNEAKIER THAN TALKING BEHIND SOMEONE'S BACK!

Panel 7: WELL, **ALMOST** NOTHING...

SHH! THEY'RE MAKING FUN OF OUR FURNITURE!

KIRKMAN & SCOTT

Panel 8: WELL! HOW DO YOU LIKE THAT? BUTCH AND BUNNY THINK OUR LAWN IS AN EYESORE!

THAT REALLY BURNS ME UP!

Panel 9: YEAH! THEY COULD HAVE **SAID** SOMETHING!

I KNOW — WHY TALK BEHIND SOMEBODY'S BACK? WHY PRETEND TO LIKE SOMETHING WHEN YOU REALLY DON'T?

Panel 10: I GUESS YOU NEVER REALLY KNOW HOW HONEST PEOPLE ARE UNTIL YOU EAVESDROP ON THEM.

KIRKMAN & SCOTT

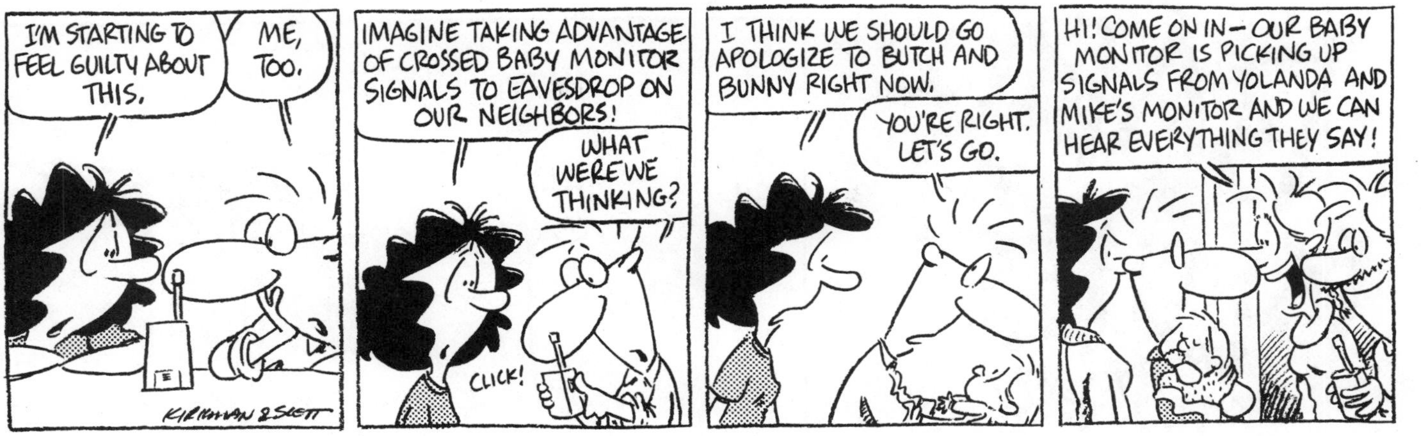
I'M STARTING TO FEEL GUILTY ABOUT THIS.
ME, TOO.
KIRKMAN & SCOTT
IMAGINE TAKING ADVANTAGE OF CROSSED BABY MONITOR SIGNALS TO EAVESDROP ON OUR NEIGHBORS!
WHAT WERE WE THINKING?
CLICK!
I THINK WE SHOULD GO APOLOGIZE TO BUTCH AND BUNNY RIGHT NOW.
YOU'RE RIGHT. LET'S GO.
HI! COME ON IN— OUR BABY MONITOR IS PICKING UP SIGNALS FROM YOLANDA AND MIKE'S MONITOR AND WE CAN HEAR EVERYTHING THEY SAY!

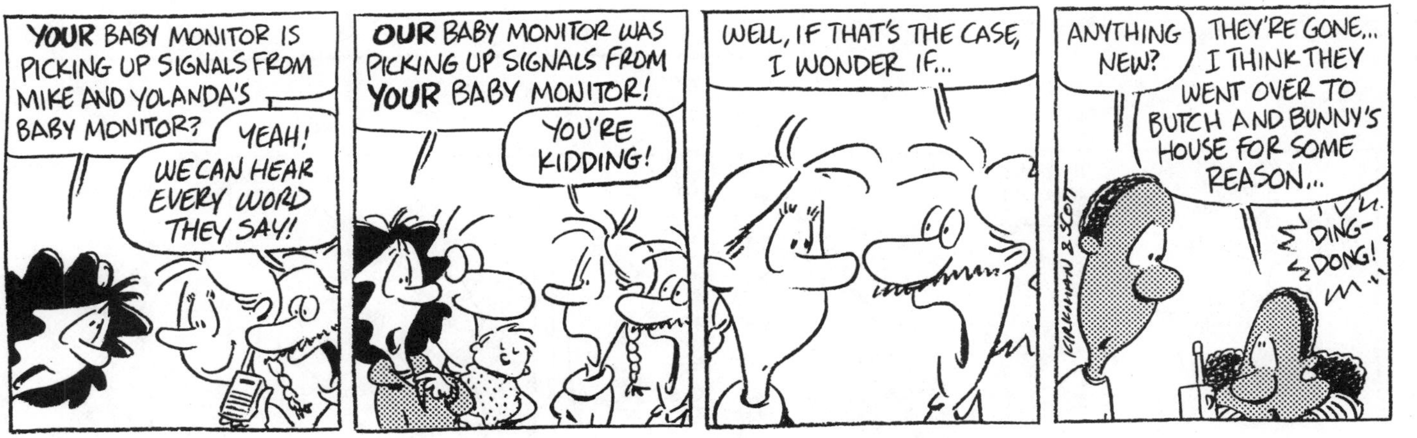
YOUR BABY MONITOR IS PICKING UP SIGNALS FROM MIKE AND YOLANDA'S BABY MONITOR?
YEAH! WE CAN HEAR EVERY WORD THEY SAY!
OUR BABY MONITOR WAS PICKING UP SIGNALS FROM **YOUR** BABY MONITOR!
YOU'RE KIDDING!
WELL, IF THAT'S THE CASE, I WONDER IF...
ANYTHING NEW?
THEY'RE GONE... I THINK THEY WENT OVER TO BUTCH AND BUNNY'S HOUSE FOR SOME REASON...
DING-DONG!
KIRKMAN & SCOTT

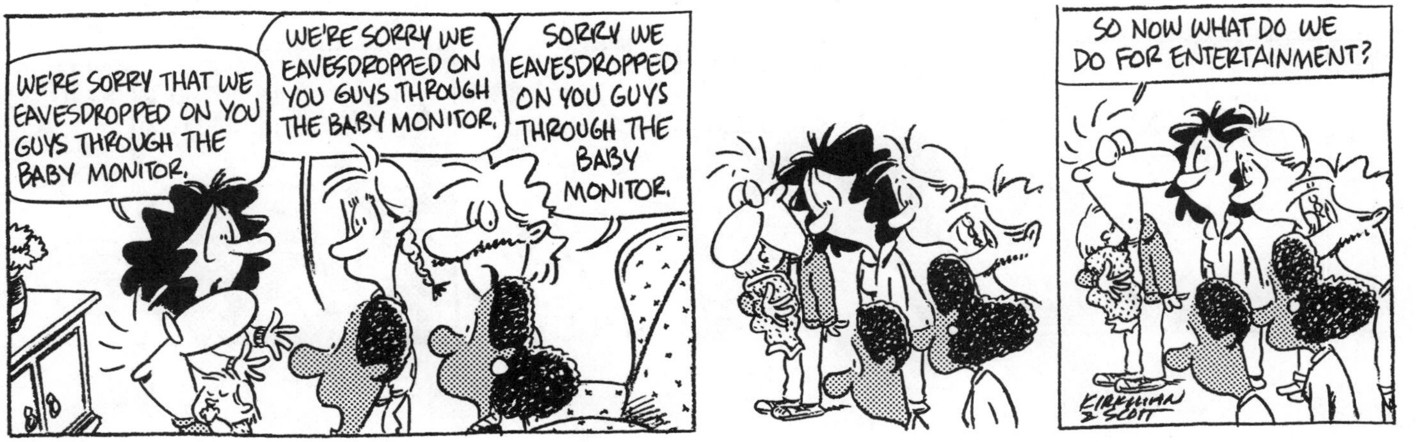
WE'RE SORRY THAT WE EAVESDROPPED ON YOU GUYS THROUGH THE BABY MONITOR.
WE'RE SORRY WE EAVESDROPPED ON YOU GUYS THROUGH THE BABY MONITOR.
SORRY WE EAVESDROPPED ON YOU GUYS THROUGH THE BABY MONITOR.
SO NOW WHAT DO WE DO FOR ENTERTAINMENT?
KIRKMAN & SCOTT

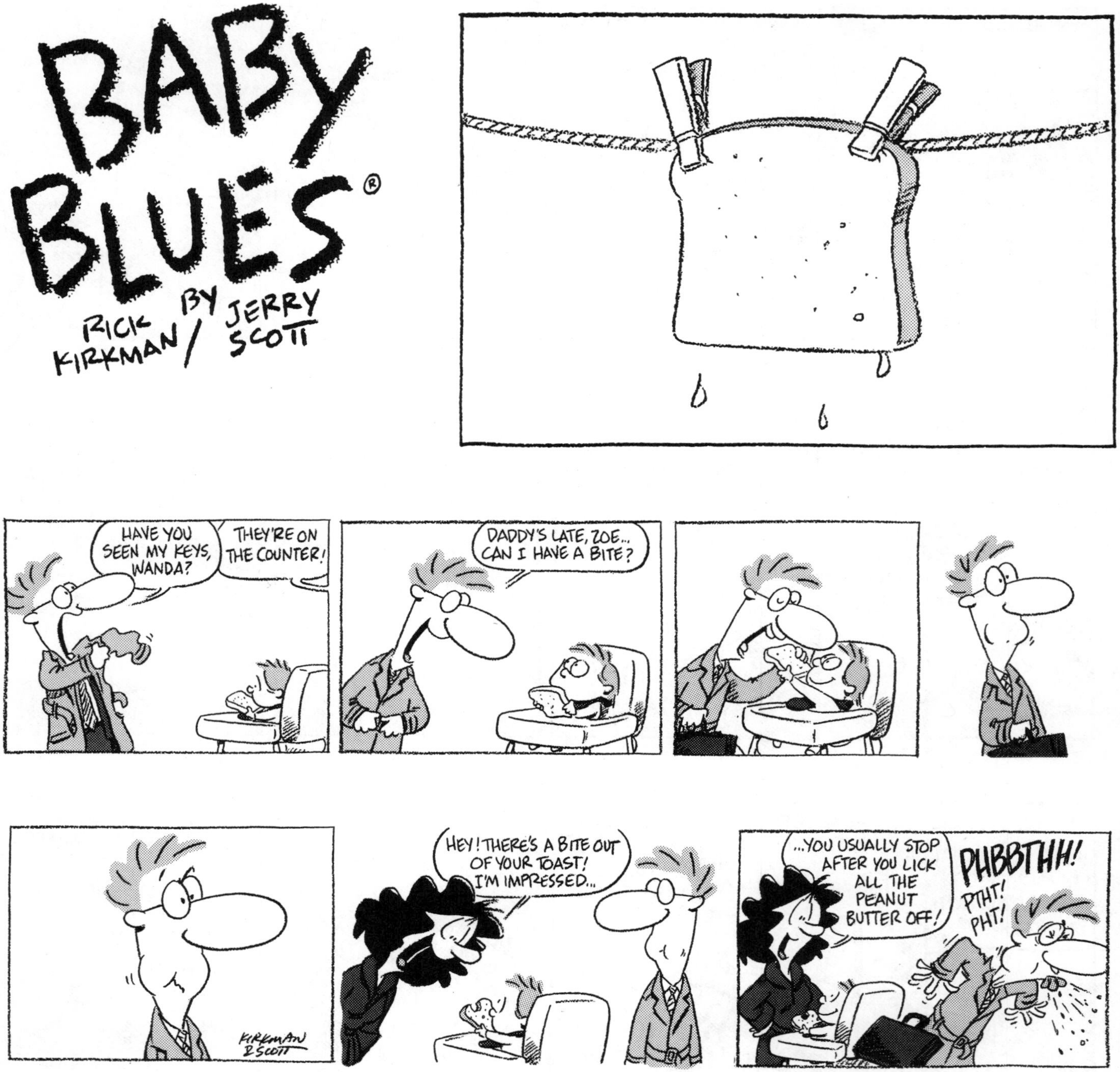
BABY BLUES®
BY RICK KIRKMAN / JERRY SCOTT
HAVE YOU SEEN MY KEYS, WANDA?
THEY'RE ON THE COUNTER!
DADDY'S LATE, ZOE... CAN I HAVE A BITE?
KIRKMAN & SCOTT
HEY! THERE'S A BITE OUT OF YOUR TOAST! I'M IMPRESSED...
...YOU USUALLY STOP AFTER YOU LICK ALL THE PEANUT BUTTER OFF!
PHBBTHH!
PTHT!
PHT!

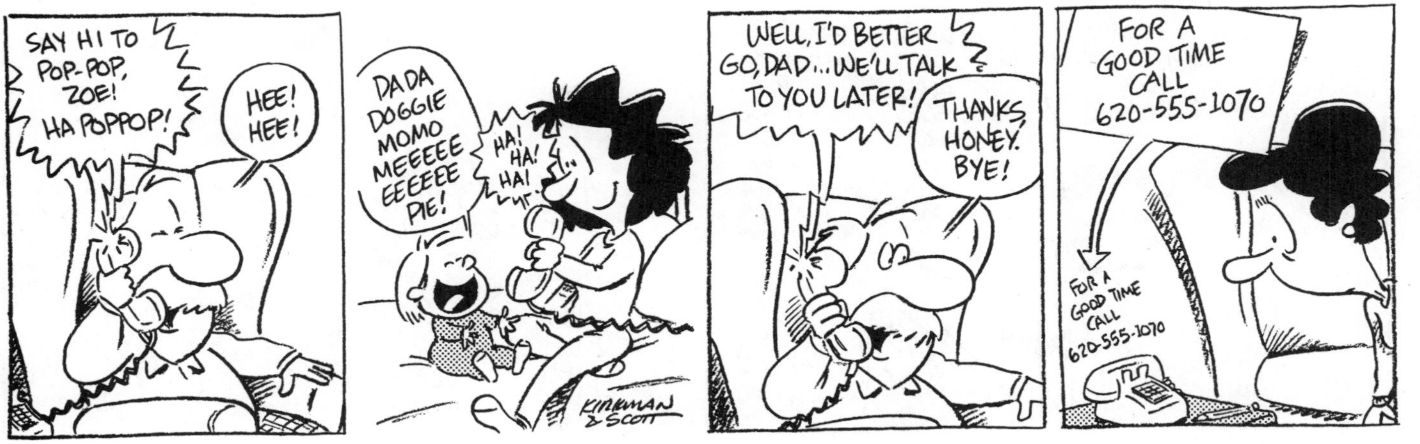
SAY HI TO POP-POP, ZOE! HA POPPOP!
HEE! HEE!
DADA DOGGIE MOMO MEEEEE EEEEEE PIE!
HA! HA! HA!
KIRKMAN & SCOTT
WELL, I'D BETTER GO, DAD... WE'LL TALK TO YOU LATER!
THANKS, HONEY. BYE!
FOR A GOOD TIME CALL 620-555-1070
FOR A GOOD TIME CALL 620-555-1070

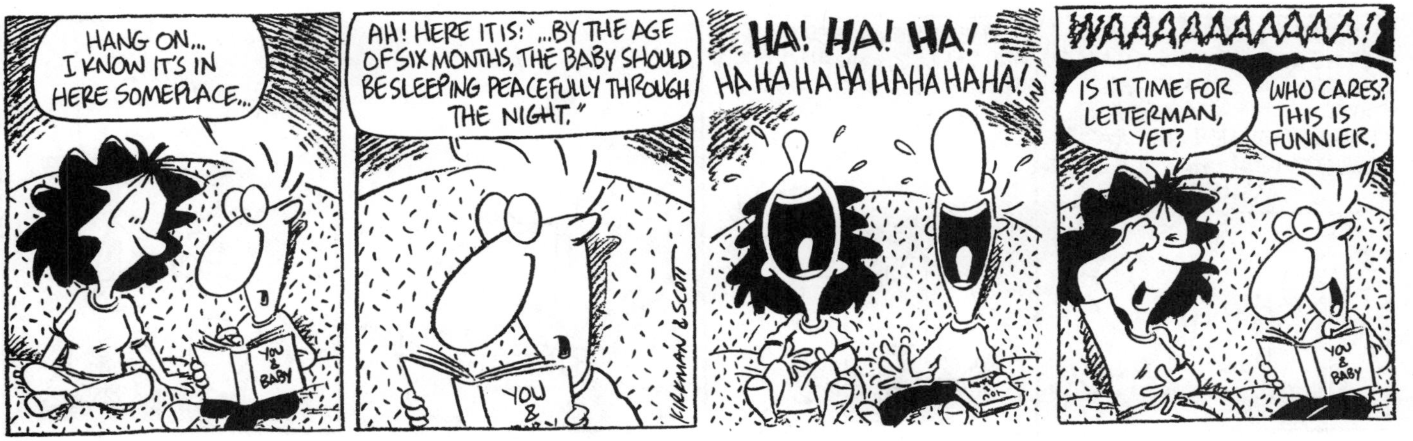
HANG ON... I KNOW IT'S IN HERE SOMEPLACE...
YOU & BABY
AH! HERE IT IS: "...BY THE AGE OF SIX MONTHS, THE BABY SHOULD BE SLEEPING PEACEFULLY THROUGH THE NIGHT."
KIRKMAN & SCOTT
HA! HA! HA! HA HA HA HA HA HA HA HA HA!
WAAAAAAAAAA!
IS IT TIME FOR LETTERMAN, YET?
WHO CARES? THIS IS FUNNIER.
YOU & BABY

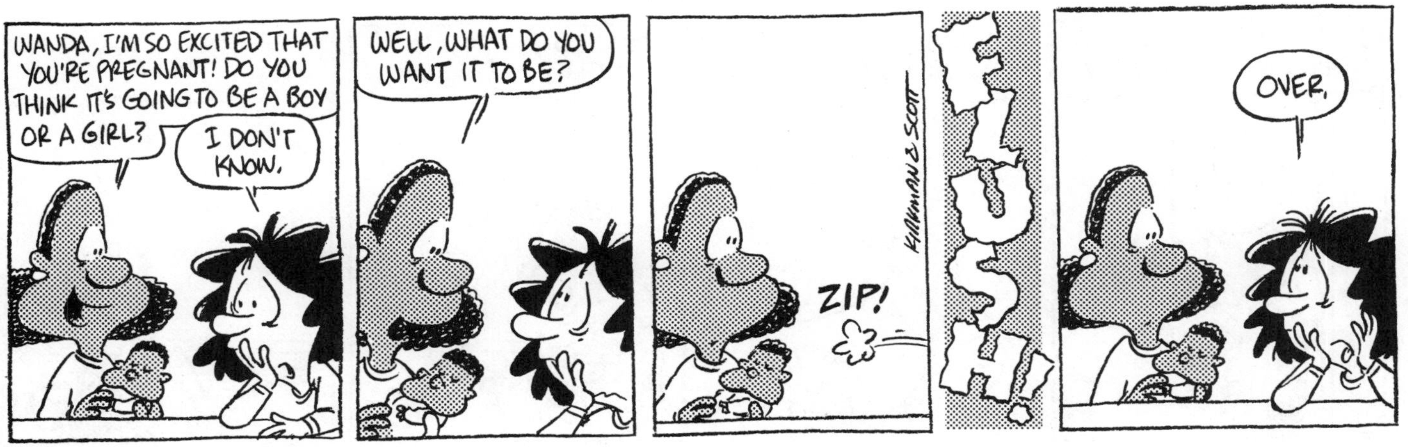
WANDA, I'M SO EXCITED THAT YOU'RE PREGNANT! DO YOU THINK IT'S GOING TO BE A BOY OR A GIRL?
I DON'T KNOW.
WELL, WHAT DO YOU WANT IT TO BE?
KIRKMAN & SCOTT
ZIP!
FLUSH!
OVER.

Panel 1: WANDA, HAVE YOU SEEN MY CAR KEYS? / I THOUGHT THEY WERE SITTING BY YOUR SUNGLASSES.

Panel 2: THEY WERE... BUT I DON'T SEE ANY SUNGLASSES, EITHER. / WEREN'T THEY ON TOP OF YOUR BRIEFCASE?

Panel 3: YEAH, BUT WHERE...?

Panel 4: ...IS IT JUST ME, OR IS THERE A PATTERN DEVELOPING HERE?

Panel 5: WHAT A MORNING! ZOE STOLE MY KEYS, TRASHED MY SUNGLASSES, SPILLED APPLE JUICE IN MY BRIEFCASE AND POUNDED MY NEW CALCULATOR TO PIECES WITH HER XYLOPHONE MALLET.

Panel 6: THEN SHE LOOKED UP AND SMILED, AND ALL I COULD THINK ABOUT WAS WHAT A LUCKY GUY I AM.

Panel 7: SIP!

Panel 8: WHAT'S HAPPENED TO ME??

Panel 9: I GOT SOME GREAT VIDEOTAPE OF ZOE AT THE PARK TODAY!

Panel 10: WE SHOULD MAKE COPIES AND SEND ONE TO EACH OF OUR FOLKS.

Panel 11: CAN YOU DO THAT? / NO SWEAT!

Panel 12: SWEAT!

KIRKMAN & SCOTT

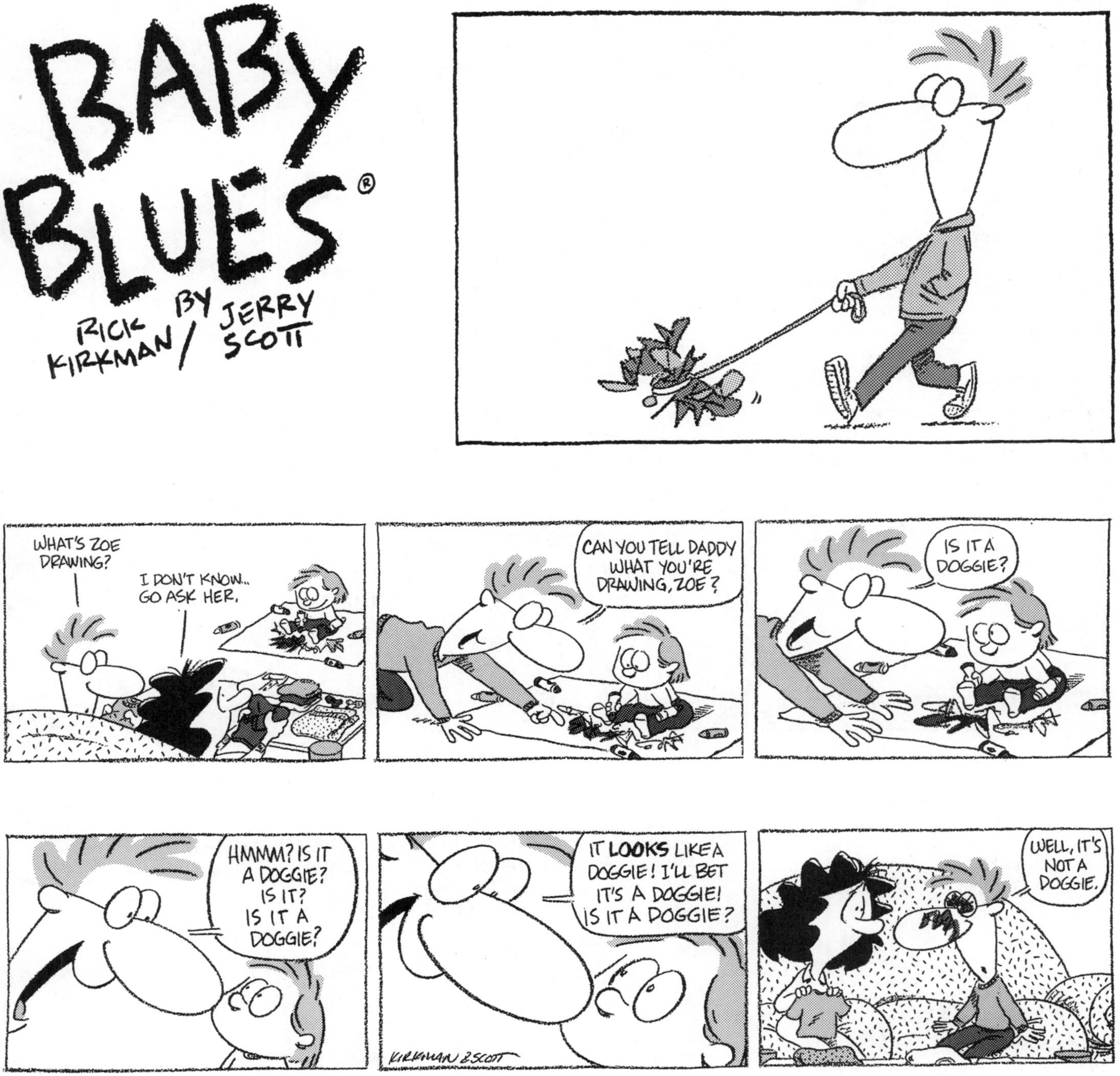
BABY BLUES®
BY RICK KIRKMAN / JERRY SCOTT
WHAT'S ZOE DRAWING?
I DON'T KNOW.. GO ASK HER.
CAN YOU TELL DADDY WHAT YOU'RE DRAWING, ZOE?
IS IT A DOGGIE?
HMMM? IS IT A DOGGIE? IS IT? IS IT A DOGGIE?
IT LOOKS LIKE A DOGGIE! I'LL BET IT'S A DOGGIE! IS IT A DOGGIE?
KIRKMAN & SCOTT
WELL, IT'S NOT A DOGGIE.

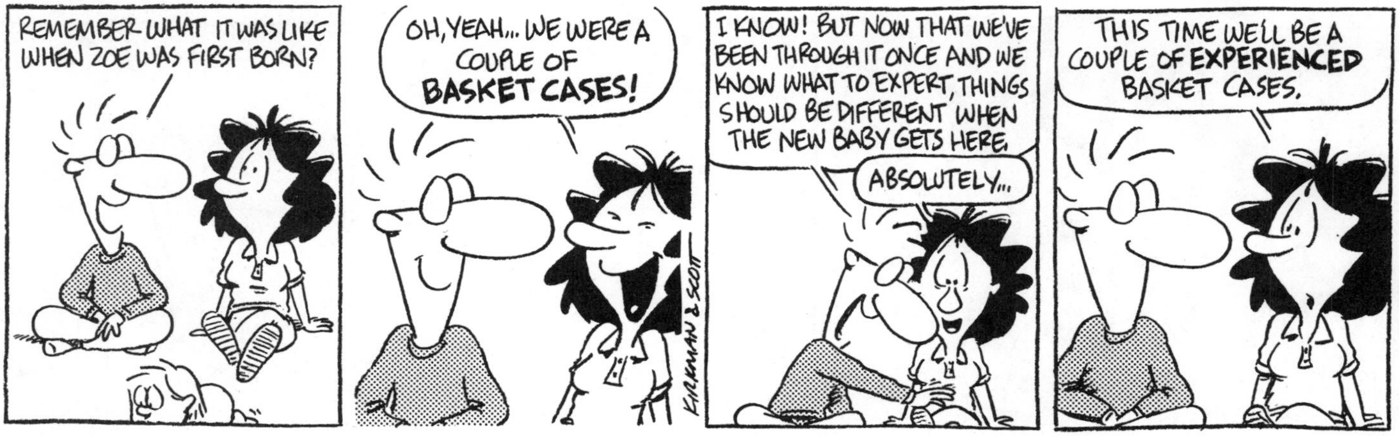
REMEMBER WHAT IT WAS LIKE WHEN ZOE WAS FIRST BORN?
OH, YEAH... WE WERE A COUPLE OF **BASKET CASES!**
I KNOW! BUT NOW THAT WE'VE BEEN THROUGH IT ONCE AND WE KNOW WHAT TO EXPERT, THINGS SHOULD BE DIFFERENT WHEN THE NEW BABY GETS HERE.
ABSOLUTELY...
THIS TIME WE'LL BE A COUPLE OF **EXPERIENCED** BASKET CASES.
KIRKMAN & SCOTT

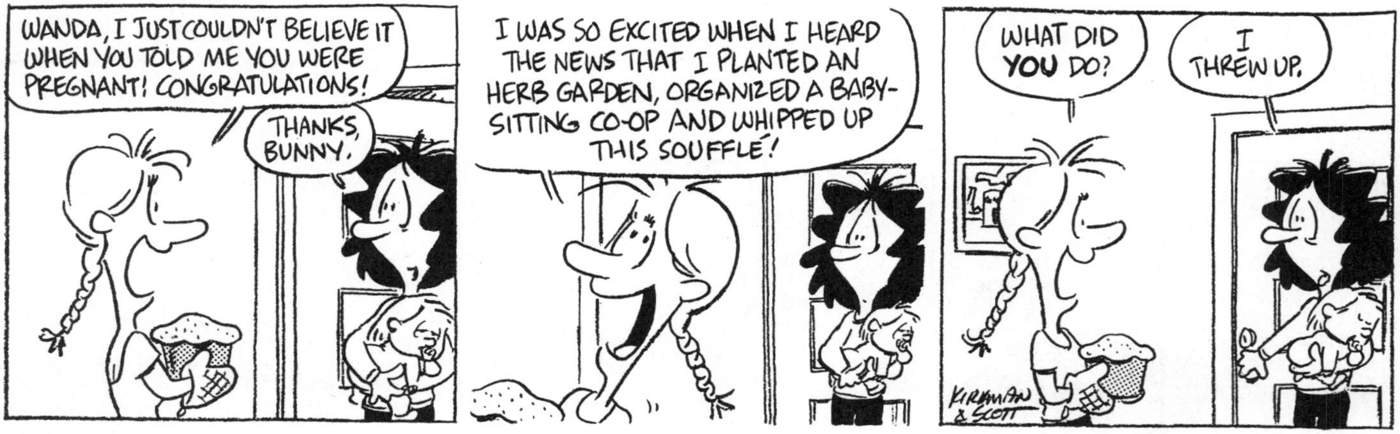
WANDA, I JUST COULDN'T BELIEVE IT WHEN YOU TOLD ME YOU WERE PREGNANT! CONGRATULATIONS!
THANKS, BUNNY.
I WAS SO EXCITED WHEN I HEARD THE NEWS THAT I PLANTED AN HERB GARDEN, ORGANIZED A BABY-SITTING CO-OP AND WHIPPED UP THIS SOUFFLÉ!
WHAT DID **YOU** DO?
I THREW UP.
KIRKMAN & SCOTT

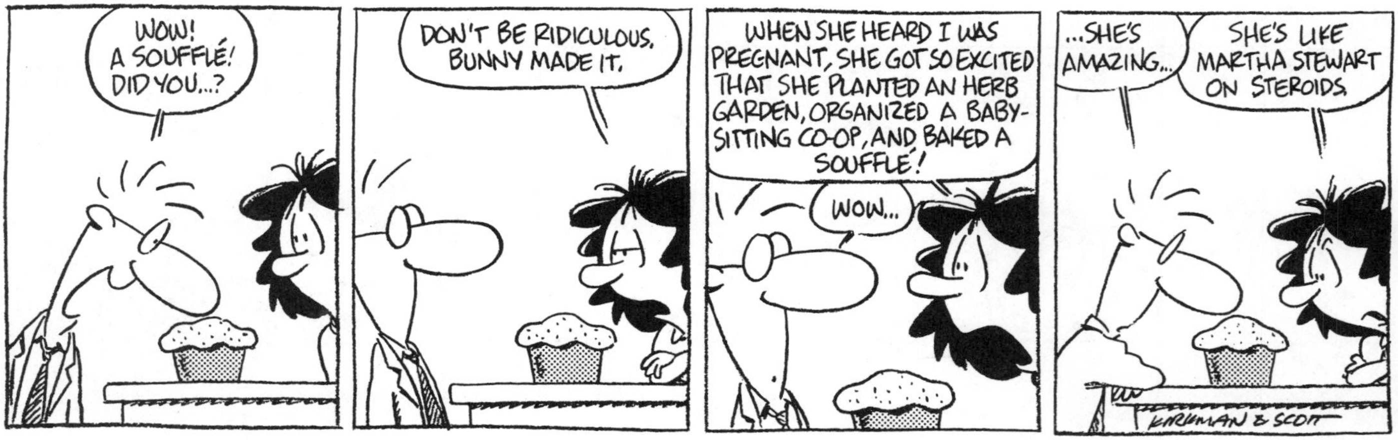
WOW! A SOUFFLÉ! DID YOU...?
DON'T BE RIDICULOUS. BUNNY MADE IT.
WHEN SHE HEARD I WAS PREGNANT, SHE GOT SO EXCITED THAT SHE PLANTED AN HERB GARDEN, ORGANIZED A BABY-SITTING CO-OP, AND BAKED A SOUFFLÉ!
WOW...
...SHE'S AMAZING...
SHE'S LIKE MARTHA STEWART ON STEROIDS.
KIRKMAN & SCOTT

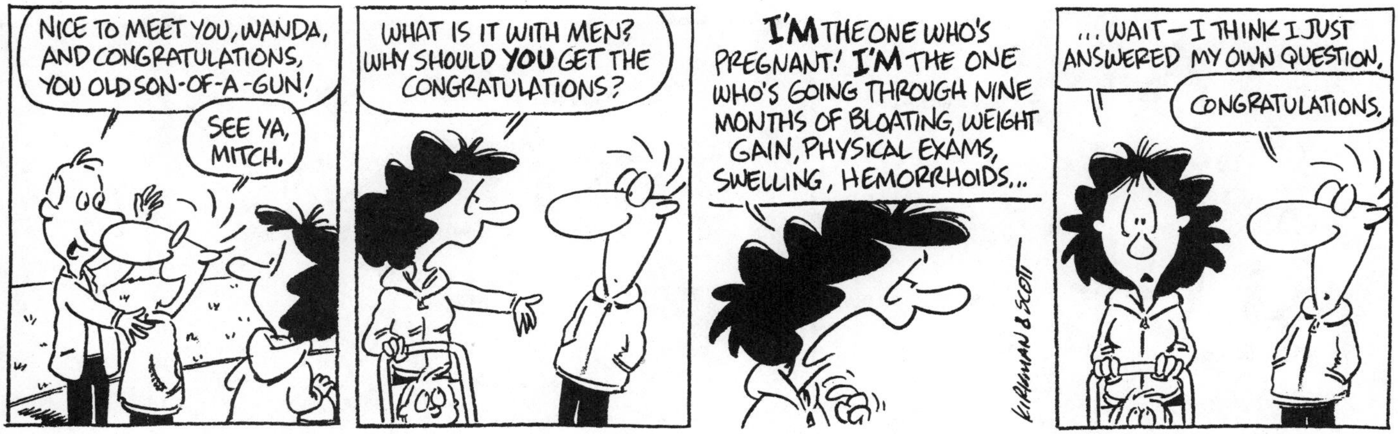
NICE TO MEET YOU, WANDA, AND CONGRATULATIONS, YOU OLD SON-OF-A-GUN!
SEE YA, MITCH.
WHAT IS IT WITH MEN? WHY SHOULD YOU GET THE CONGRATULATIONS?
I'M THE ONE WHO'S PREGNANT! I'M THE ONE WHO'S GOING THROUGH NINE MONTHS OF BLOATING, WEIGHT GAIN, PHYSICAL EXAMS, SWELLING, HEMORRHOIDS...
KIRKMAN & SCOTT
...WAIT—I THINK I JUST ANSWERED MY OWN QUESTION.
CONGRATULATIONS.

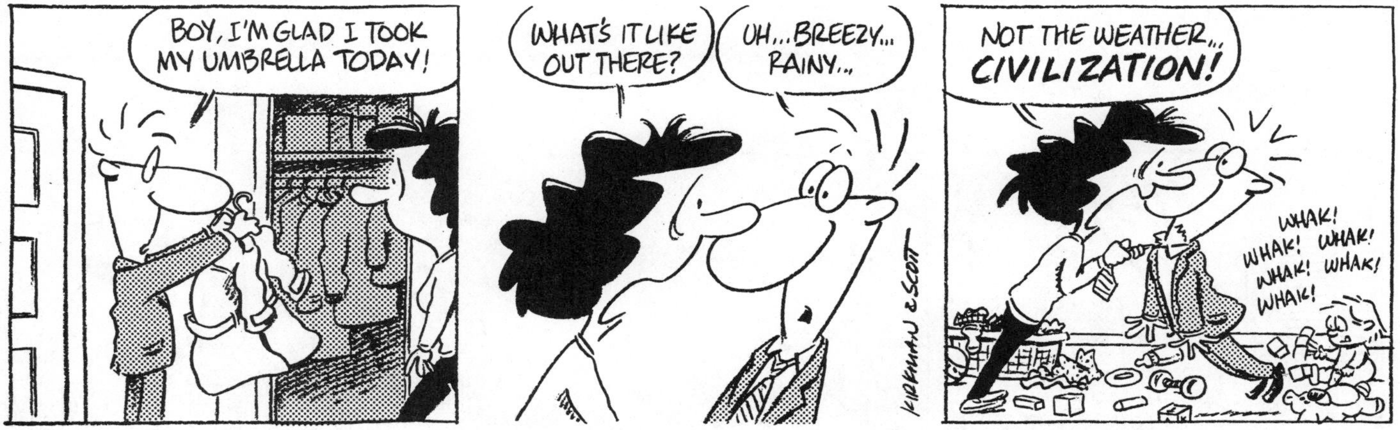
BOY, I'M GLAD I TOOK MY UMBRELLA TODAY!
WHAT'S IT LIKE OUT THERE?
UH... BREEZY... RAINY...
KIRKMAN & SCOTT
NOT THE WEATHER... CIVILIZATION!
WHAK! WHAK! WHAK! WHAK! WHAK! WHAK!

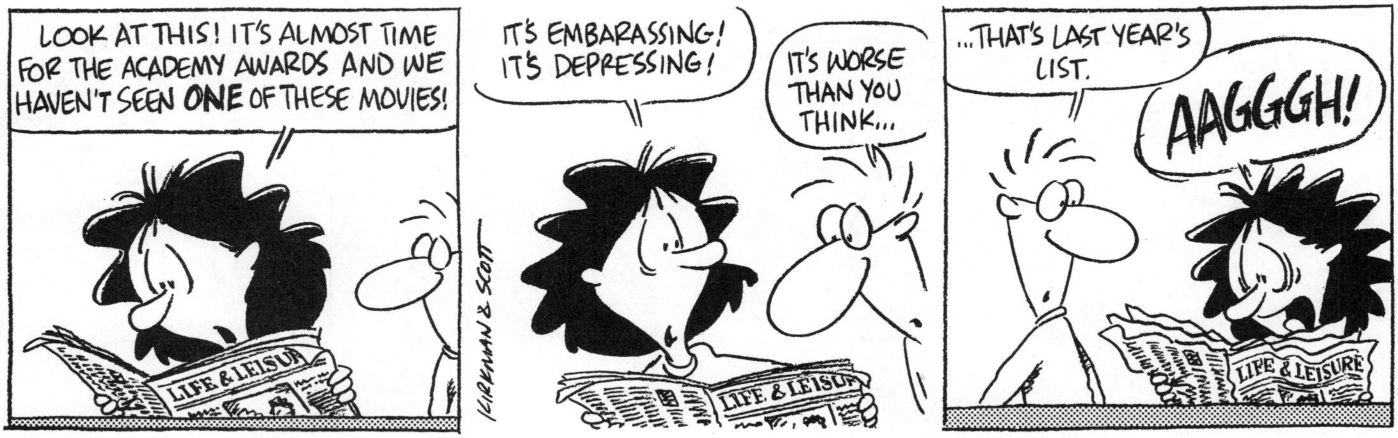
LOOK AT THIS! IT'S ALMOST TIME FOR THE ACADEMY AWARDS AND WE HAVEN'T SEEN ONE OF THESE MOVIES!
LIFE & LEISURE
KIRKMAN & SCOTT
IT'S EMBARASSING! IT'S DEPRESSING!
IT'S WORSE THAN YOU THINK...
LIFE & LEISURE
...THAT'S LAST YEAR'S LIST.
AAGGGH!
LIFE & LEISURE

BABY BLUES®

RICK KIRKMAN / JERRY SCOTT BY

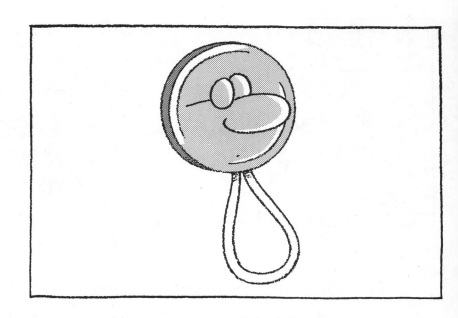

DINK!

NO, ZOE... THIS IS DADDY'S GLASS. YOUR JUICE IS RIGHT THERE.

DA-DA
OOOH, NO, YOU DON'T!

DON'T THINK YOU CAN USE THAT INNOCENT (HEE! HEE!) LOOK AND THAT SWEET LITTLE (AWWWW...) VOICE TO GET ME TO (YOU'RE SOOO CUTE!) UH... TRY... TO... UM... AH...

SIGH!

WHAT WAS I SAYING?
YOU'RE DOOMED.
THLURP! THLUP! THLUP!

KIRKMAN & SCOTT

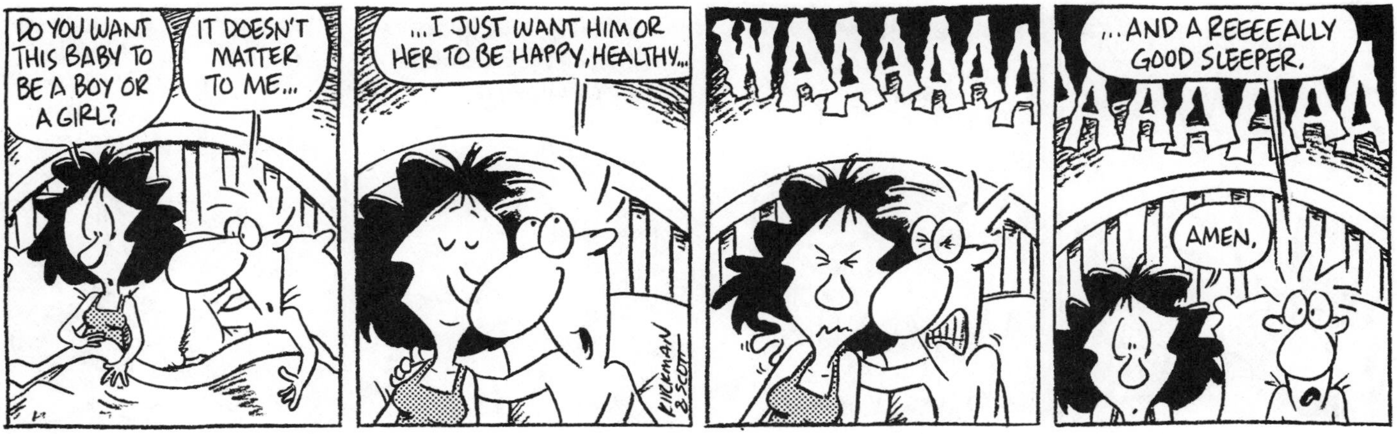
DO YOU WANT THIS BABY TO BE A BOY OR A GIRL?
IT DOESN'T MATTER TO ME...
...I JUST WANT HIM OR HER TO BE HAPPY, HEALTHY...
KIRKMAN & SCOTT
WAAAAAAAAAAAAA
...AND A REEEEALLY GOOD SLEEPER.
AMEN.

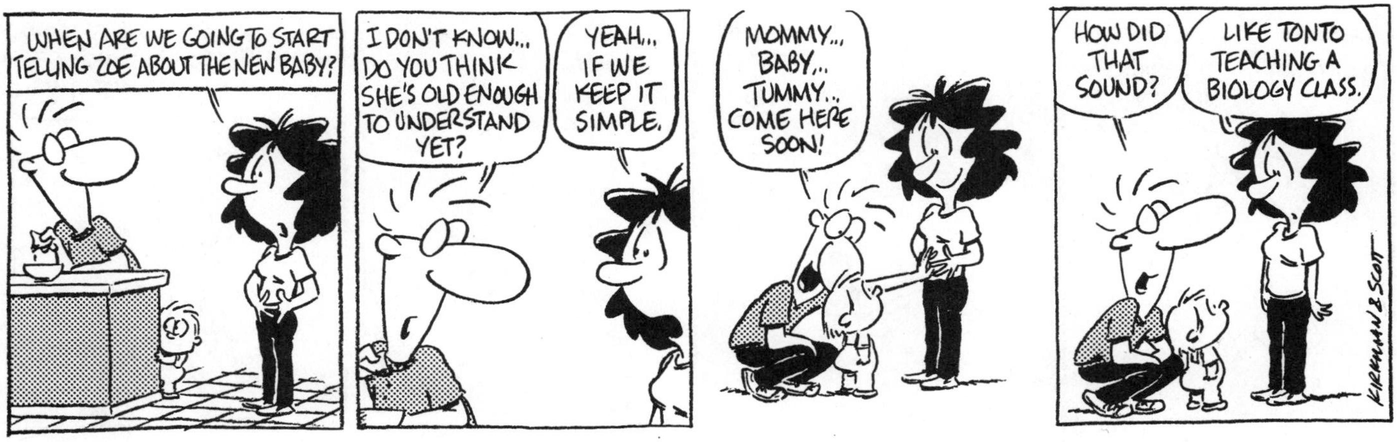
WHEN ARE WE GOING TO START TELLING ZOE ABOUT THE NEW BABY?
I DON'T KNOW... DO YOU THINK SHE'S OLD ENOUGH TO UNDERSTAND YET?
YEAH... IF WE KEEP IT SIMPLE.
MOMMY... BABY... TUMMY... COME HERE SOON!
HOW DID THAT SOUND?
LIKE TONTO TEACHING A BIOLOGY CLASS.
KIRKMAN & SCOTT

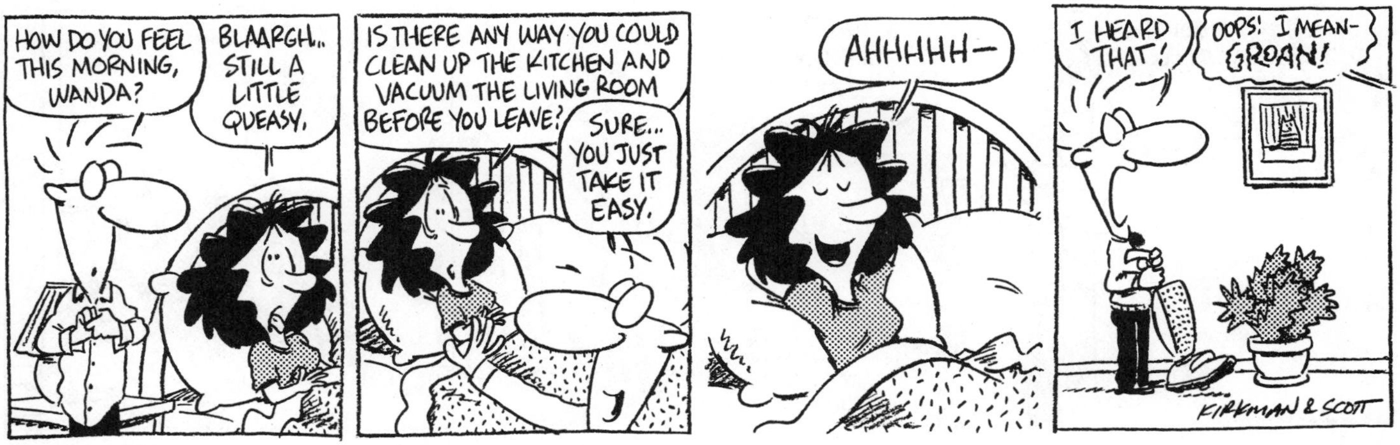
HOW DO YOU FEEL THIS MORNING, WANDA?
BLAARGH... STILL A LITTLE QUEASY.
IS THERE ANY WAY YOU COULD CLEAN UP THE KITCHEN AND VACUUM THE LIVING ROOM BEFORE YOU LEAVE?
SURE... YOU JUST TAKE IT EASY.
AHHHHH-
I HEARD THAT!
OOPS! I MEAN- GROAN!
KIRKMAN & SCOTT

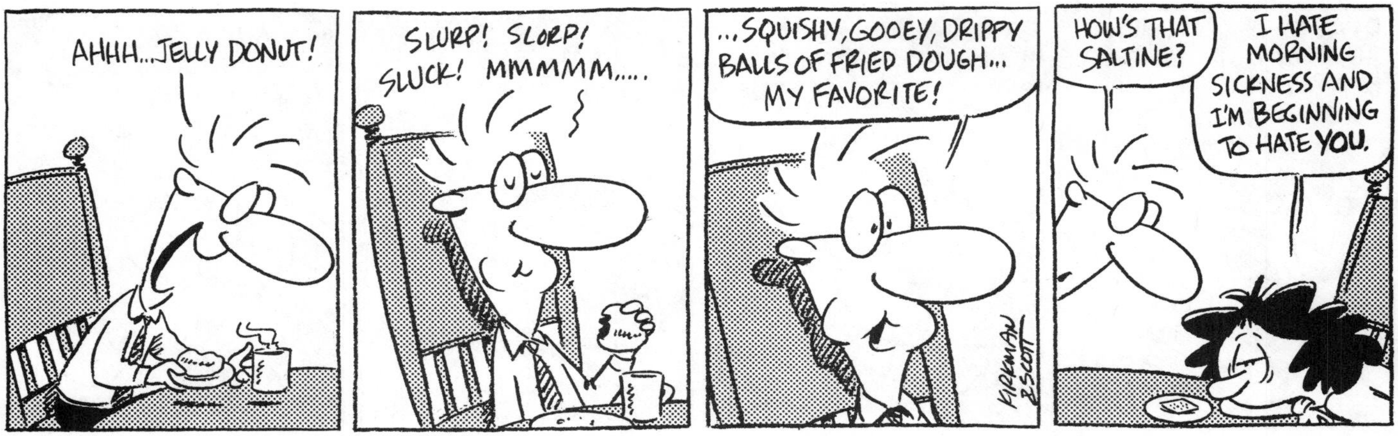
AHHH...JELLY DONUT!
SLURP! SLORP! SLUCK! MMMMM.....
...SQUISHY, GOOEY, DRIPPY BALLS OF FRIED DOUGH... MY FAVORITE!
KIRKMAN & SCOTT
HOW'S THAT SALTINE?
I HATE MORNING SICKNESS AND I'M BEGINNING TO HATE **YOU**.

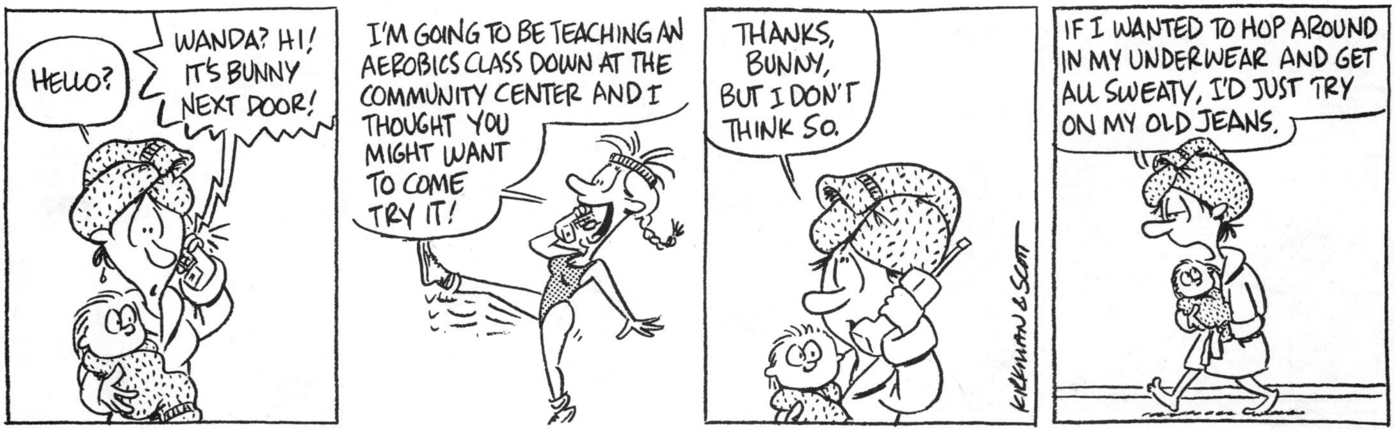
HELLO?
WANDA? HI! IT'S BUNNY NEXT DOOR!
I'M GOING TO BE TEACHING AN AEROBICS CLASS DOWN AT THE COMMUNITY CENTER AND I THOUGHT YOU MIGHT WANT TO COME TRY IT!
THANKS, BUNNY, BUT I DON'T THINK SO.
KIRKMAN & SCOTT
IF I WANTED TO HOP AROUND IN MY UNDERWEAR AND GET ALL SWEATY, I'D JUST TRY ON MY OLD JEANS.

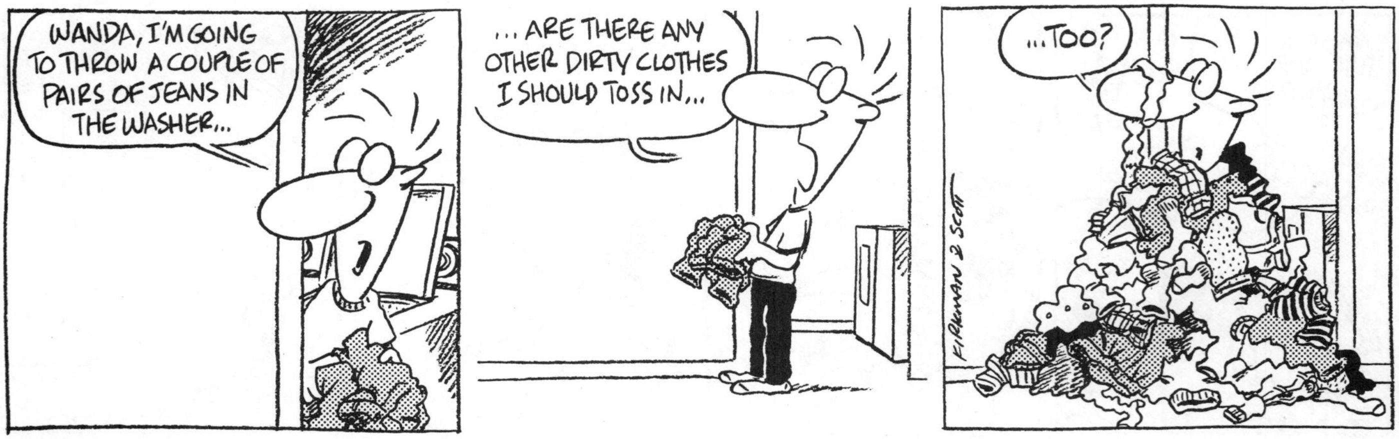
WANDA, I'M GOING TO THROW A COUPLE OF PAIRS OF JEANS IN THE WASHER...
...ARE THERE ANY OTHER DIRTY CLOTHES I SHOULD TOSS IN...
KIRKMAN & SCOTT
...TOO?

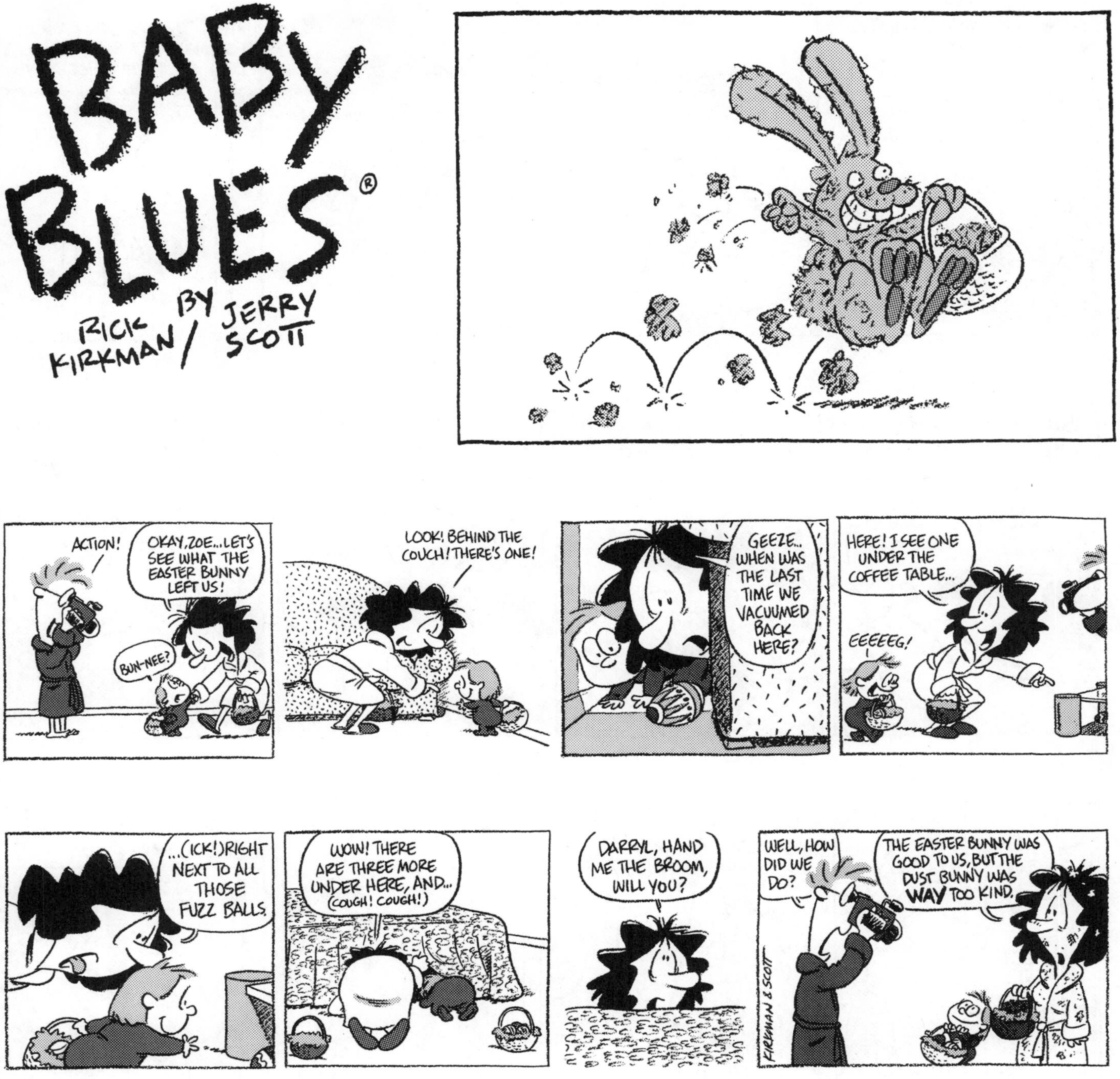
BABY BLUES®
BY RICK KIRKMAN / JERRY SCOTT
ACTION!
OKAY, ZOE... LET'S SEE WHAT THE EASTER BUNNY LEFT US!
BUN-NEE?
LOOK! BEHIND THE COUCH! THERE'S ONE!
GEEZE... WHEN WAS THE LAST TIME WE VACUUMED BACK HERE?
HERE! I SEE ONE UNDER THE COFFEE TABLE...
EEEEEG!
...(ICK!) RIGHT NEXT TO ALL THOSE FUZZ BALLS.
WOW! THERE ARE THREE MORE UNDER HERE, AND... (COUGH! COUGH!)
DARRYL, HAND ME THE BROOM, WILL YOU?
KIRKMAN & SCOTT
WELL, HOW DID WE DO?
THE EASTER BUNNY WAS GOOD TO US, BUT THE DUST BUNNY WAS WAY TOO KIND.

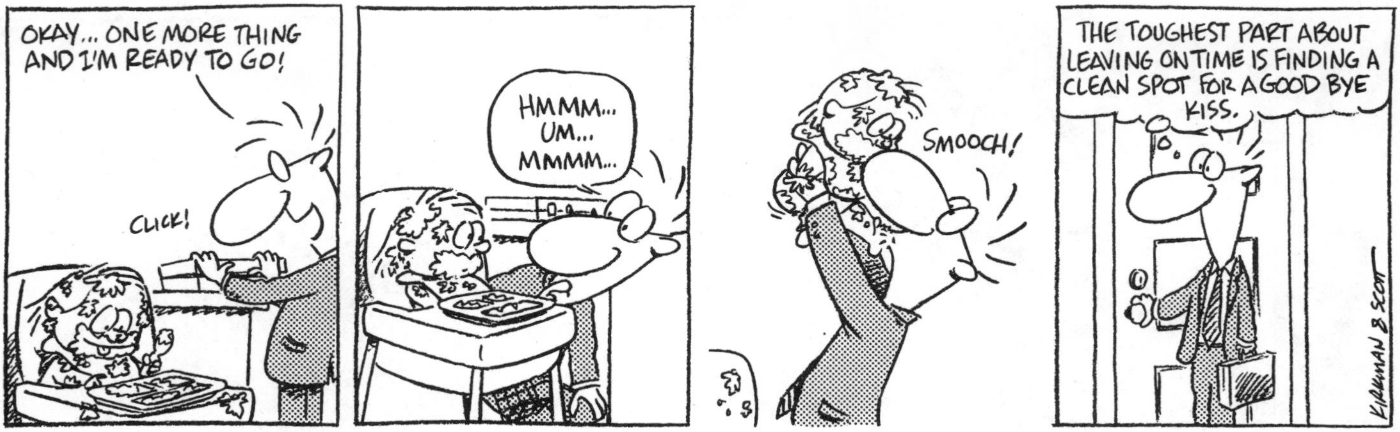
OKAY... ONE MORE THING AND I'M READY TO GO!
CLICK!
HMMM... UM... MMMM...
SMOOCH!
THE TOUGHEST PART ABOUT LEAVING ON TIME IS FINDING A CLEAN SPOT FOR A GOOD BYE KISS.
KIRKMAN & SCOTT

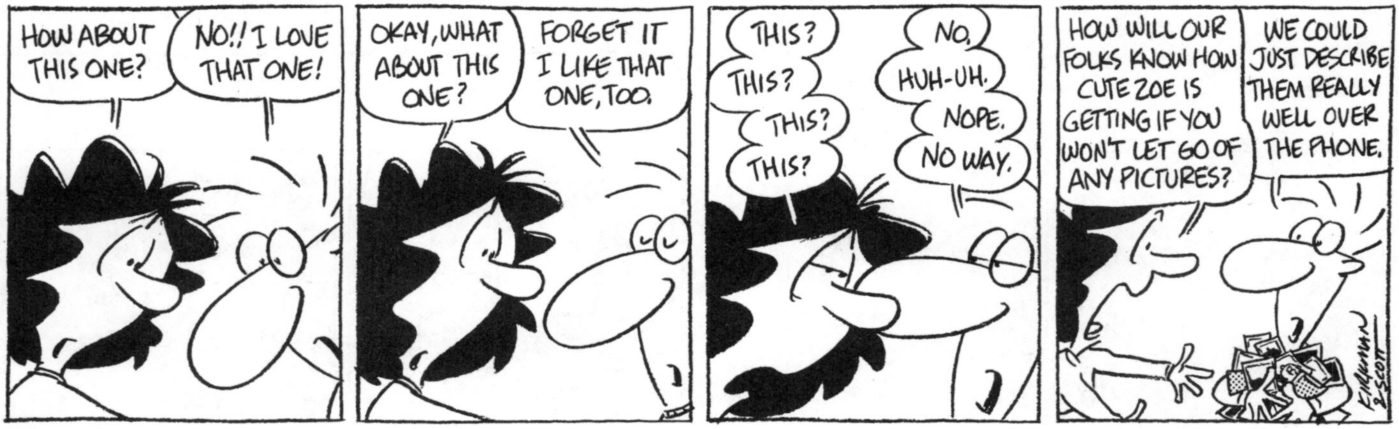
HOW ABOUT THIS ONE?
NO!! I LOVE THAT ONE!
OKAY, WHAT ABOUT THIS ONE?
FORGET IT I LIKE THAT ONE, TOO.
THIS? THIS? THIS? THIS?
NO. HUH-UH. NOPE. NO WAY.
HOW WILL OUR FOLKS KNOW HOW CUTE ZOE IS GETTING IF YOU WON'T LET GO OF ANY PICTURES?
WE COULD JUST DESCRIBE THEM REALLY WELL OVER THE PHONE.
KIRKMAN & SCOTT

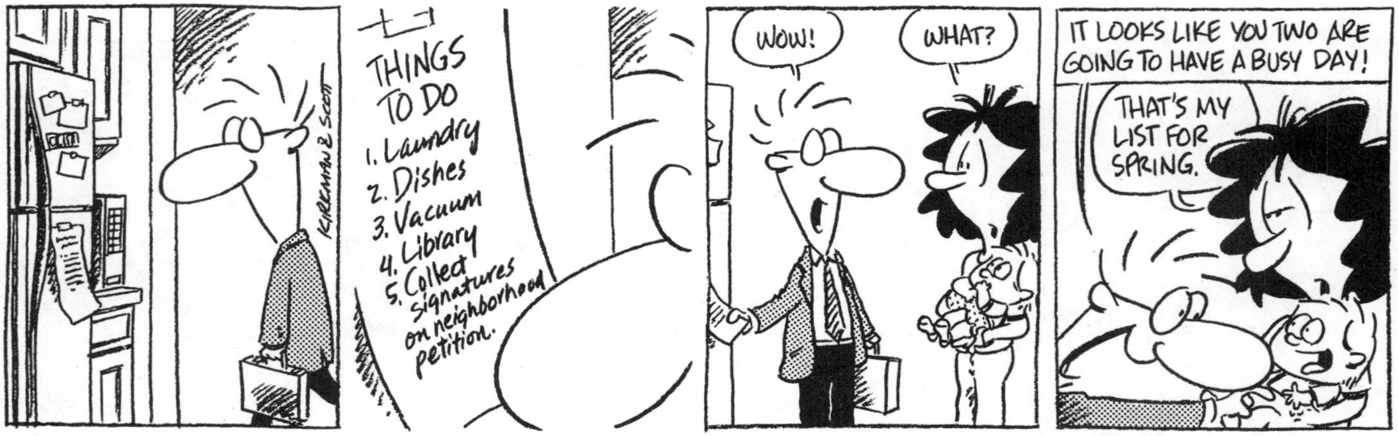
KIRKMAN & SCOTT
THINGS TO DO
1. Laundry
2. Dishes
3. Vacuum
4. Library
5. Collect signatures on neighborhood petition.
WOW!
WHAT?
IT LOOKS LIKE YOU TWO ARE GOING TO HAVE A BUSY DAY!
THAT'S MY LIST FOR SPRING.

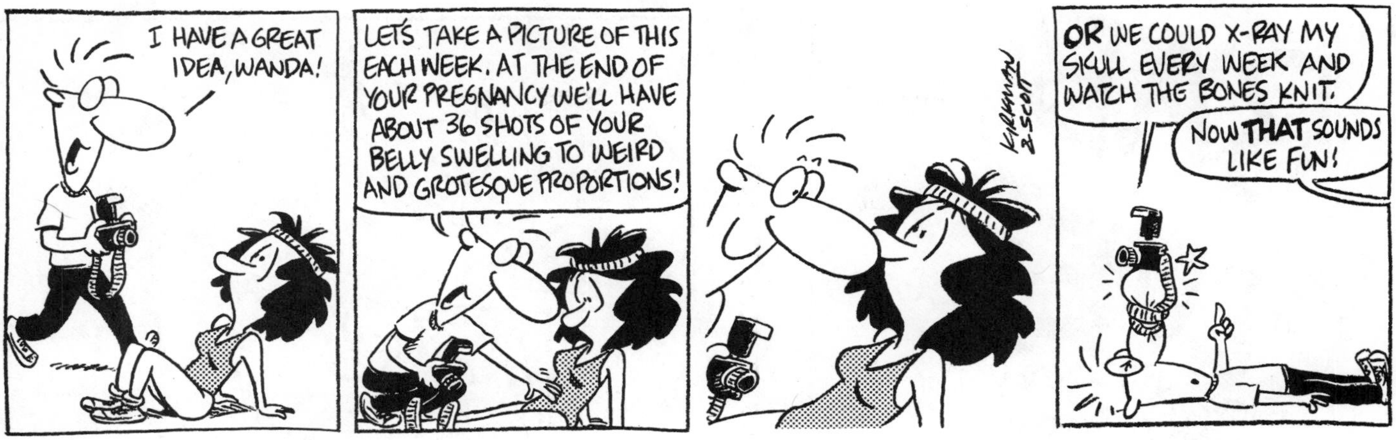
I HAVE A GREAT IDEA, WANDA!
LET'S TAKE A PICTURE OF THIS EACH WEEK. AT THE END OF YOUR PREGNANCY WE'LL HAVE ABOUT 36 SHOTS OF YOUR BELLY SWELLING TO WEIRD AND GROTESQUE PROPORTIONS!
KIRKMAN & SCOTT
OR WE COULD X-RAY MY SKULL EVERY WEEK AND WATCH THE BONES KNIT.
NOW THAT SOUNDS LIKE FUN!

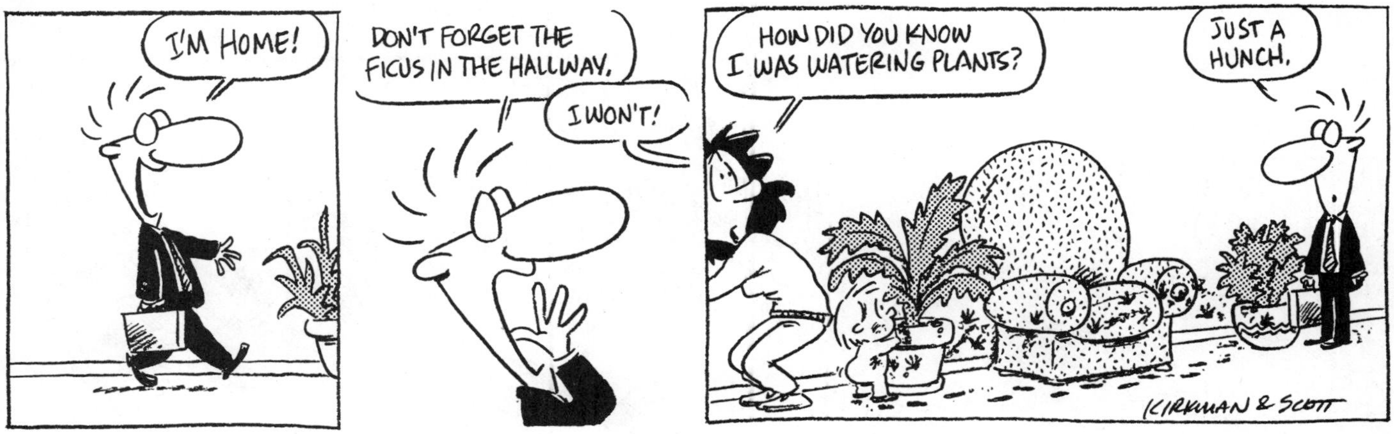
I'M HOME!
DON'T FORGET THE FICUS IN THE HALLWAY.
I WON'T!
HOW DID YOU KNOW I WAS WATERING PLANTS?
JUST A HUNCH.
KIRKMAN & SCOTT

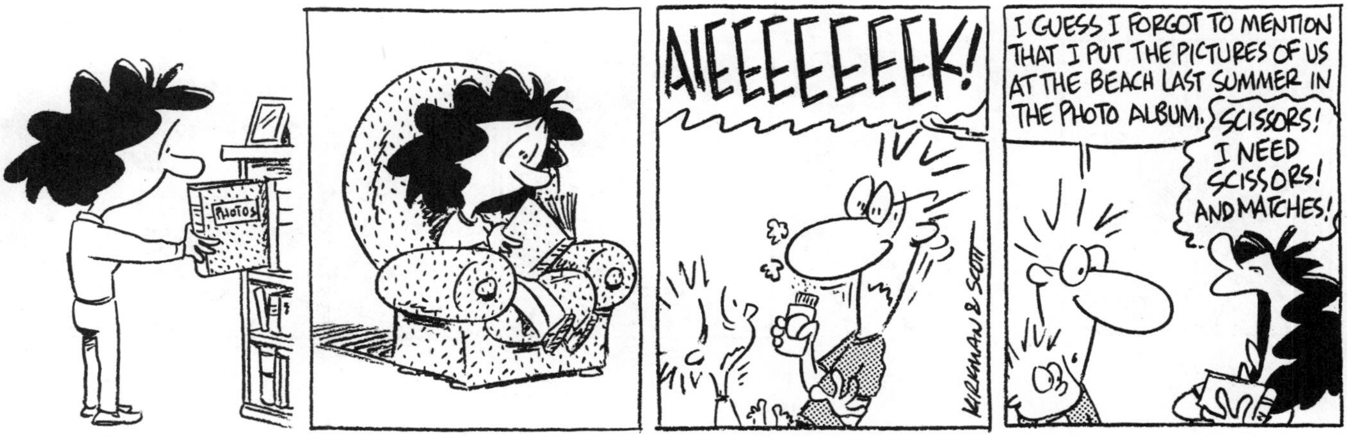
PHOTOS
AIEEEEEEEEK!
KIRKMAN & SCOTT
I GUESS I FORGOT TO MENTION THAT I PUT THE PICTURES OF US AT THE BEACH LAST SUMMER IN THE PHOTO ALBUM.
SCISSORS! I NEED SCISSORS! AND MATCHES!

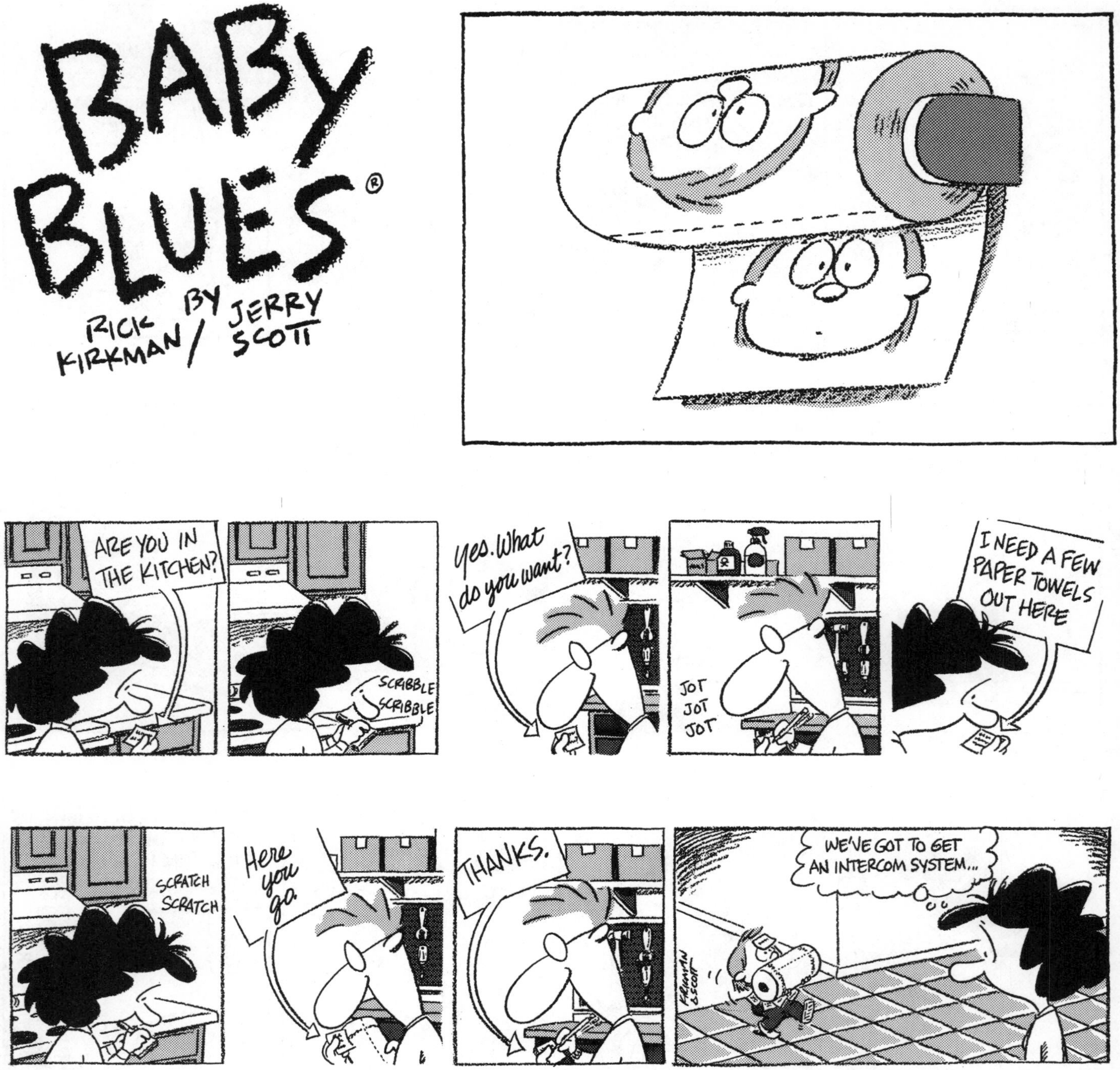
BABY BLUES®
BY RICK KIRKMAN / JERRY SCOTT
ARE YOU IN THE KITCHEN?
SCRIBBLE SCRIBBLE
Yes. What do you want?
JOT JOT JOT
I NEED A FEW PAPER TOWELS OUT HERE
SCRATCH SCRATCH
Here you go.
THANKS.
WE'VE GOT TO GET AN INTERCOM SYSTEM...

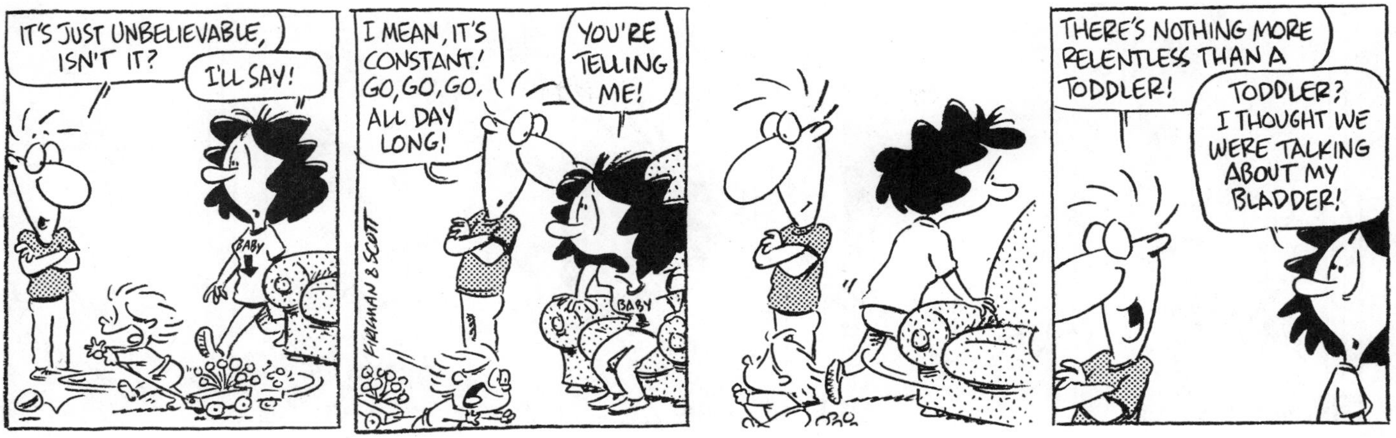
IT'S JUST UNBELIEVABLE, ISN'T IT?
I'LL SAY!
BABY
I MEAN, IT'S CONSTANT! GO, GO, GO, ALL DAY LONG!
YOU'RE TELLING ME!
KIRKMAN & SCOTT
BABY
THERE'S NOTHING MORE RELENTLESS THAN A TODDLER!
TODDLER? I THOUGHT WE WERE TALKING ABOUT MY BLADDER!

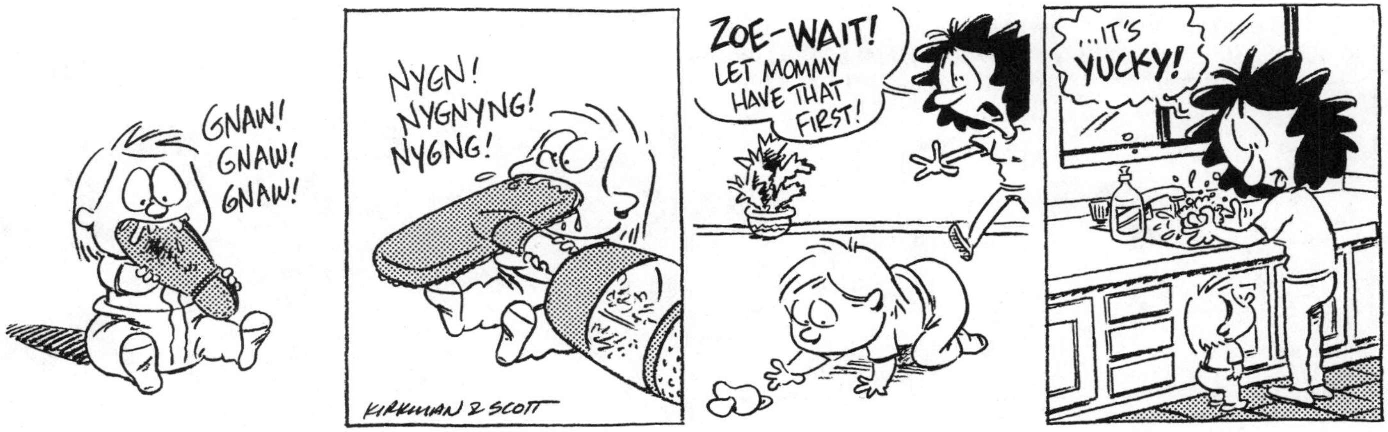
GNAW! GNAW! GNAW!
NYGN! NYGNYNG! NYGNG!
KIRKMAN & SCOTT
ZOE-WAIT! LET MOMMY HAVE THAT FIRST!
...IT'S YUCKY!

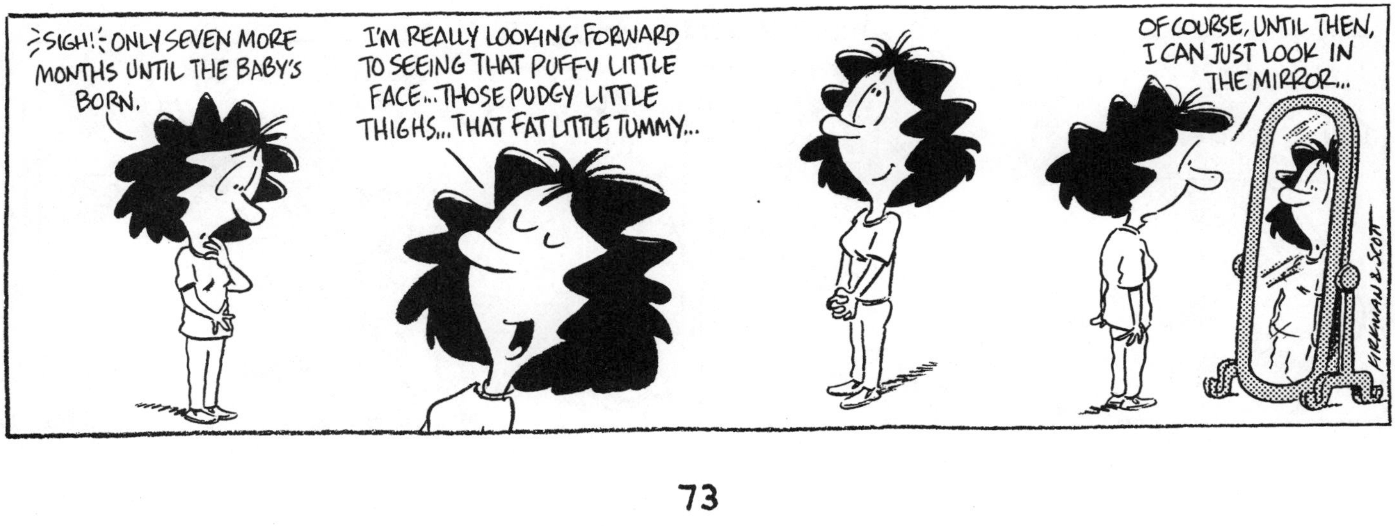
SIGH! ONLY SEVEN MORE MONTHS UNTIL THE BABY'S BORN.
I'M REALLY LOOKING FORWARD TO SEEING THAT PUFFY LITTLE FACE... THOSE PUDGY LITTLE THIGHS... THAT FAT LITTLE TUMMY...
OF COURSE, UNTIL THEN, I CAN JUST LOOK IN THE MIRROR...
KIRKMAN & SCOTT

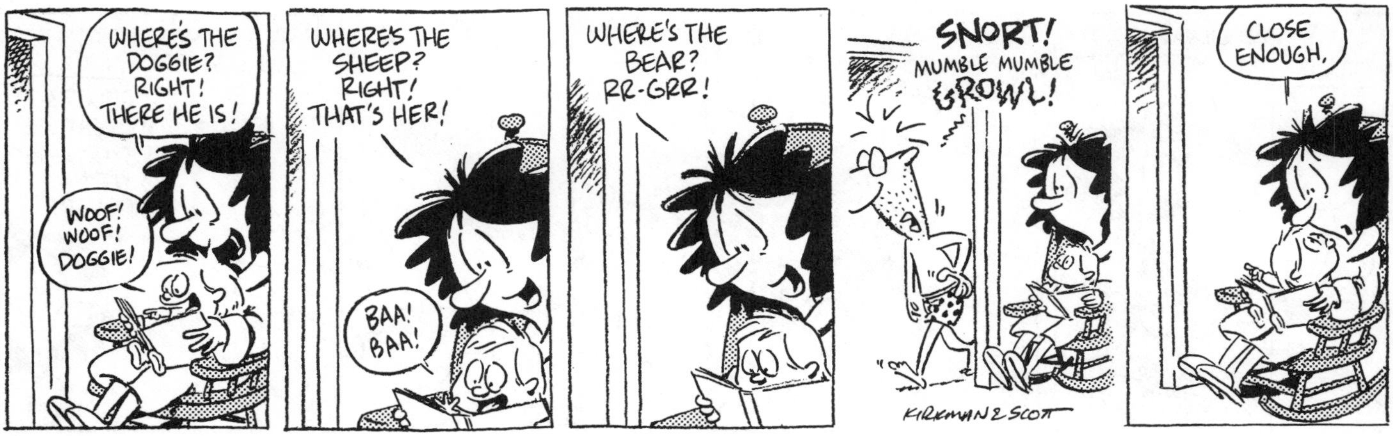
WHERE'S THE DOGGIE? RIGHT! THERE HE IS!
WOOF! WOOF! DOGGIE!
WHERE'S THE SHEEP? RIGHT! THAT'S HER!
BAA! BAA!
WHERE'S THE BEAR? RR-GRR!
SNORT! MUMBLE MUMBLE GROWL!
KIRKMAN & SCOTT
CLOSE ENOUGH.

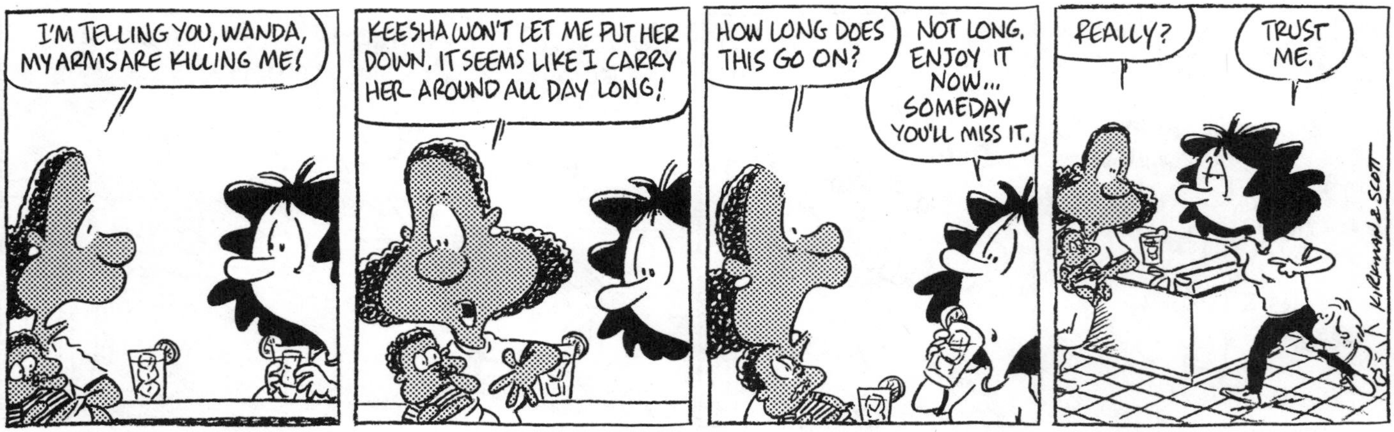
I'M TELLING YOU, WANDA, MY ARMS ARE KILLING ME!
KEESHA WON'T LET ME PUT HER DOWN. IT SEEMS LIKE I CARRY HER AROUND ALL DAY LONG!
HOW LONG DOES THIS GO ON?
NOT LONG. ENJOY IT NOW... SOMEDAY YOU'LL MISS IT.
REALLY?
TRUST ME.
KIRKMAN & SCOTT

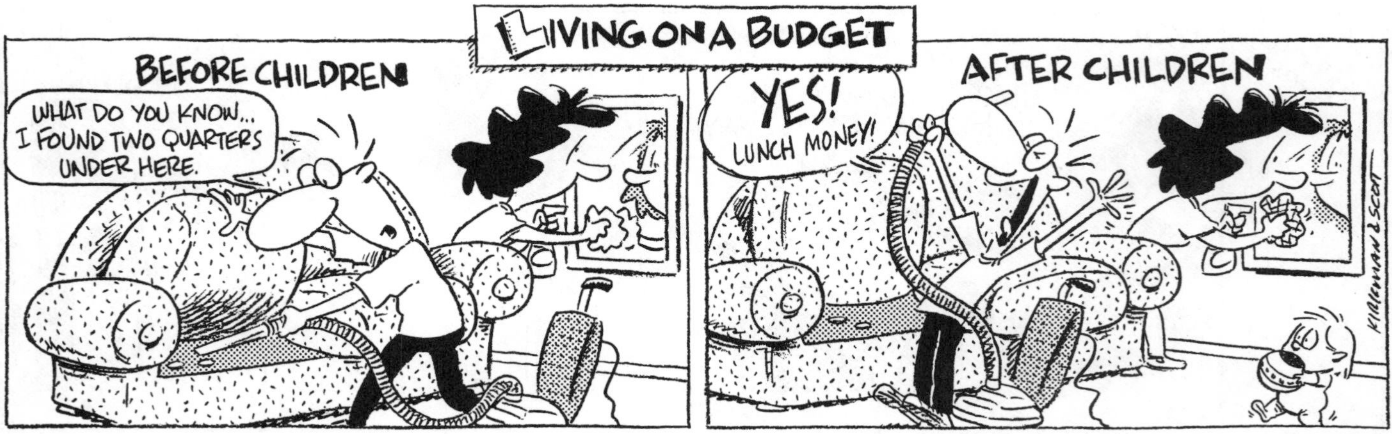
LIVING ON A BUDGET
BEFORE CHILDREN
WHAT DO YOU KNOW... I FOUND TWO QUARTERS UNDER HERE.
AFTER CHILDREN
YES! LUNCH MONEY!
KIRKMAN & SCOTT

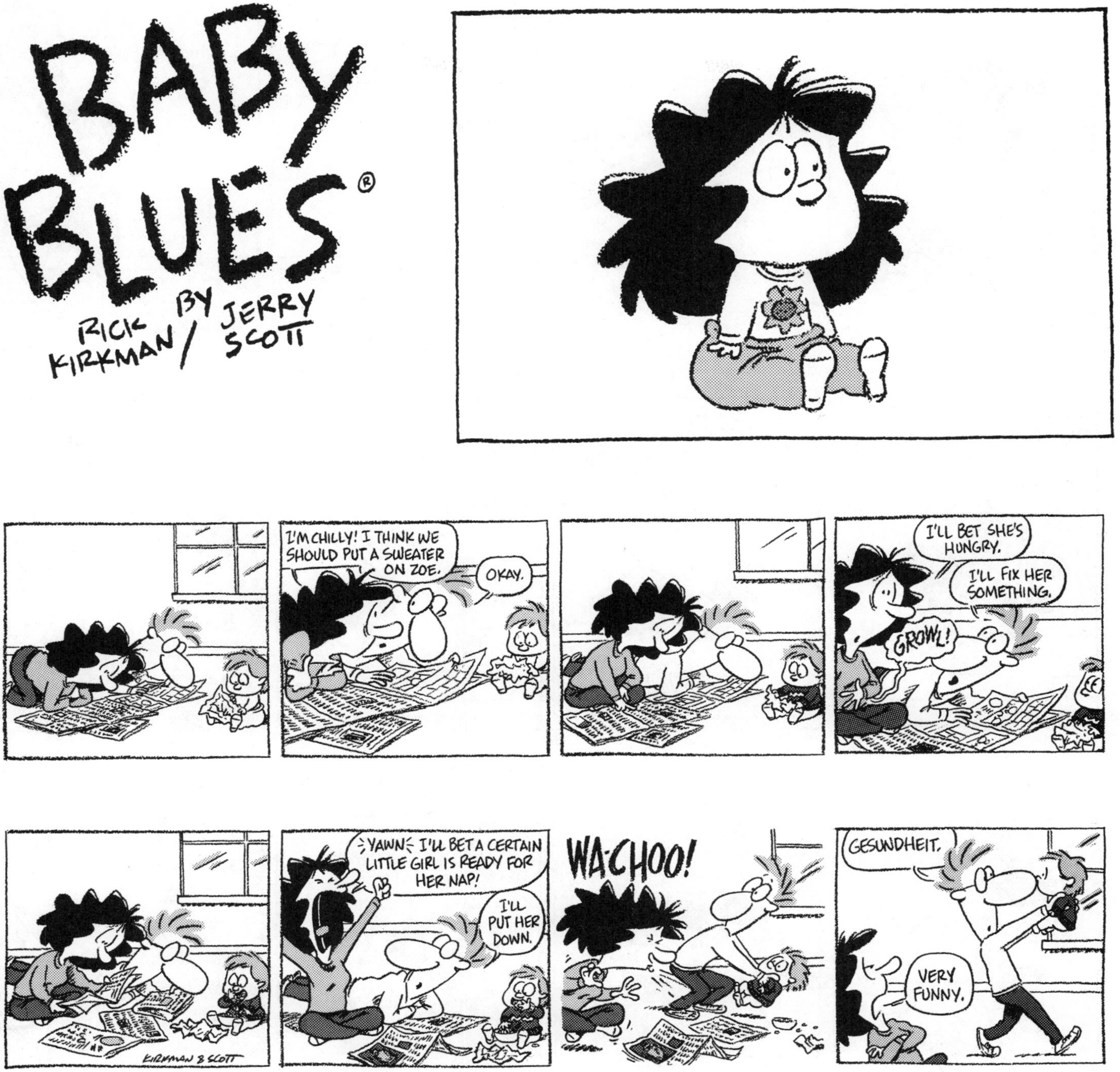
BABY BLUES®
BY RICK KIRKMAN / JERRY SCOTT
I'M CHILLY! I THINK WE SHOULD PUT A SWEATER ON ZOE.
OKAY.
I'LL BET SHE'S HUNGRY.
I'LL FIX HER SOMETHING.
GROWL!
KIRKMAN & SCOTT
≷YAWN≶ I'LL BET A CERTAIN LITTLE GIRL IS READY FOR HER NAP!
I'LL PUT HER DOWN.
WA-CHOO!
GESUNDHEIT.
VERY FUNNY.

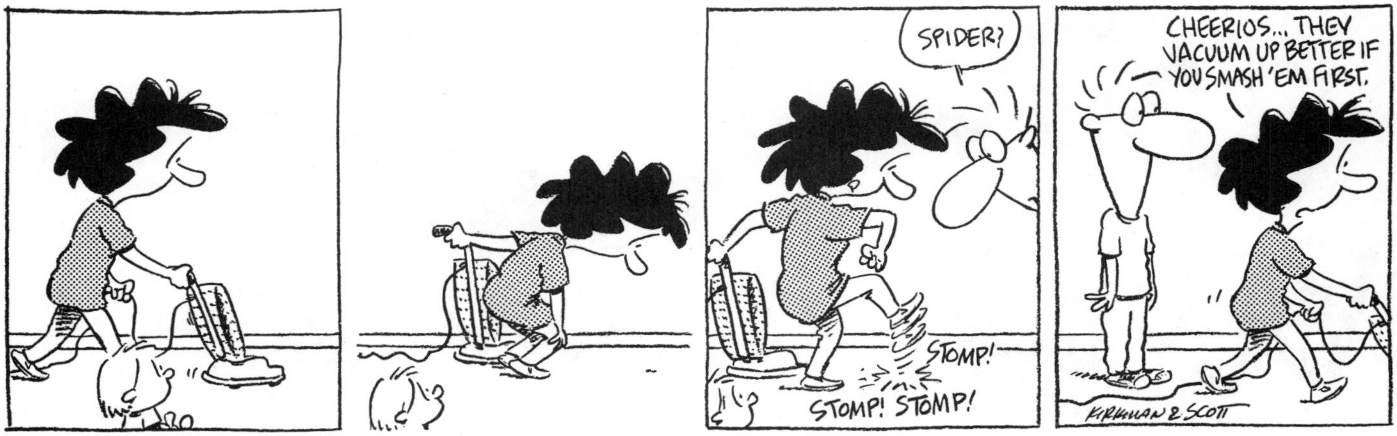
SPIDER?
STOMP!
STOMP! STOMP!
CHEERIOS... THEY VACUUM UP BETTER IF YOU SMASH 'EM FIRST.
KIRKMAN & SCOTT

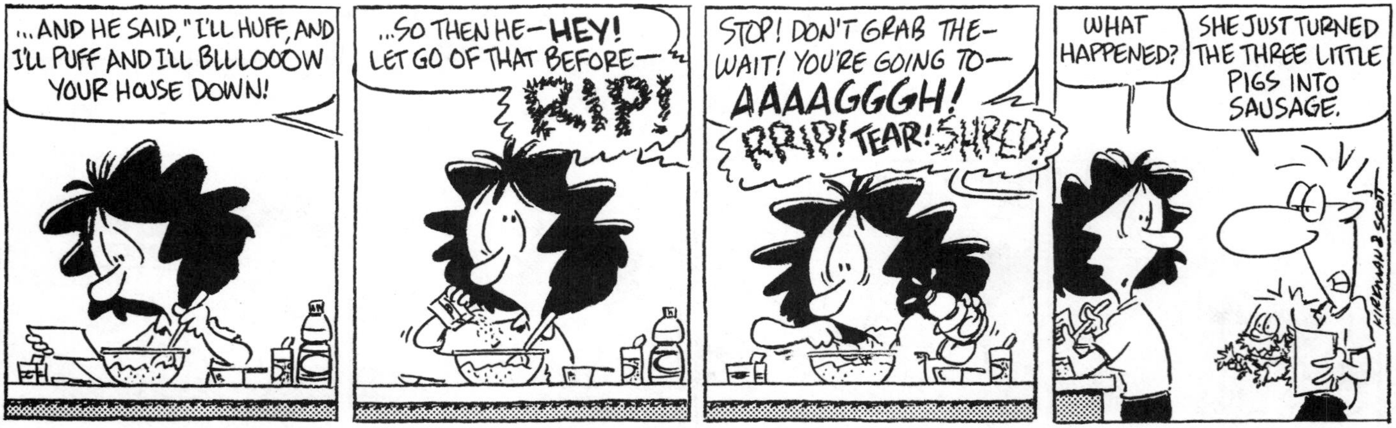
...AND HE SAID, "I'LL HUFF, AND I'LL PUFF AND I'LL BLLLOOOW YOUR HOUSE DOWN!
...SO THEN HE—HEY! LET GO OF THAT BEFORE—
RIP!
STOP! DON'T GRAB THE—WAIT! YOU'RE GOING TO—AAAAGGGH!
RRIP! TEAR! SHRED!
WHAT HAPPENED?
SHE JUST TURNED THE THREE LITTLE PIGS INTO SAUSAGE.
KIRKMAN & SCOTT

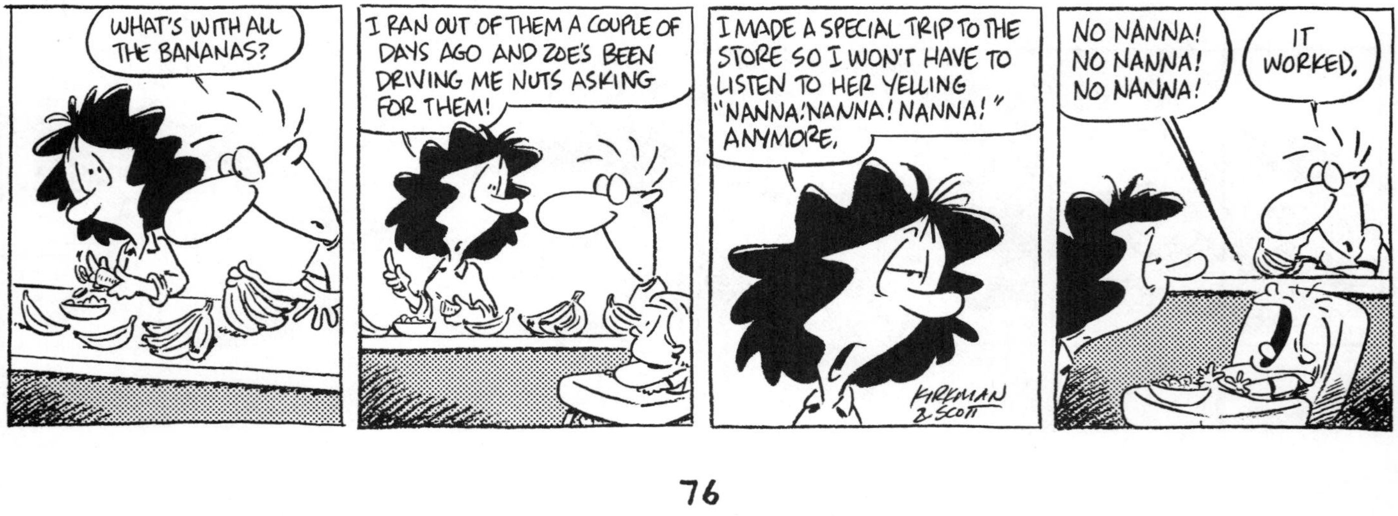
WHAT'S WITH ALL THE BANANAS?
I RAN OUT OF THEM A COUPLE OF DAYS AGO AND ZOE'S BEEN DRIVING ME NUTS ASKING FOR THEM!
I MADE A SPECIAL TRIP TO THE STORE SO I WON'T HAVE TO LISTEN TO HER YELLING "NANNA! NANNA! NANNA!" ANYMORE.
KIRKMAN & SCOTT
NO NANNA! NO NANNA! NO NANNA!
IT WORKED.

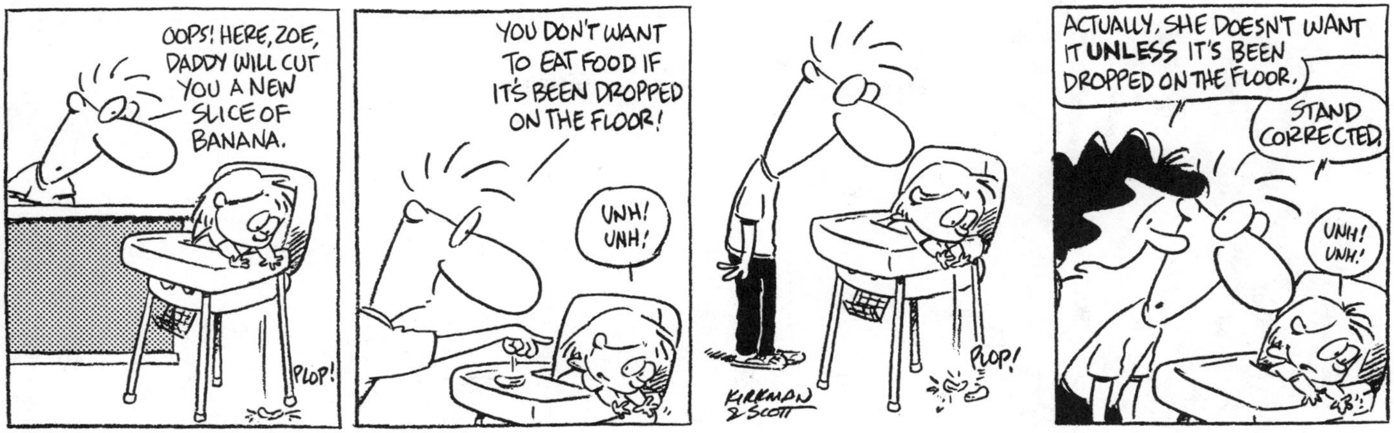
OOPS! HERE, ZOE, DADDY WILL CUT YOU A NEW SLICE OF BANANA.
PLOP!
YOU DON'T WANT TO EAT FOOD IF IT'S BEEN DROPPED ON THE FLOOR!
UNH! UNH!
PLOP!
KIRKMAN & SCOTT
ACTUALLY, SHE DOESN'T WANT IT **UNLESS** IT'S BEEN DROPPED ON THE FLOOR.
STAND CORRECTED.
UNH! UNH!

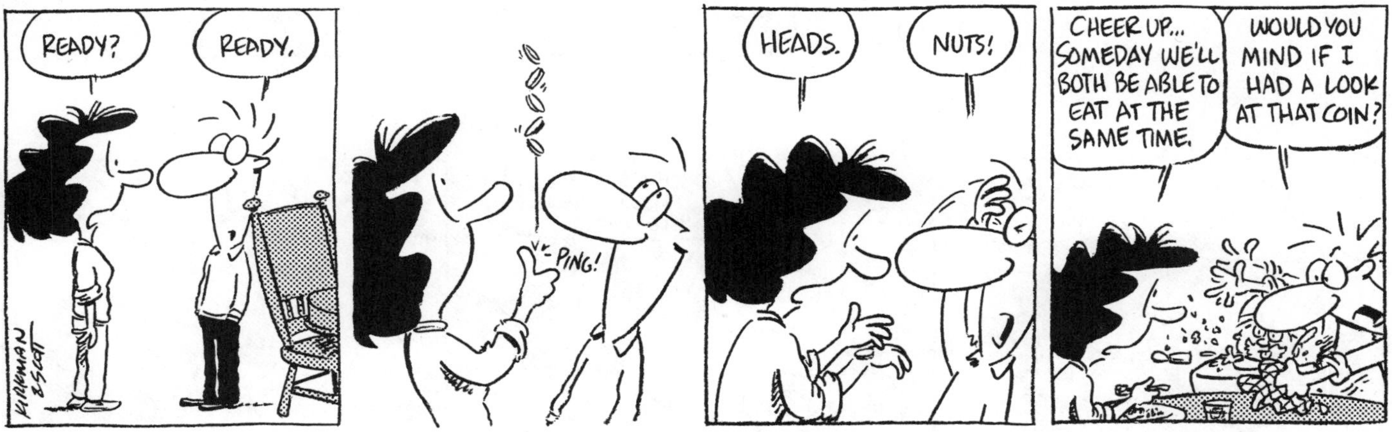
READY?
READY.
KIRKMAN & SCOTT
PING!
HEADS.
NUTS!
CHEER UP... SOMEDAY WE'LL BOTH BE ABLE TO EAT AT THE SAME TIME.
WOULD YOU MIND IF I HAD A LOOK AT THAT COIN?

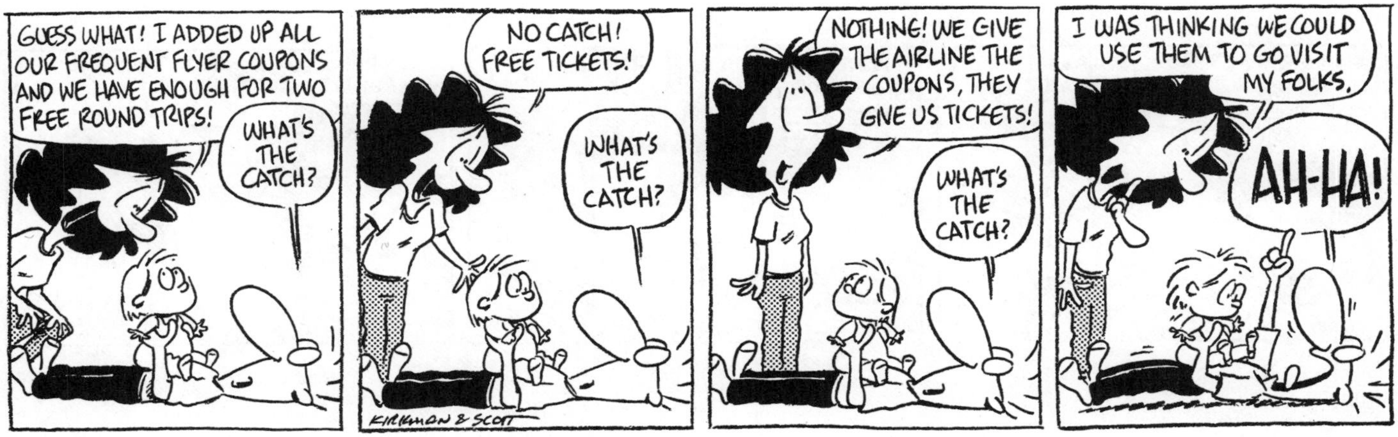
GUESS WHAT! I ADDED UP ALL OUR FREQUENT FLYER COUPONS AND WE HAVE ENOUGH FOR TWO FREE ROUND TRIPS!
WHAT'S THE CATCH?
NO CATCH! FREE TICKETS!
WHAT'S THE CATCH?
KIRKMAN & SCOTT
NOTHING! WE GIVE THE AIRLINE THE COUPONS, THEY GIVE US TICKETS!
WHAT'S THE CATCH?
I WAS THINKING WE COULD USE THEM TO GO VISIT MY FOLKS.
AH-HA!

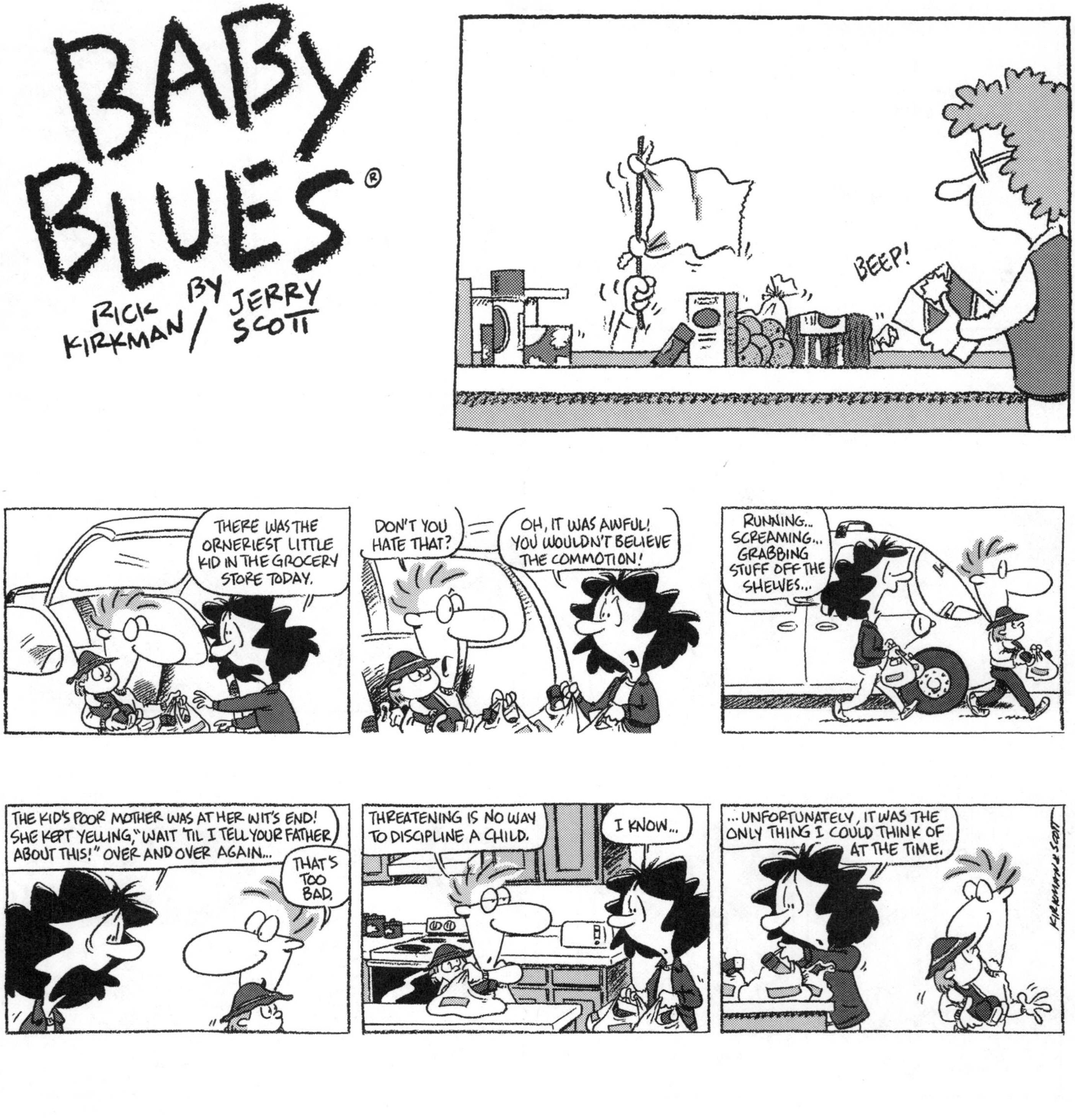
BABY BLUES®
BY RICK KIRKMAN / JERRY SCOTT
BEEP!
THERE WAS THE ORNERIEST LITTLE KID IN THE GROCERY STORE TODAY.
DON'T YOU HATE THAT?
OH, IT WAS AWFUL! YOU WOULDN'T BELIEVE THE COMMOTION!
RUNNING... SCREAMING... GRABBING STUFF OFF THE SHELVES...
THE KID'S POOR MOTHER WAS AT HER WIT'S END! SHE KEPT YELLING, "WAIT 'TIL I TELL YOUR FATHER ABOUT THIS!" OVER AND OVER AGAIN...
THAT'S TOO BAD.
THREATENING IS NO WAY TO DISCIPLINE A CHILD.
I KNOW...
...UNFORTUNATELY, IT WAS THE ONLY THING I COULD THINK OF AT THE TIME.
KIRKMAN & SCOTT

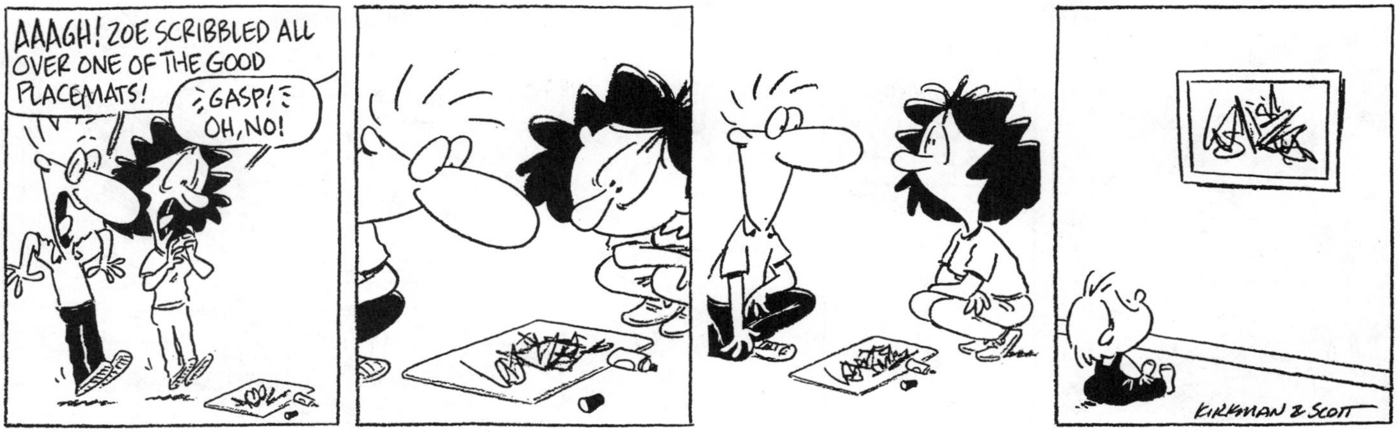
AAAGH! ZOE SCRIBBLED ALL OVER ONE OF THE GOOD PLACEMATS!
GASP! OH, NO!
KIRKMAN & SCOTT

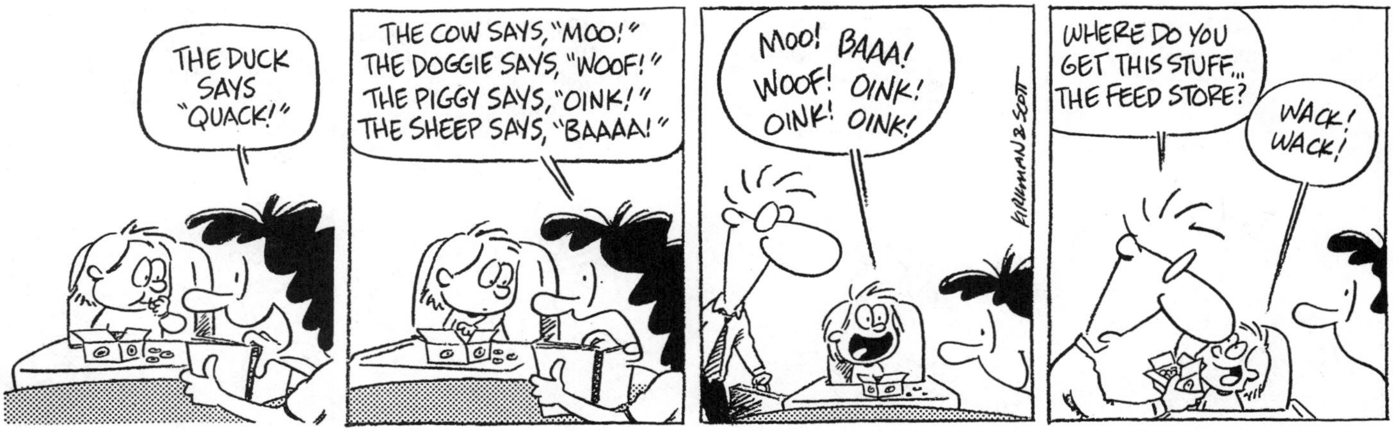
THE DUCK SAYS "QUACK!"
THE COW SAYS, "MOO!" THE DOGGIE SAYS, "WOOF!" THE PIGGY SAYS, "OINK!" THE SHEEP SAYS, "BAAAA!"
MOO! BAAA! WOOF! OINK! OINK! OINK!
KIRKMAN & SCOTT
WHERE DO YOU GET THIS STUFF... THE FEED STORE?
WACK! WACK!

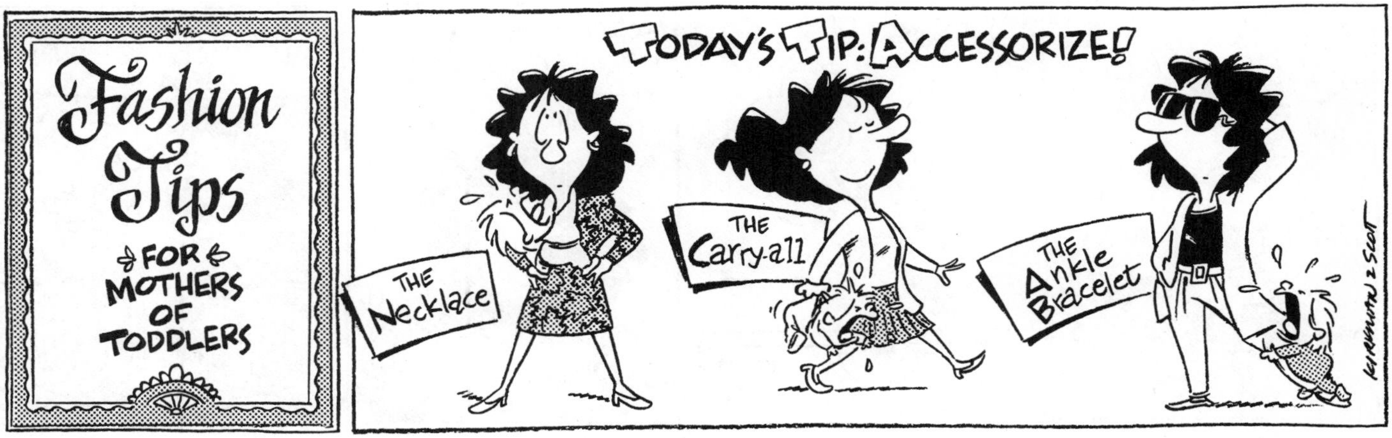
Fashion Tips FOR MOTHERS OF TODDLERS
TODAY'S TIP: ACCESSORIZE!
THE Necklace
THE Carry-all
THE Ankle Bracelet
KIRKMAN & SCOTT

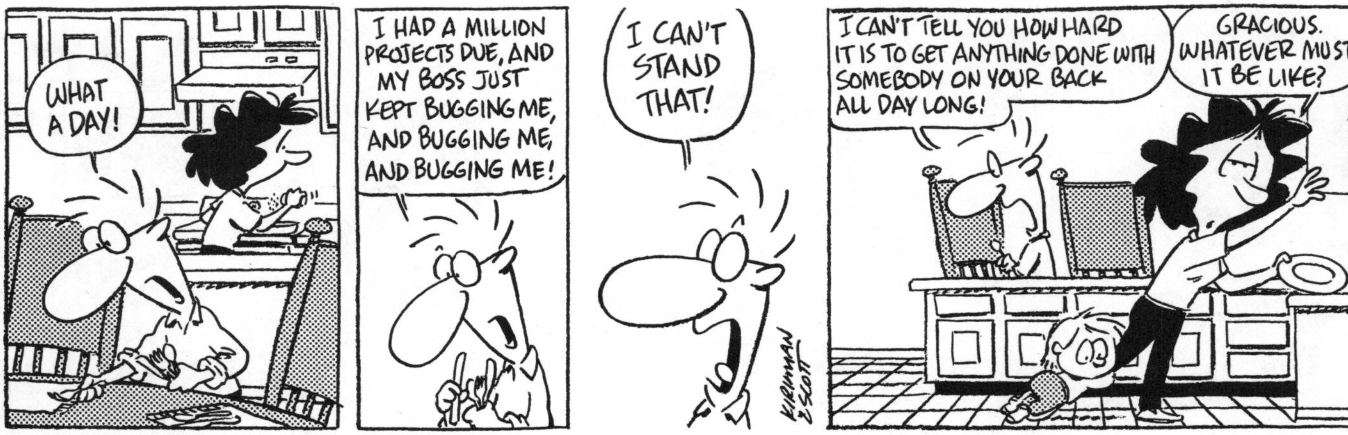
WHAT A DAY!
I HAD A MILLION PROJECTS DUE, AND MY BOSS JUST KEPT BUGGING ME, AND BUGGING ME, AND BUGGING ME!
I CAN'T STAND THAT!
KIRKMAN & SCOTT
I CAN'T TELL YOU HOW HARD IT IS TO GET ANYTHING DONE WITH SOMEBODY ON YOUR BACK ALL DAY LONG!
GRACIOUS. WHATEVER MUST IT BE LIKE?

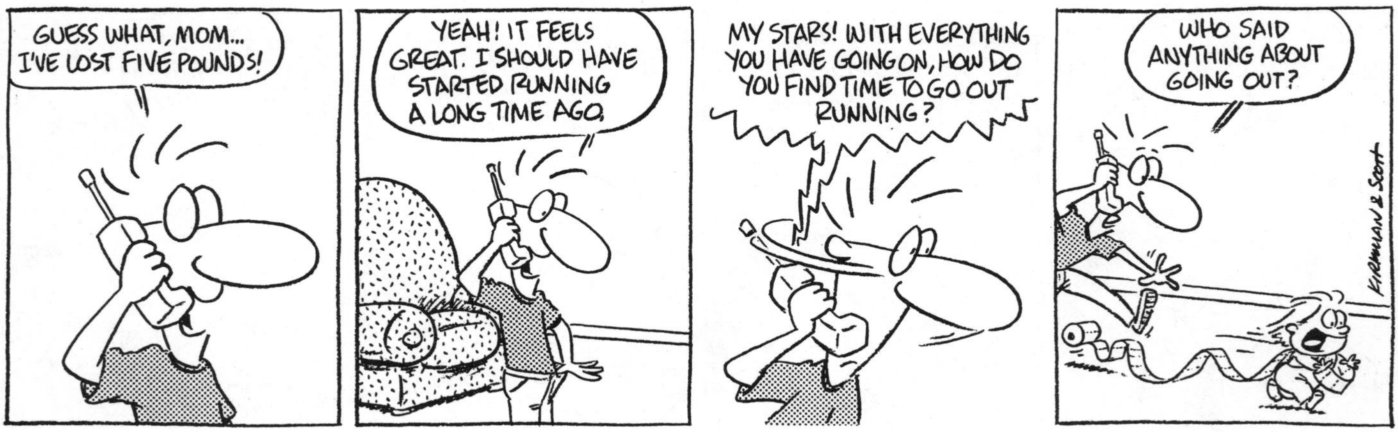
GUESS WHAT, MOM... I'VE LOST FIVE POUNDS!
YEAH! IT FEELS GREAT. I SHOULD HAVE STARTED RUNNING A LONG TIME AGO.
MY STARS! WITH EVERYTHING YOU HAVE GOING ON, HOW DO YOU FIND TIME TO GO OUT RUNNING?
WHO SAID ANYTHING ABOUT GOING OUT?
KIRKMAN & SCOTT

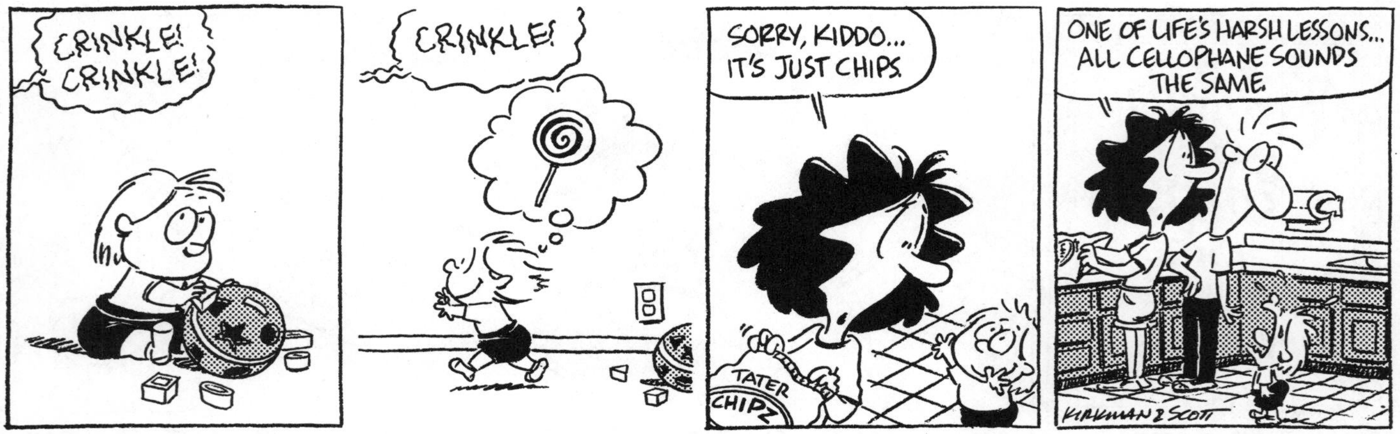
CRINKLE! CRINKLE!
CRINKLE!
SORRY, KIDDO... IT'S JUST CHIPS.
TATER CHIPZ
ONE OF LIFE'S HARSH LESSONS... ALL CELLOPHANE SOUNDS THE SAME.
KIRKMAN & SCOTT

BABY BLUES®
BY RICK KIRKMAN / JERRY SCOTT
AHHHH
UH-OH.
BONK!
PLOP!
I'LL GET IT!
YUCKK! THIS THING IS COVERED WITH GRASS AND TWIGS. BETTER GIVE ZOE ANOTHER LOLLIPOP.
KIRKMAN & SCOTT
HERE YOU GO, SWEETHEART...
WAAAAAAAAAAAAAAH
NO GOOD...SHE WANTS THE PURPLE ONE, AND THAT'S THE LAST ONE WE HAVE.
WHAT AM I SUPPOSED TO DO...LICK ALL THE JUNK OFF THIS ONE AND GIVE IT BACK TO HER?
WAAAAAAAA
WAAAAAAAAA
SOMETIMES I WONDER, ARE WE RAISING HER, OR IS SHE RAISING US?
ACK! PPPTH! BLEAH!

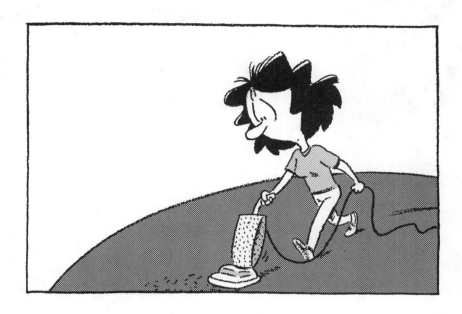

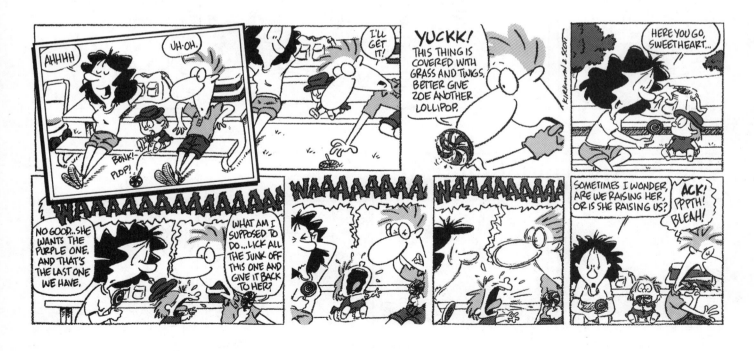

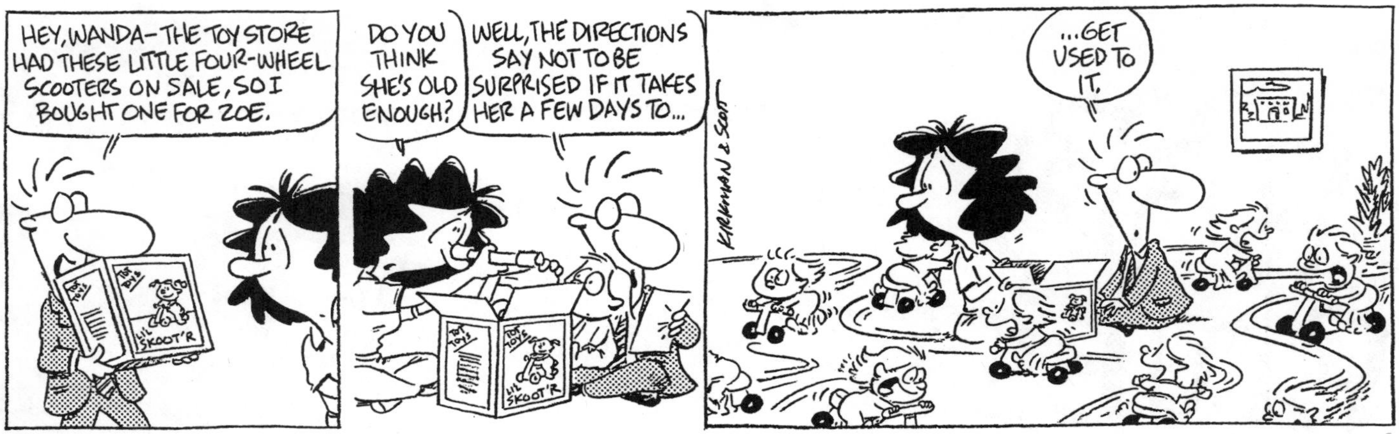
HEY, WANDA–THE TOY STORE HAD THESE LITTLE FOUR-WHEEL SCOOTERS ON SALE, SO I BOUGHT ONE FOR ZOE.
DO YOU THINK SHE'S OLD ENOUGH?
WELL, THE DIRECTIONS SAY NOT TO BE SURPRISED IF IT TAKES HER A FEW DAYS TO...
KIRKMAN & SCOTT
...GET USED TO IT.

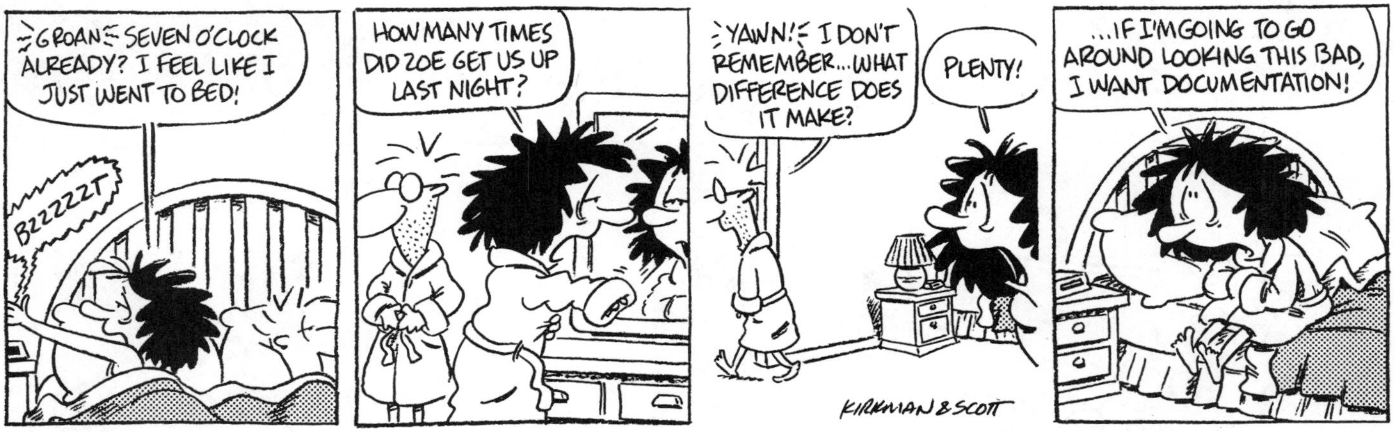
~GROAN~ SEVEN O'CLOCK ALREADY? I FEEL LIKE I JUST WENT TO BED!
BZZZZZT
HOW MANY TIMES DID ZOE GET US UP LAST NIGHT?
~YAWN!~ I DON'T REMEMBER... WHAT DIFFERENCE DOES IT MAKE?
PLENTY!
KIRKMAN & SCOTT
...IF I'M GOING TO GO AROUND LOOKING THIS BAD, I WANT DOCUMENTATION!

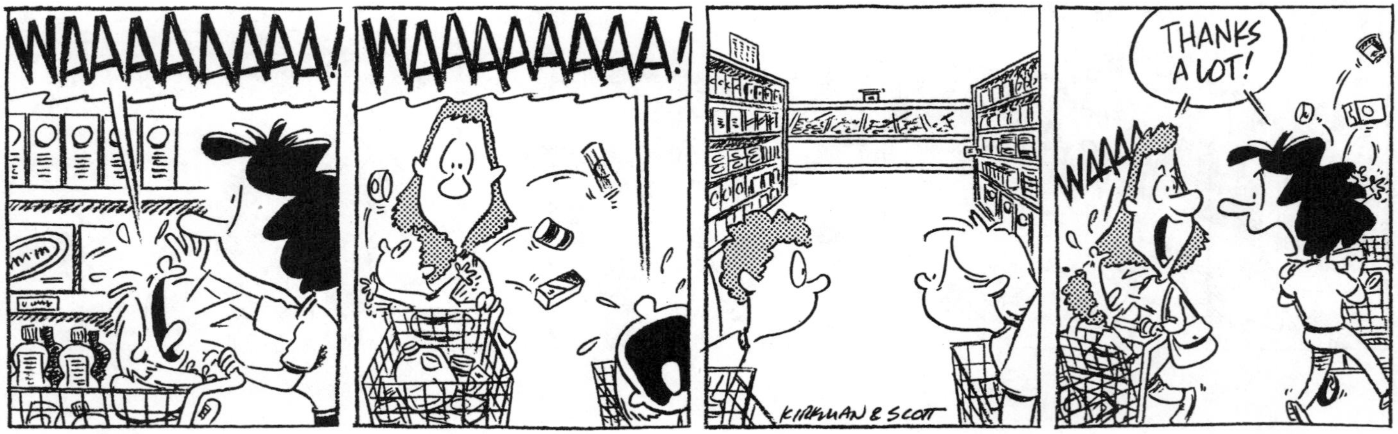
WAAAAAAAA!
WAAAAAAAAA!
KIRKMAN & SCOTT
WAAA
THANKS A LOT!

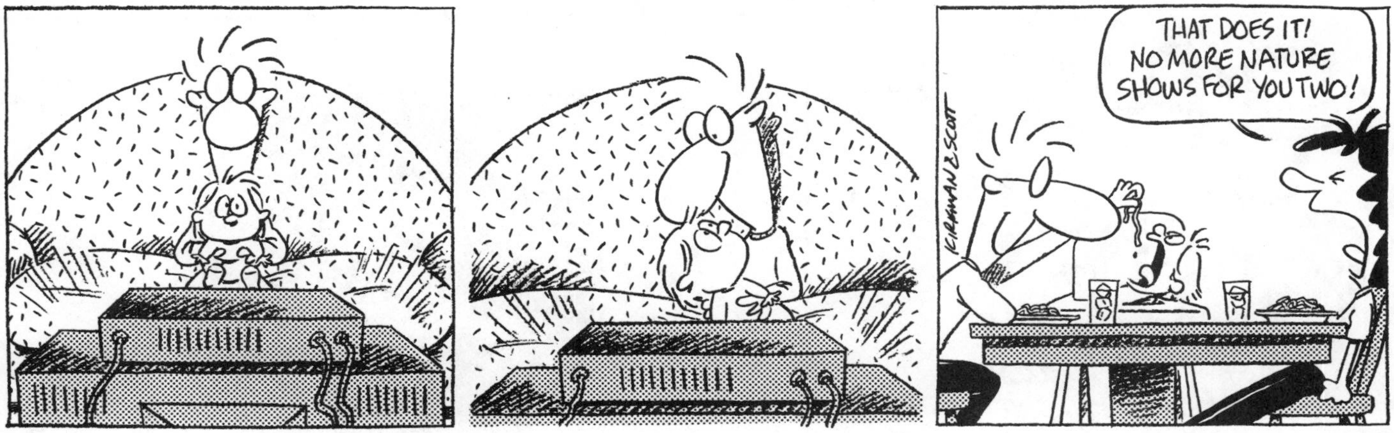
KIRKMAN & SCOTT
THAT DOES IT! NO MORE NATURE SHOWS FOR YOU TWO!

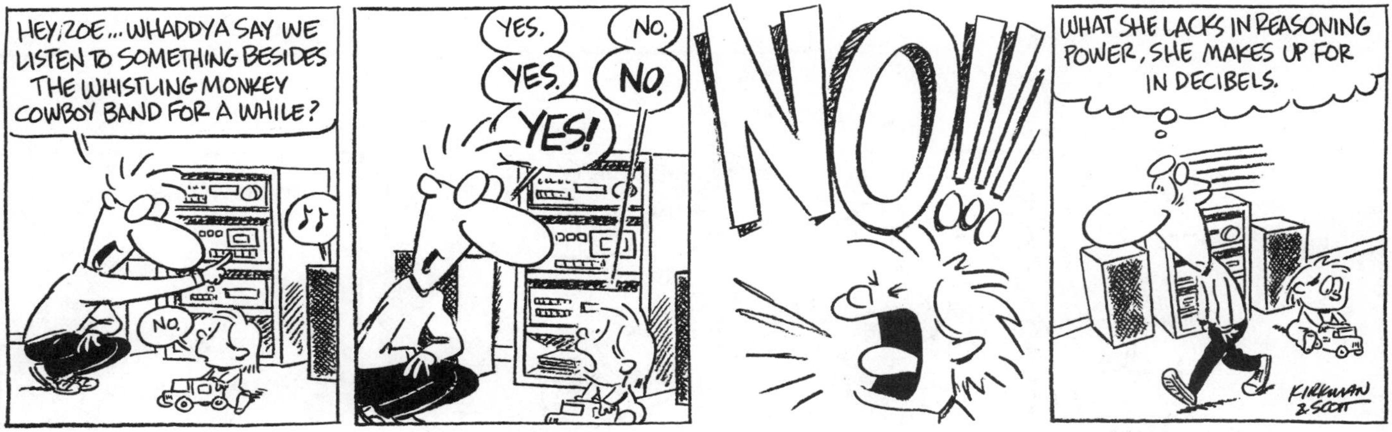
HEY, ZOE... WHADDYA SAY WE LISTEN TO SOMETHING BESIDES THE WHISTLING MONKEY COWBOY BAND FOR A WHILE?
NO.
YES.
NO.
YES.
NO.
YES!
NO!!!
WHAT SHE LACKS IN REASONING POWER, SHE MAKES UP FOR IN DECIBELS.
KIRKMAN & SCOTT

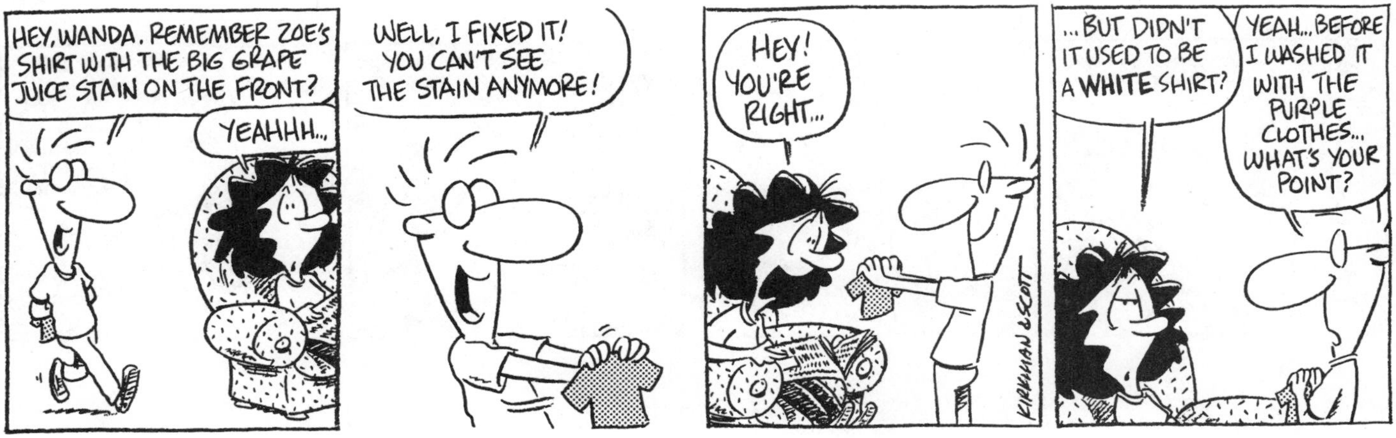
HEY, WANDA. REMEMBER ZOE'S SHIRT WITH THE BIG GRAPE JUICE STAIN ON THE FRONT?
YEAHHH...
WELL, I FIXED IT! YOU CAN'T SEE THE STAIN ANYMORE!
HEY! YOU'RE RIGHT...
KIRKMAN & SCOTT
...BUT DIDN'T IT USED TO BE A WHITE SHIRT?
YEAH... BEFORE I WASHED IT WITH THE PURPLE CLOTHES... WHAT'S YOUR POINT?

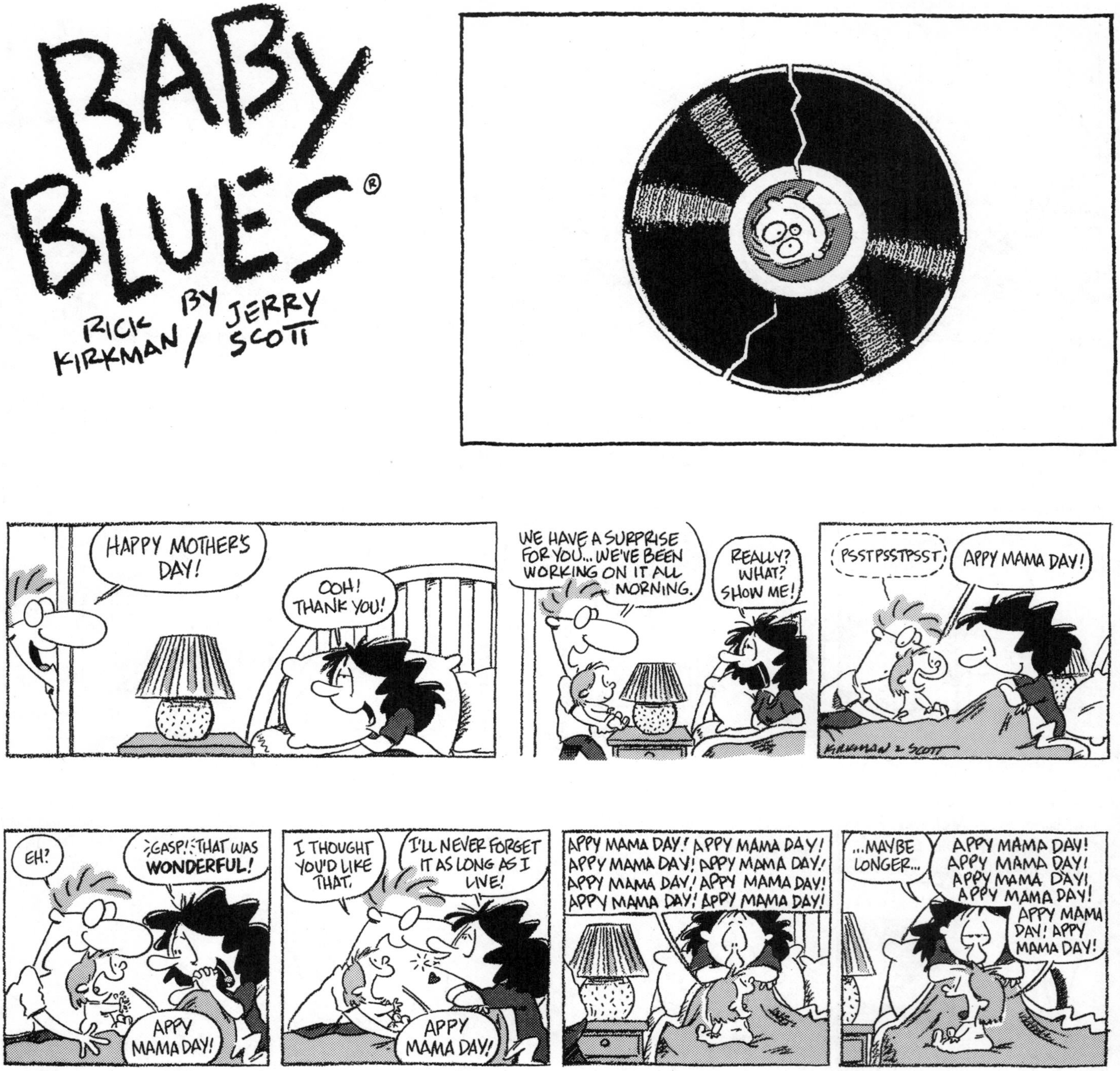
BABY BLUES®
BY RICK KIRKMAN / JERRY SCOTT
HAPPY MOTHER'S DAY!
OOH! THANK YOU!
WE HAVE A SURPRISE FOR YOU... WE'VE BEEN WORKING ON IT ALL MORNING.
REALLY? WHAT? SHOW ME!
PSSTPSSTPSST
APPY MAMA DAY!
KIRKMAN & SCOTT
EH?
GASP! THAT WAS **WONDERFUL!**
APPY MAMA DAY!
I THOUGHT YOU'D LIKE THAT.
I'LL NEVER FORGET IT AS LONG AS I LIVE!
APPY MAMA DAY!
APPY MAMA DAY! APPY MAMA DAY! APPY MAMA DAY! APPY MAMA DAY! APPY MAMA DAY! APPY MAMA DAY! APPY MAMA DAY! APPY MAMA DAY!
...MAYBE LONGER...
APPY MAMA DAY! APPY MAMA DAY! APPY MAMA DAY! APPY MAMA DAY! APPY MAMA DAY! APPY MAMA DAY!

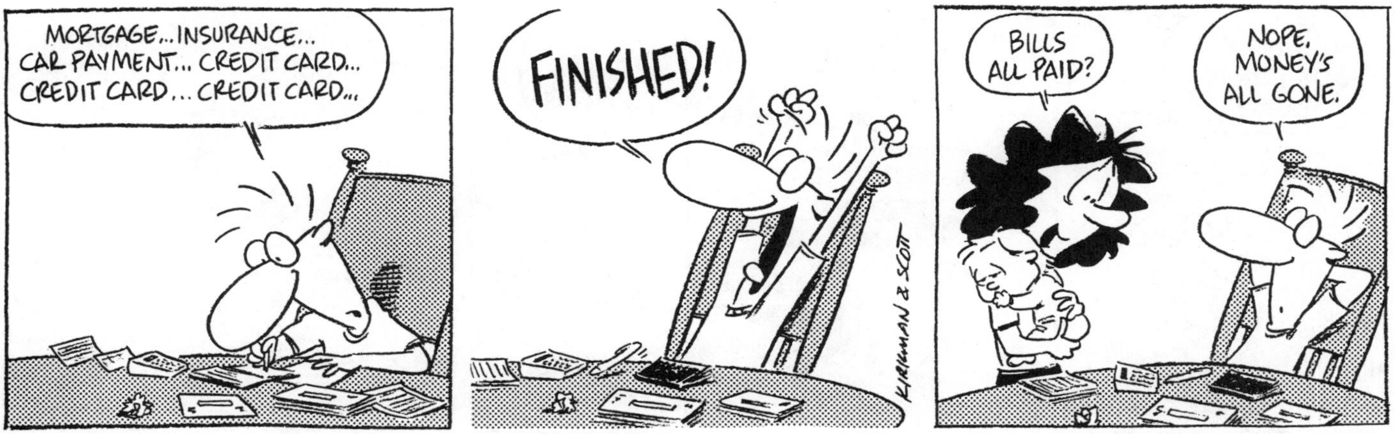
MORTGAGE... INSURANCE... CAR PAYMENT... CREDIT CARD... CREDIT CARD... CREDIT CARD...
FINISHED!
KIRKMAN & SCOTT
BILLS ALL PAID?
NOPE. MONEY'S ALL GONE.

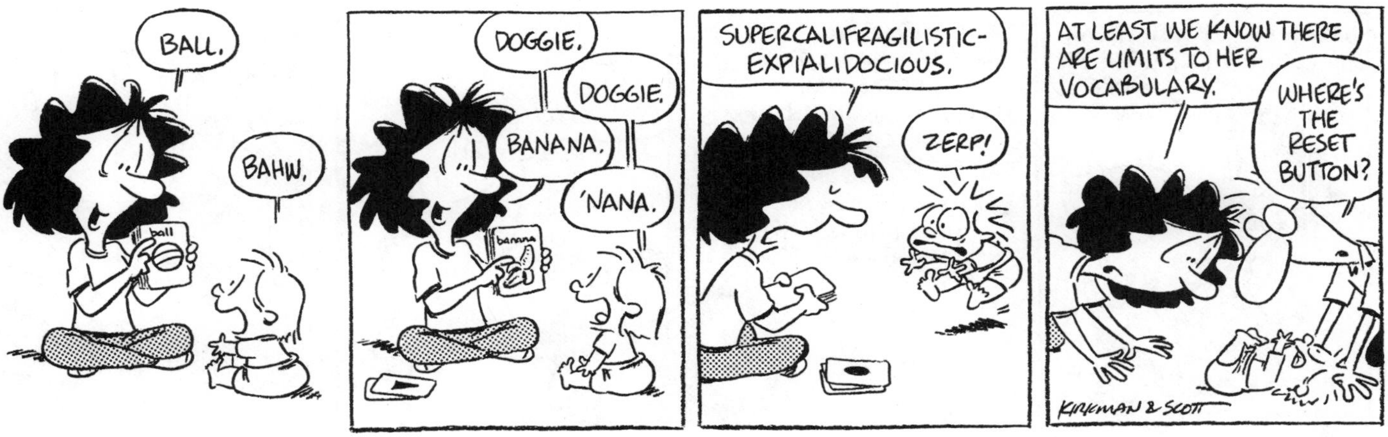
BALL.
BAHW.
ball
DOGGIE.
DOGGIE.
BANANA.
'NANA.
banana
SUPERCALIFRAGILISTIC-EXPIALIDOCIOUS.
ZERP!
AT LEAST WE KNOW THERE ARE LIMITS TO HER VOCABULARY.
WHERE'S THE RESET BUTTON?
KIRKMAN & SCOTT

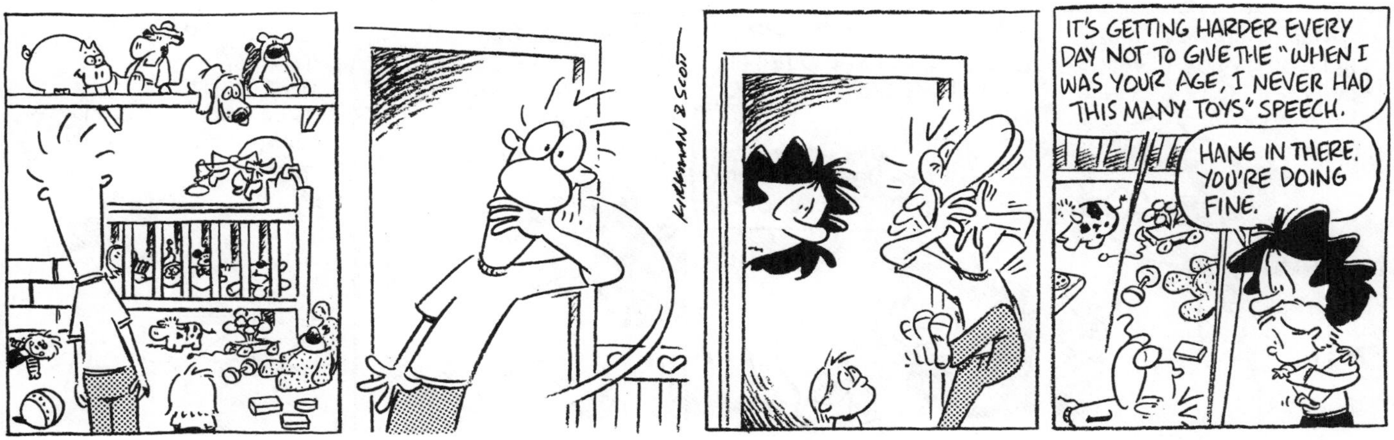
KIRKMAN & SCOTT
IT'S GETTING HARDER EVERY DAY NOT TO GIVE THE "WHEN I WAS YOUR AGE, I NEVER HAD THIS MANY TOYS" SPEECH.
HANG IN THERE. YOU'RE DOING FINE.

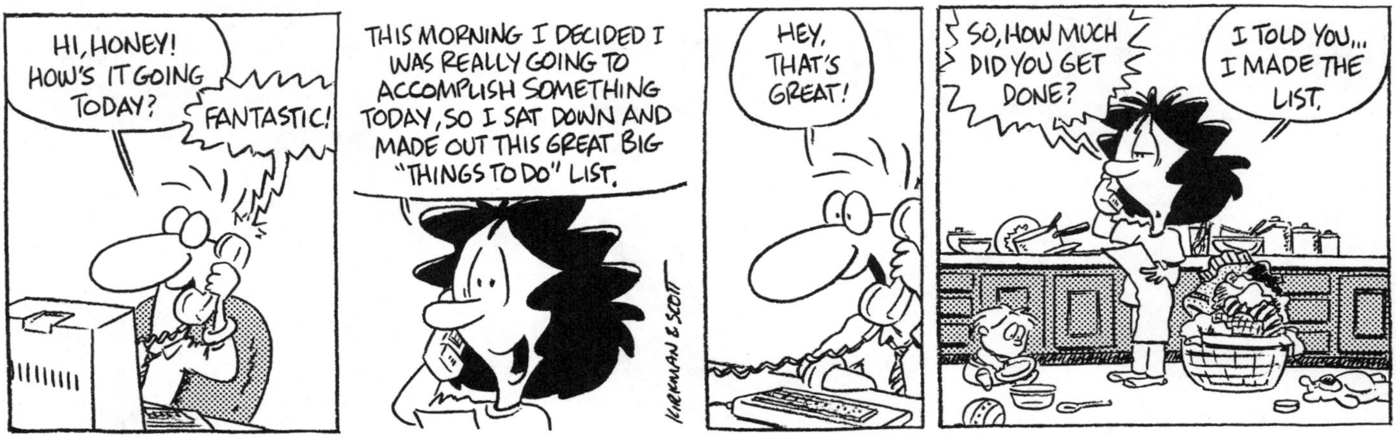
HI, HONEY! HOW'S IT GOING TODAY?
FANTASTIC!
THIS MORNING I DECIDED I WAS REALLY GOING TO ACCOMPLISH SOMETHING TODAY, SO I SAT DOWN AND MADE OUT THIS GREAT BIG "THINGS TO DO" LIST.
HEY, THAT'S GREAT!
SO, HOW MUCH DID YOU GET DONE?
I TOLD YOU... I MADE THE LIST.

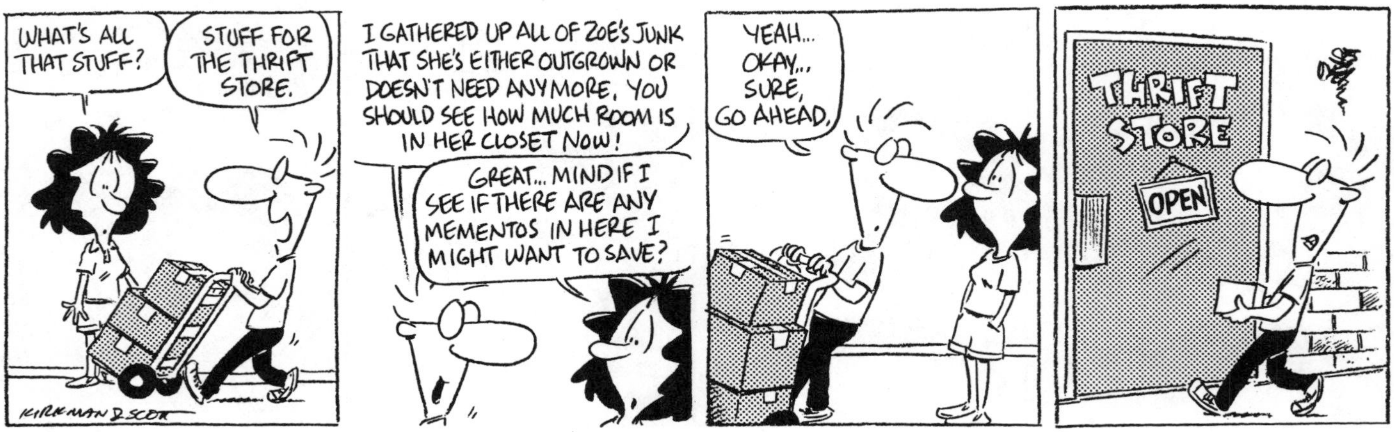
WHAT'S ALL THAT STUFF?
STUFF FOR THE THRIFT STORE.
I GATHERED UP ALL OF ZOE'S JUNK THAT SHE'S EITHER OUTGROWN OR DOESN'T NEED ANYMORE. YOU SHOULD SEE HOW MUCH ROOM IS IN HER CLOSET NOW!
GREAT... MIND IF I SEE IF THERE ARE ANY MEMENTOS IN HERE I MIGHT WANT TO SAVE?
YEAH... OKAY..., SURE, GO AHEAD.
THRIFT STORE
OPEN

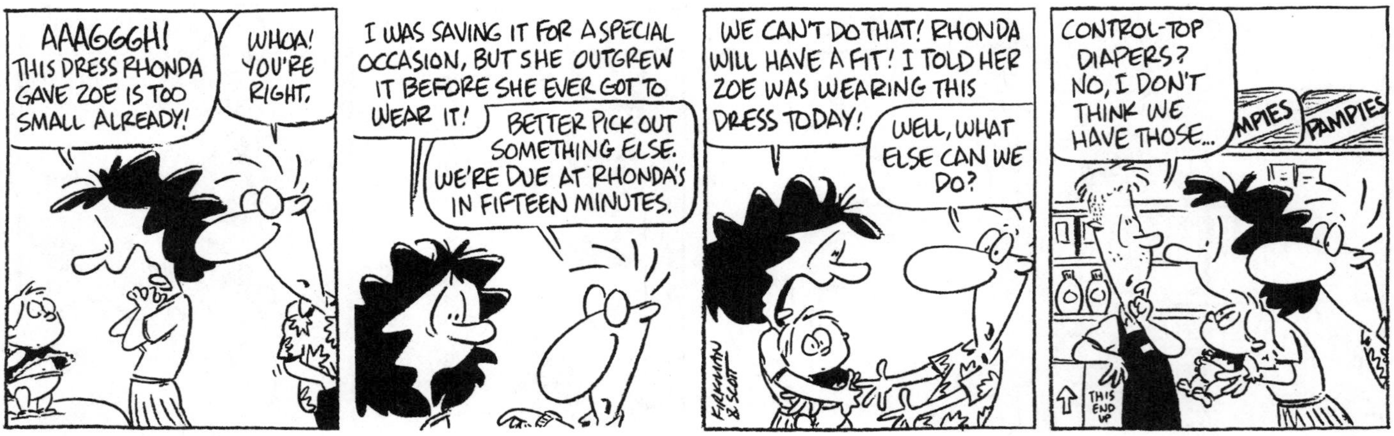
AAAGGGH! THIS DRESS RHONDA GAVE ZOE IS TOO SMALL ALREADY!
WHOA! YOU'RE RIGHT.
I WAS SAVING IT FOR A SPECIAL OCCASION, BUT SHE OUTGREW IT BEFORE SHE EVER GOT TO WEAR IT!
BETTER PICK OUT SOMETHING ELSE. WE'RE DUE AT RHONDA'S IN FIFTEEN MINUTES.
WE CAN'T DO THAT! RHONDA WILL HAVE A FIT! I TOLD HER ZOE WAS WEARING THIS DRESS TODAY!
WELL, WHAT ELSE CAN WE DO?
CONTROL-TOP DIAPERS? NO, I DON'T THINK WE HAVE THOSE...
PAMPIES
THIS END UP

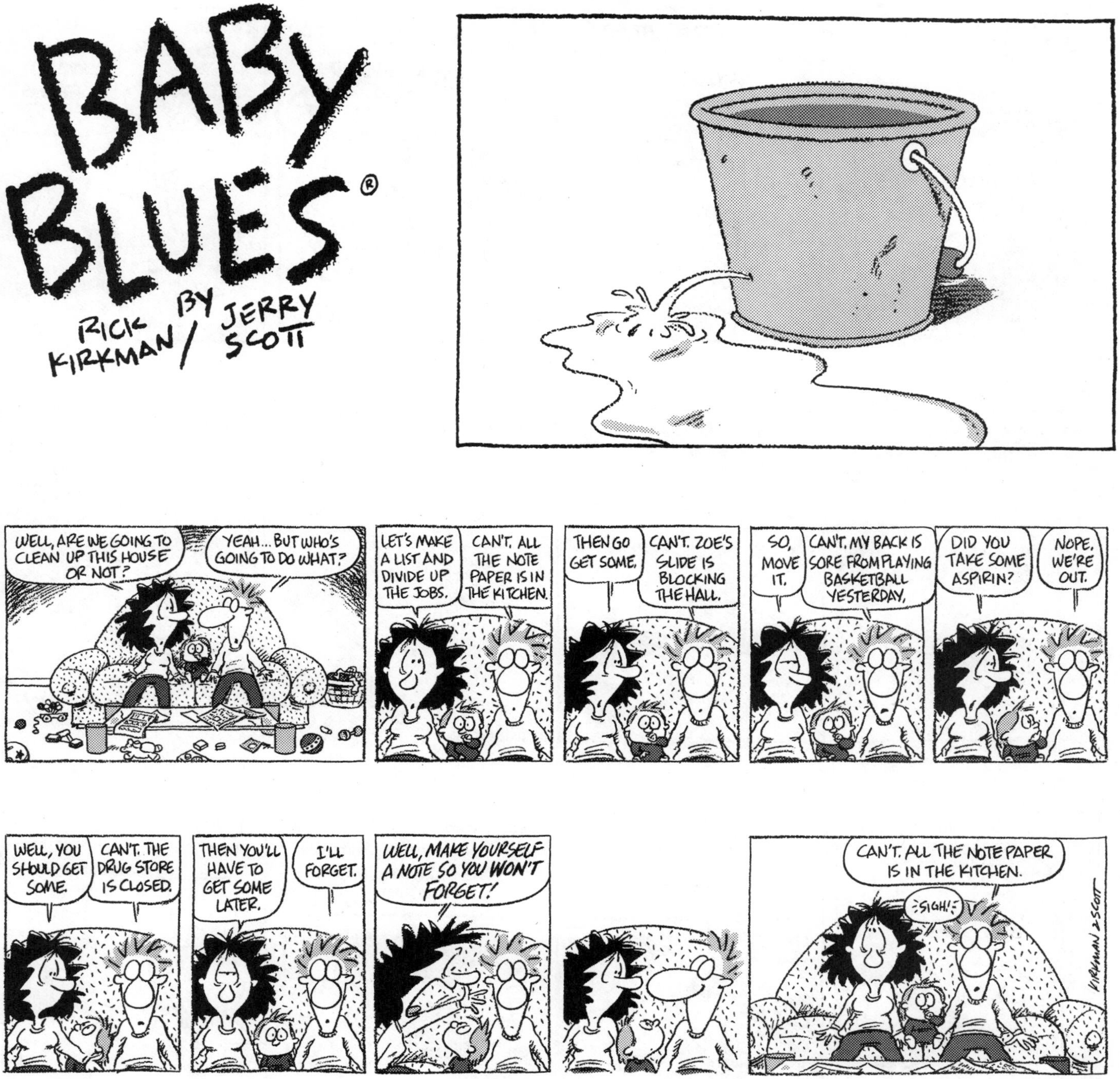
BABY BLUES®
BY RICK KIRKMAN / JERRY SCOTT
WELL, ARE WE GOING TO CLEAN UP THIS HOUSE OR NOT?
YEAH... BUT WHO'S GOING TO DO WHAT?
LET'S MAKE A LIST AND DIVIDE UP THE JOBS.
CAN'T. ALL THE NOTE PAPER IS IN THE KITCHEN.
THEN GO GET SOME.
CAN'T. ZOE'S SLIDE IS BLOCKING THE HALL.
SO, MOVE IT.
CAN'T. MY BACK IS SORE FROM PLAYING BASKETBALL YESTERDAY.
DID YOU TAKE SOME ASPIRIN?
NOPE. WE'RE OUT.
WELL, YOU SHOULD GET SOME.
CAN'T. THE DRUG STORE IS CLOSED.
THEN YOU'LL HAVE TO GET SOME LATER.
I'LL FORGET.
WELL, MAKE YOURSELF A NOTE SO YOU WON'T FORGET!
CAN'T. ALL THE NOTE PAPER IS IN THE KITCHEN.
SIGH!
KIRKMAN & SCOTT

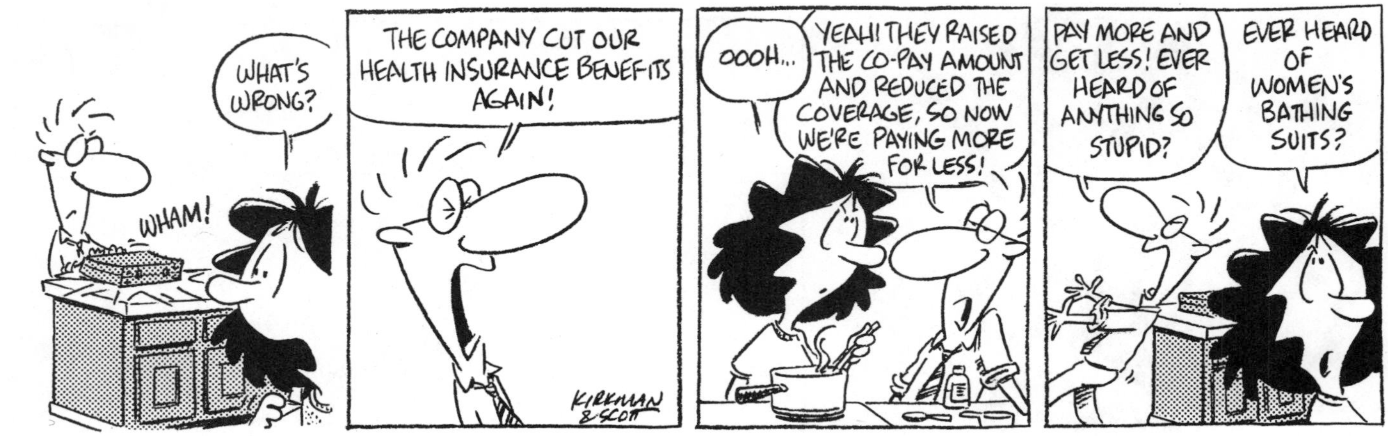
WHAT'S WRONG?
WHAM!
THE COMPANY CUT OUR HEALTH INSURANCE BENEFITS AGAIN!
KIRKMAN & SCOTT
OOOH...
YEAH! THEY RAISED THE CO-PAY AMOUNT AND REDUCED THE COVERAGE, SO NOW WE'RE PAYING MORE FOR LESS!
PAY MORE AND GET LESS! EVER HEARD OF ANYTHING SO STUPID?
EVER HEARD OF WOMEN'S BATHING SUITS?

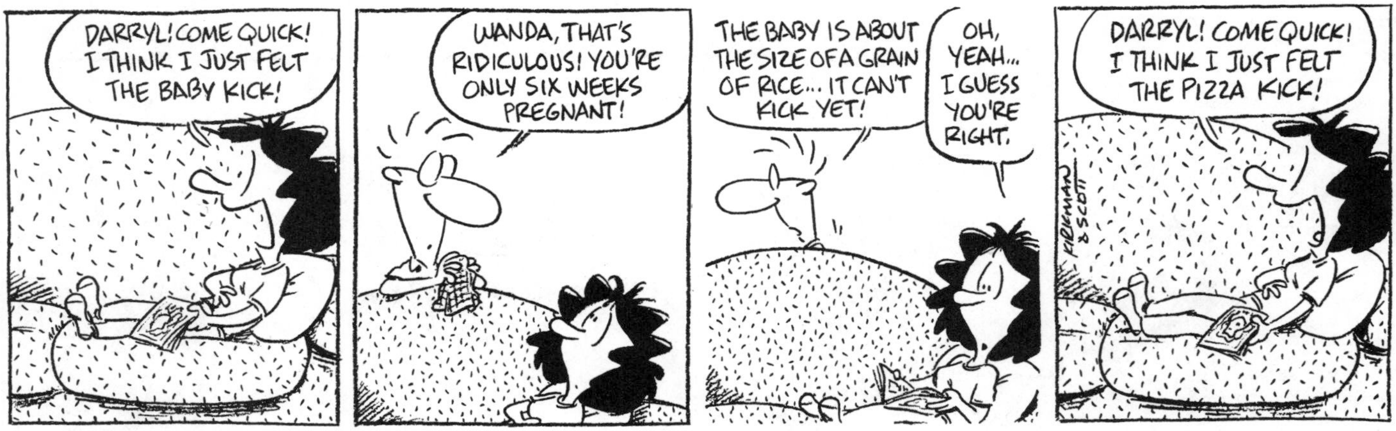
DARRYL! COME QUICK! I THINK I JUST FELT THE BABY KICK!
WANDA, THAT'S RIDICULOUS! YOU'RE ONLY SIX WEEKS PREGNANT!
THE BABY IS ABOUT THE SIZE OF A GRAIN OF RICE... IT CAN'T KICK YET!
OH, YEAH... I GUESS YOU'RE RIGHT.
KIRKMAN & SCOTT
DARRYL! COME QUICK! I THINK I JUST FELT THE PIZZA KICK!

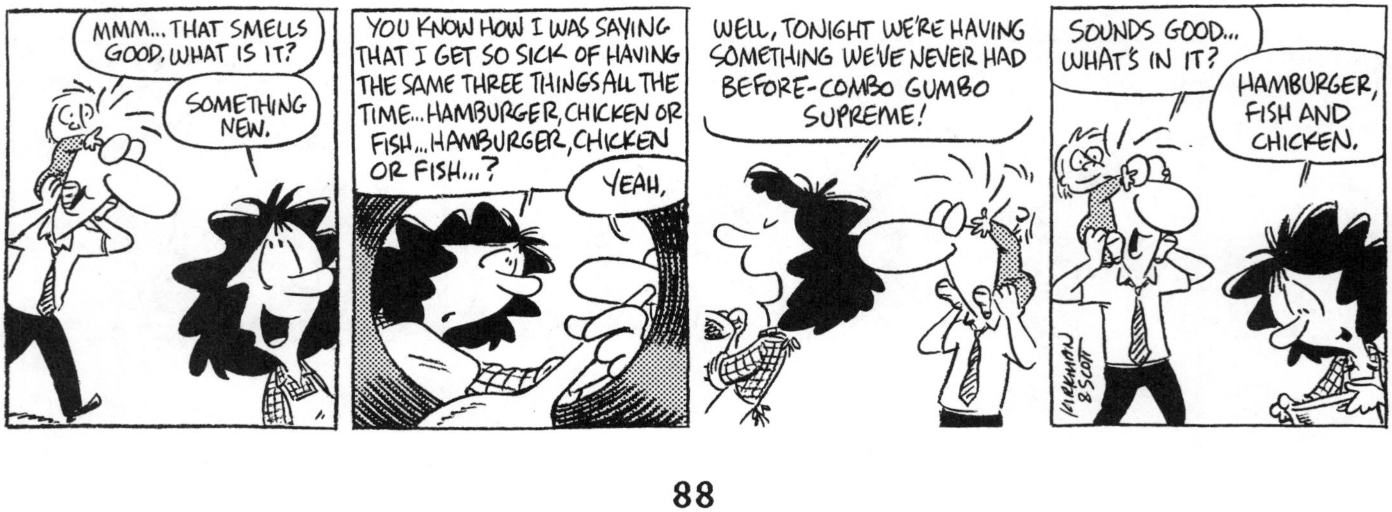
MMM... THAT SMELLS GOOD. WHAT IS IT?
SOMETHING NEW.
YOU KNOW HOW I WAS SAYING THAT I GET SO SICK OF HAVING THE SAME THREE THINGS ALL THE TIME... HAMBURGER, CHICKEN OR FISH... HAMBURGER, CHICKEN OR FISH...?
YEAH.
WELL, TONIGHT WE'RE HAVING SOMETHING WE'VE NEVER HAD BEFORE-COMBO GUMBO SUPREME!
SOUNDS GOOD... WHAT'S IN IT?
HAMBURGER, FISH AND CHICKEN.
KIRKMAN & SCOTT

I AM REALLY SPACING-OUT THESE DAYS!
I JUST PUT IT DOWN HERE A SECOND AGO, AND NOW I CAN'T FIND IT ANYWHERE!
PUT WHAT DOWN?
DANG!
BOY! YOU REALLY ARE SPACING-OUT, AREN'T YOU?
KIRKMAN & SCOTT

LOOK AT THAT... CAN YOU BELIEVE IT?
DISGUSTING!
THERE'S BUNNY—MRS. PERFECT—GATHERING FRESH HERBS FROM HER OWN HERB GARDEN.
SHE'S SO SMUG.
IF SHE THINKS SHE'S THE ONLY ONE WHO CAN COOK WITH GARDEN-FRESH HERBS, I'VE GOT NEWS FOR HER... VOILA!
WOW! I'M IMPRESSED! I DIDN'T KNOW YOU HAD AN HERB GARDEN.
I DON'T... I SWIPED 'EM FROM HERS.
WOW! NOW I'M REALLY IMPRESSED!
KIRKMAN & SCOTT

I CAN'T BELIEVE HOW FAT AND UGLY MY BODY IS!
KIRKMAN & SCOTT
HUH? OH... NO WAY, HON...
I CAN'T BELIEVE HOW BAD MY TIMING IS!

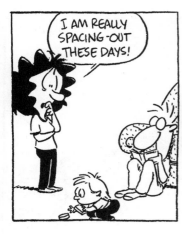

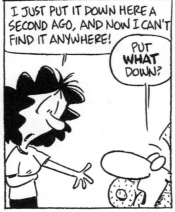

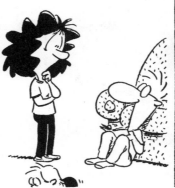

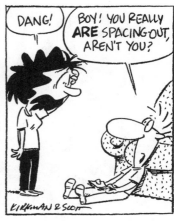

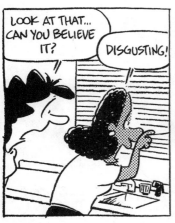

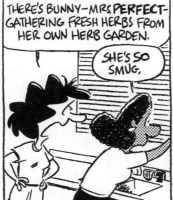

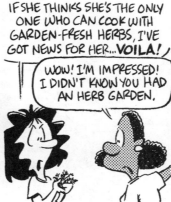

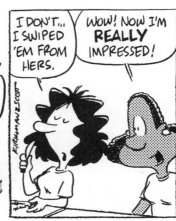

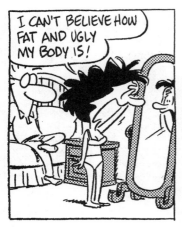

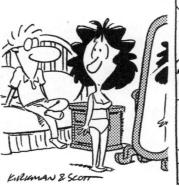

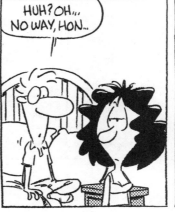

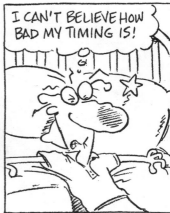

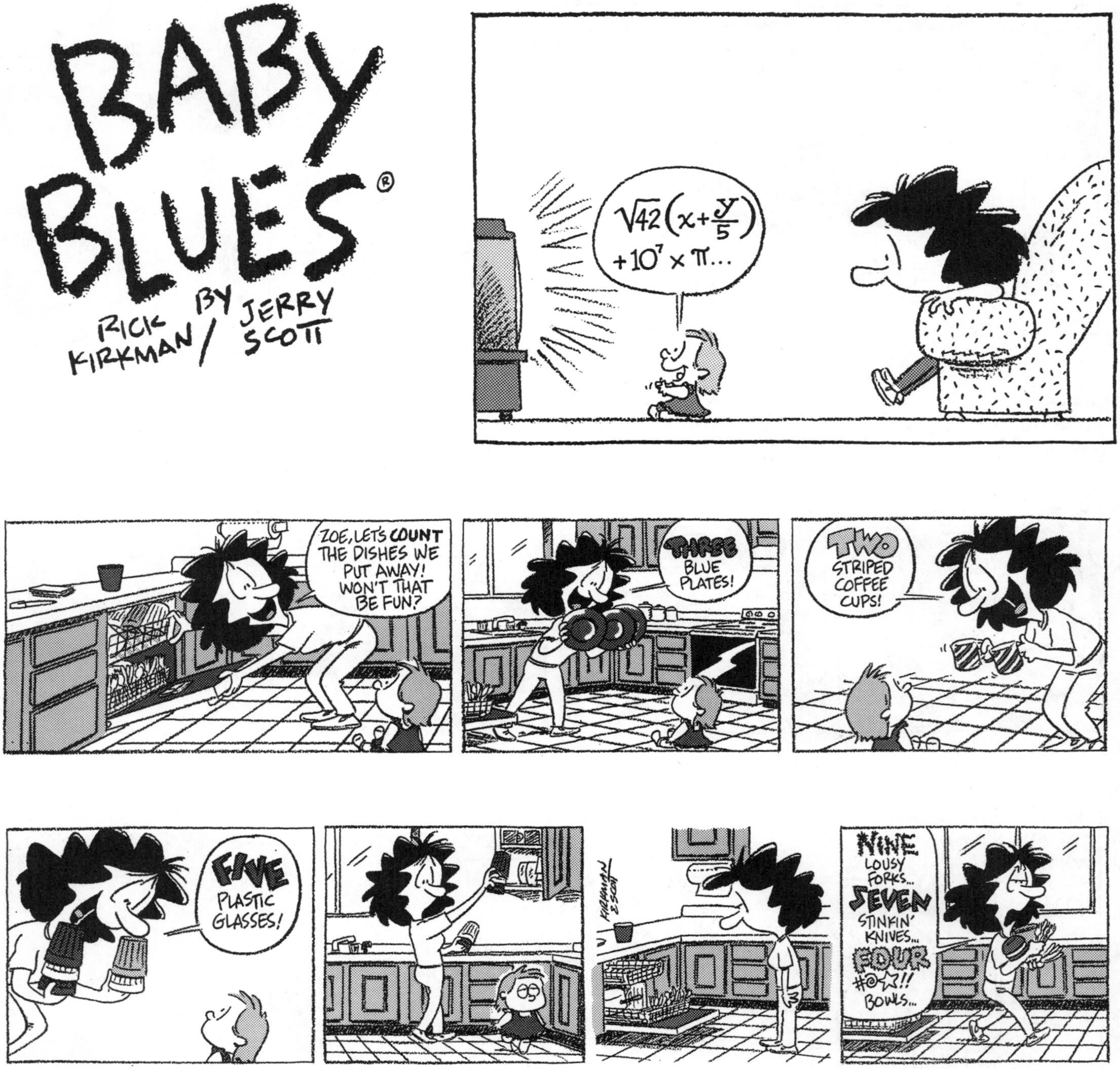
BABY BLUES®
BY RICK KIRKMAN / JERRY SCOTT
√42(x + y/5) + 10⁷ × π...
ZOE, LET'S COUNT THE DISHES WE PUT AWAY! WON'T THAT BE FUN?
THREE BLUE PLATES!
TWO STRIPED COFFEE CUPS!
FIVE PLASTIC GLASSES!
NINE LOUSY FORKS... SEVEN STINKIN' KNIVES... FOUR #@☆!! BOWLS...

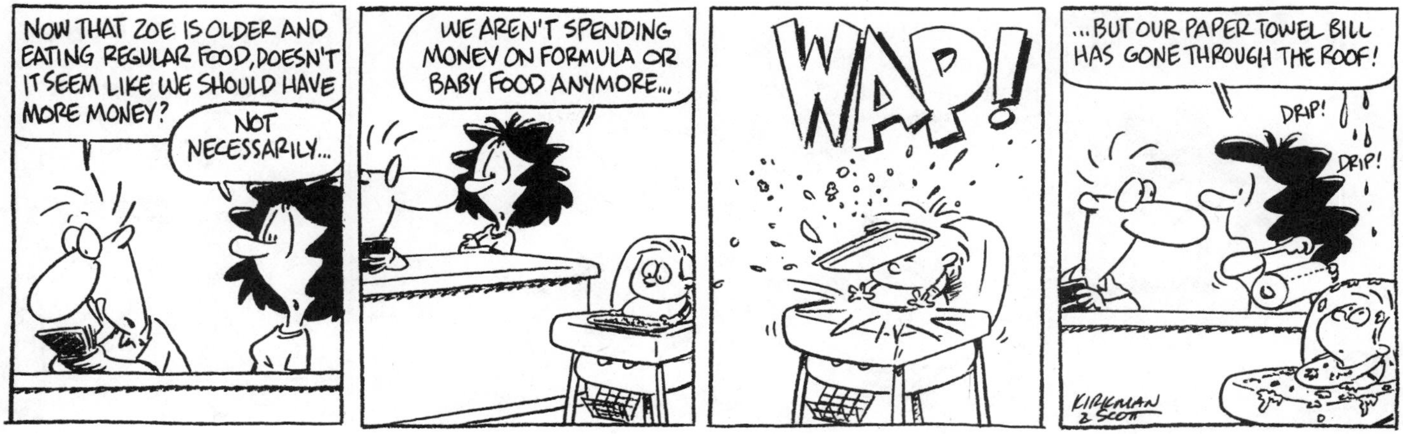
NOW THAT ZOE IS OLDER AND EATING REGULAR FOOD, DOESN'T IT SEEM LIKE WE SHOULD HAVE MORE MONEY?
NOT NECESSARILY...
WE AREN'T SPENDING MONEY ON FORMULA OR BABY FOOD ANYMORE...
WAP!
...BUT OUR PAPER TOWEL BILL HAS GONE THROUGH THE ROOF!
DRIP!
DRIP!
KIRKMAN & SCOTT

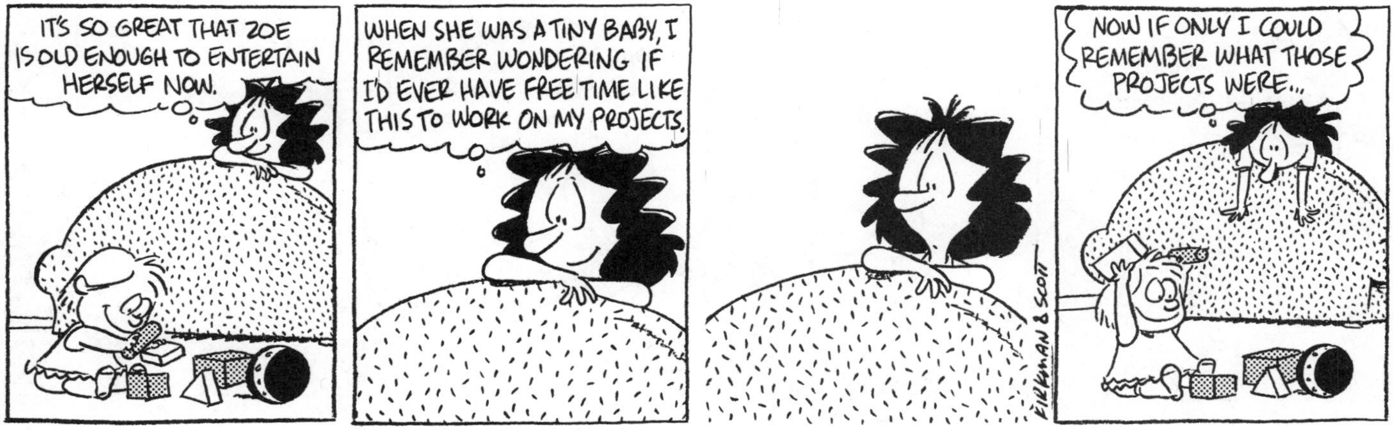
IT'S SO GREAT THAT ZOE IS OLD ENOUGH TO ENTERTAIN HERSELF NOW.
WHEN SHE WAS A TINY BABY, I REMEMBER WONDERING IF I'D EVER HAVE FREE TIME LIKE THIS TO WORK ON MY PROJECTS.
KIRKMAN & SCOTT
NOW IF ONLY I COULD REMEMBER WHAT THOSE PROJECTS WERE...

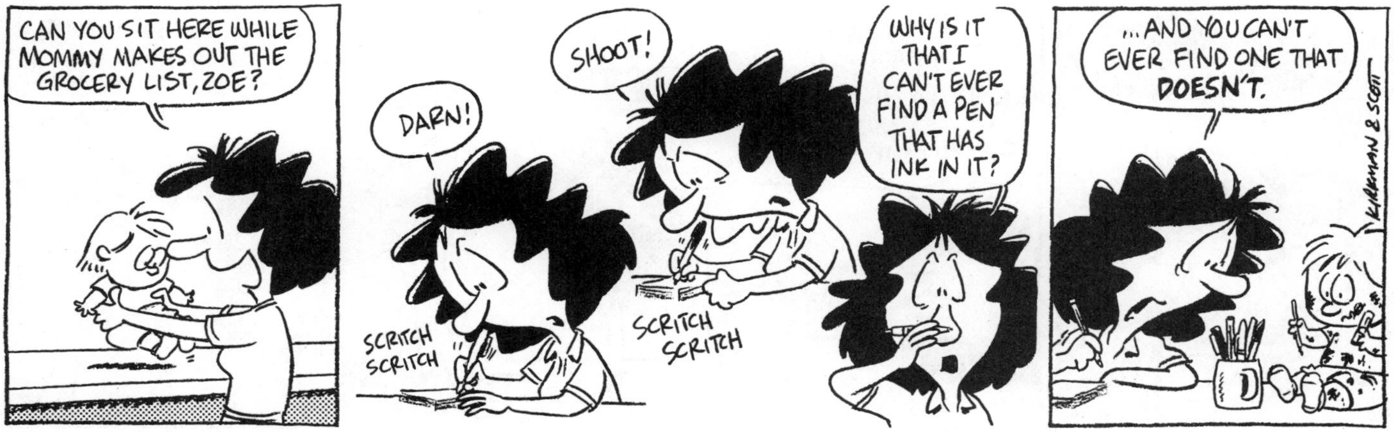
CAN YOU SIT HERE WHILE MOMMY MAKES OUT THE GROCERY LIST, ZOE?
DARN!
SCRITCH SCRITCH
SHOOT!
SCRITCH SCRITCH
WHY IS IT THAT I CAN'T EVER FIND A PEN THAT HAS INK IN IT?
...AND YOU CAN'T EVER FIND ONE THAT **DOESN'T.**
KIRKMAN & SCOTT

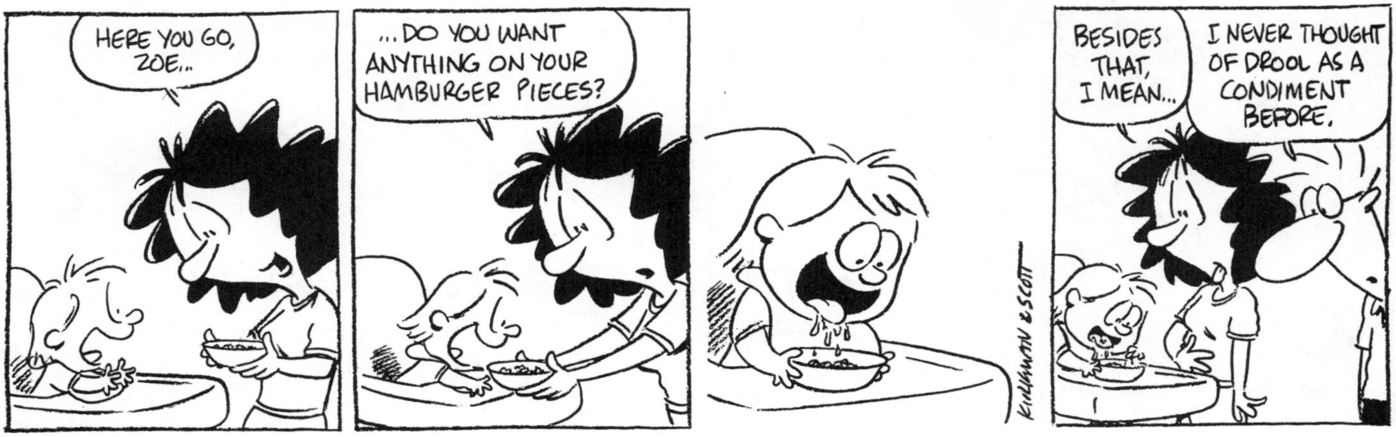
HERE YOU GO, ZOE...
...DO YOU WANT ANYTHING ON YOUR HAMBURGER PIECES?
BESIDES THAT, I MEAN...
I NEVER THOUGHT OF DROOL AS A CONDIMENT BEFORE.
KIRKMAN & SCOTT

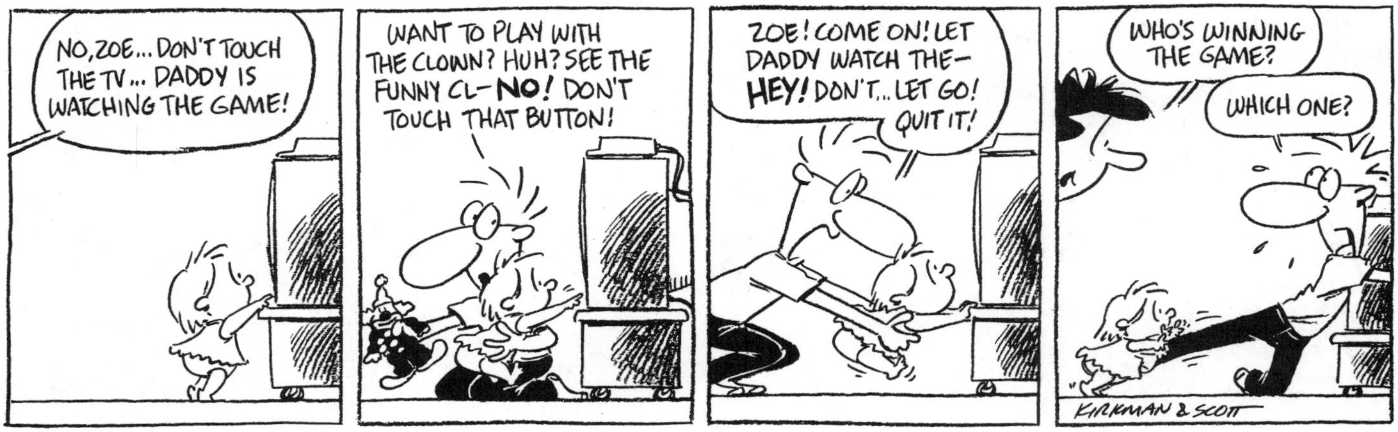
NO, ZOE... DON'T TOUCH THE TV... DADDY IS WATCHING THE GAME!
WANT TO PLAY WITH THE CLOWN? HUH? SEE THE FUNNY CL-**NO!** DON'T TOUCH THAT BUTTON!
ZOE! COME ON! LET DADDY WATCH THE-**HEY!** DON'T... LET GO! QUIT IT!
WHO'S WINNING THE GAME?
WHICH ONE?
KIRKMAN & SCOTT

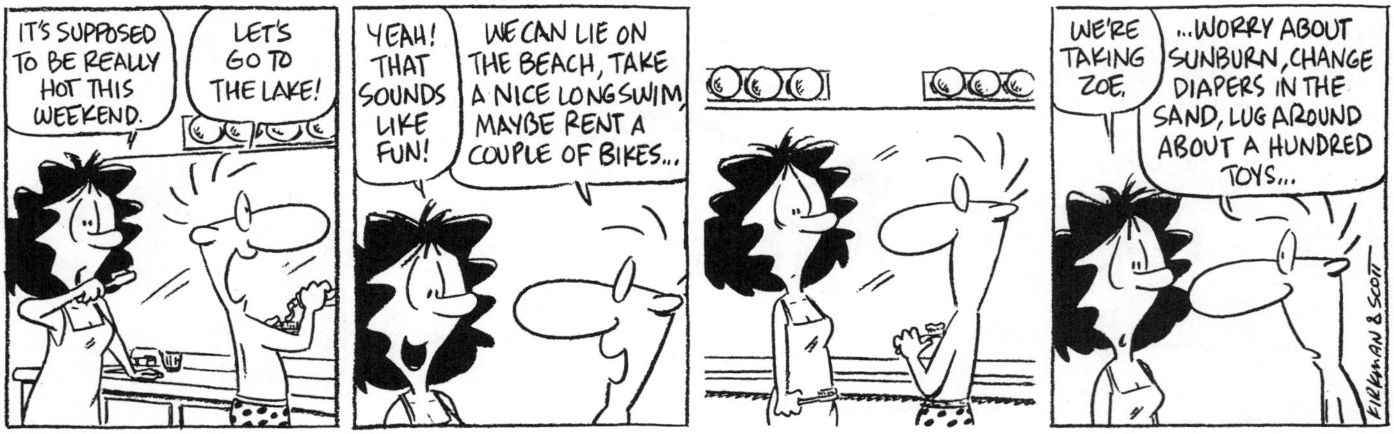
IT'S SUPPOSED TO BE REALLY HOT THIS WEEKEND.
LET'S GO TO THE LAKE!
YEAH! THAT SOUNDS LIKE FUN!
WE CAN LIE ON THE BEACH, TAKE A NICE LONG SWIM, MAYBE RENT A COUPLE OF BIKES...
WE'RE TAKING ZOE.
...WORRY ABOUT SUNBURN, CHANGE DIAPERS IN THE SAND, LUG AROUND ABOUT A HUNDRED TOYS...
KIRKMAN & SCOTT

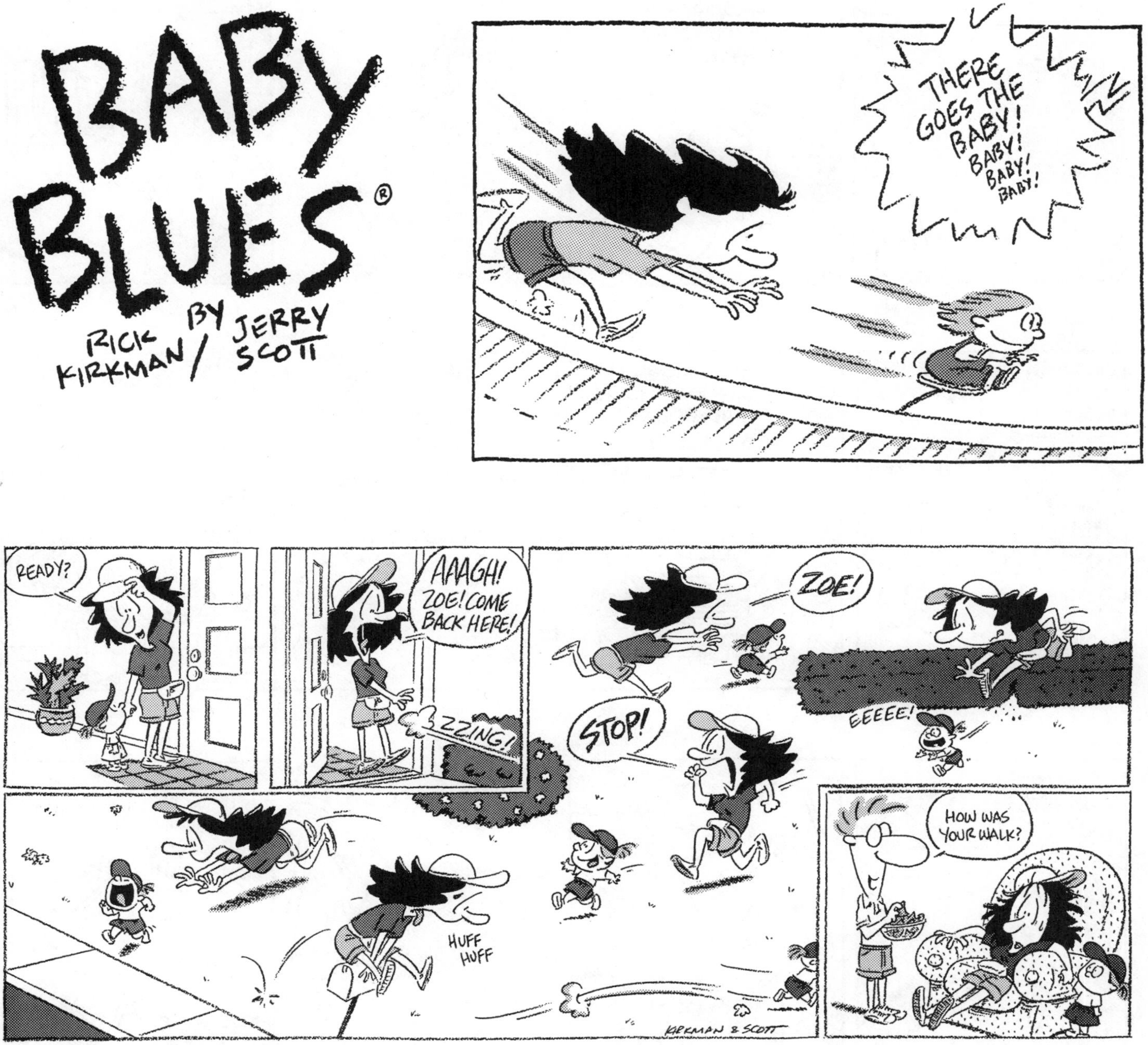
BABY BLUES®
BY RICK KIRKMAN / JERRY SCOTT
THERE GOES THE BABY! BABY! BABY! BABY!
READY?
AAAGH! ZOE! COME BACK HERE!
ZZZING!
ZOE!
STOP!
EEEEE!
HUFF HUFF
KIRKMAN & SCOTT
HOW WAS YOUR WALK?

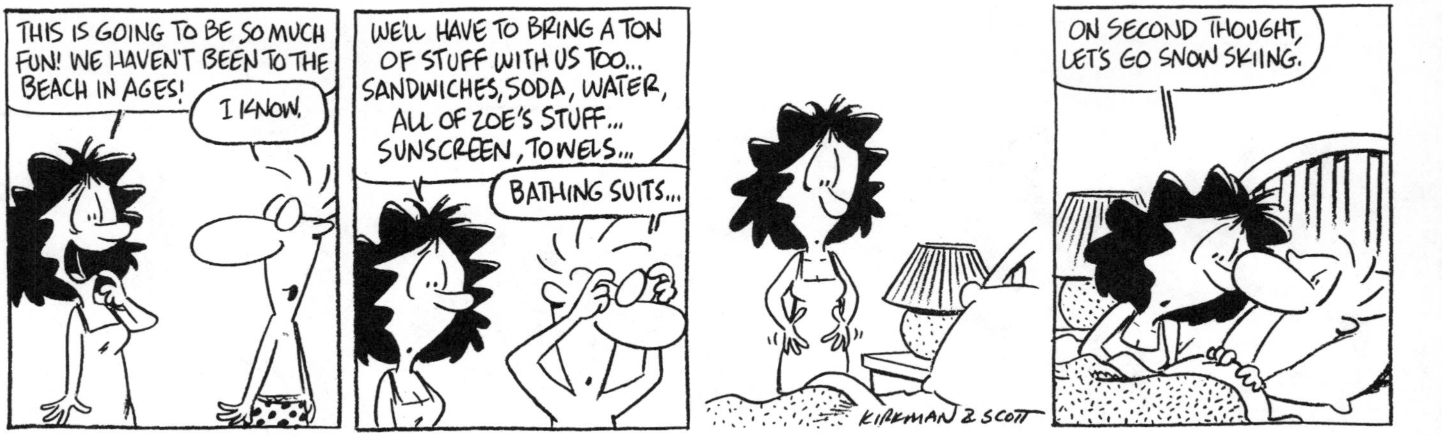
THIS IS GOING TO BE SO MUCH FUN! WE HAVEN'T BEEN TO THE BEACH IN AGES!
I KNOW.
WE'LL HAVE TO BRING A TON OF STUFF WITH US TOO... SANDWICHES, SODA, WATER, ALL OF ZOE'S STUFF... SUNSCREEN, TOWELS...
BATHING SUITS...
KIRKMAN & SCOTT
ON SECOND THOUGHT, LET'S GO SNOW SKIING.

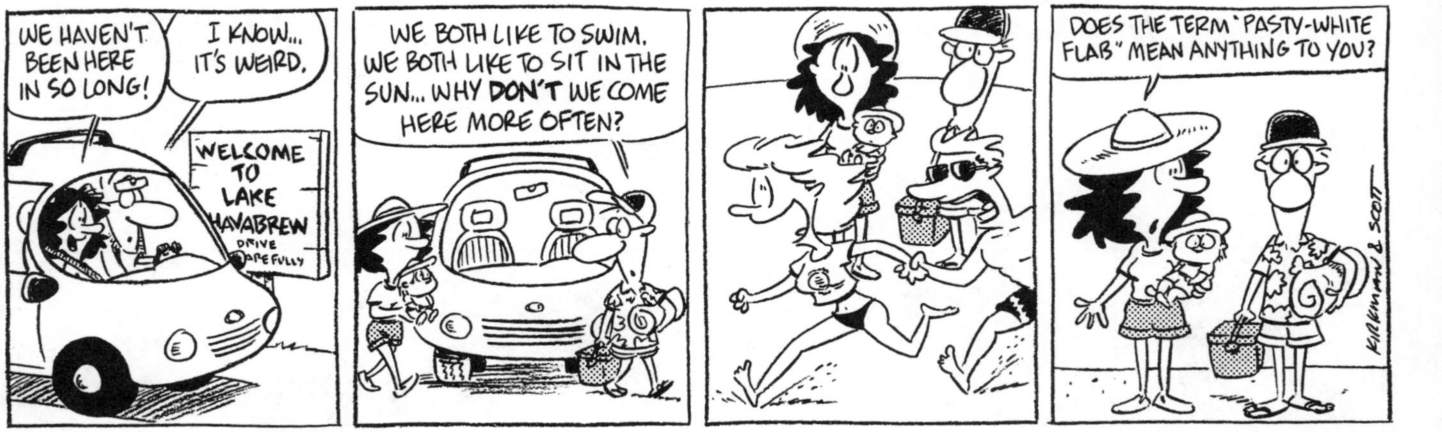
WE HAVEN'T BEEN HERE IN SO LONG!
I KNOW... IT'S WEIRD.
WELCOME TO LAKE HAVABREW
DRIVE SAFEFULLY
WE BOTH LIKE TO SWIM. WE BOTH LIKE TO SIT IN THE SUN... WHY DON'T WE COME HERE MORE OFTEN?
DOES THE TERM "PASTY-WHITE FLAB" MEAN ANYTHING TO YOU?
KIRKMAN & SCOTT

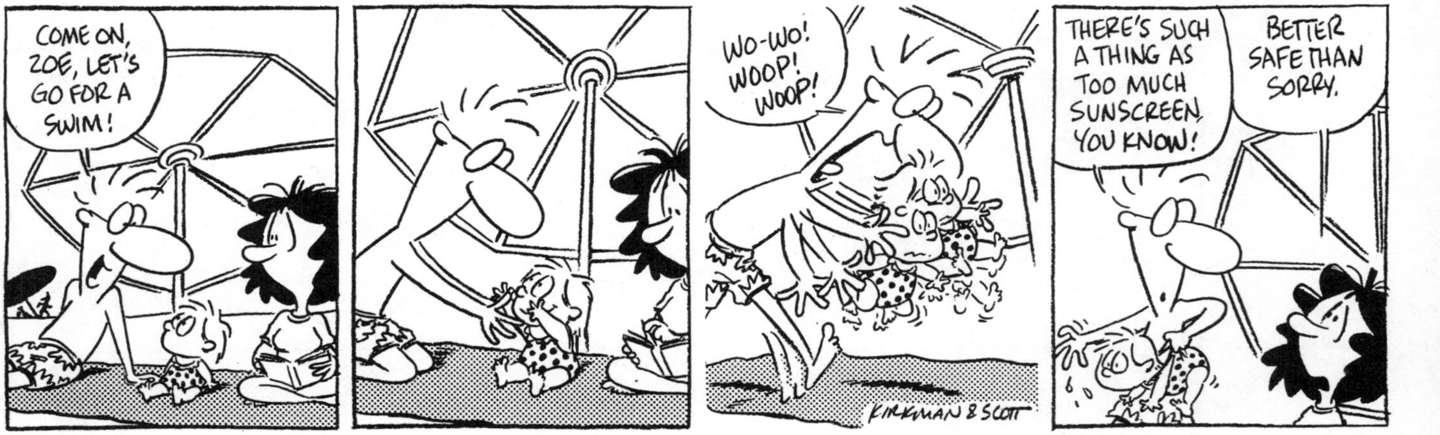
COME ON, ZOE, LET'S GO FOR A SWIM!
WO-WO! WOOP! WOOP!
KIRKMAN & SCOTT
THERE'S SUCH A THING AS TOO MUCH SUNSCREEN, YOU KNOW!
BETTER SAFE THAN SORRY.

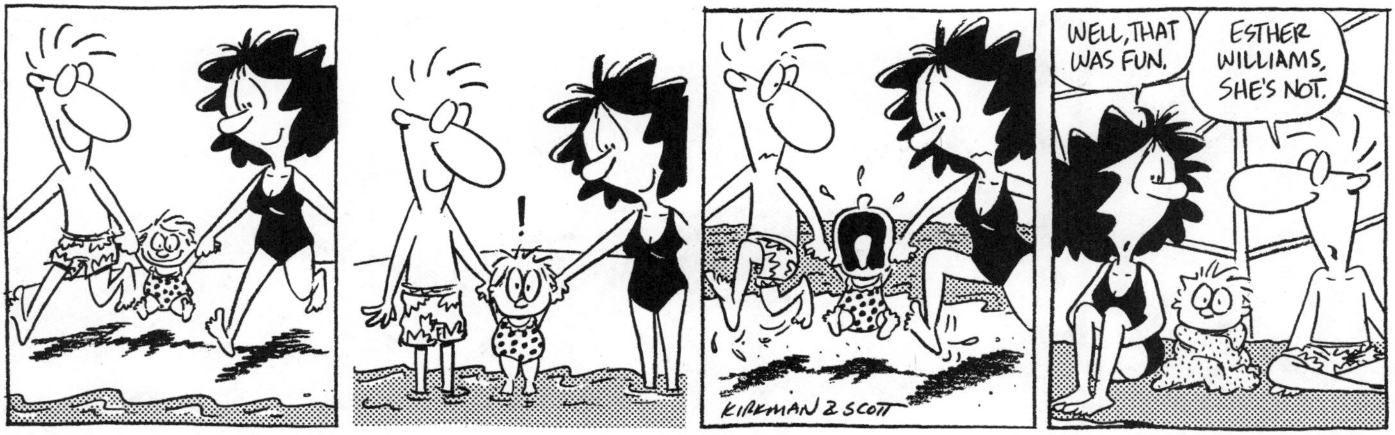
!
KIRKMAN & SCOTT
WELL, THAT WAS FUN.
ESTHER WILLIAMS, SHE'S NOT.

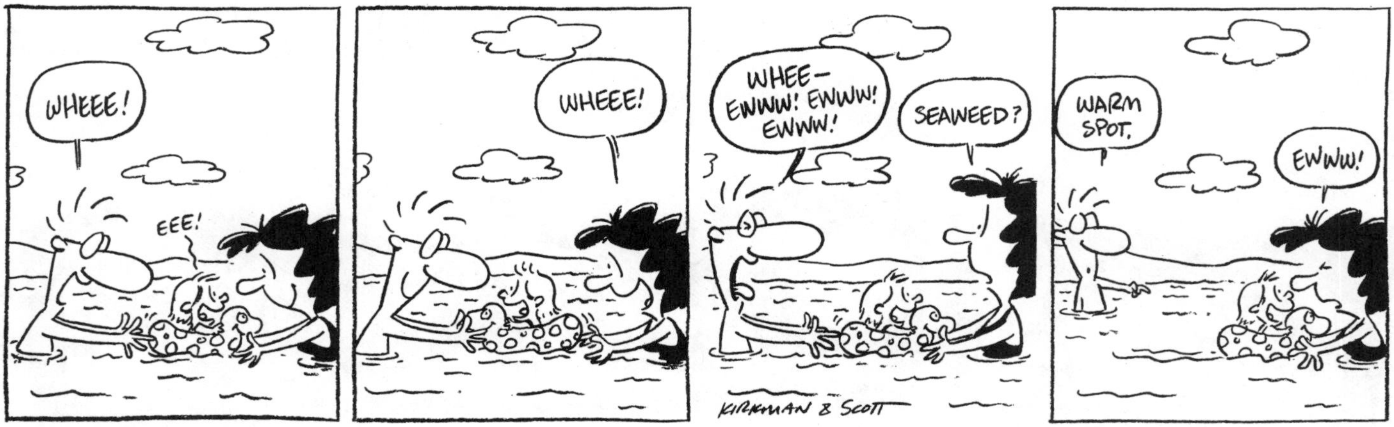
WHEEE!
EEE!
WHEEE!
WHEE-EWWW! EWWW! EWWW!
SEAWEED?
KIRKMAN & SCOTT
WARM SPOT.
EWWW!

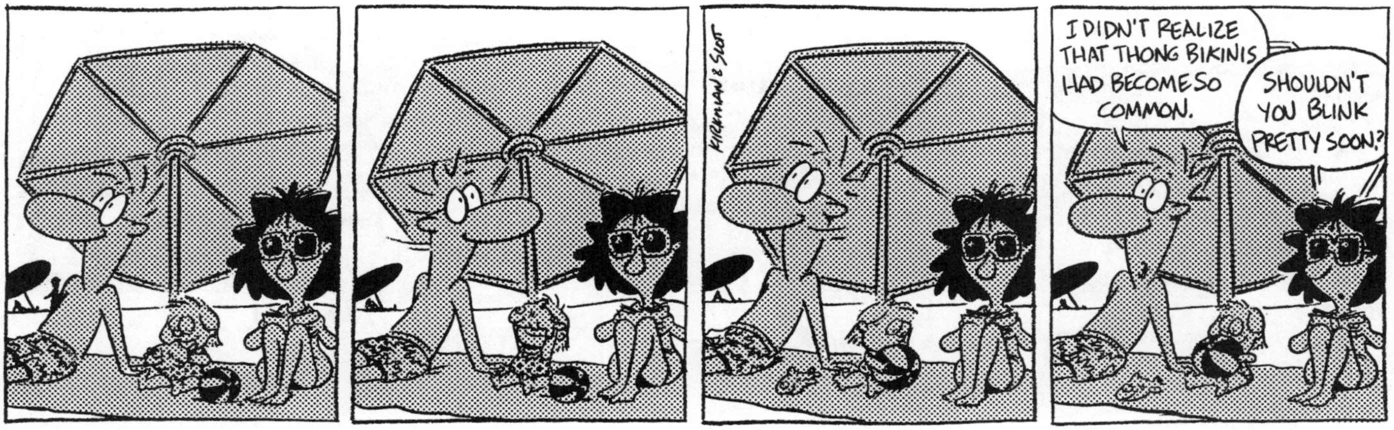
KIRKMAN & SCOTT
I DIDN'T REALIZE THAT THONG BIKINIS HAD BECOME SO COMMON.
SHOULDN'T YOU BLINK PRETTY SOON?

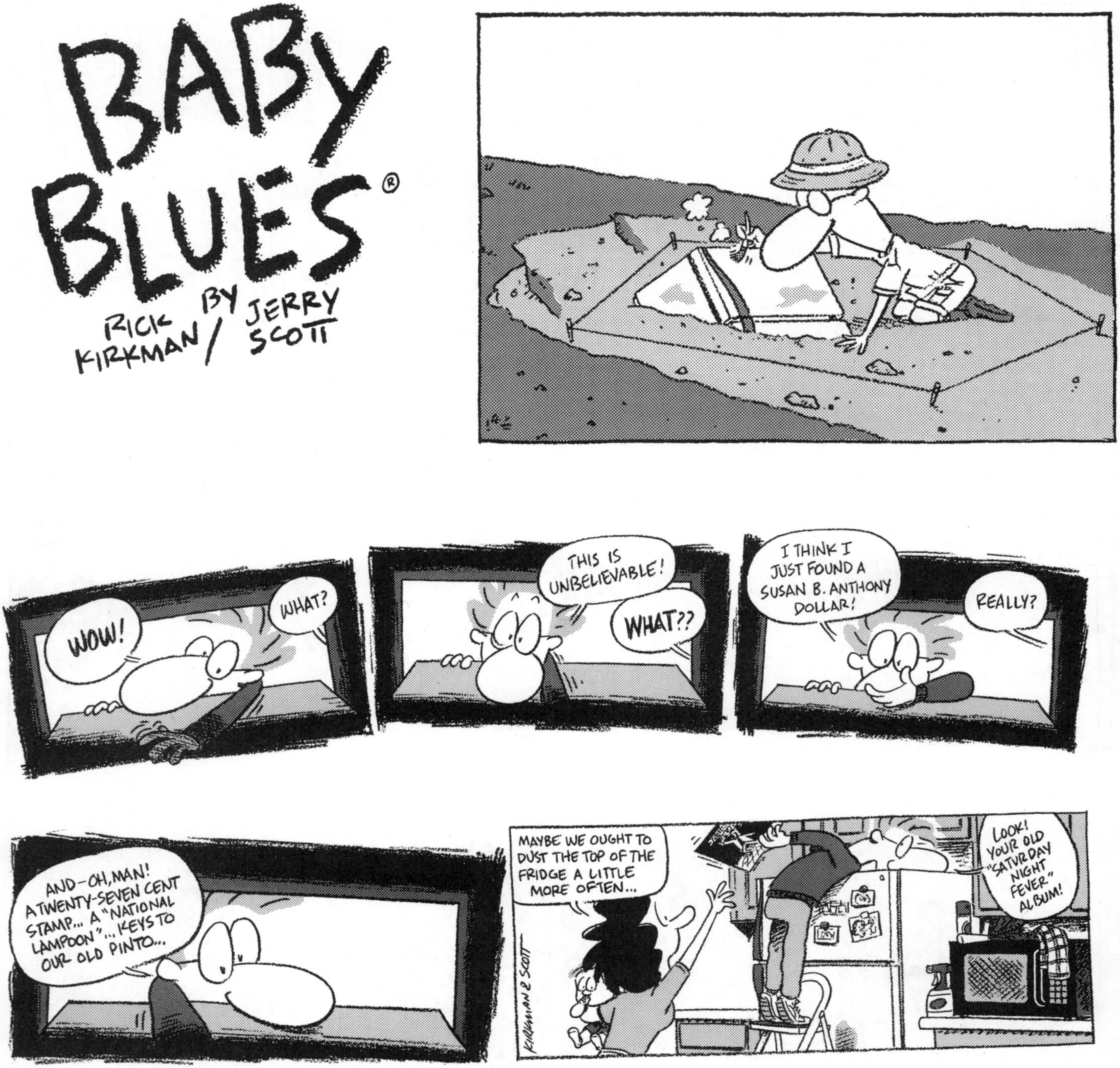
BABY BLUES®
BY RICK KIRKMAN / JERRY SCOTT
WOW!
WHAT?
THIS IS UNBELIEVABLE!
WHAT??
I THINK I JUST FOUND A SUSAN B. ANTHONY DOLLAR!
REALLY?
AND–OH, MAN! A TWENTY-SEVEN CENT STAMP... A "NATIONAL LAMPOON"... KEYS TO OUR OLD PINTO...
MAYBE WE OUGHT TO DUST THE TOP OF THE FRIDGE A LITTLE MORE OFTEN...
LOOK! YOUR OLD "SATURDAY NIGHT FEVER" ALBUM!
KIRKMAN & SCOTT

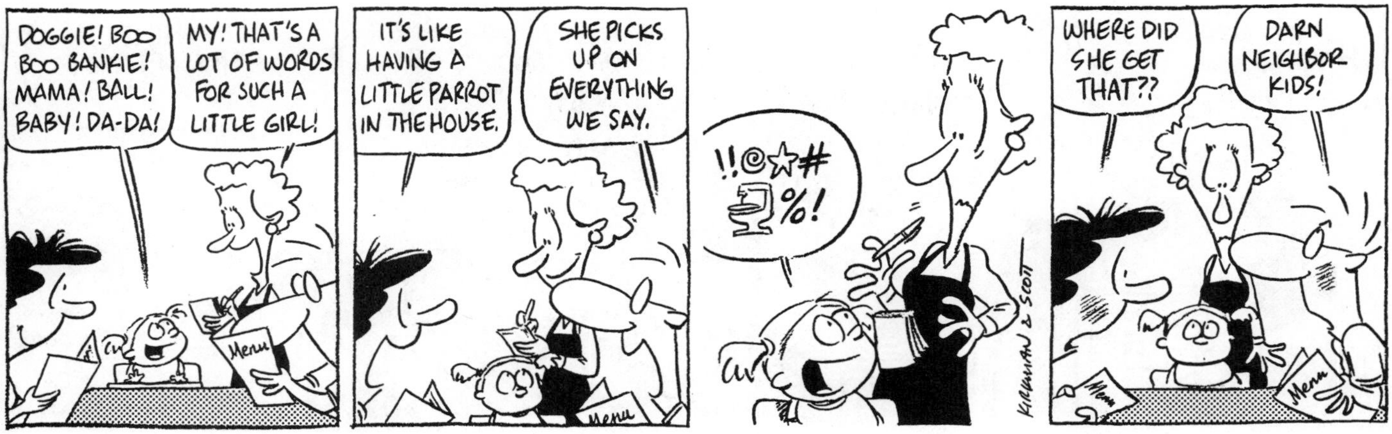
DOGGIE! BOO BOO BANKIE! MAMA! BALL! BABY! DA-DA!
MY! THAT'S A LOT OF WORDS FOR SUCH A LITTLE GIRL!
Menu
IT'S LIKE HAVING A LITTLE PARROT IN THE HOUSE.
SHE PICKS UP ON EVERYTHING WE SAY.
Menu
!!@☆# %!
KIRKMAN & SCOTT
WHERE DID SHE GET THAT??
DARN NEIGHBOR KIDS!
Menu
Menu

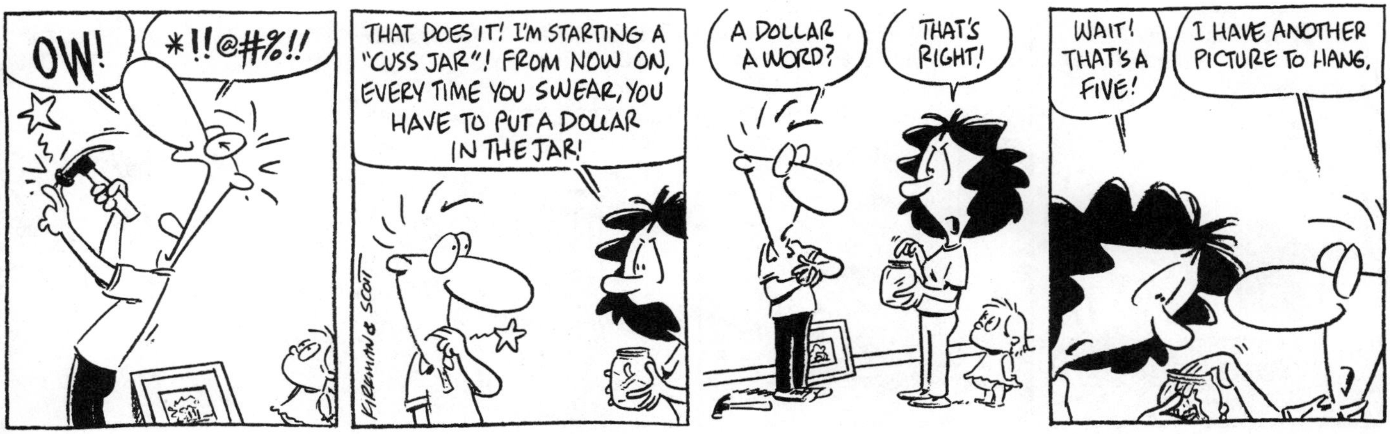
OW!
*!!@#%!!
THAT DOES IT! I'M STARTING A "CUSS JAR"! FROM NOW ON, EVERY TIME YOU SWEAR, YOU HAVE TO PUT A DOLLAR IN THE JAR!
KIRKMAN & SCOTT
A DOLLAR A WORD?
THAT'S RIGHT!
WAIT! THAT'S A FIVE!
I HAVE ANOTHER PICTURE TO HANG.

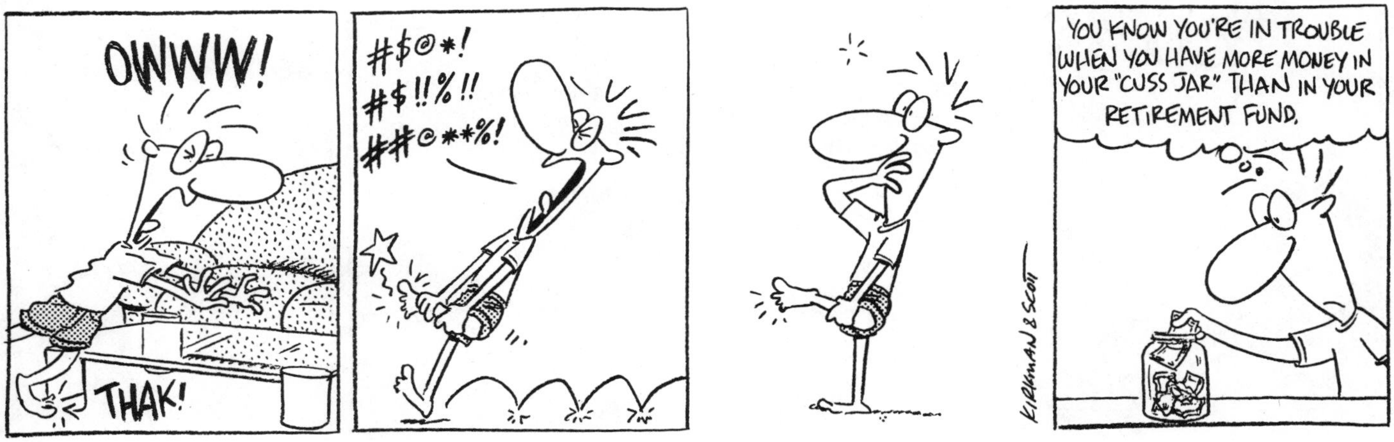
OWWW!
THAK!
#$@*!
#$!!%!!
##@**%!
KIRKMAN & SCOTT
YOU KNOW YOU'RE IN TROUBLE WHEN YOU HAVE MORE MONEY IN YOUR "CUSS JAR" THAN IN YOUR RETIREMENT FUND.

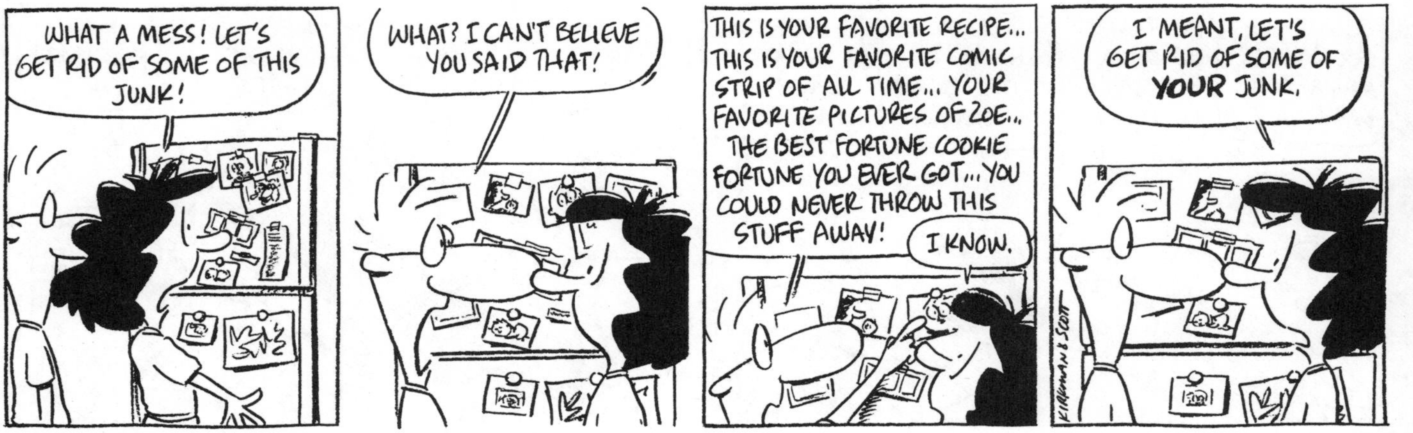
WHAT A MESS! LET'S GET RID OF SOME OF THIS JUNK!
WHAT? I CAN'T BELIEVE YOU SAID THAT!
THIS IS YOUR FAVORITE RECIPE... THIS IS YOUR FAVORITE COMIC STRIP OF ALL TIME... YOUR FAVORITE PICTURES OF ZOE... THE BEST FORTUNE COOKIE FORTUNE YOU EVER GOT... YOU COULD NEVER THROW THIS STUFF AWAY!
I KNOW.
KIRKMAN & SCOTT
I MEANT, LET'S GET RID OF SOME OF **YOUR** JUNK.

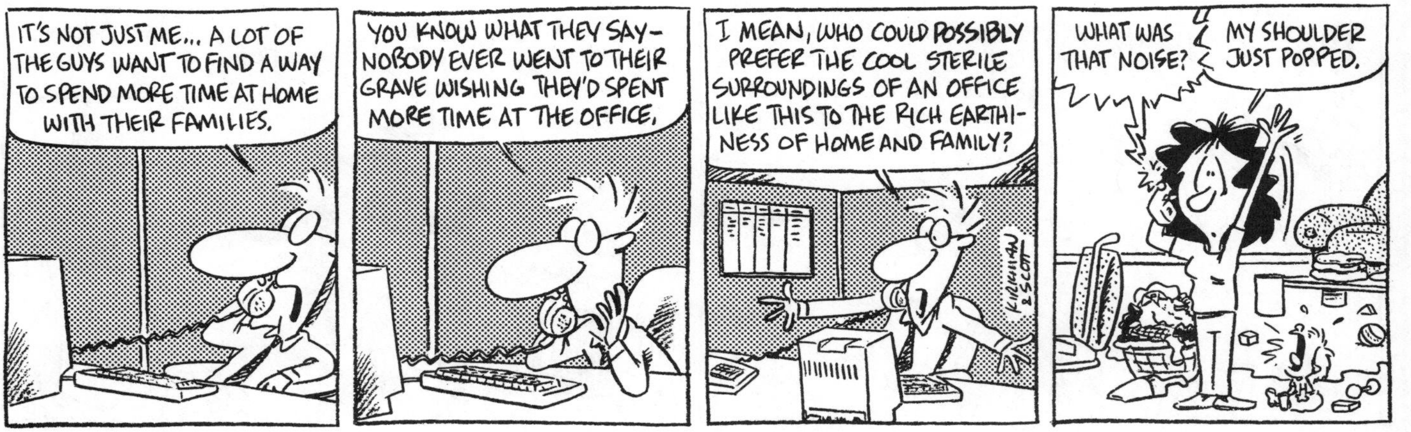
IT'S NOT JUST ME... A LOT OF THE GUYS WANT TO FIND A WAY TO SPEND MORE TIME AT HOME WITH THEIR FAMILIES.
YOU KNOW WHAT THEY SAY- NOBODY EVER WENT TO THEIR GRAVE WISHING THEY'D SPENT MORE TIME AT THE OFFICE.
I MEAN, WHO COULD **POSSIBLY** PREFER THE COOL STERILE SURROUNDINGS OF AN OFFICE LIKE THIS TO THE RICH EARTHINESS OF HOME AND FAMILY?
KIRKMAN & SCOTT
WHAT WAS THAT NOISE?
MY SHOULDER JUST POPPED.

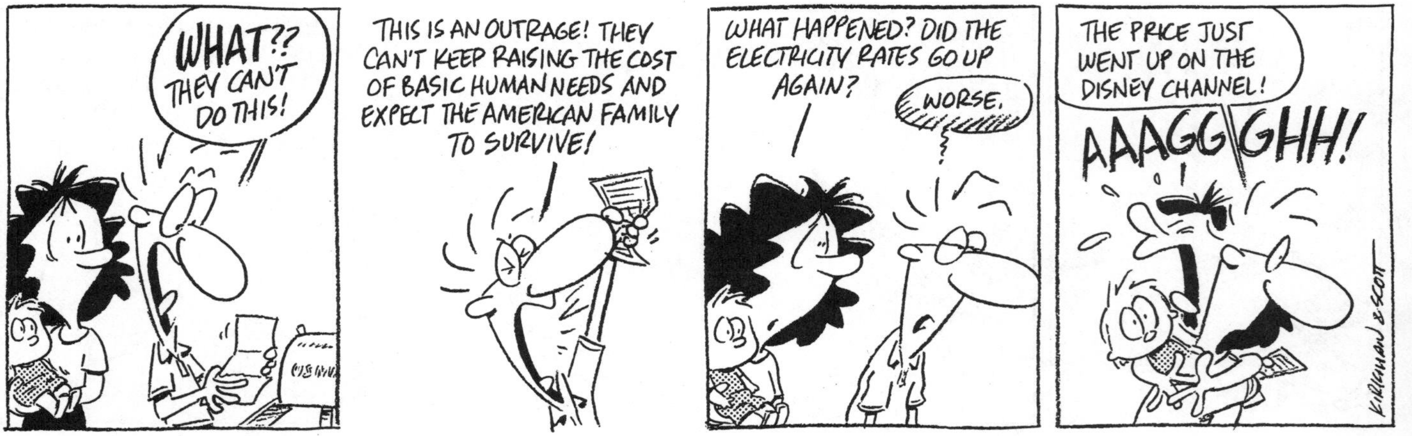
WHAT?? THEY CAN'T DO THIS!
THIS IS AN OUTRAGE! THEY CAN'T KEEP RAISING THE COST OF BASIC HUMAN NEEDS AND EXPECT THE AMERICAN FAMILY TO SURVIVE!
WHAT HAPPENED? DID THE ELECTRICITY RATES GO UP AGAIN?
WORSE.
THE PRICE JUST WENT UP ON THE DISNEY CHANNEL!
AAAGGGHH!
KIRKMAN & SCOTT

BABY BLUES®

BY RICK KIRKMAN / JERRY SCOTT

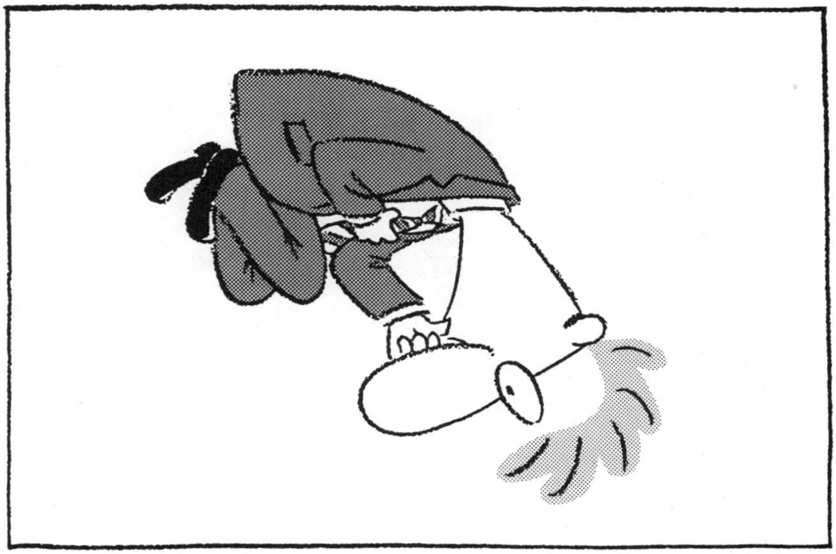

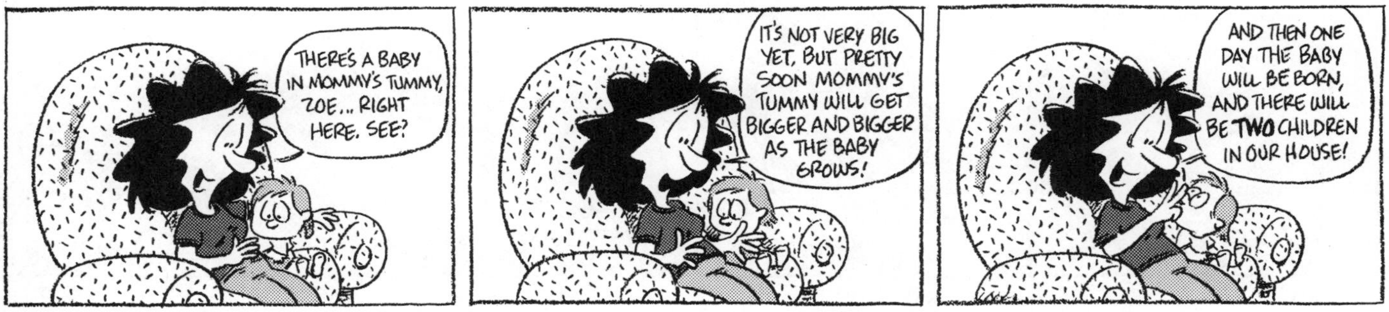

THERE'S A BABY IN MOMMY'S TUMMY, ZOE... RIGHT HERE. SEE?
IT'S NOT VERY BIG YET, BUT PRETTY SOON MOMMY'S TUMMY WILL GET BIGGER AND BIGGER AS THE BABY GROWS!
AND THEN ONE DAY THE BABY WILL BE BORN, AND THERE WILL BE **TWO** CHILDREN IN OUR HOUSE!

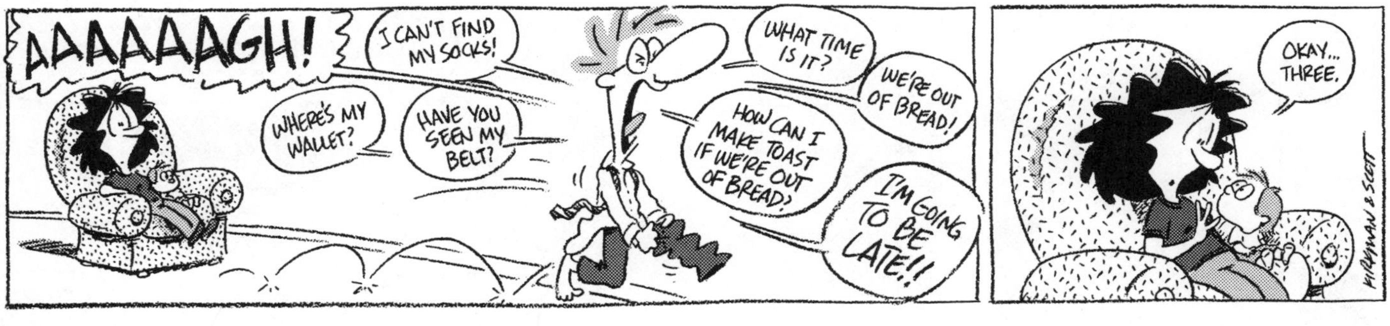

AAAAAAGH!
I CAN'T FIND MY SOCKS!
WHERE'S MY WALLET?
HAVE YOU SEEN MY BELT?
WHAT TIME IS IT?
WE'RE OUT OF BREAD!
HOW CAN I MAKE TOAST IF WE'RE OUT OF BREAD?
I'M GOING TO BE LATE!!
OKAY... THREE.
KIRKMAN & SCOTT

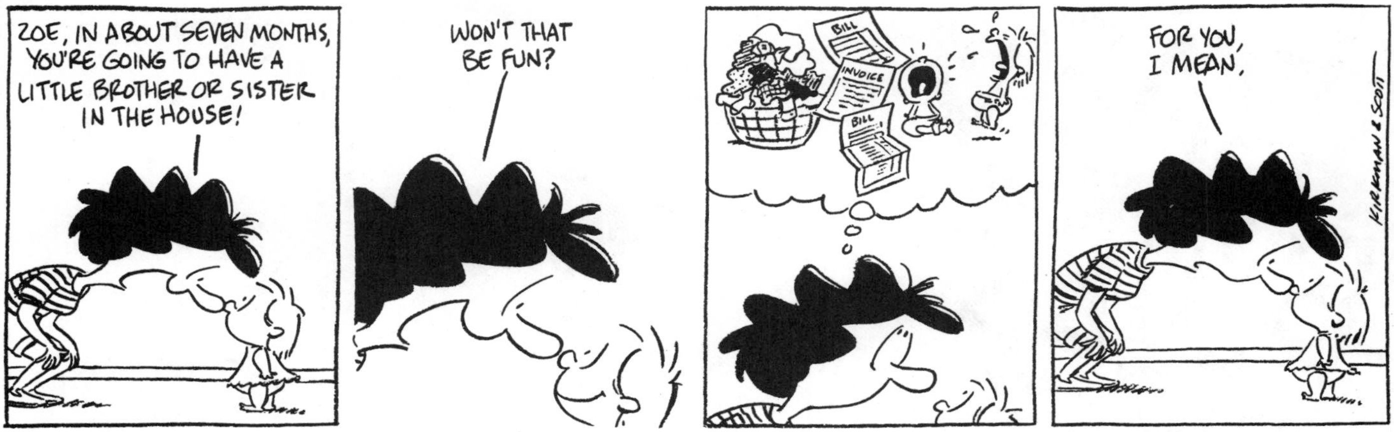
ZOE, IN ABOUT SEVEN MONTHS, YOU'RE GOING TO HAVE A LITTLE BROTHER OR SISTER IN THE HOUSE!
WON'T THAT BE FUN?
BILL
INVOICE
BILL
FOR YOU, I MEAN.
KIRKMAN & SCOTT

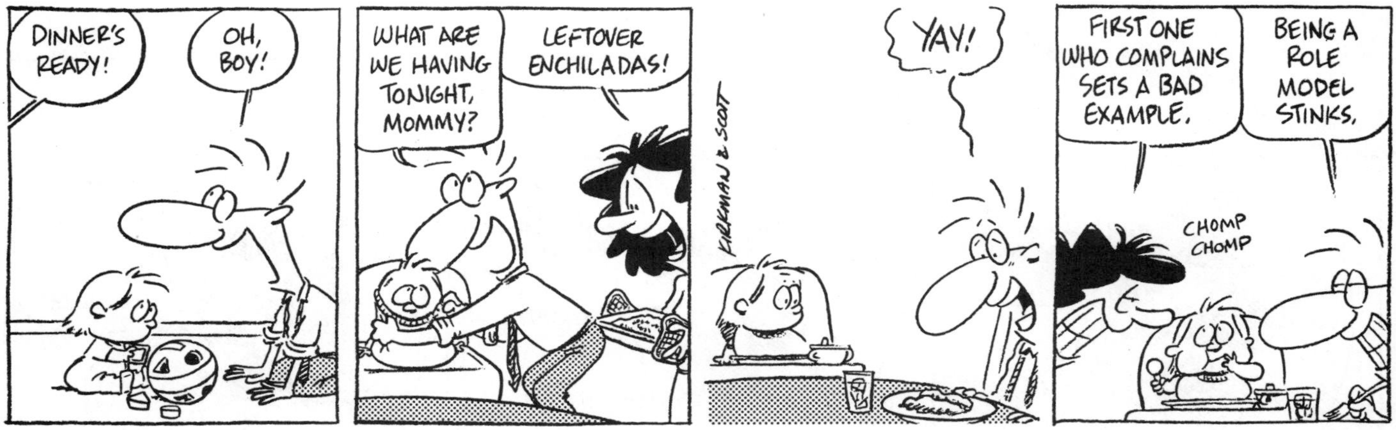
DINNER'S READY!
OH, BOY!
WHAT ARE WE HAVING TONIGHT, MOMMY?
LEFTOVER ENCHILADAS!
KIRKMAN & SCOTT
YAY!
FIRST ONE WHO COMPLAINS SETS A BAD EXAMPLE.
BEING A ROLE MODEL STINKS.
CHOMP CHOMP

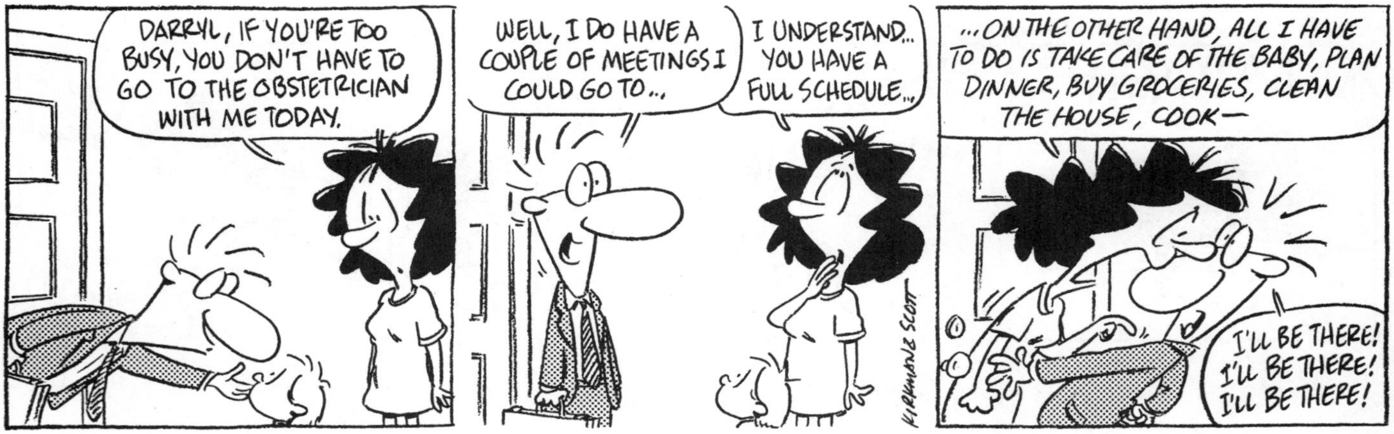
DARRYL, IF YOU'RE TOO BUSY, YOU DON'T HAVE TO GO TO THE OBSTETRICIAN WITH ME TODAY.
WELL, I DO HAVE A COUPLE OF MEETINGS I COULD GO TO...
I UNDERSTAND... YOU HAVE A FULL SCHEDULE...
KIRKMAN & SCOTT
...ON THE OTHER HAND, ALL I HAVE TO DO IS TAKE CARE OF THE BABY, PLAN DINNER, BUY GROCERIES, CLEAN THE HOUSE, COOK—
I'LL BE THERE! I'LL BE THERE! I'LL BE THERE!

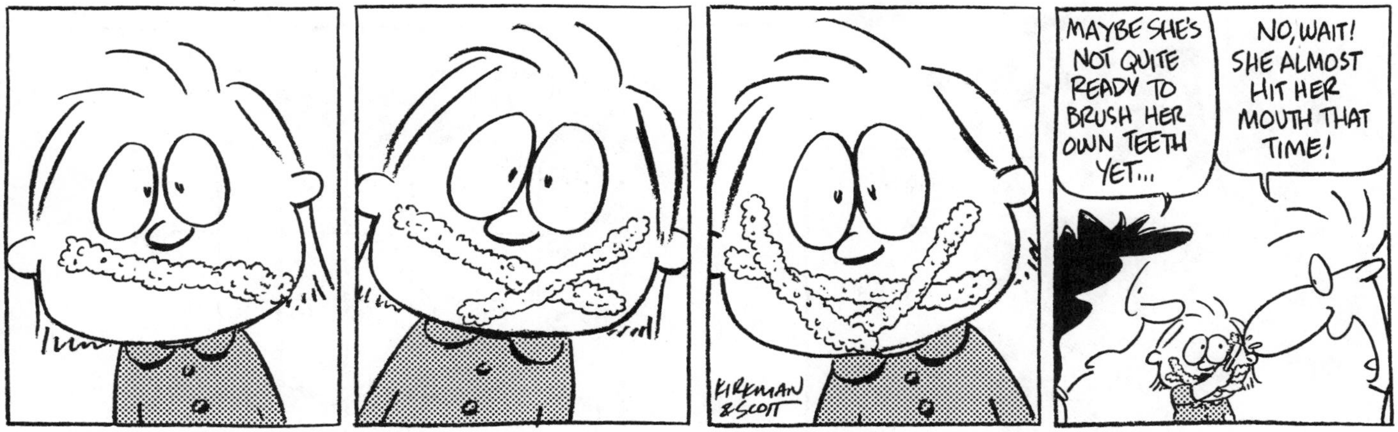
KIRKMAN & SCOTT
MAYBE SHE'S NOT QUITE READY TO BRUSH HER OWN TEETH YET...
NO, WAIT! SHE ALMOST HIT HER MOUTH THAT TIME!

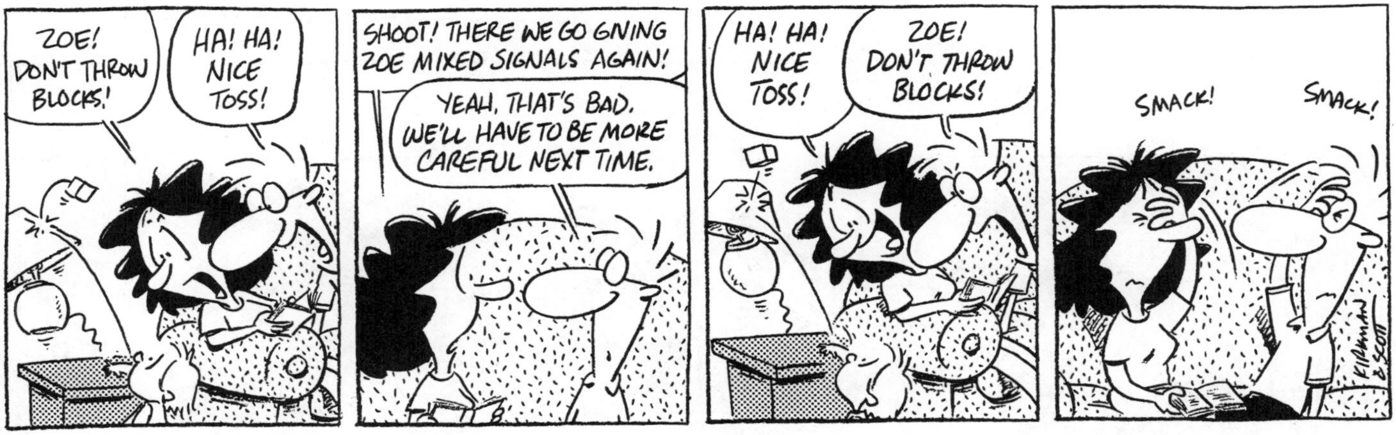
ZOE! DON'T THROW BLOCKS!
HA! HA! NICE TOSS!
SHOOT! THERE WE GO GIVING ZOE MIXED SIGNALS AGAIN!
YEAH, THAT'S BAD. WE'LL HAVE TO BE MORE CAREFUL NEXT TIME.
HA! HA! NICE TOSS!
ZOE! DON'T THROW BLOCKS!
SMACK!
SMACK!
KIRKMAN & SCOTT

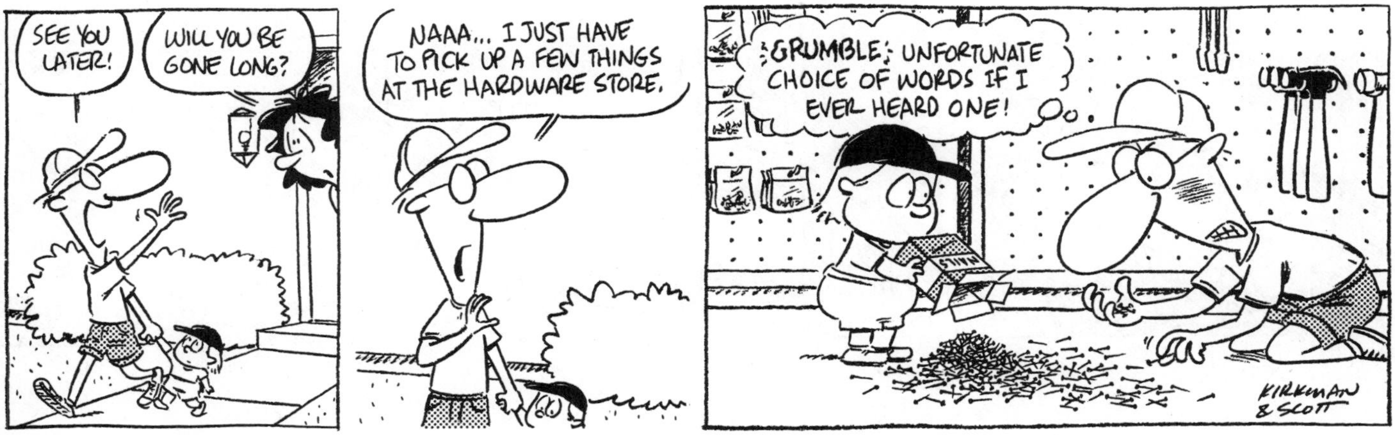
SEE YOU LATER!
WILL YOU BE GONE LONG?
NAAA... I JUST HAVE TO PICK UP A FEW THINGS AT THE HARDWARE STORE.
GRUMBLE UNFORTUNATE CHOICE OF WORDS IF I EVER HEARD ONE!
NAILS
KIRKMAN & SCOTT

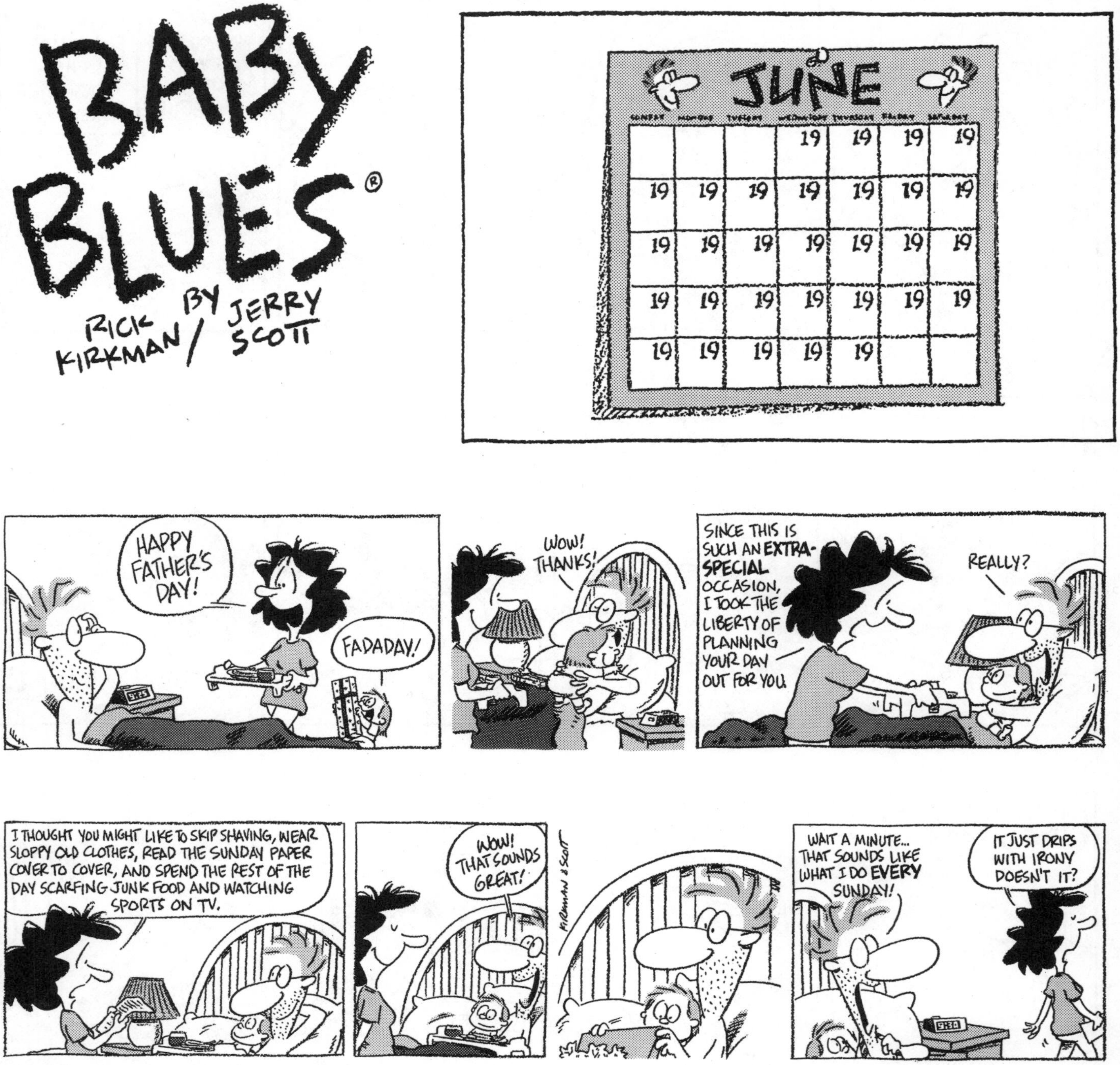
BABY BLUES®
BY RICK KIRKMAN / JERRY SCOTT
JUNE
HAPPY FATHER'S DAY!
FADADAY!
WOW! THANKS!
SINCE THIS IS SUCH AN **EXTRA-SPECIAL** OCCASION, I TOOK THE LIBERTY OF PLANNING YOUR DAY OUT FOR YOU.
REALLY?
I THOUGHT YOU MIGHT LIKE TO SKIP SHAVING, WEAR SLOPPY OLD CLOTHES, READ THE SUNDAY PAPER COVER TO COVER, AND SPEND THE REST OF THE DAY SCARFING JUNK FOOD AND WATCHING SPORTS ON TV.
WOW! THAT SOUNDS GREAT!
WAIT A MINUTE... THAT SOUNDS LIKE WHAT I DO **EVERY** SUNDAY!
IT JUST DRIPS WITH IRONY DOESN'T IT?

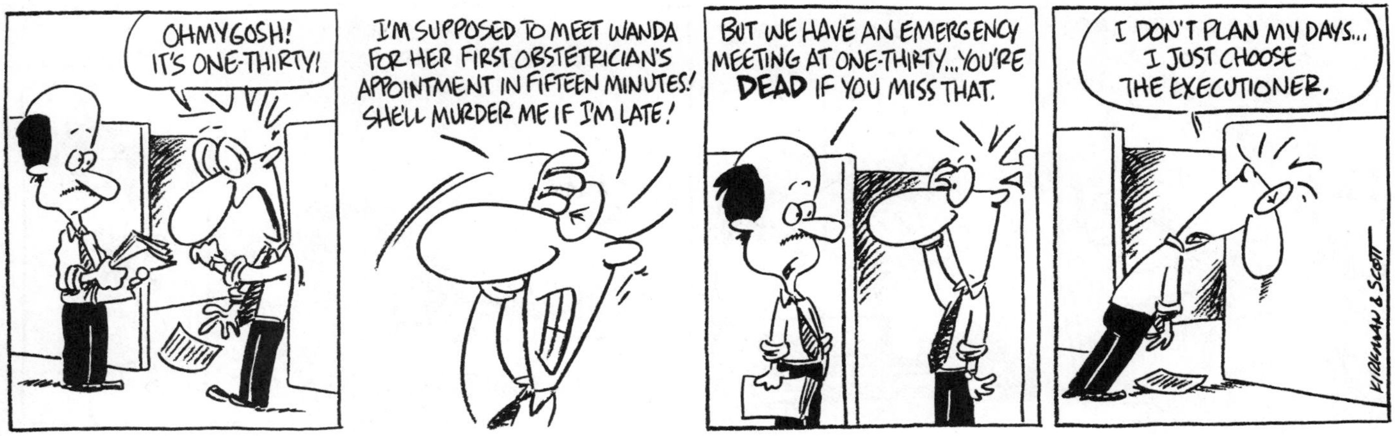
OHMYGOSH! IT'S ONE-THIRTY!
I'M SUPPOSED TO MEET WANDA FOR HER FIRST OBSTETRICIAN'S APPOINTMENT IN FIFTEEN MINUTES! SHE'LL MURDER ME IF I'M LATE!
BUT WE HAVE AN EMERGENCY MEETING AT ONE-THIRTY... YOU'RE **DEAD** IF YOU MISS THAT.
I DON'T PLAN MY DAYS... I JUST CHOOSE THE EXECUTIONER.
KIRKMAN & SCOTT

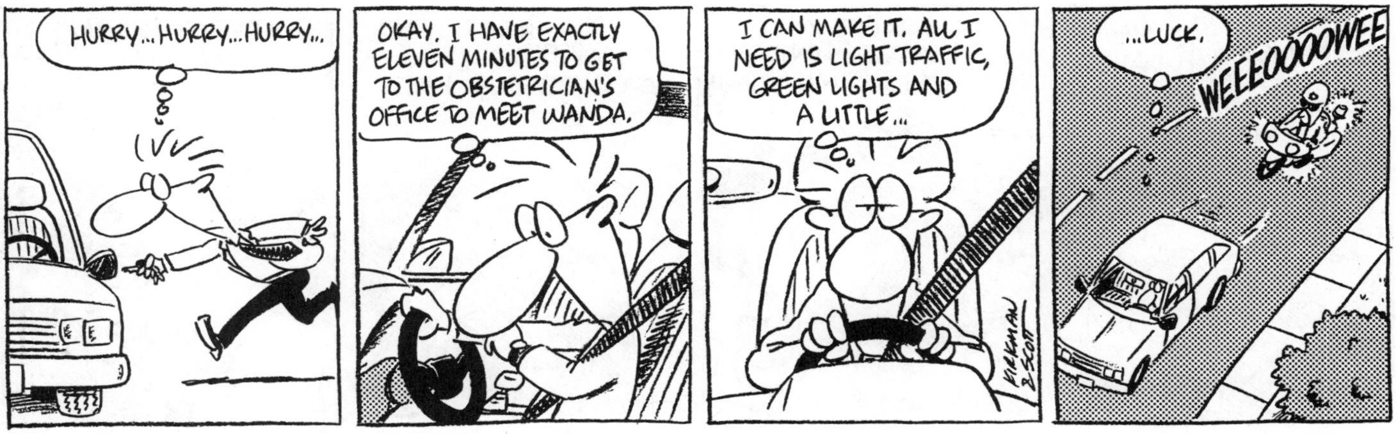
HURRY... HURRY... HURRY...
OKAY. I HAVE EXACTLY ELEVEN MINUTES TO GET TO THE OBSTETRICIAN'S OFFICE TO MEET WANDA.
I CAN MAKE IT. ALL I NEED IS LIGHT TRAFFIC, GREEN LIGHTS AND A LITTLE...
KIRKMAN & SCOTT
...LUCK.
WEEEOOOOWEE

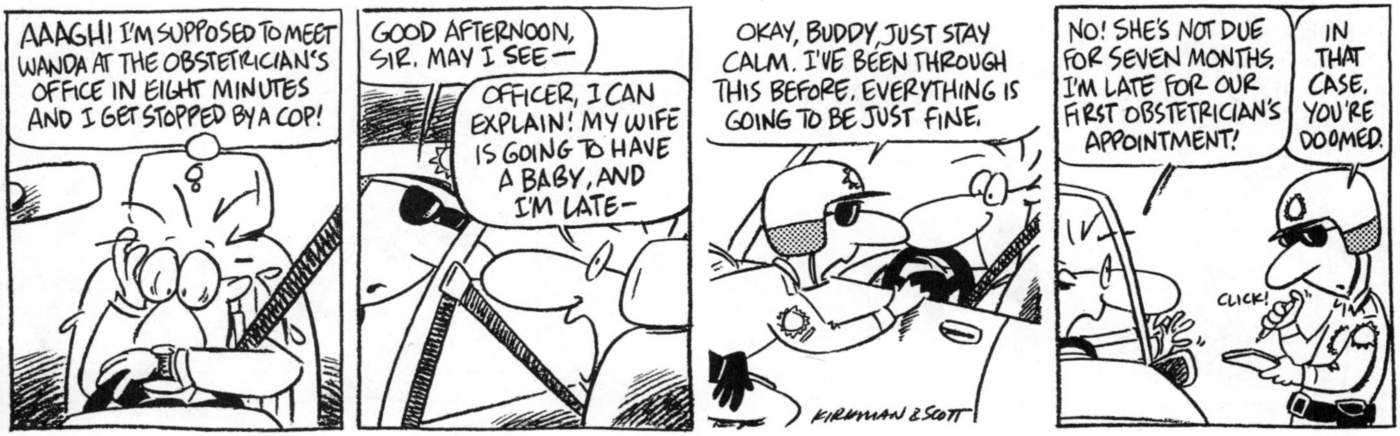
AAAGH! I'M SUPPOSED TO MEET WANDA AT THE OBSTETRICIAN'S OFFICE IN EIGHT MINUTES AND I GET STOPPED BY A COP!
GOOD AFTERNOON, SIR. MAY I SEE—
OFFICER, I CAN EXPLAIN! MY WIFE IS GOING TO HAVE A BABY, AND I'M LATE—
OKAY, BUDDY, JUST STAY CALM. I'VE BEEN THROUGH THIS BEFORE. EVERYTHING IS GOING TO BE JUST FINE.
KIRKMAN & SCOTT
NO! SHE'S NOT DUE FOR SEVEN MONTHS. I'M LATE FOR OUR FIRST OBSTETRICIAN'S APPOINTMENT!
IN THAT CASE, YOU'RE DOOMED.
CLICK!

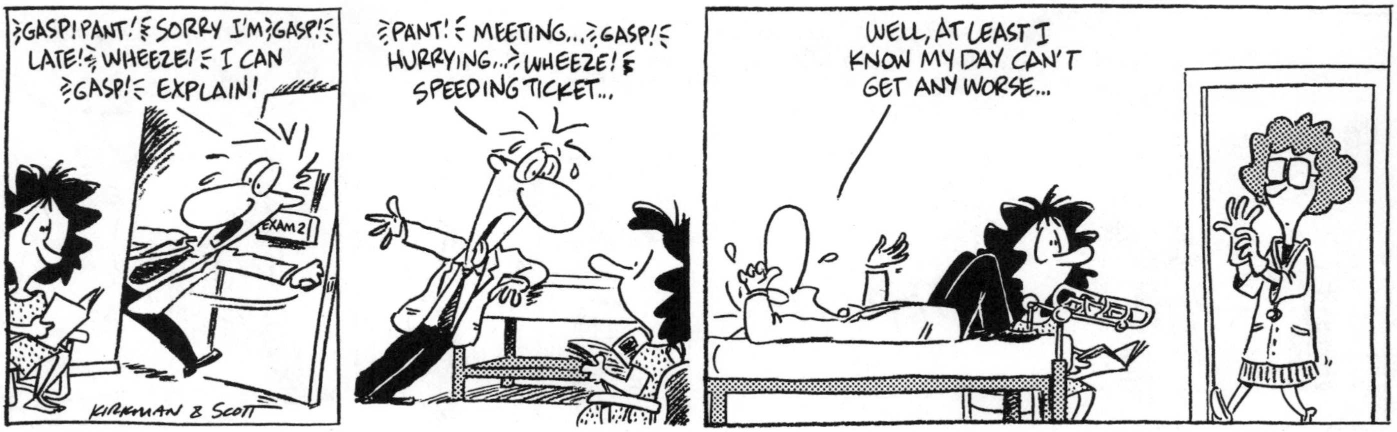
GASP! PANT! SORRY I'M GASP! LATE! WHEEZE! I CAN GASP! EXPLAIN!
EXAM 2
KIRKMAN & SCOTT
PANT! MEETING... GASP! HURRYING... WHEEZE! SPEEDING TICKET...
WELL, AT LEAST I KNOW MY DAY CAN'T GET ANY WORSE...

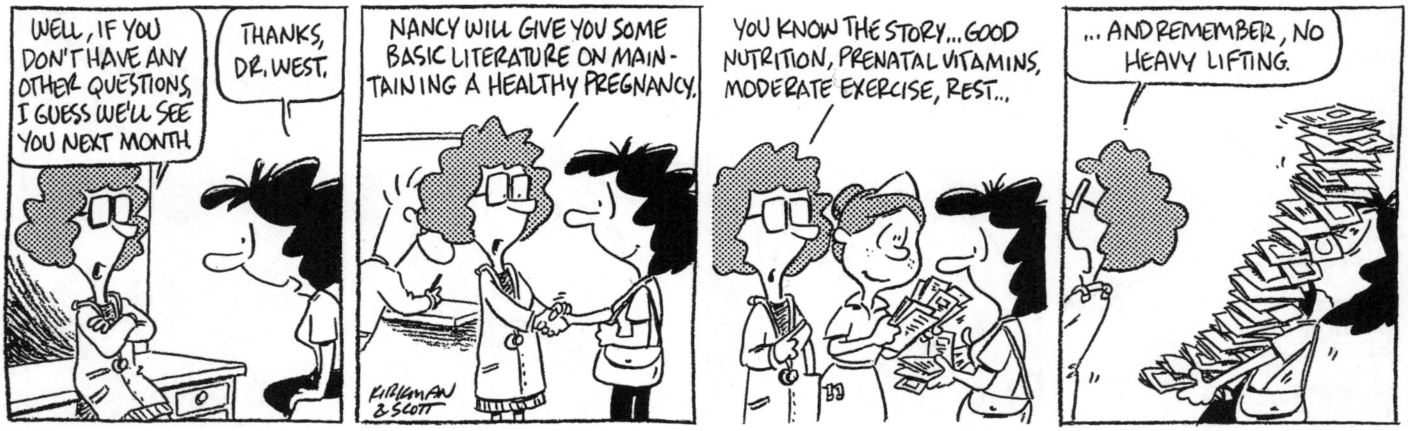
WELL, IF YOU DON'T HAVE ANY OTHER QUESTIONS, I GUESS WE'LL SEE YOU NEXT MONTH.
THANKS, DR. WEST.
NANCY WILL GIVE YOU SOME BASIC LITERATURE ON MAINTAINING A HEALTHY PREGNANCY.
KIRKMAN & SCOTT
YOU KNOW THE STORY... GOOD NUTRITION, PRENATAL VITAMINS, MODERATE EXERCISE, REST...
... AND REMEMBER, NO HEAVY LIFTING.

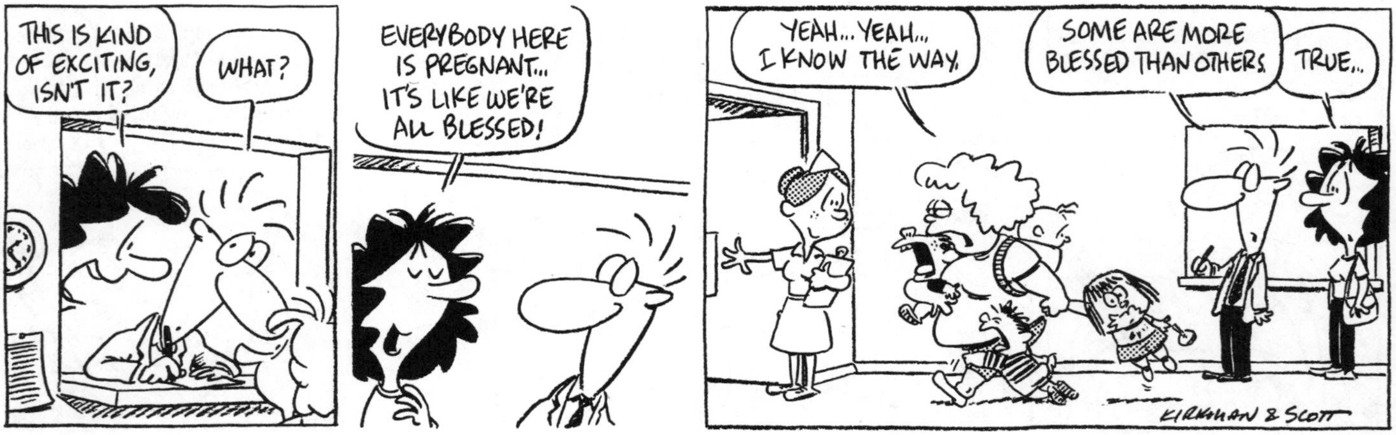
THIS IS KIND OF EXCITING, ISN'T IT?
WHAT?
EVERYBODY HERE IS PREGNANT... IT'S LIKE WE'RE ALL BLESSED!
YEAH... YEAH... I KNOW THE WAY.
SOME ARE MORE BLESSED THAN OTHERS.
TRUE...
KIRKMAN & SCOTT

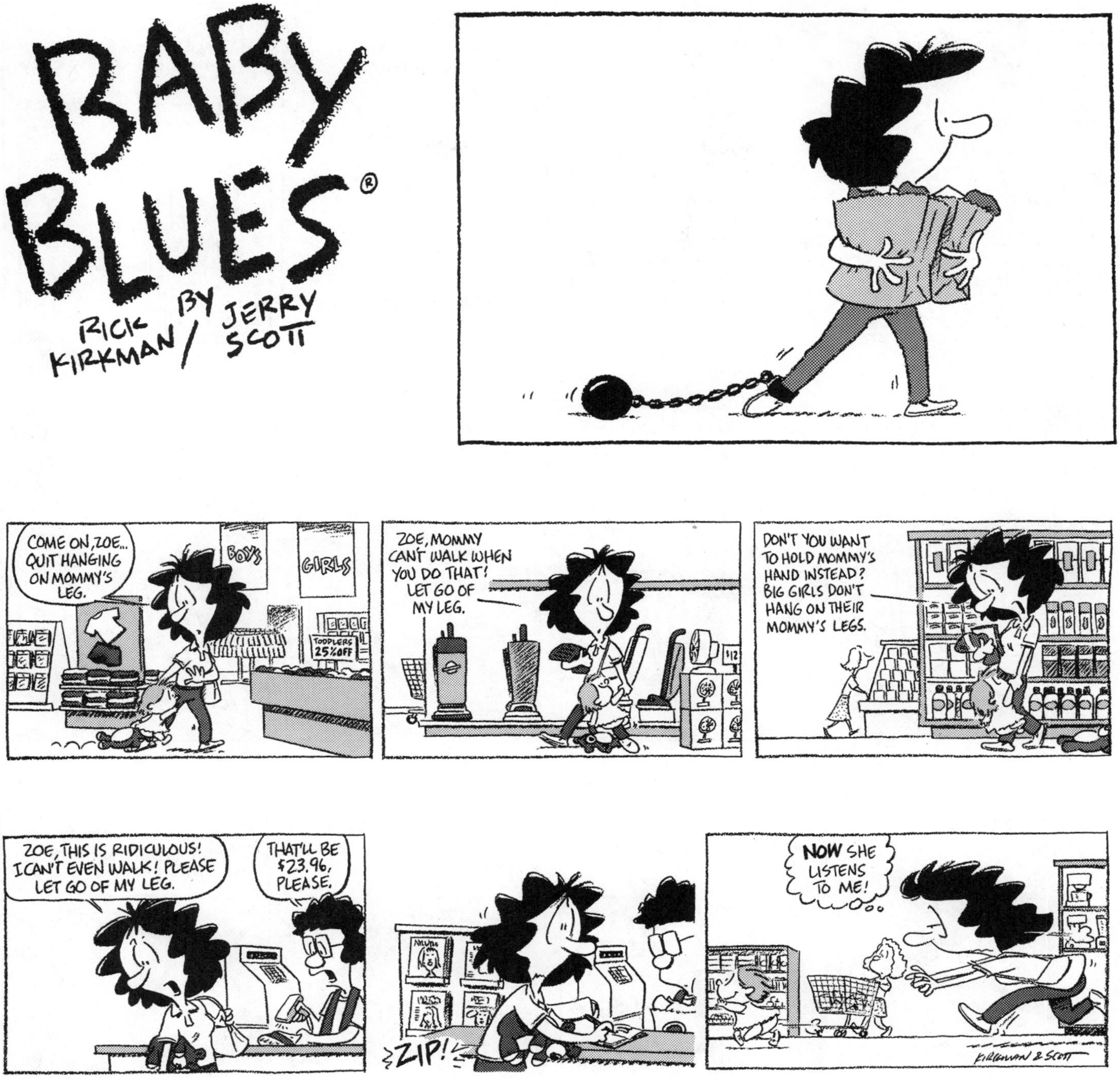
BABY BLUES®
BY RICK KIRKMAN / JERRY SCOTT
COME ON, ZOE... QUIT HANGING ON MOMMY'S LEG.
BOYS
GIRLS
TODDLERS 25% OFF
ZOE, MOMMY CAN'T WALK WHEN YOU DO THAT! LET GO OF MY LEG.
DON'T YOU WANT TO HOLD MOMMY'S HAND INSTEAD? BIG GIRLS DON'T HANG ON THEIR MOMMY'S LEGS.
ZOE, THIS IS RIDICULOUS! I CAN'T EVEN WALK! PLEASE LET GO OF MY LEG.
THAT'LL BE $23.96, PLEASE.
ZIP!
NOW SHE LISTENS TO ME!
KIRKMAN & SCOTT

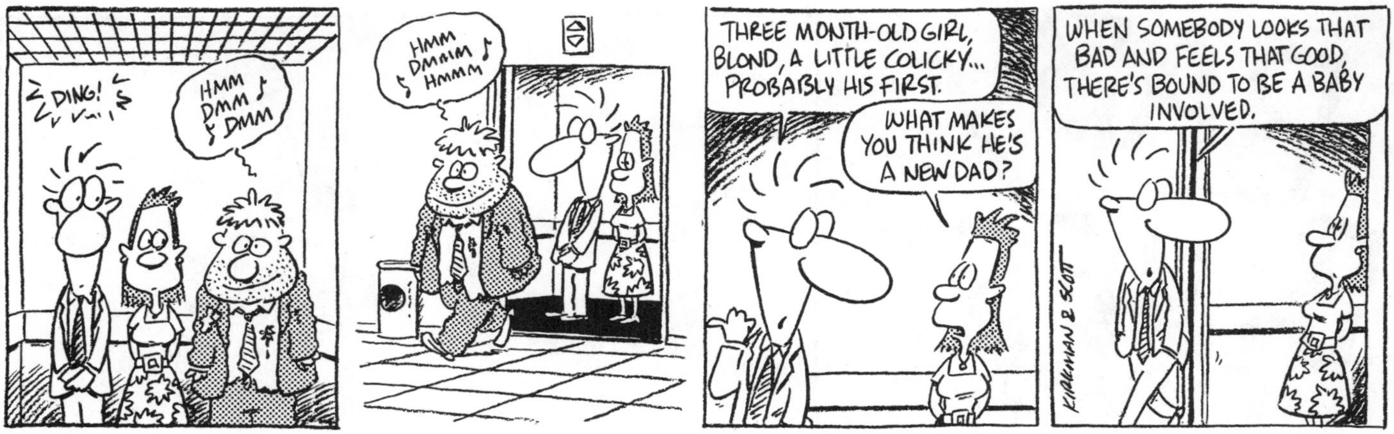
DING!
HMM DMM DMM
HMM DMMM HMMM
THREE MONTH-OLD GIRL, BLOND, A LITTLE COLICKY... PROBABLY HIS FIRST.
WHAT MAKES YOU THINK HE'S A NEW DAD?
WHEN SOMEBODY LOOKS THAT BAD AND FEELS THAT GOOD, THERE'S BOUND TO BE A BABY INVOLVED.
KIRKMAN & SCOTT

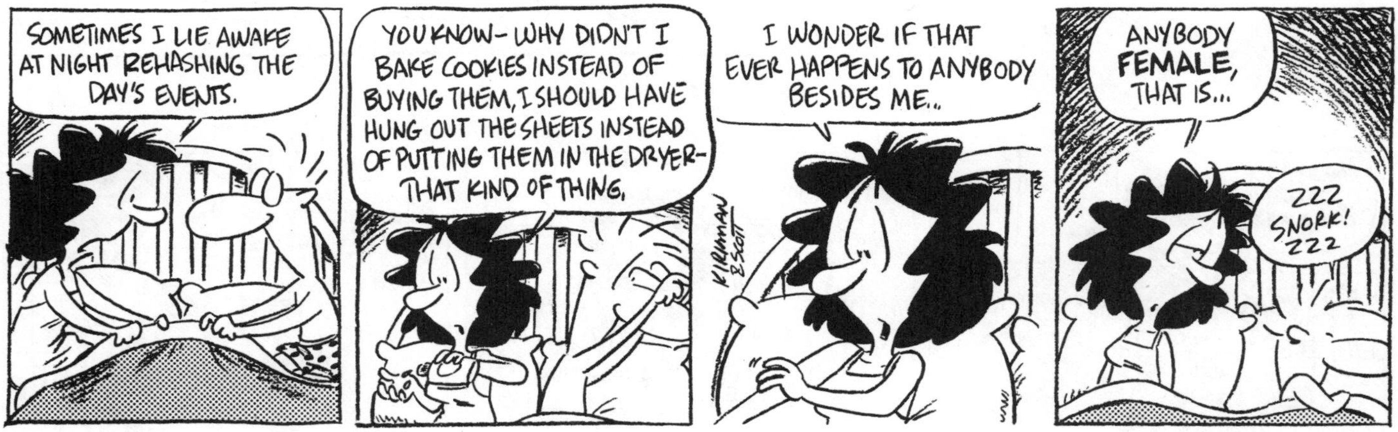
SOMETIMES I LIE AWAKE AT NIGHT REHASHING THE DAY'S EVENTS.
YOU KNOW- WHY DIDN'T I BAKE COOKIES INSTEAD OF BUYING THEM, I SHOULD HAVE HUNG OUT THE SHEETS INSTEAD OF PUTTING THEM IN THE DRYER- THAT KIND OF THING.
I WONDER IF THAT EVER HAPPENS TO ANYBODY BESIDES ME..
KIRKMAN & SCOTT
ANYBODY **FEMALE**, THAT IS...
ZZZ SNORK! ZZZ

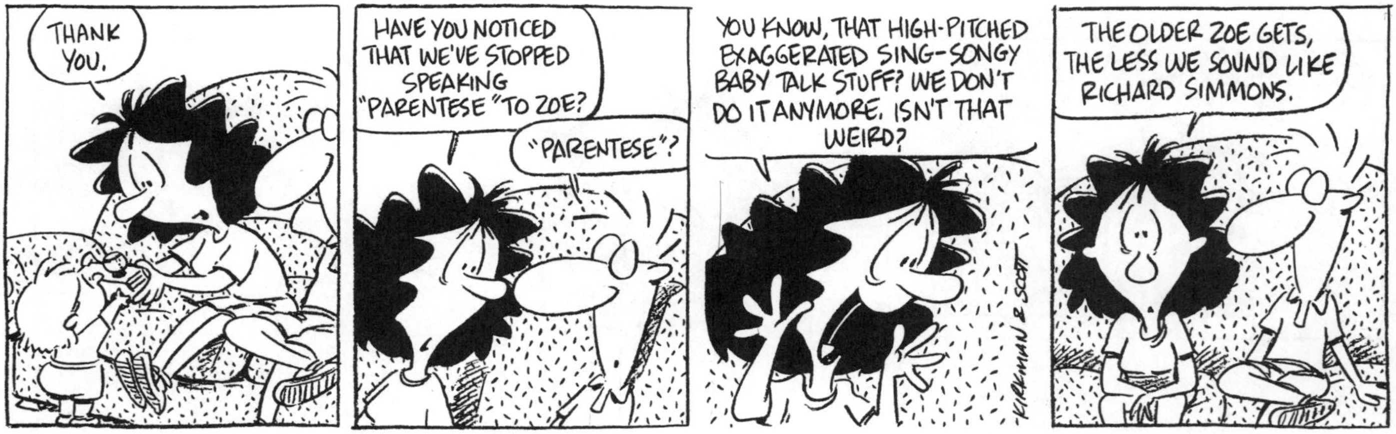
THANK YOU.
HAVE YOU NOTICED THAT WE'VE STOPPED SPEAKING "PARENTESE" TO ZOE?
"PARENTESE"?
YOU KNOW, THAT HIGH-PITCHED EXAGGERATED SING-SONGY BABY TALK STUFF? WE DON'T DO IT ANYMORE. ISN'T THAT WEIRD?
KIRKMAN & SCOTT
THE OLDER ZOE GETS, THE LESS WE SOUND LIKE RICHARD SIMMONS.

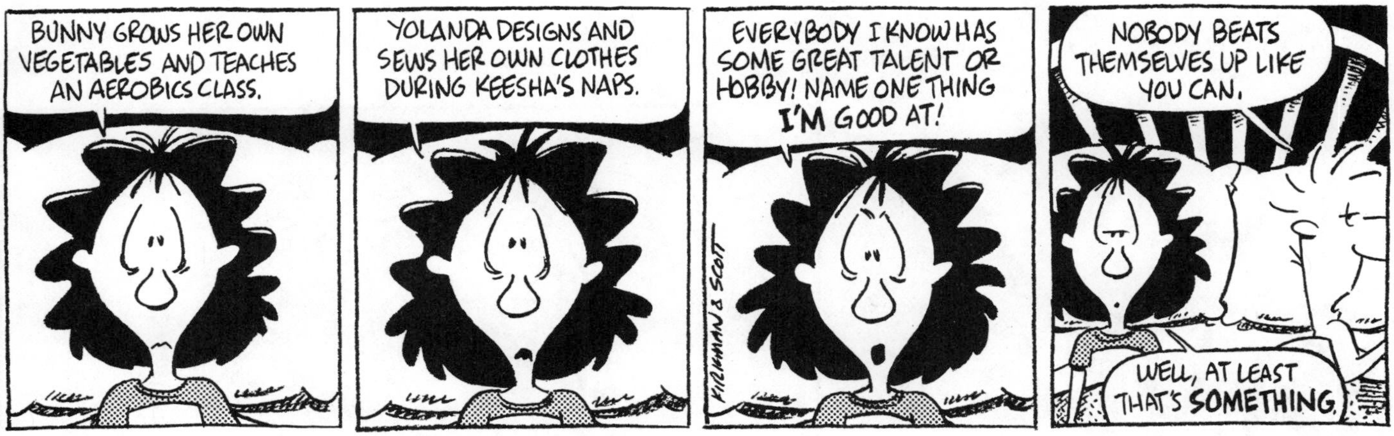
BUNNY GROWS HER OWN VEGETABLES AND TEACHES AN AEROBICS CLASS.
YOLANDA DESIGNS AND SEWS HER OWN CLOTHES DURING KEESHA'S NAPS.
EVERYBODY I KNOW HAS SOME GREAT TALENT OR HOBBY! NAME ONE THING I'M GOOD AT!
KIRKMAN & SCOTT
NOBODY BEATS THEMSELVES UP LIKE YOU CAN.
WELL, AT LEAST THAT'S SOMETHING.

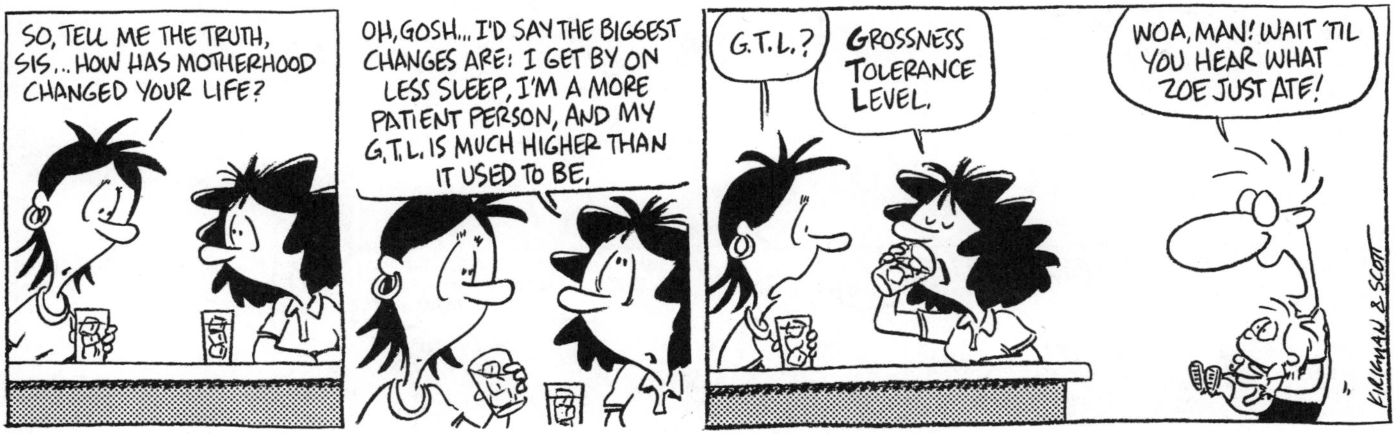
SO, TELL ME THE TRUTH, SIS... HOW HAS MOTHERHOOD CHANGED YOUR LIFE?
OH, GOSH... I'D SAY THE BIGGEST CHANGES ARE: I GET BY ON LESS SLEEP, I'M A MORE PATIENT PERSON, AND MY G.T.L. IS MUCH HIGHER THAN IT USED TO BE.
G.T.L.?
GROSSNESS TOLERANCE LEVEL.
WOA, MAN! WAIT 'TIL YOU HEAR WHAT ZOE JUST ATE!
KIRKMAN & SCOTT

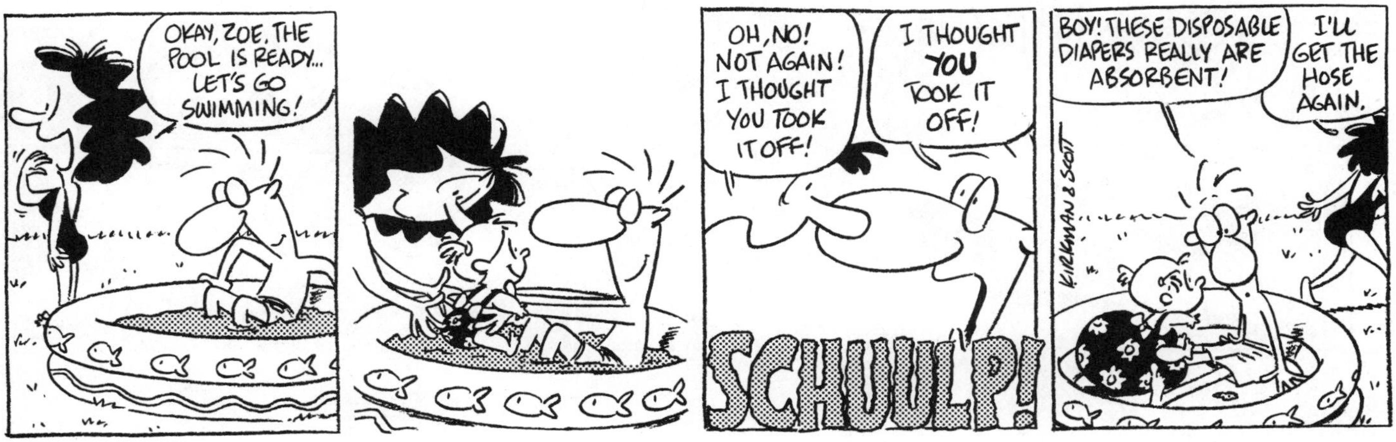
OKAY, ZOE, THE POOL IS READY... LET'S GO SWIMMING!
OH, NO! NOT AGAIN! I THOUGHT YOU TOOK IT OFF!
I THOUGHT YOU TOOK IT OFF!
SCHUULP!
KIRKMAN & SCOTT
BOY! THESE DISPOSABLE DIAPERS REALLY ARE ABSORBENT!
I'LL GET THE HOSE AGAIN.

BABY BLUES®

BY
RICK KIRKMAN / JERRY SCOTT

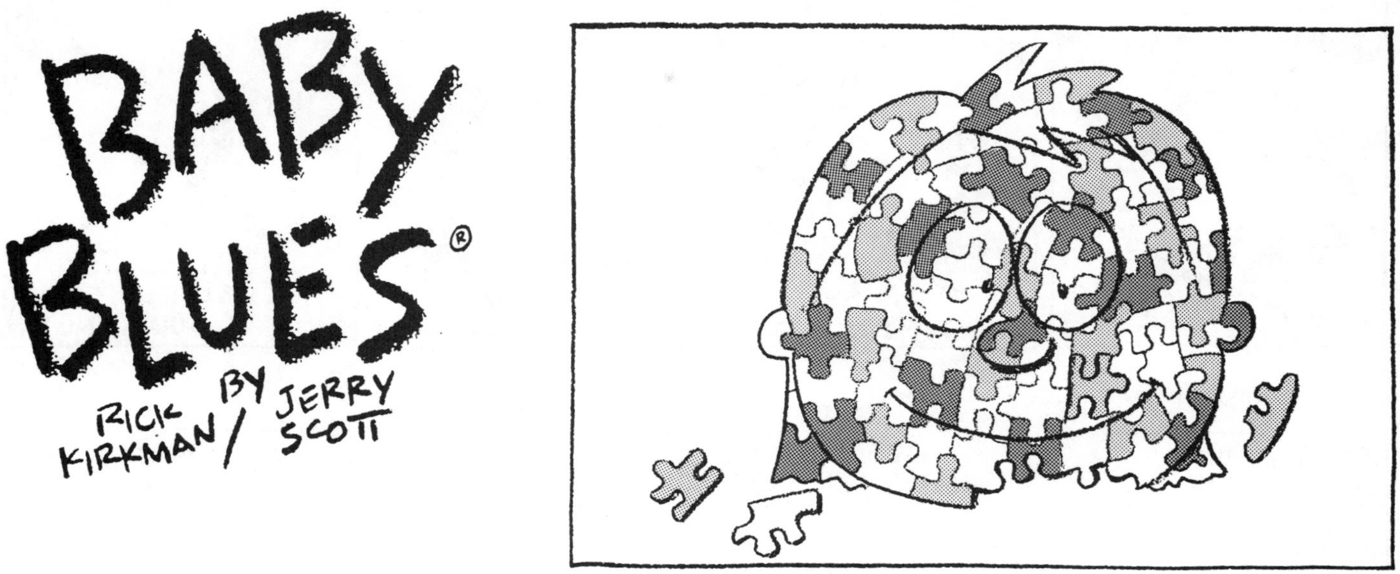

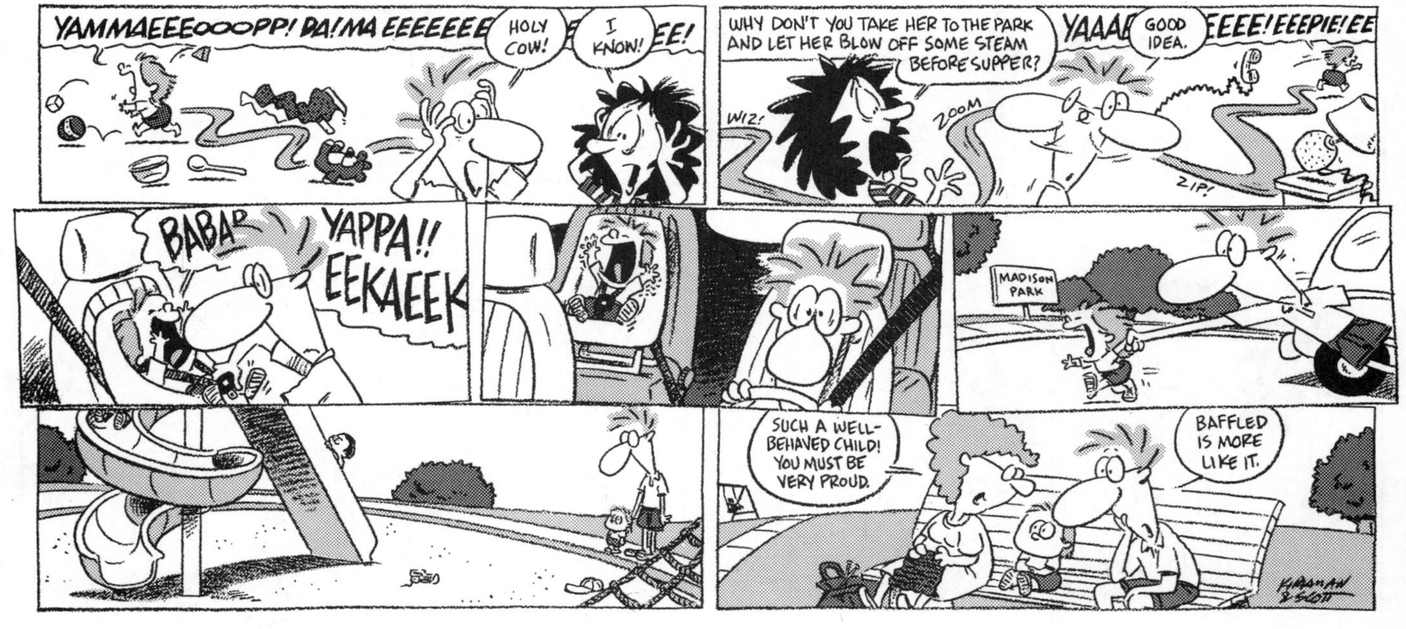
YAMMAEEEoooPP! DA!MA EEEEEEE
HOLY COW!
I KNOW!
EE!
WHY DON'T YOU TAKE HER TO THE PARK AND LET HER BLOW OFF SOME STEAM BEFORE SUPPER?
GOOD IDEA.
EEEE! EEEPIE! EE
WIZ!
ZOOM
ZIP!
BABAB
YAPPA!! EEKAEEEK
MADISON PARK
SUCH A WELL-BEHAVED CHILD! YOU MUST BE VERY PROUD.
BAFFLED IS MORE LIKE IT.
KIRKMAN & SCOTT

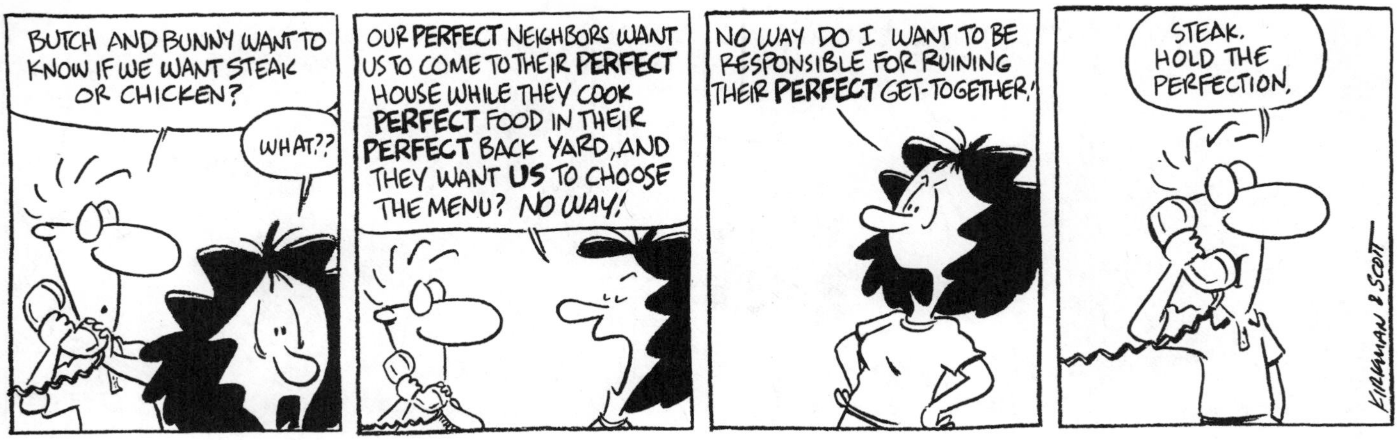
BUTCH AND BUNNY WANT TO KNOW IF WE WANT STEAK OR CHICKEN?
WHAT??
OUR **PERFECT** NEIGHBORS WANT US TO COME TO THEIR **PERFECT** HOUSE WHILE THEY COOK **PERFECT** FOOD IN THEIR **PERFECT** BACK YARD, AND THEY WANT **US** TO CHOOSE THE MENU? NO WAY!
NO WAY DO I WANT TO BE RESPONSIBLE FOR RUINING THEIR **PERFECT** GET-TOGETHER!
STEAK. HOLD THE PERFECTION.
KIRKMAN & SCOTT

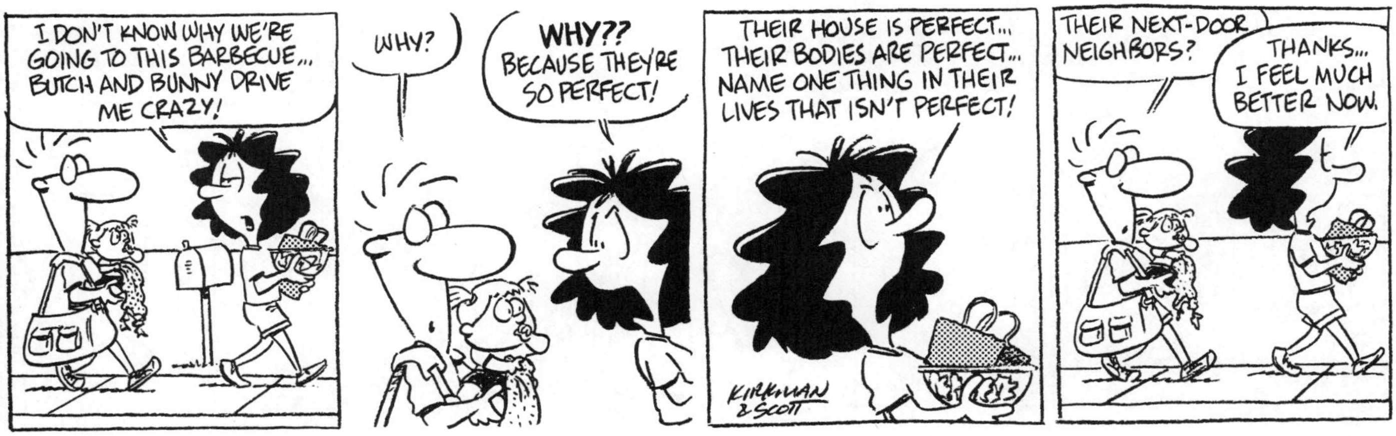
I DON'T KNOW WHY WE'RE GOING TO THIS BARBECUE... BUTCH AND BUNNY DRIVE ME CRAZY!
WHY?
WHY?? BECAUSE THEY'RE SO PERFECT!
THEIR HOUSE IS PERFECT... THEIR BODIES ARE PERFECT... NAME ONE THING IN THEIR LIVES THAT ISN'T PERFECT!
KIRKMAN & SCOTT
THEIR NEXT-DOOR NEIGHBORS?
THANKS... I FEEL MUCH BETTER NOW.

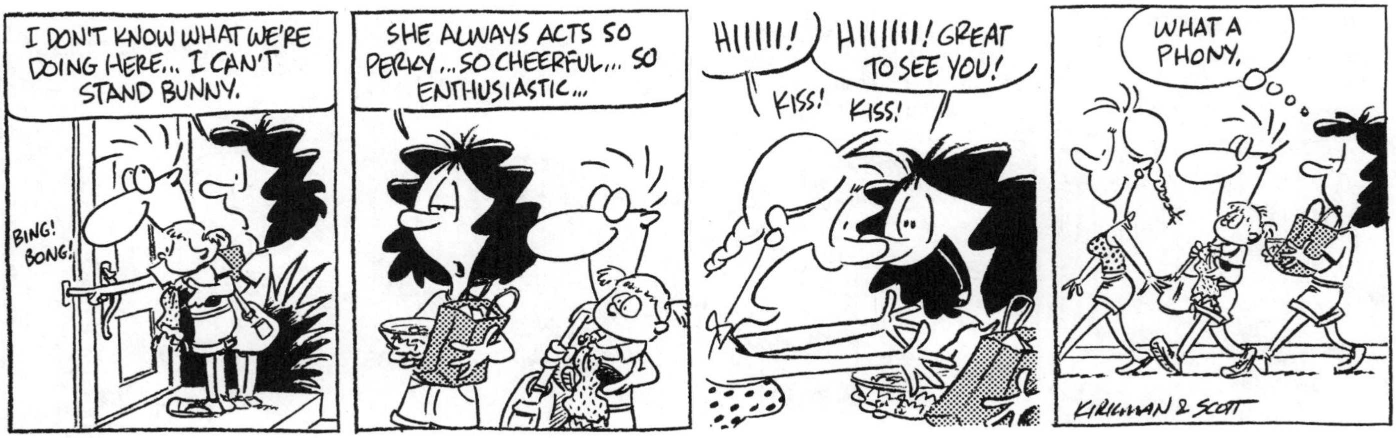
I DON'T KNOW WHAT WE'RE DOING HERE... I CAN'T STAND BUNNY.
BING! BONG!
SHE ALWAYS ACTS SO PERKY... SO CHEERFUL... SO ENTHUSIASTIC...
HI!!!!!
HI!!!!!! GREAT TO SEE YOU!
KISS! KISS!
WHAT A PHONY.
KIRKMAN & SCOTT

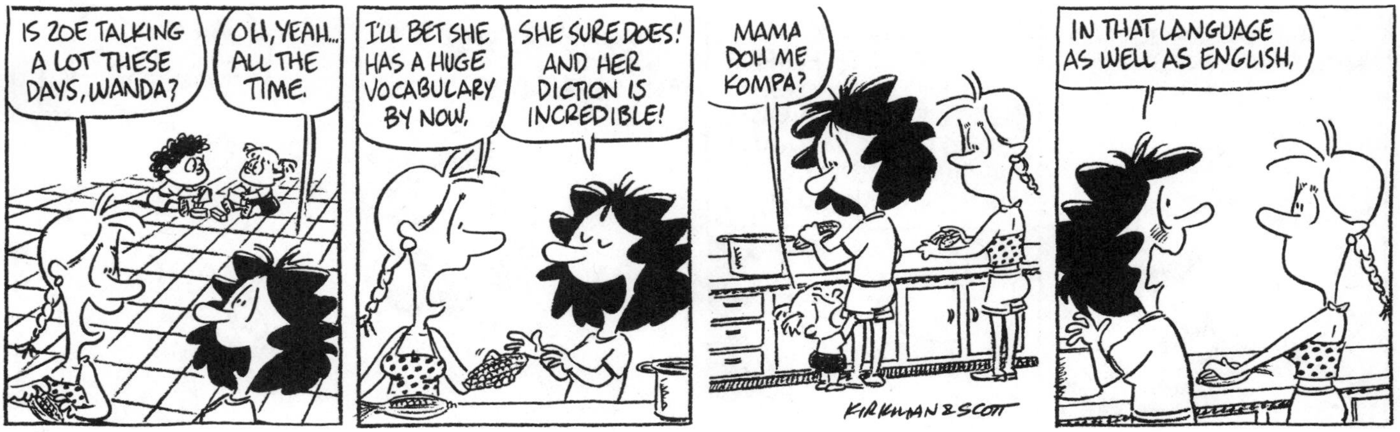
IS ZOE TALKING A LOT THESE DAYS, WANDA?
OH, YEAH... ALL THE TIME.
I'LL BET SHE HAS A HUGE VOCABULARY BY NOW.
SHE SURE DOES! AND HER DICTION IS INCREDIBLE!
MAMA DOH ME KOMPA?
KIRKMAN & SCOTT
IN THAT LANGUAGE AS WELL AS ENGLISH.

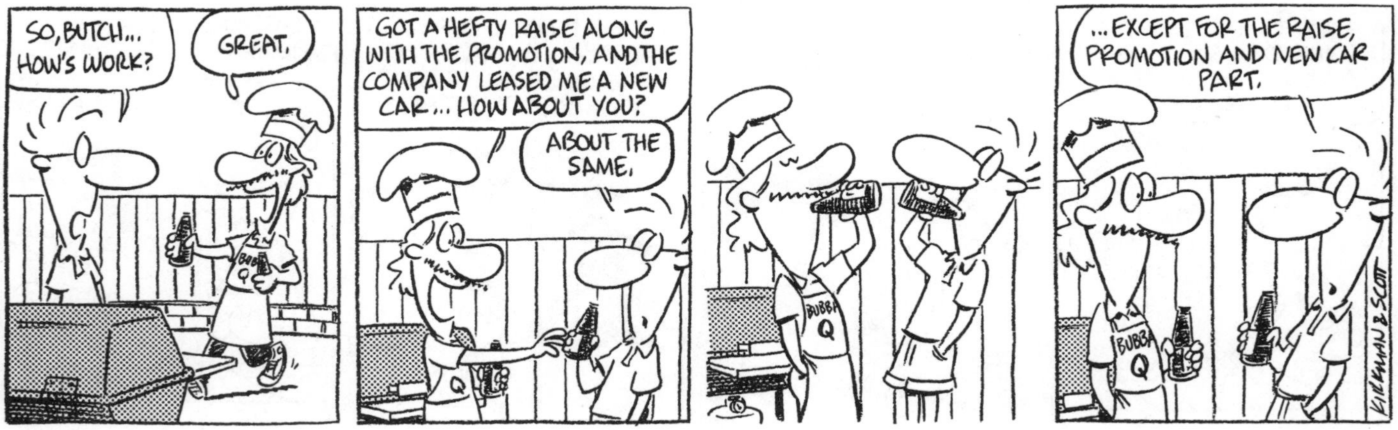
SO, BUTCH... HOW'S WORK?
GREAT.
GOT A HEFTY RAISE ALONG WITH THE PROMOTION, AND THE COMPANY LEASED ME A NEW CAR... HOW ABOUT YOU?
ABOUT THE SAME.
BUBBA Q
...EXCEPT FOR THE RAISE, PROMOTION AND NEW CAR PART.
KIRKMAN & SCOTT

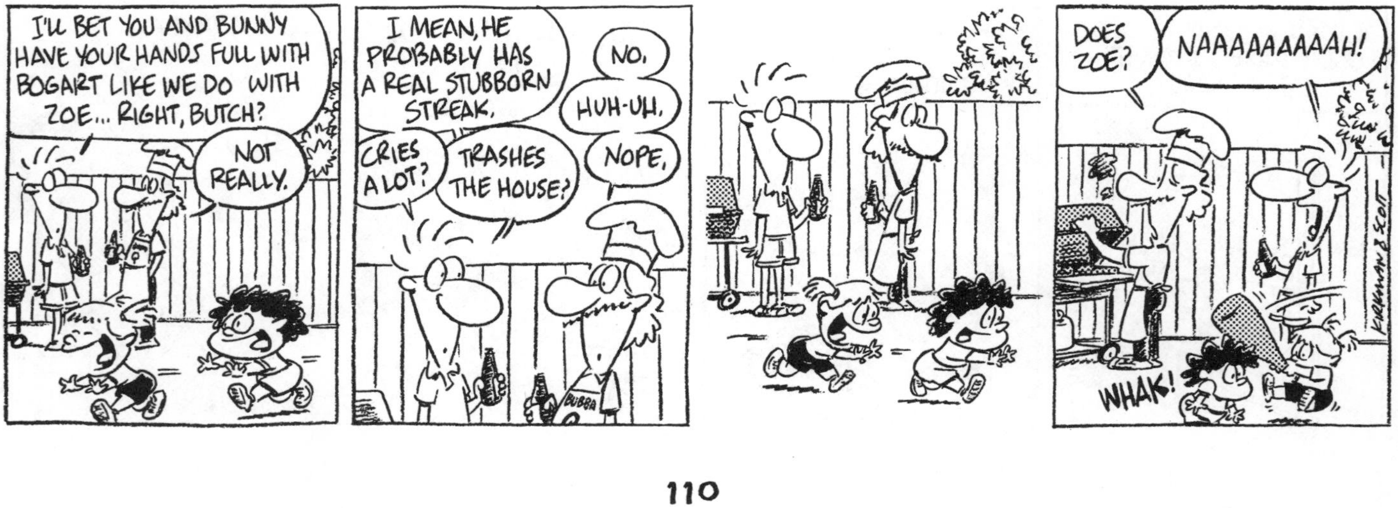
I'LL BET YOU AND BUNNY HAVE YOUR HANDS FULL WITH BOGART LIKE WE DO WITH ZOE... RIGHT, BUTCH?
NOT REALLY.
I MEAN, HE PROBABLY HAS A REAL STUBBORN STREAK.
NO.
CRIES A LOT?
HUH-UH.
TRASHES THE HOUSE?
NOPE.
DOES ZOE?
NAAAAAAAAH!
WHAK!
KIRKMAN & SCOTT

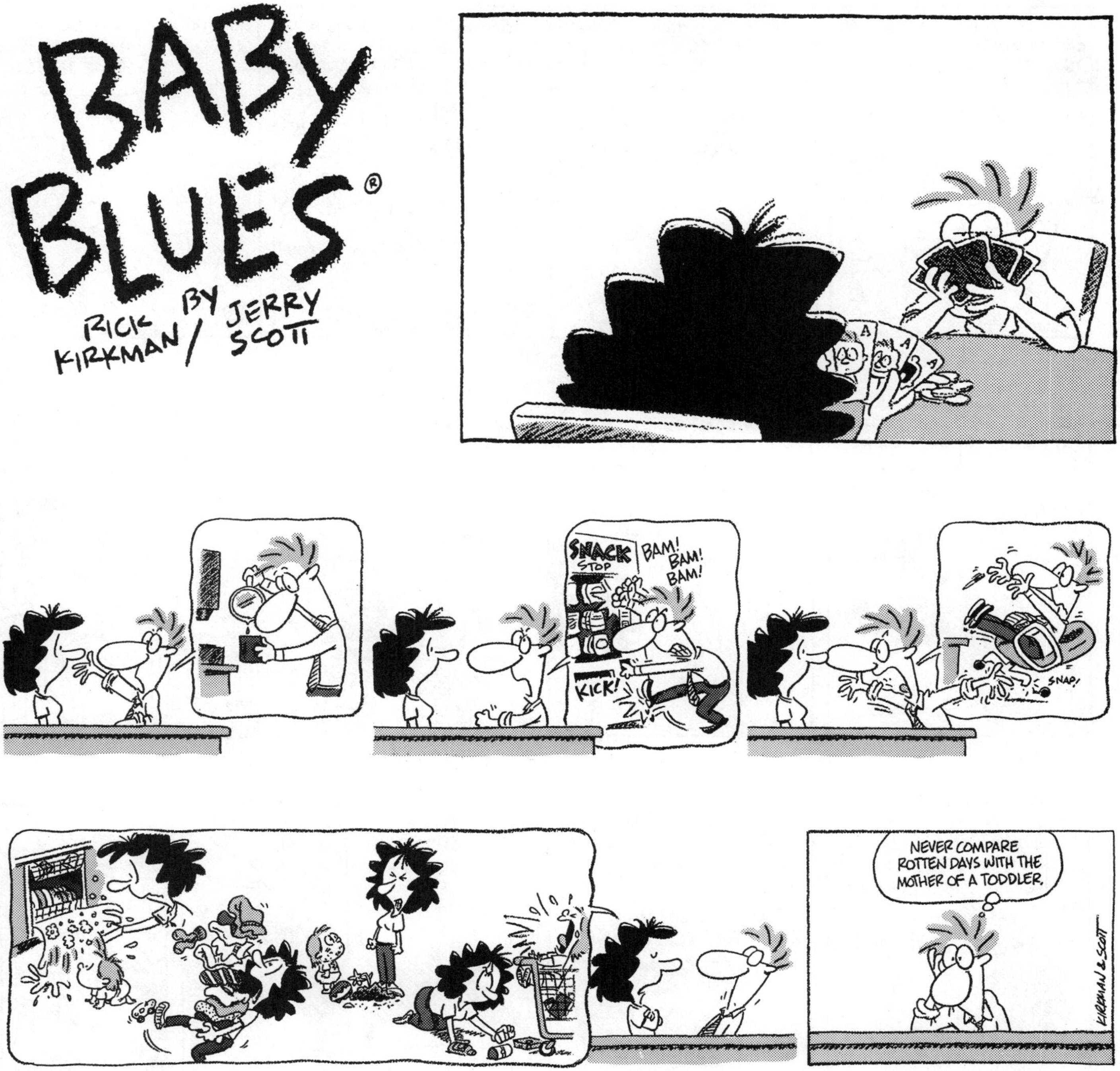
BABY BLUES®
BY RICK KIRKMAN / JERRY SCOTT
SNACK STOP
BAM! BAM! BAM!
KICK!
SNAP!
NEVER COMPARE ROTTEN DAYS WITH THE MOTHER OF A TODDLER.
KIRKMAN & SCOTT

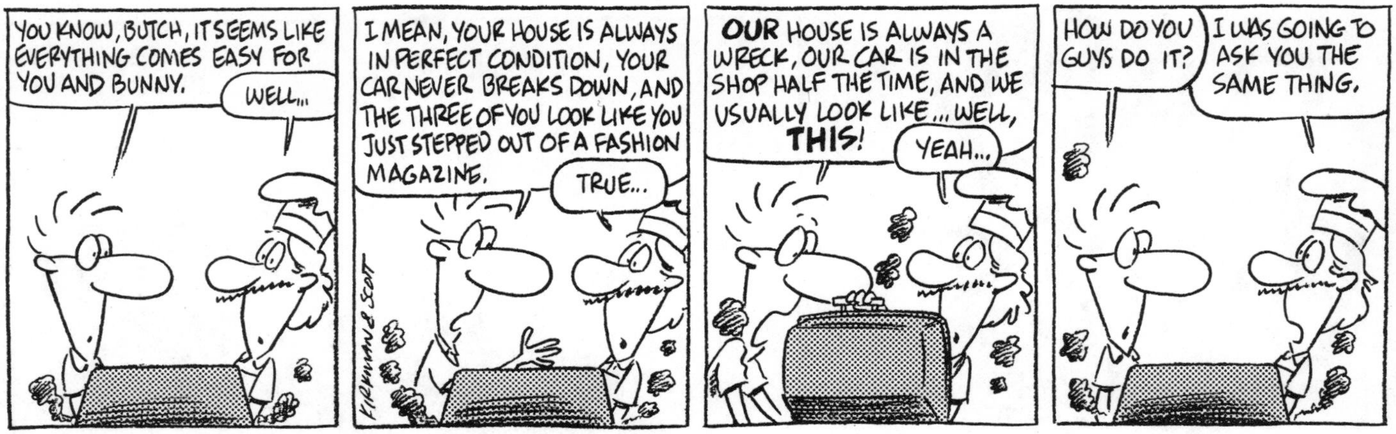
YOU KNOW, BUTCH, IT SEEMS LIKE EVERYTHING COMES EASY FOR YOU AND BUNNY.
WELL...
I MEAN, YOUR HOUSE IS ALWAYS IN PERFECT CONDITION, YOUR CAR NEVER BREAKS DOWN, AND THE THREE OF YOU LOOK LIKE YOU JUST STEPPED OUT OF A FASHION MAGAZINE.
TRUE...
KIRKMAN & SCOTT
OUR HOUSE IS ALWAYS A WRECK, OUR CAR IS IN THE SHOP HALF THE TIME, AND WE USUALLY LOOK LIKE... WELL, THIS!
YEAH...
HOW DO YOU GUYS DO IT?
I WAS GOING TO ASK YOU THE SAME THING.

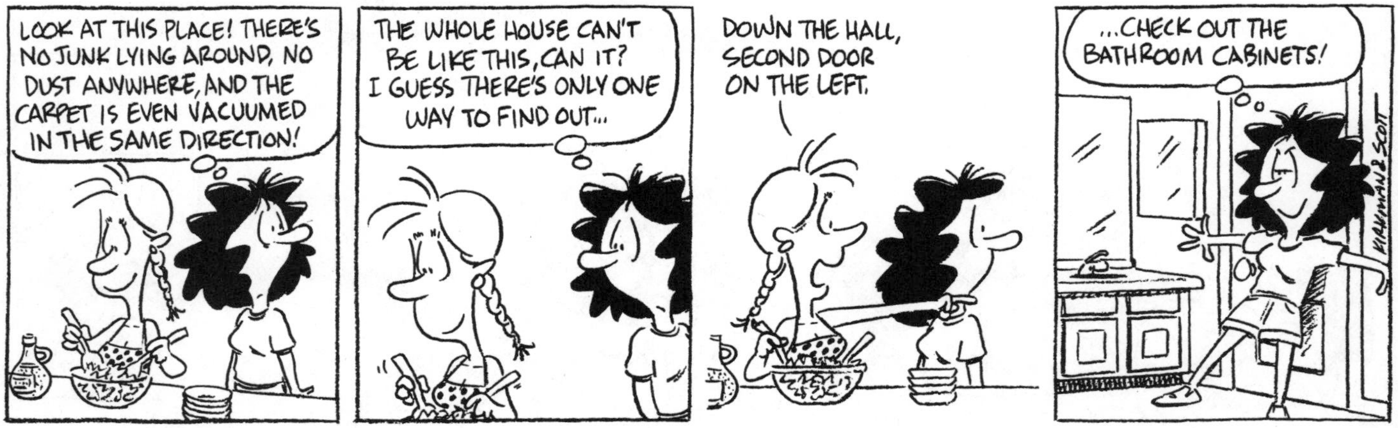
LOOK AT THIS PLACE! THERE'S NO JUNK LYING AROUND, NO DUST ANYWHERE, AND THE CARPET IS EVEN VACUUMED IN THE SAME DIRECTION!
THE WHOLE HOUSE CAN'T BE LIKE THIS, CAN IT? I GUESS THERE'S ONLY ONE WAY TO FIND OUT...
DOWN THE HALL, SECOND DOOR ON THE LEFT.
...CHECK OUT THE BATHROOM CABINETS!
KIRKMAN & SCOTT

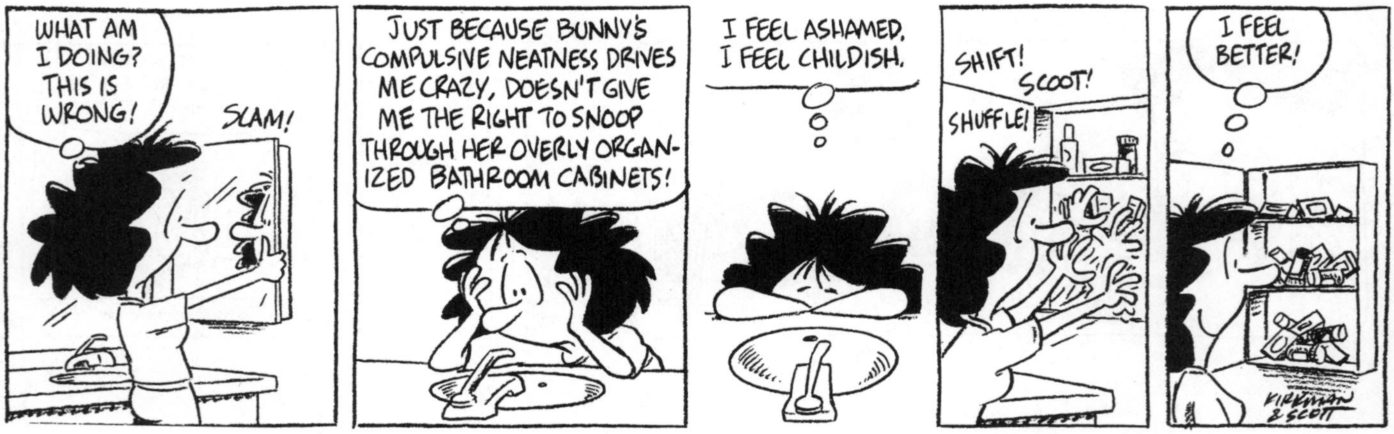
WHAT AM I DOING? THIS IS WRONG!
SLAM!
JUST BECAUSE BUNNY'S COMPULSIVE NEATNESS DRIVES ME CRAZY, DOESN'T GIVE ME THE RIGHT TO SNOOP THROUGH HER OVERLY ORGAN-IZED BATHROOM CABINETS!
I FEEL ASHAMED. I FEEL CHILDISH.
SHIFT!
SCOOT!
SHUFFLE!
I FEEL BETTER!
KIRKMAN & SCOTT

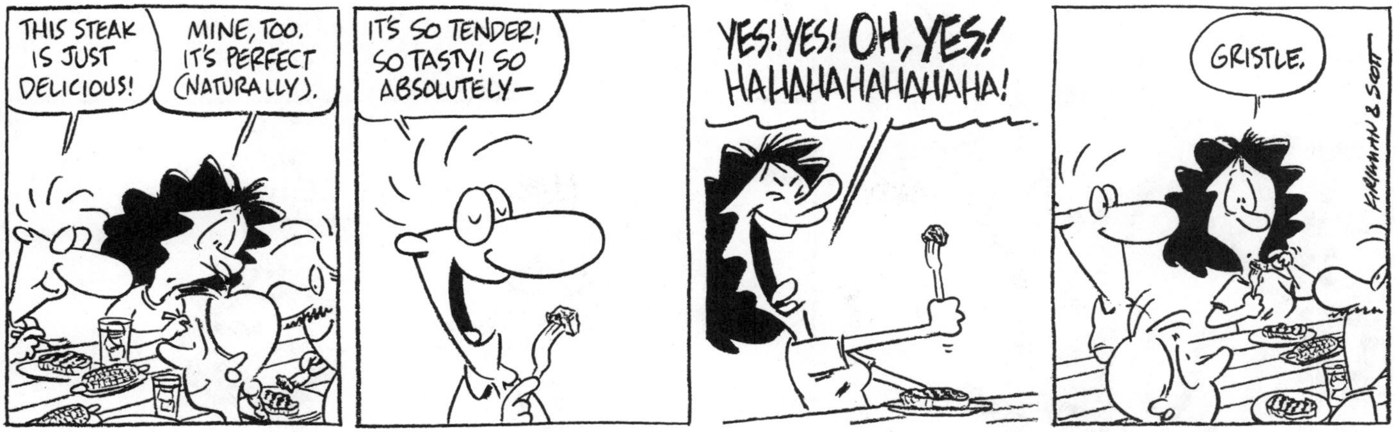
THIS STEAK IS JUST DELICIOUS!
MINE, TOO. IT'S PERFECT (NATURALLY).
IT'S SO TENDER! SO TASTY! SO ABSOLUTELY—
YES! YES! OH, YES! HAHAHAHAHAHAHA!
GRISTLE.
KIRKMAN & SCOTT

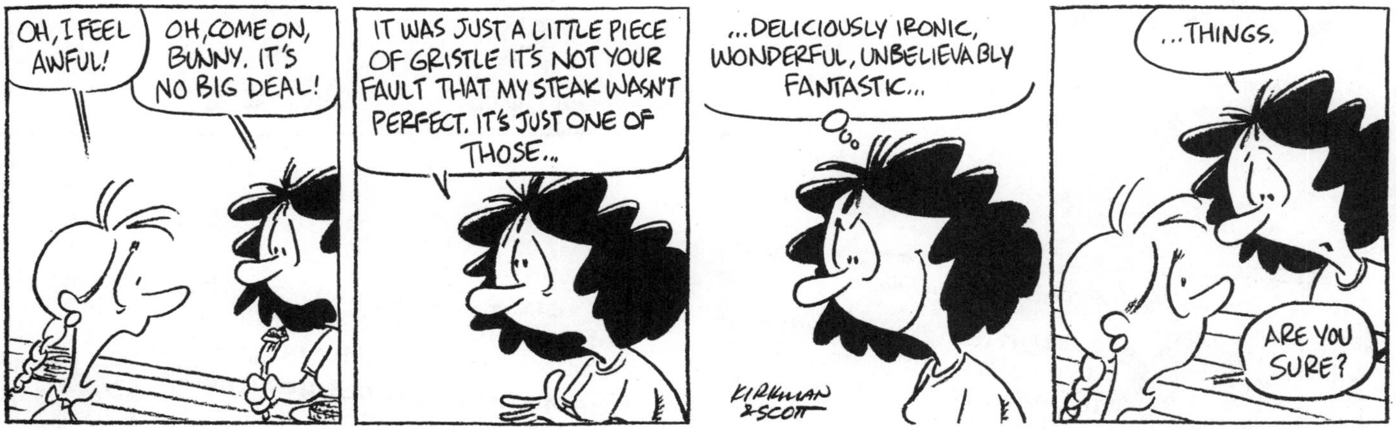
OH, I FEEL AWFUL!
OH, COME ON, BUNNY. IT'S NO BIG DEAL!
IT WAS JUST A LITTLE PIECE OF GRISTLE IT'S NOT YOUR FAULT THAT MY STEAK WASN'T PERFECT. IT'S JUST ONE OF THOSE...
...DELICIOUSLY IRONIC, WONDERFUL, UNBELIEVABLY FANTASTIC...
KIRKMAN & SCOTT
...THINGS.
ARE YOU SURE?

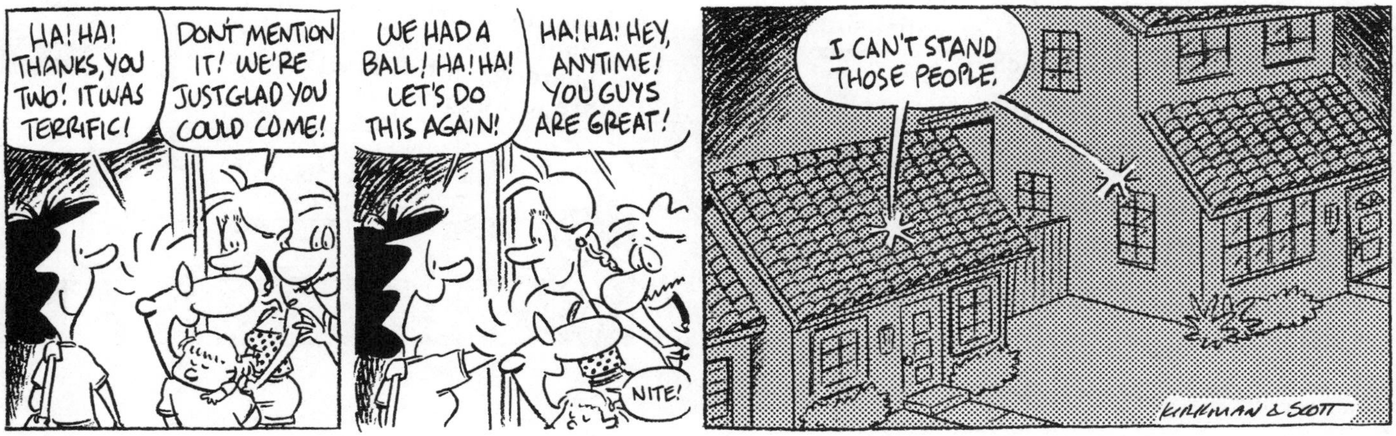
HA! HA! THANKS, YOU TWO! IT WAS TERRIFIC!
DON'T MENTION IT! WE'RE JUST GLAD YOU COULD COME!
WE HAD A BALL! HA! HA! LET'S DO THIS AGAIN!
HA! HA! HEY, ANYTIME! YOU GUYS ARE GREAT!
NITE!
I CAN'T STAND THOSE PEOPLE.
KIRKMAN & SCOTT

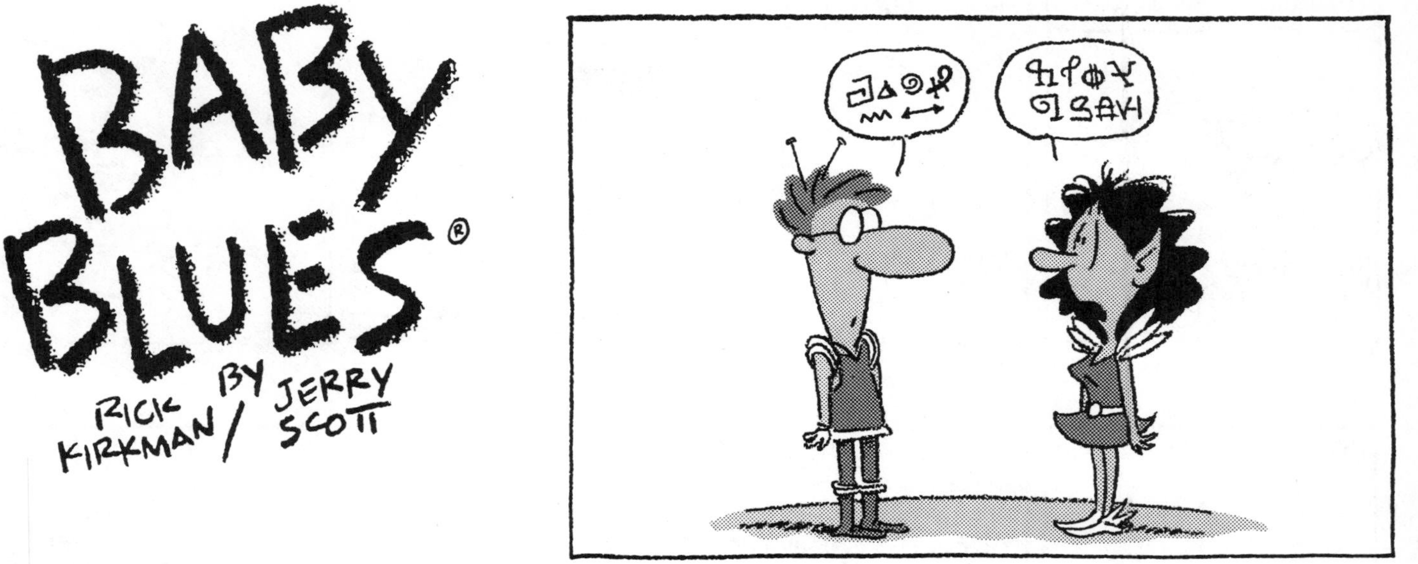
BABY BLUES®
BY
RICK KIRKMAN / JERRY SCOTT

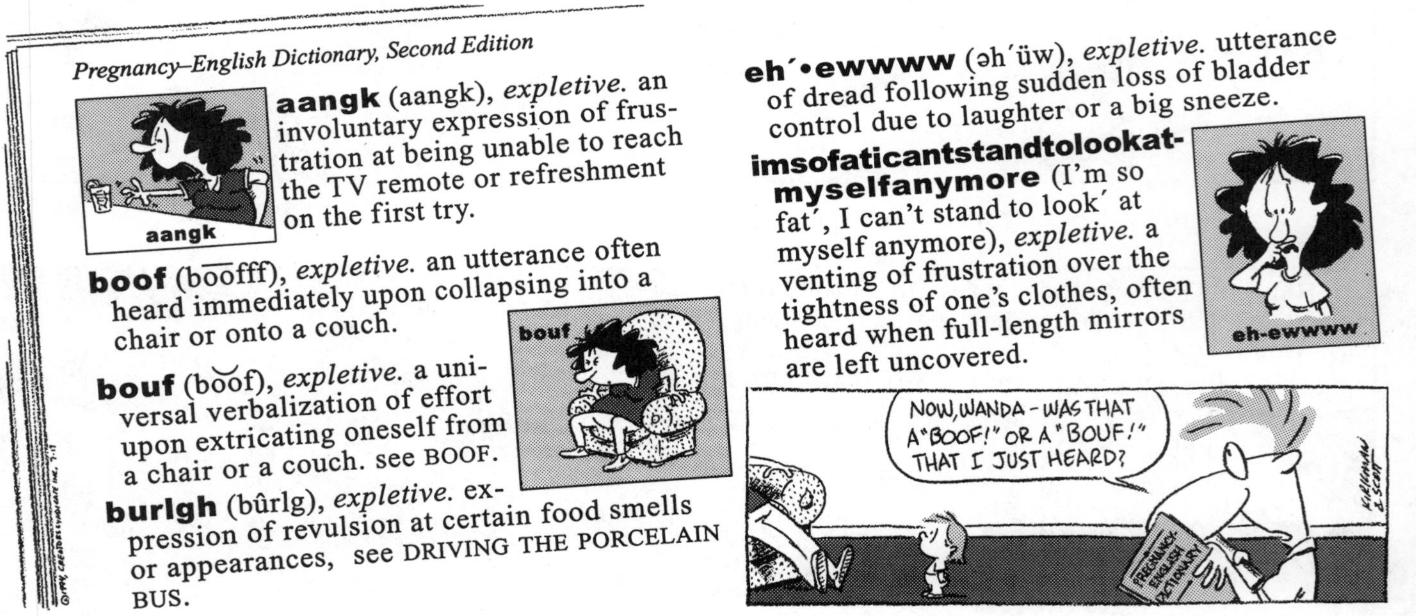
Pregnancy–English Dictionary, Second Edition
aangk
aangk (aangk), expletive. an involuntary expression of frustration at being unable to reach the TV remote or refreshment on the first try.
boof (bōōfff), expletive. an utterance often heard immediately upon collapsing into a chair or onto a couch.
bouf
bouf (bŏŏf), expletive. a universal verbalization of effort upon extricating oneself from a chair or a couch. see BOOF.
burlgh (bûrlg), expletive. expression of revulsion at certain food smells or appearances, see DRIVING THE PORCELAIN BUS.
eh´•ewwww (əh´üw), expletive. utterance of dread following sudden loss of bladder control due to laughter or a big sneeze.
imsofaticantstandtolookatmyselfanymore (I'm so fat´, I can't stand to look´ at myself anymore), expletive. a venting of frustration over the tightness of one's clothes, often heard when full-length mirrors are left uncovered.
eh-ewwww
NOW, WANDA - WAS THAT A "BOOF!" OR A "BOUF!" THAT I JUST HEARD?
PREGNANCY ENGLISH DICTIONARY
KIRKMAN & SCOTT

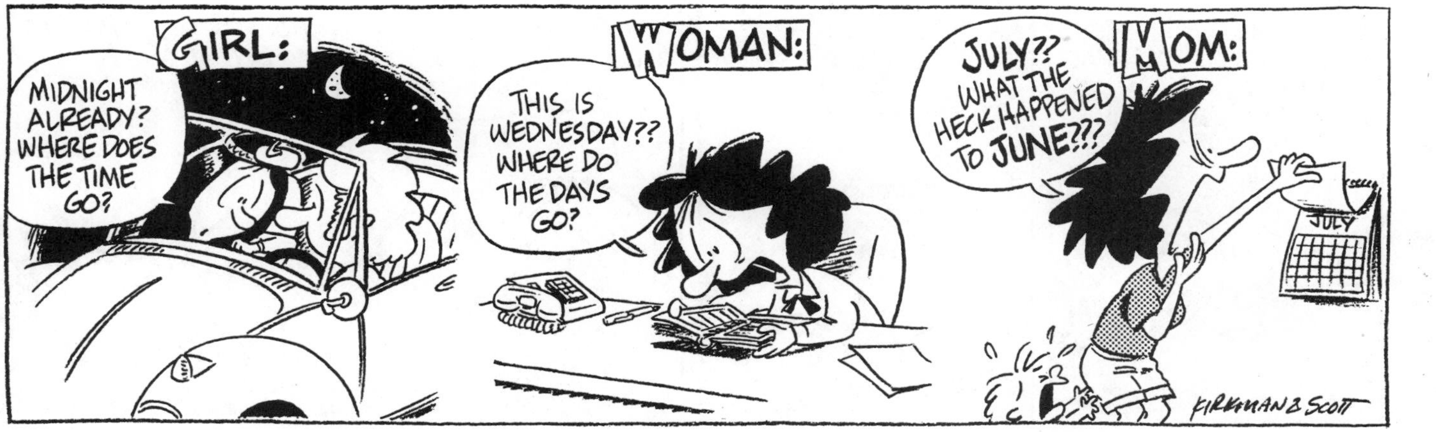
GIRL:
MIDNIGHT ALREADY? WHERE DOES THE TIME GO?
WOMAN:
THIS IS WEDNESDAY?? WHERE DO THE DAYS GO?
MOM:
JULY?? WHAT THE HECK HAPPENED TO JUNE???
JULY
KIRKMAN & SCOTT

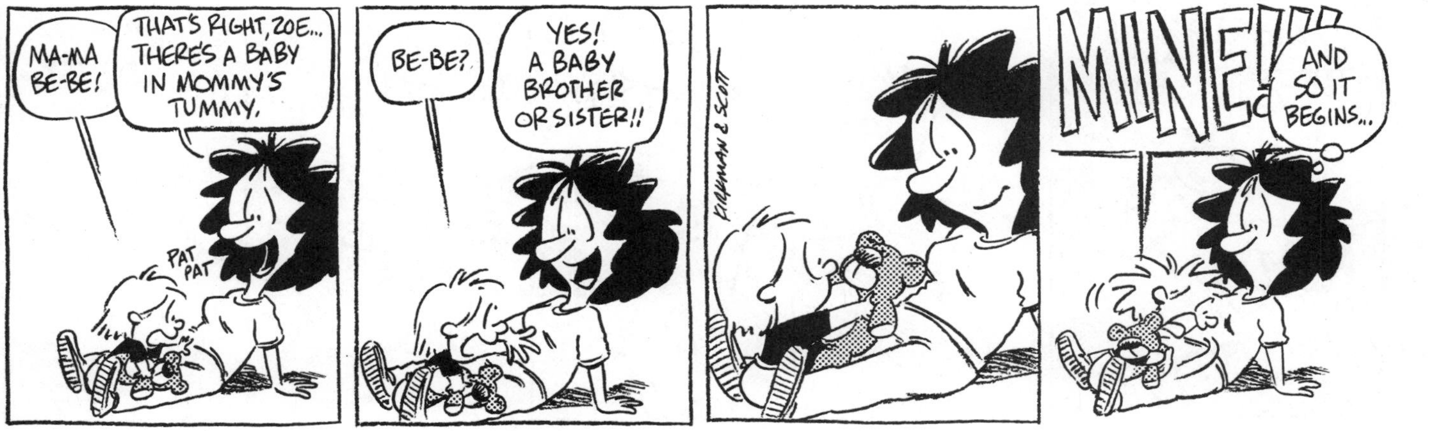
MA-MA BE-BE!
THAT'S RIGHT, ZOE... THERE'S A BABY IN MOMMY'S TUMMY.
PAT PAT
BE-BE?
YES! A BABY BROTHER OR SISTER!!
KIRKMAN & SCOTT
MINE!!
AND SO IT BEGINS...

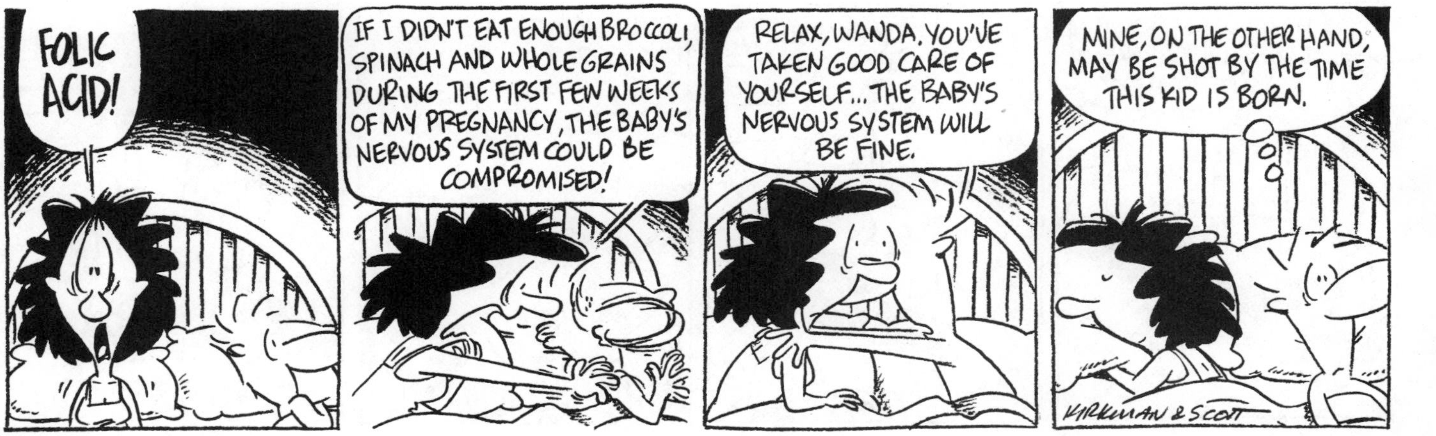
FOLIC ACID!
IF I DIDN'T EAT ENOUGH BROCCOLI, SPINACH AND WHOLE GRAINS DURING THE FIRST FEW WEEKS OF MY PREGNANCY, THE BABY'S NERVOUS SYSTEM COULD BE COMPROMISED!
RELAX, WANDA. YOU'VE TAKEN GOOD CARE OF YOURSELF... THE BABY'S NERVOUS SYSTEM WILL BE FINE.
MINE, ON THE OTHER HAND, MAY BE SHOT BY THE TIME THIS KID IS BORN.
KIRKMAN & SCOTT

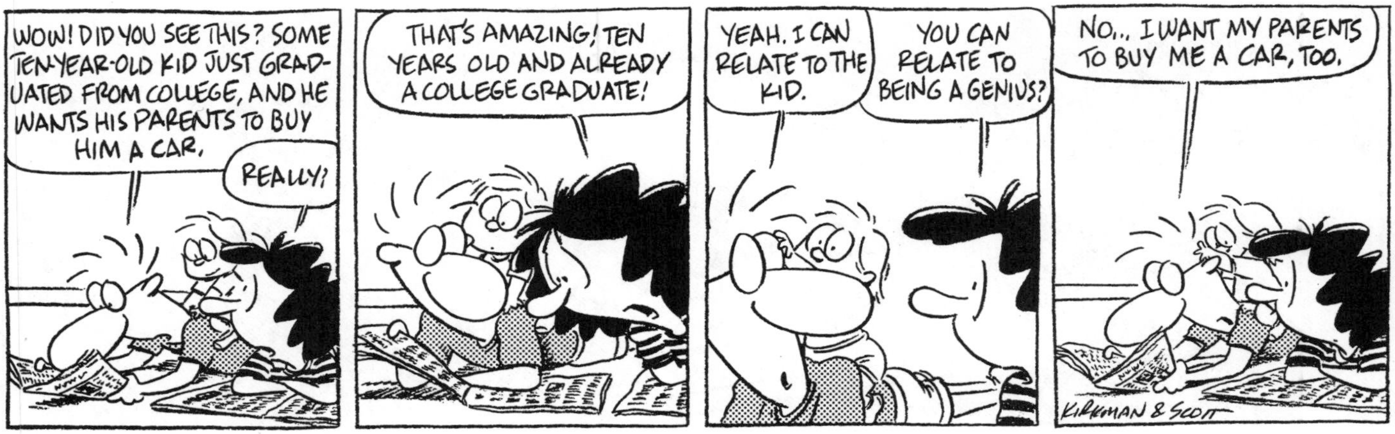
WOW! DID YOU SEE THIS? SOME TEN-YEAR-OLD KID JUST GRADUATED FROM COLLEGE, AND HE WANTS HIS PARENTS TO BUY HIM A CAR.
REALLY?
THAT'S AMAZING! TEN YEARS OLD AND ALREADY A COLLEGE GRADUATE!
YEAH. I CAN RELATE TO THE KID.
YOU CAN RELATE TO BEING A GENIUS?
NO... I WANT MY PARENTS TO BUY ME A CAR, TOO.
KIRKMAN & SCOTT

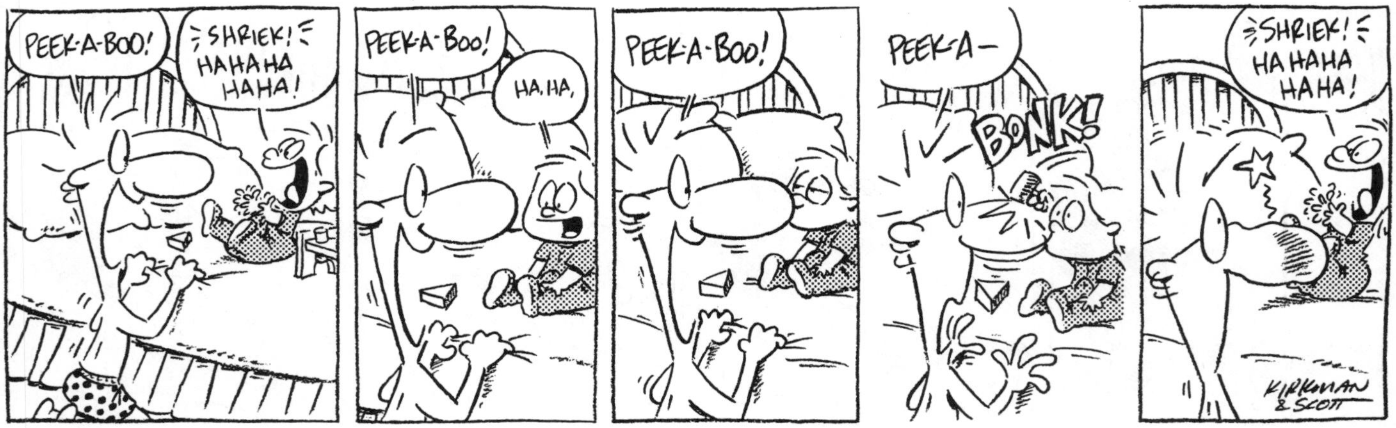
PEEK-A-BOO!
SHRIEK! HAHAHA HAHA!
PEEK-A-BOO!
HA, HA,
PEEK-A-BOO!
PEEK-A-
BONK!
SHRIEK! HA HAHA HAHA!
KIRKMAN & SCOTT

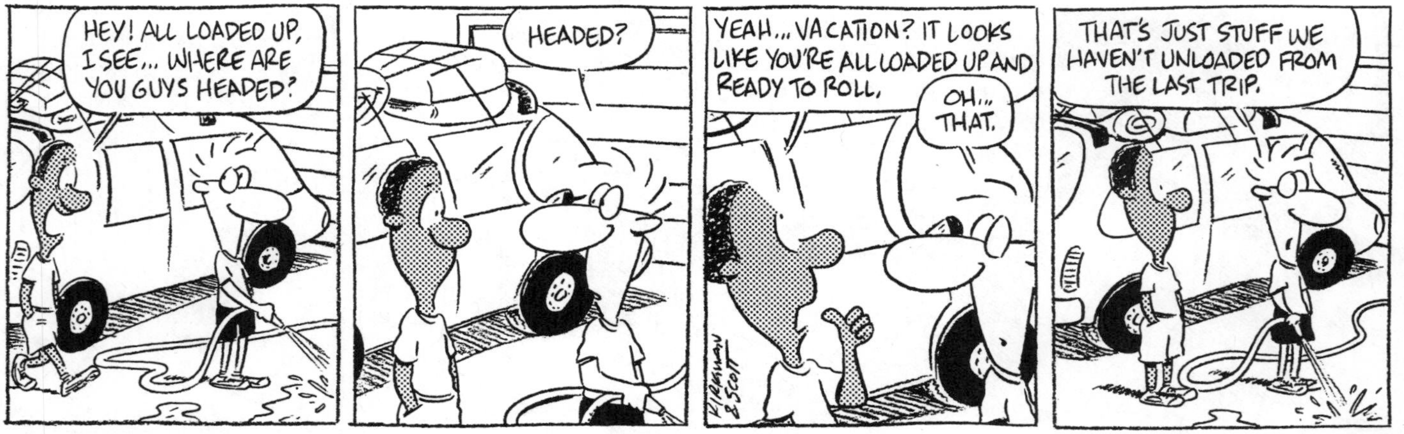
HEY! ALL LOADED UP, I SEE... WHERE ARE YOU GUYS HEADED?
HEADED?
YEAH... VACATION? IT LOOKS LIKE YOU'RE ALL LOADED UP AND READY TO ROLL.
OH... THAT.
KIRKMAN & SCOTT
THAT'S JUST STUFF WE HAVEN'T UNLOADED FROM THE LAST TRIP.

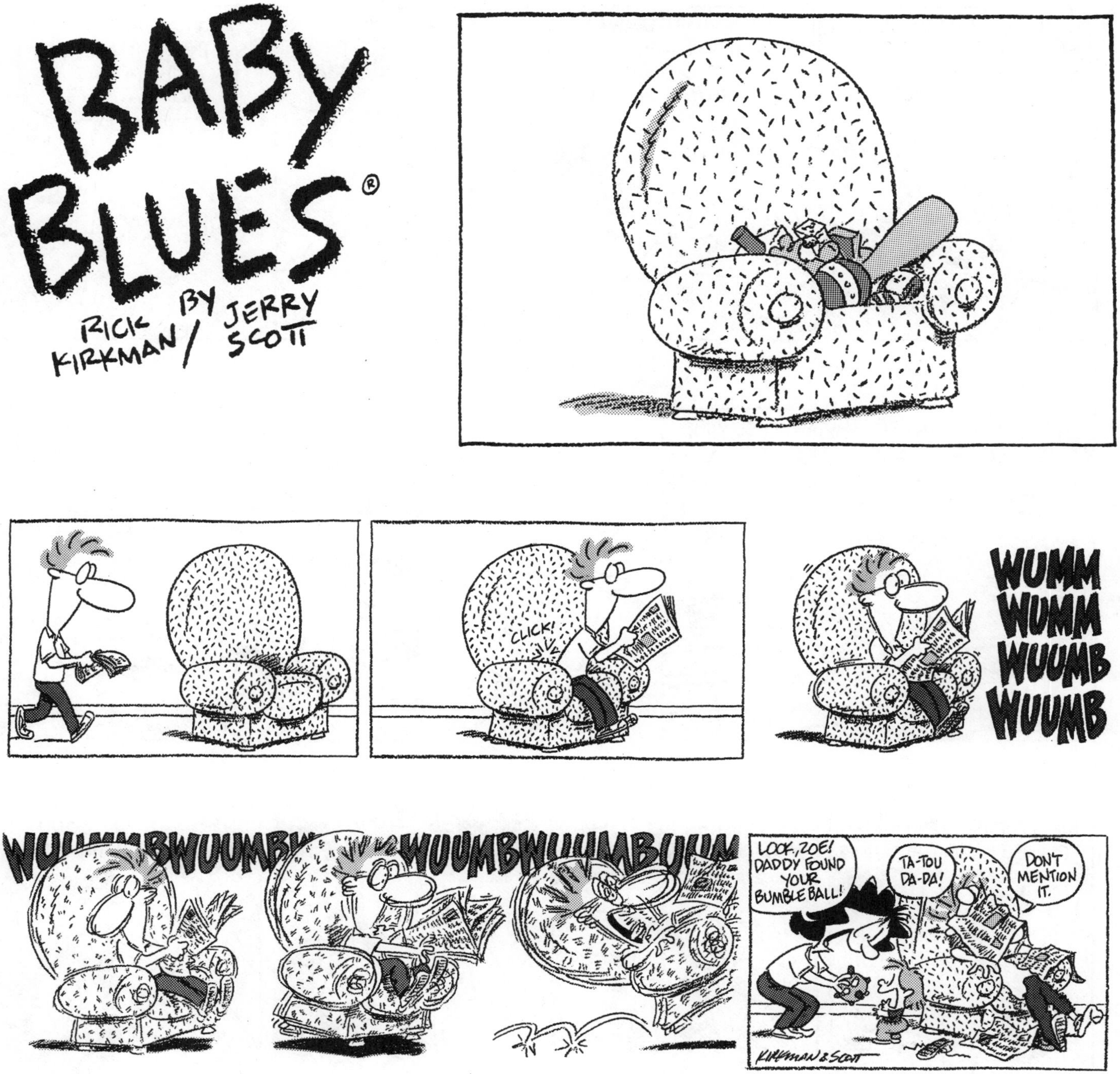
BABY BLUES®
BY RICK KIRKMAN / JERRY SCOTT
CLICK!
WUMM
WUMM
WUUMB
WUUMB
WUUMMBWUUMBW
WUUMBWUUMBUUM
LOOK, ZOE! DADDY FOUND YOUR BUMBLE BALL!
TA-TOU DA-DA!
DON'T MENTION IT.
KIRKMAN & SCOTT

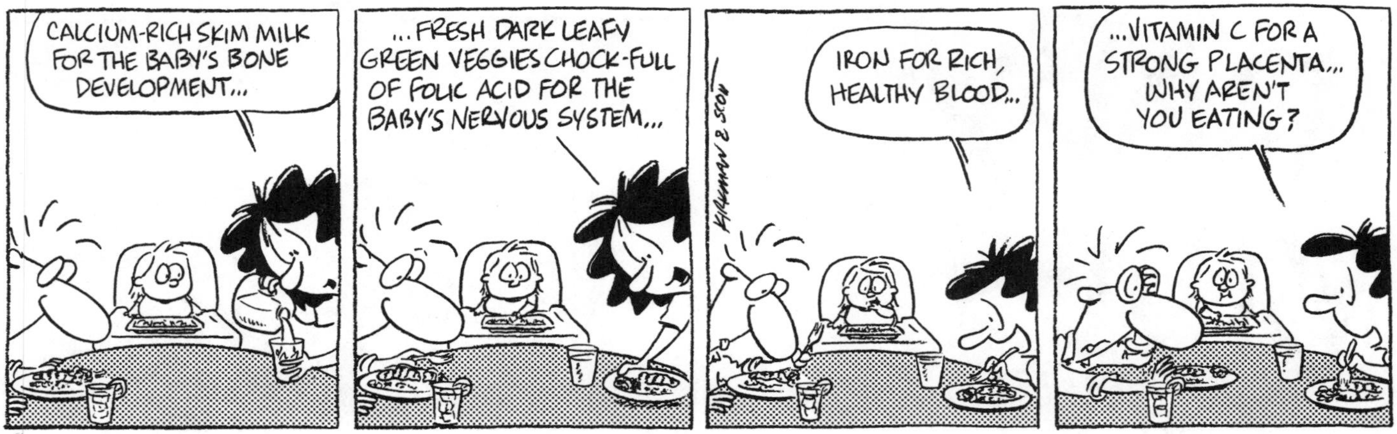
CALCIUM-RICH SKIM MILK FOR THE BABY'S BONE DEVELOPMENT...
...FRESH DARK LEAFY GREEN VEGGIES CHOCK-FULL OF FOLIC ACID FOR THE BABY'S NERVOUS SYSTEM...
IRON FOR RICH, HEALTHY BLOOD...
...VITAMIN C FOR A STRONG PLACENTA... WHY AREN'T YOU EATING?

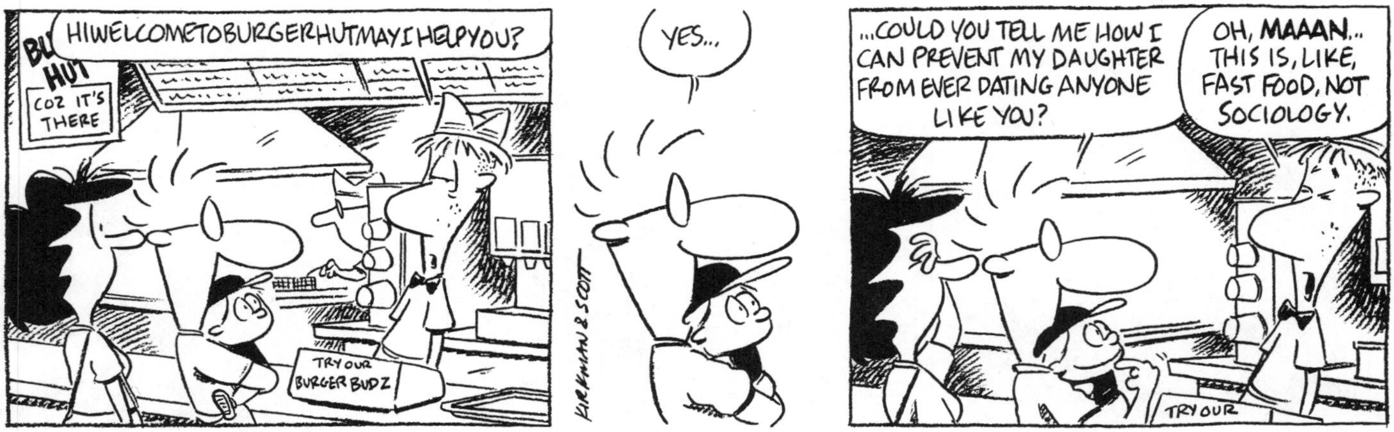
HIWELCOMETOBURGERHUTMAYIHELPYOU?
COZ IT'S THERE
TRY OUR BURGER BUDZ
KIRKMAN & SCOTT
YES...
...COULD YOU TELL ME HOW I CAN PREVENT MY DAUGHTER FROM EVER DATING ANYONE LIKE YOU?
OH, MAAAN... THIS IS, LIKE, FAST FOOD, NOT SOCIOLOGY.
TRY OUR

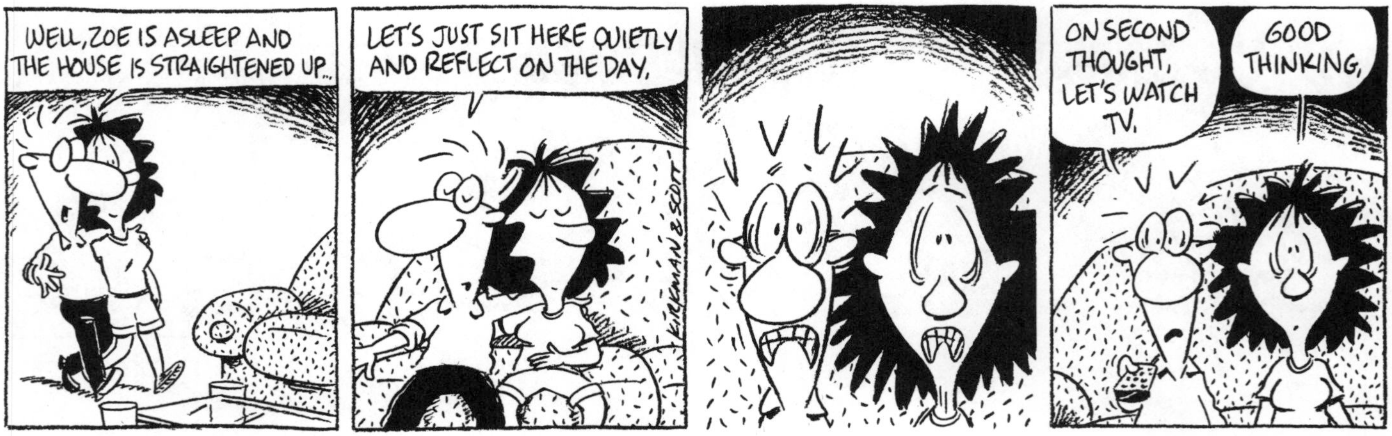
WELL, ZOE IS ASLEEP AND THE HOUSE IS STRAIGHTENED UP...
LET'S JUST SIT HERE QUIETLY AND REFLECT ON THE DAY.
KIRKMAN & SCOTT
ON SECOND THOUGHT, LET'S WATCH TV.
GOOD THINKING.

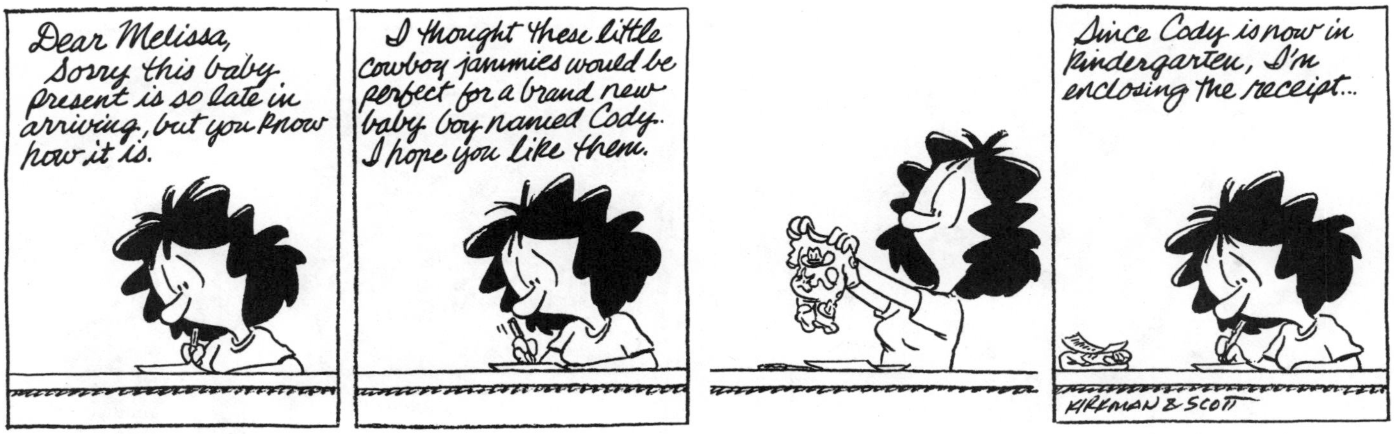
Dear Melissa,
Sorry this baby present is so late in arriving, but you know how it is.
I thought these little cowboy jammies would be perfect for a brand new baby boy named Cody. I hope you like them.
Since Cody is now in kindergarten, I'm enclosing the receipt...
KIRKMAN & SCOTT

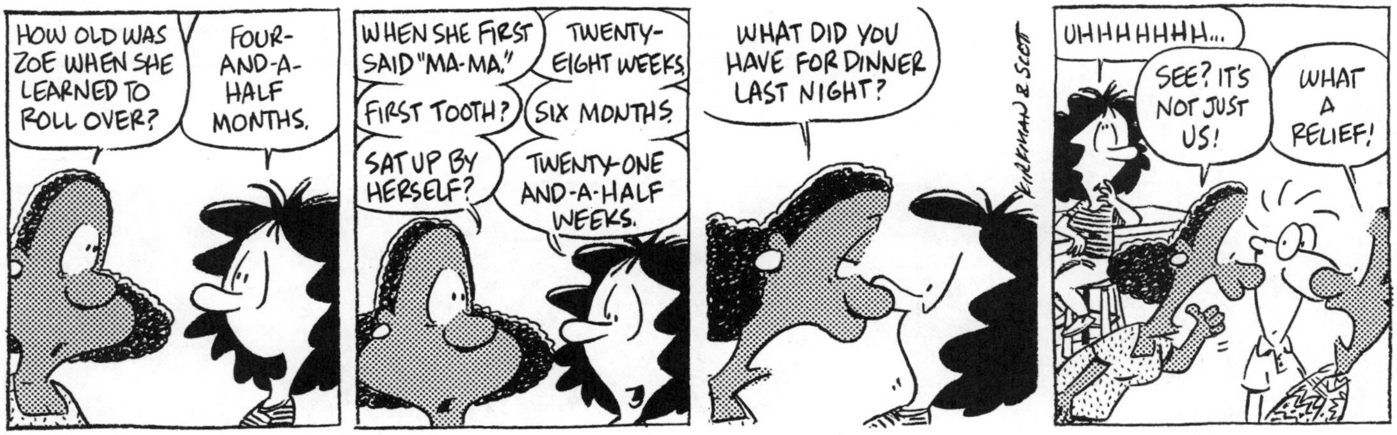
HOW OLD WAS ZOE WHEN SHE LEARNED TO ROLL OVER?
FOUR-AND-A-HALF MONTHS.
WHEN SHE FIRST SAID "MA-MA."
TWENTY-EIGHT WEEKS.
FIRST TOOTH?
SIX MONTHS.
SAT UP BY HERSELF?
TWENTY-ONE AND-A-HALF WEEKS.
WHAT DID YOU HAVE FOR DINNER LAST NIGHT?
KIRKMAN & SCOTT
UHHHHHHH...
SEE? IT'S NOT JUST US!
WHAT A RELIEF!

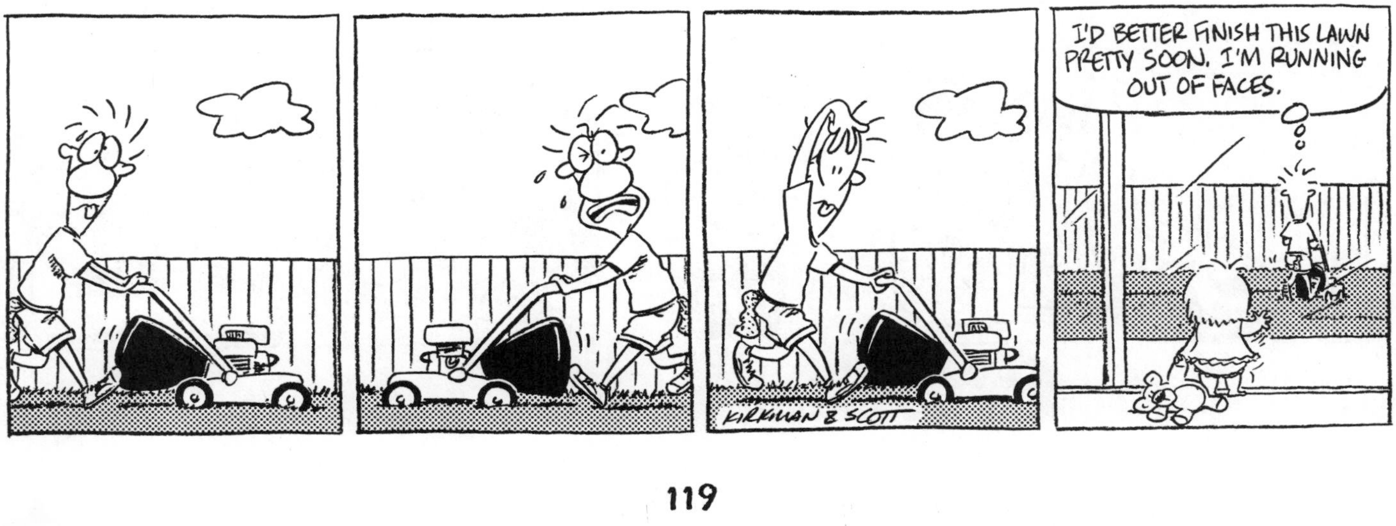
KIRKMAN & SCOTT
I'D BETTER FINISH THIS LAWN PRETTY SOON. I'M RUNNING OUT OF FACES.

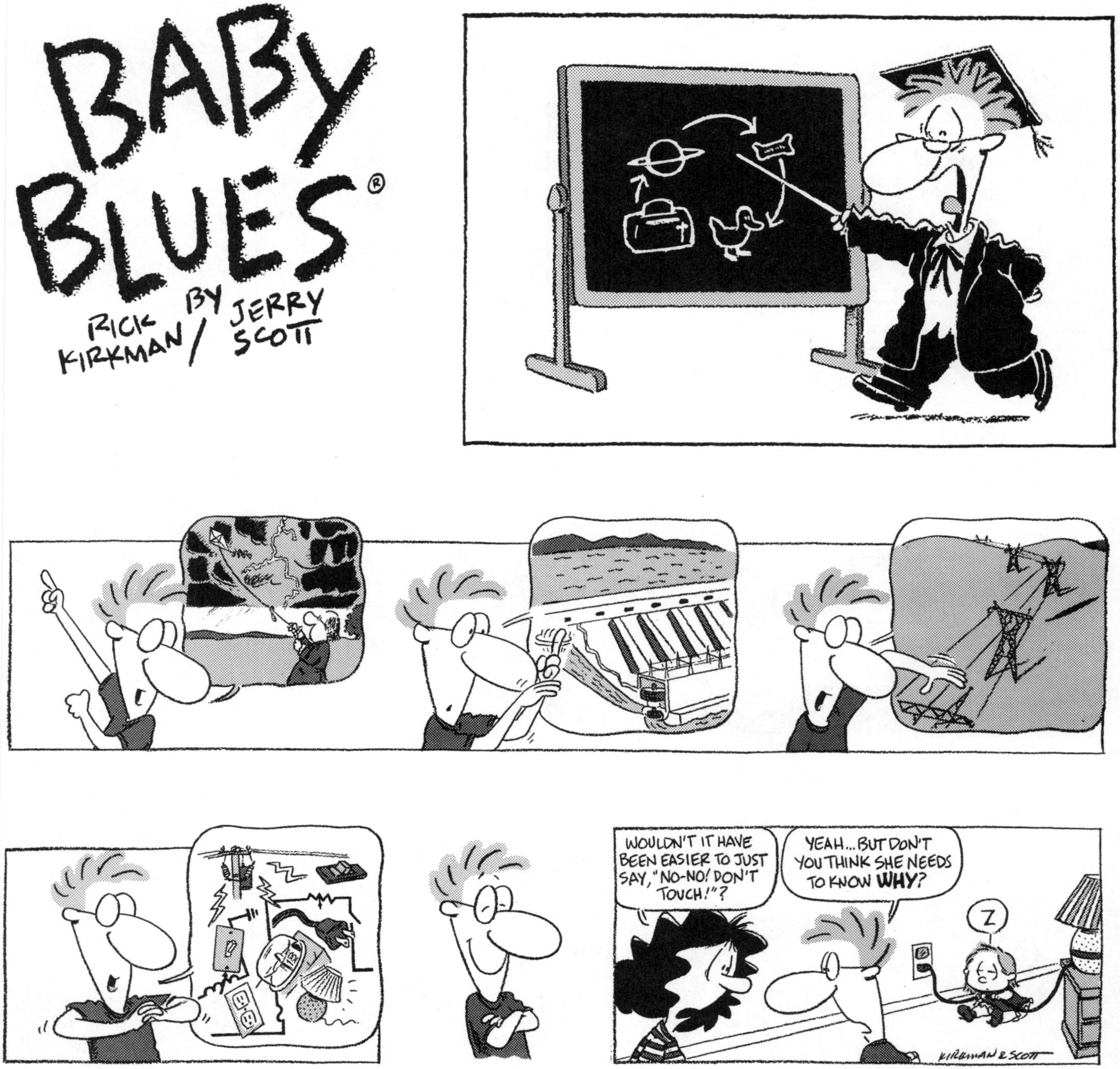
BABY BLUES®
BY RICK KIRKMAN / JERRY SCOTT
WOULDN'T IT HAVE BEEN EASIER TO JUST SAY, "NO-NO! DON'T TOUCH!"?
YEAH...BUT DON'T YOU THINK SHE NEEDS TO KNOW WHY?
Z
KIRKMAN & SCOTT

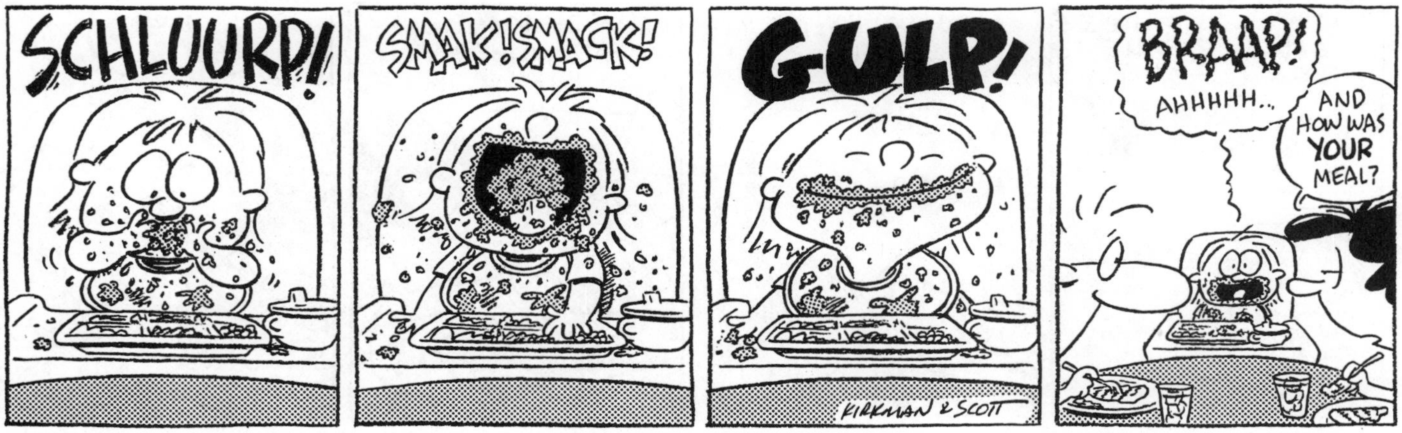
SCHLUURP!
SMAK! SMACK!
GULP!
KIRKMAN & SCOTT
BRAAP!
AHHHHH...
AND HOW WAS YOUR MEAL?

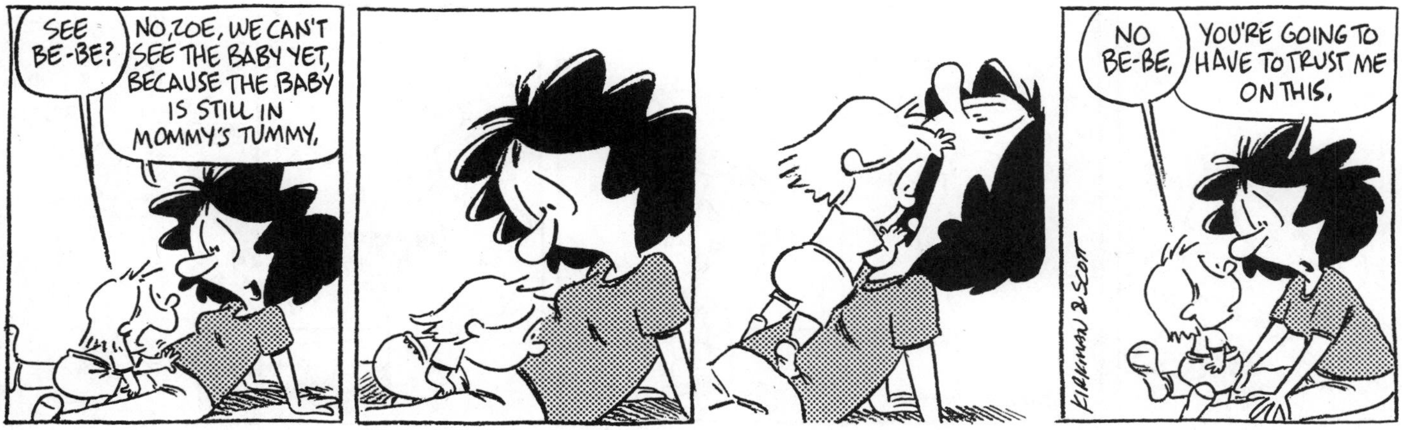
SEE BE-BE?
NO, ZOE, WE CAN'T SEE THE BABY YET, BECAUSE THE BABY IS STILL IN MOMMY'S TUMMY.
KIRKMAN & SCOTT
NO BE-BE.
YOU'RE GOING TO HAVE TO TRUST ME ON THIS.

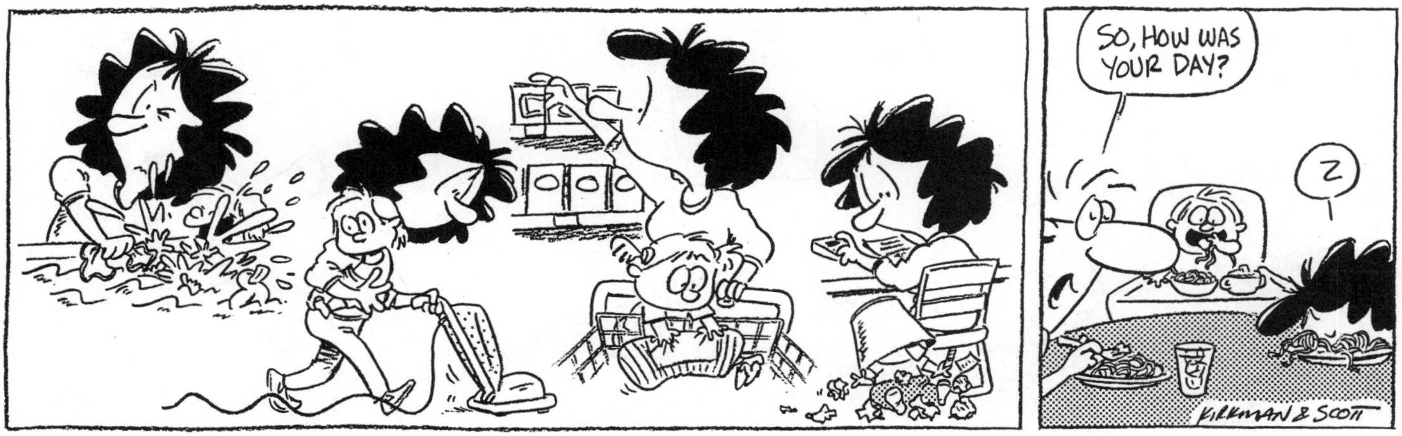
SO, HOW WAS YOUR DAY?
Z
KIRKMAN & SCOTT

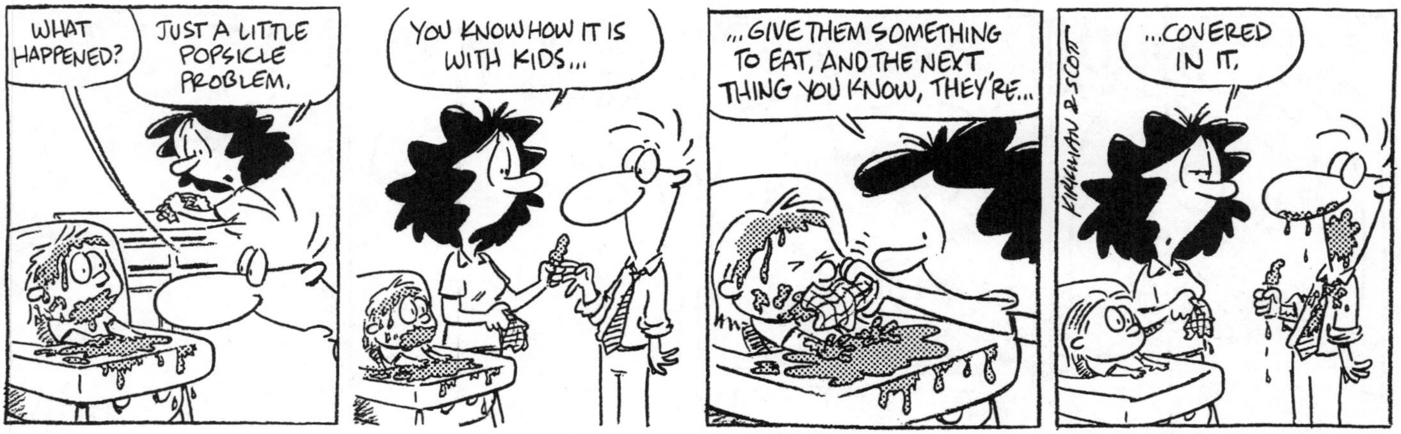
WHAT HAPPENED?
JUST A LITTLE POPSICLE PROBLEM.
YOU KNOW HOW IT IS WITH KIDS...
...GIVE THEM SOMETHING TO EAT, AND THE NEXT THING YOU KNOW, THEY'RE...
KIRKMAN & SCOTT
...COVERED IN IT.

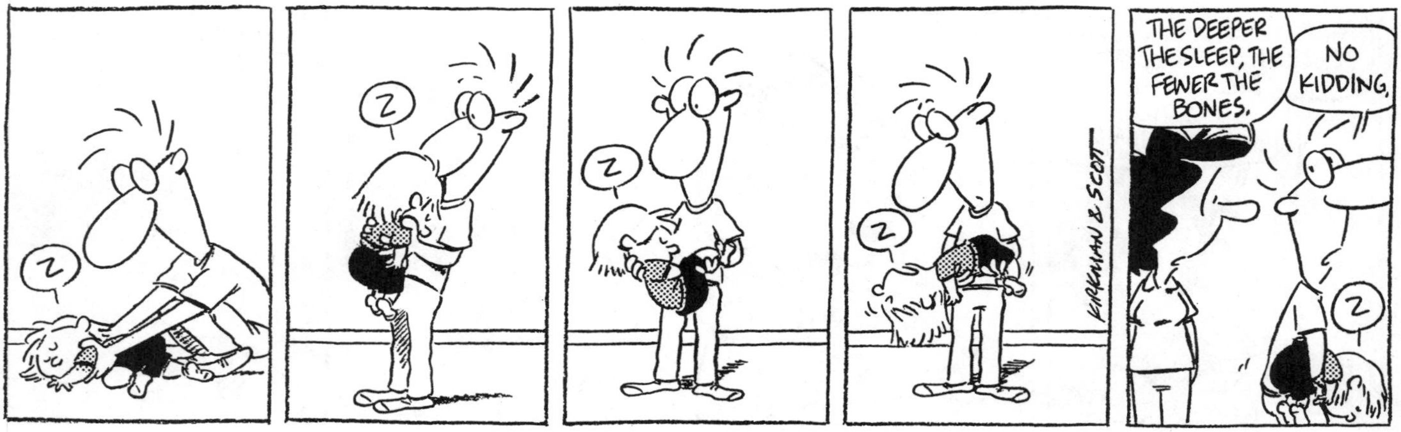
KIRKMAN & SCOTT
THE DEEPER THE SLEEP, THE FEWER THE BONES.
NO KIDDING.

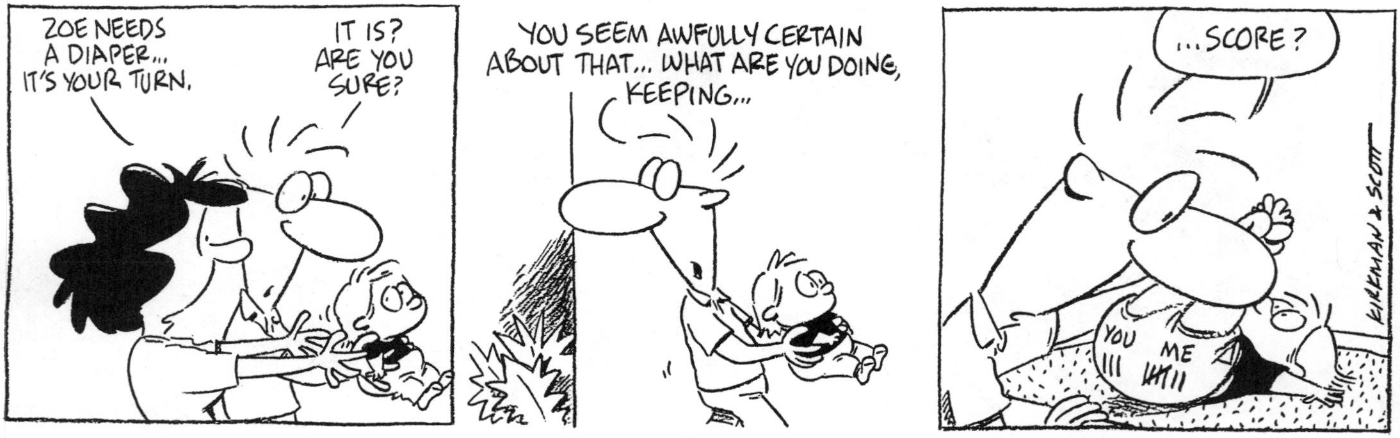
ZOE NEEDS A DIAPER... IT'S YOUR TURN.
IT IS? ARE YOU SURE?
YOU SEEM AWFULLY CERTAIN ABOUT THAT... WHAT ARE YOU DOING, KEEPING...
...SCORE?
KIRKMAN & SCOTT
YOU
ME

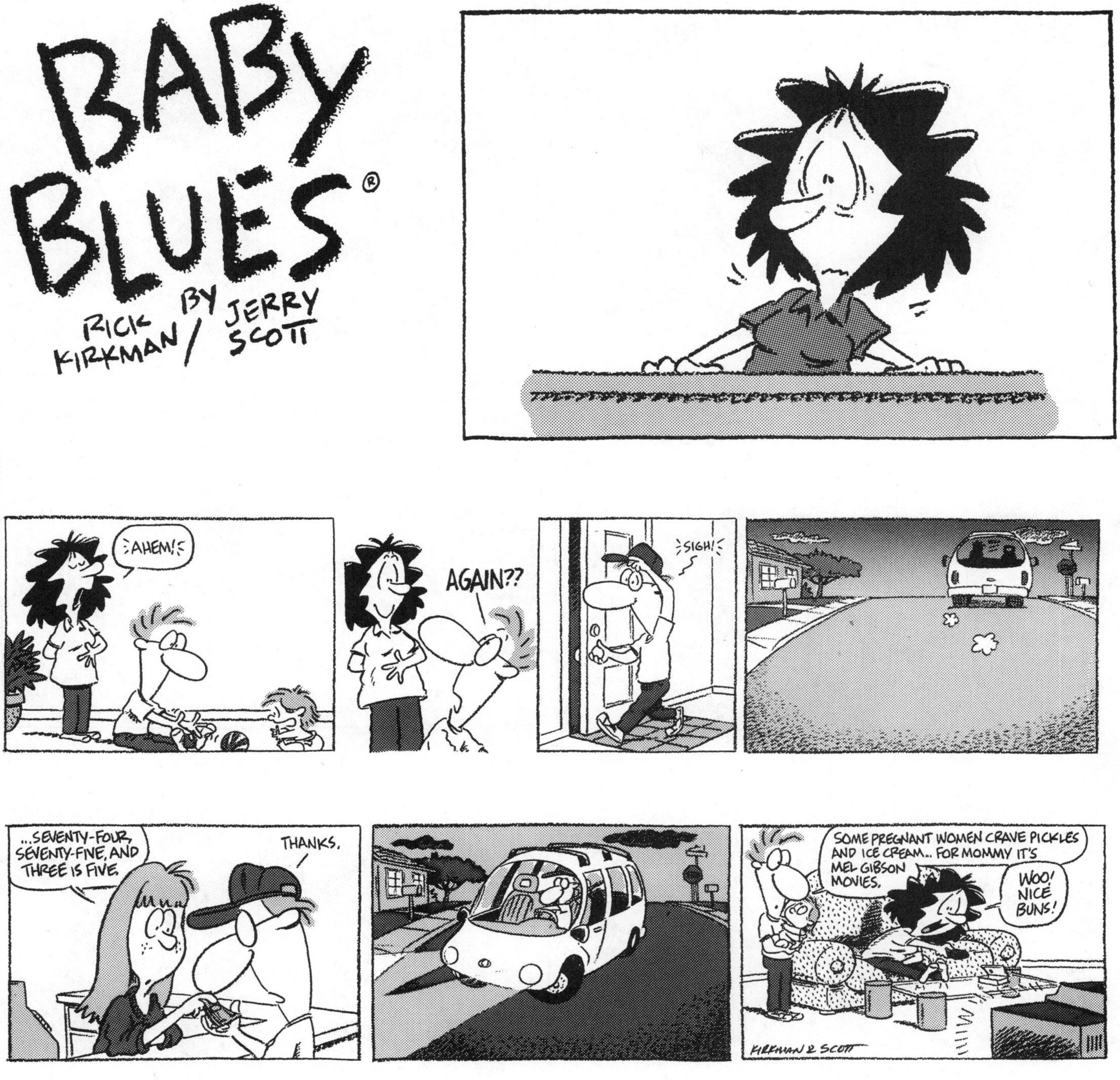
BABY BLUES®
BY RICK KIRKMAN / JERRY SCOTT
AHEM!
AGAIN??
SIGH!
...SEVENTY-FOUR, SEVENTY-FIVE, AND THREE IS FIVE.
THANKS.
SOME PREGNANT WOMEN CRAVE PICKLES AND ICE CREAM.. FOR MOMMY IT'S MEL GIBSON MOVIES.
WOO! NICE BUNS!
KIRKMAN & SCOTT

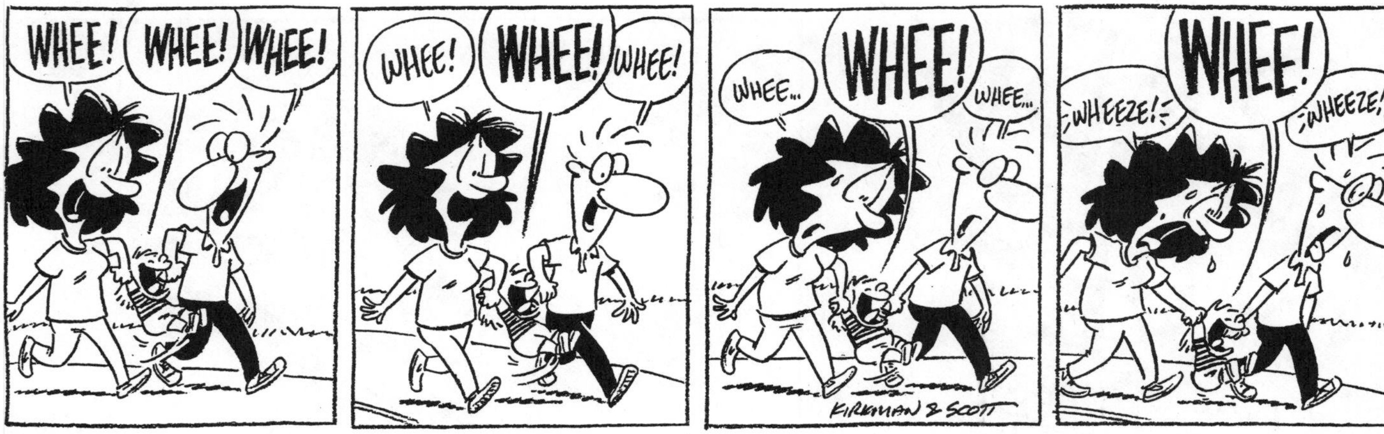
WHEE!
WHEE!
WHEE!
WHEE!
WHEE!
WHEE!
WHEE...
WHEE!
WHEE...
KIRKMAN & SCOTT
WHEEZE!
WHEE!
WHEEZE!

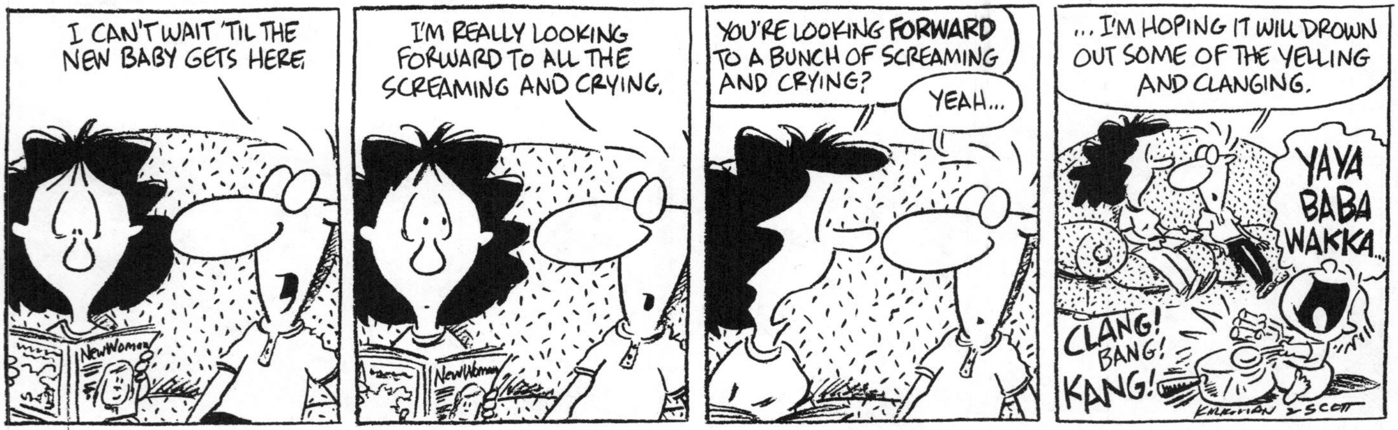
I CAN'T WAIT 'TIL THE NEW BABY GETS HERE.
NewWoman
I'M REALLY LOOKING FORWARD TO ALL THE SCREAMING AND CRYING.
YOU'RE LOOKING FORWARD TO A BUNCH OF SCREAMING AND CRYING?
YEAH...
... I'M HOPING IT WILL DROWN OUT SOME OF THE YELLING AND CLANGING.
YAYA BABA WAKKA...
CLANG! BANG! KANG!
KIRKMAN & SCOTT

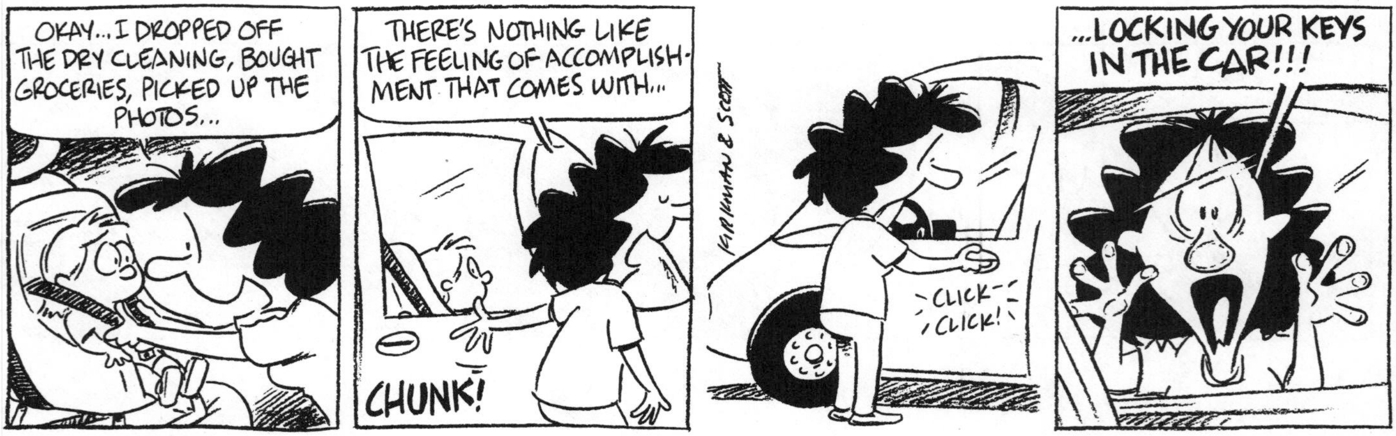
OKAY... I DROPPED OFF THE DRY CLEANING, BOUGHT GROCERIES, PICKED UP THE PHOTOS...
THERE'S NOTHING LIKE THE FEELING OF ACCOMPLISHMENT THAT COMES WITH...
CHUNK!
KIRKMAN & SCOTT
CLICK CLICK!
...LOCKING YOUR KEYS IN THE CAR!!!

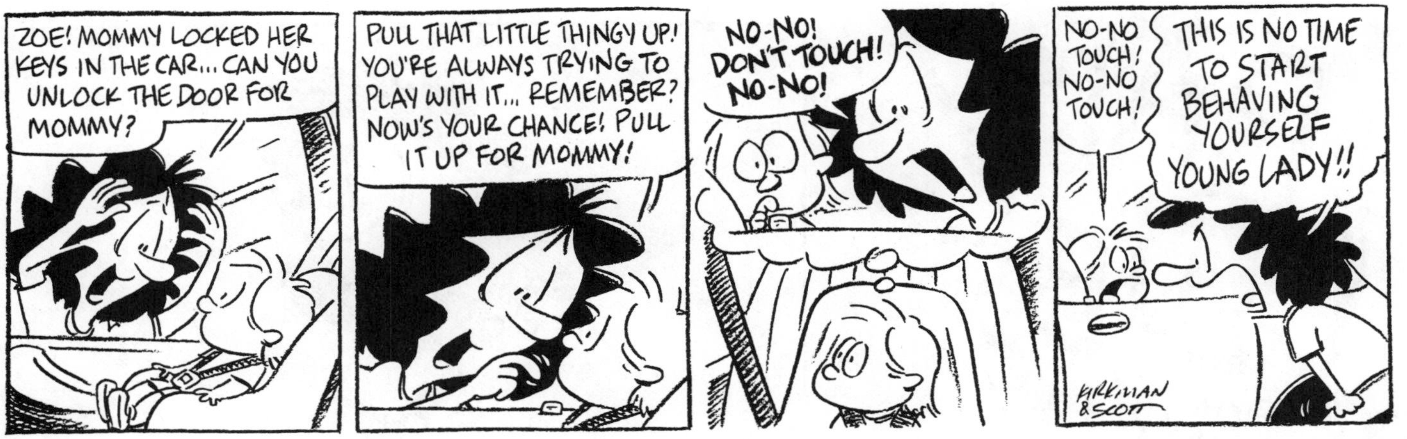
ZOE! MOMMY LOCKED HER KEYS IN THE CAR... CAN YOU UNLOCK THE DOOR FOR MOMMY?
PULL THAT LITTLE THINGY UP! YOU'RE ALWAYS TRYING TO PLAY WITH IT... REMEMBER? NOW'S YOUR CHANCE! PULL IT UP FOR MOMMY!
NO-NO! DON'T TOUCH! NO-NO!
NO-NO TOUCH! NO-NO TOUCH!
THIS IS NO TIME TO START BEHAVING YOURSELF YOUNG LADY!!
KIRKMAN & SCOTT

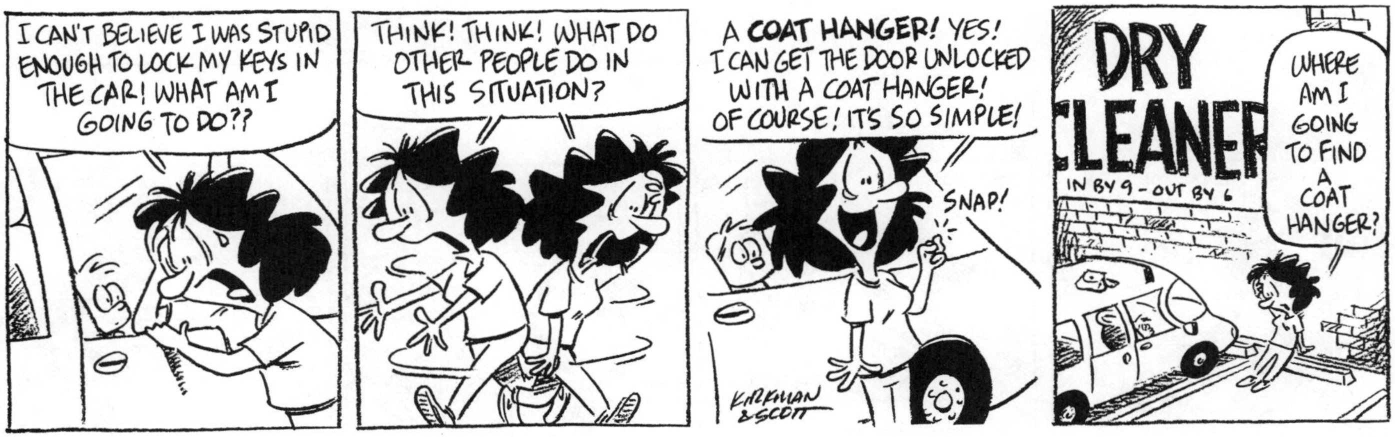
I CAN'T BELIEVE I WAS STUPID ENOUGH TO LOCK MY KEYS IN THE CAR! WHAT AM I GOING TO DO??
THINK! THINK! WHAT DO OTHER PEOPLE DO IN THIS SITUATION?
A COAT HANGER! YES! I CAN GET THE DOOR UNLOCKED WITH A COAT HANGER! OF COURSE! IT'S SO SIMPLE!
SNAP!
KIRKMAN & SCOTT
DRY CLEANER
IN BY 9 - OUT BY 6
WHERE AM I GOING TO FIND A COAT HANGER?

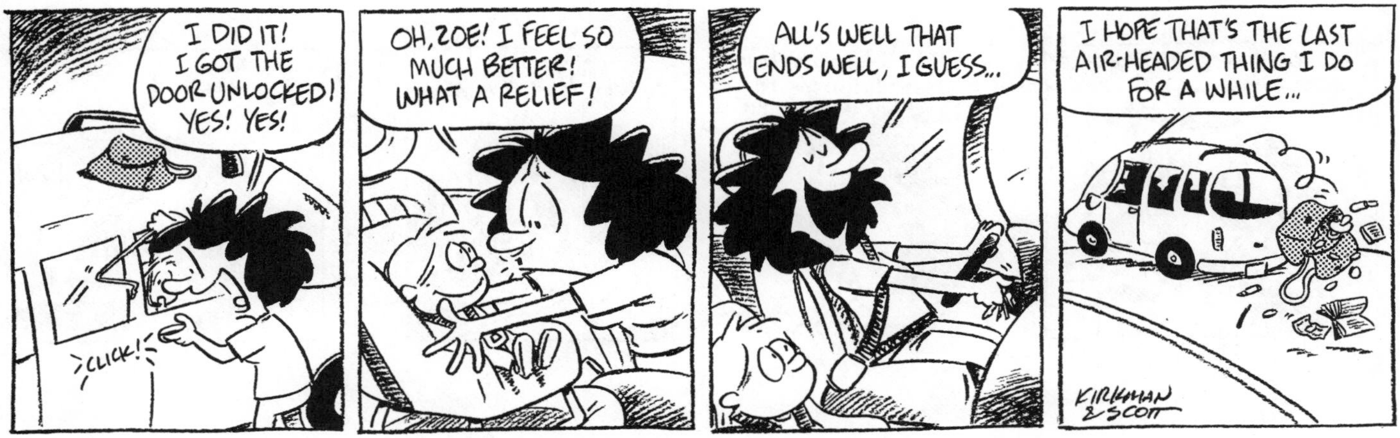
I DID IT! I GOT THE DOOR UNLOCKED! YES! YES!
CLICK!
OH, ZOE! I FEEL SO MUCH BETTER! WHAT A RELIEF!
ALL'S WELL THAT ENDS WELL, I GUESS...
I HOPE THAT'S THE LAST AIR-HEADED THING I DO FOR A WHILE...
KIRKMAN & SCOTT

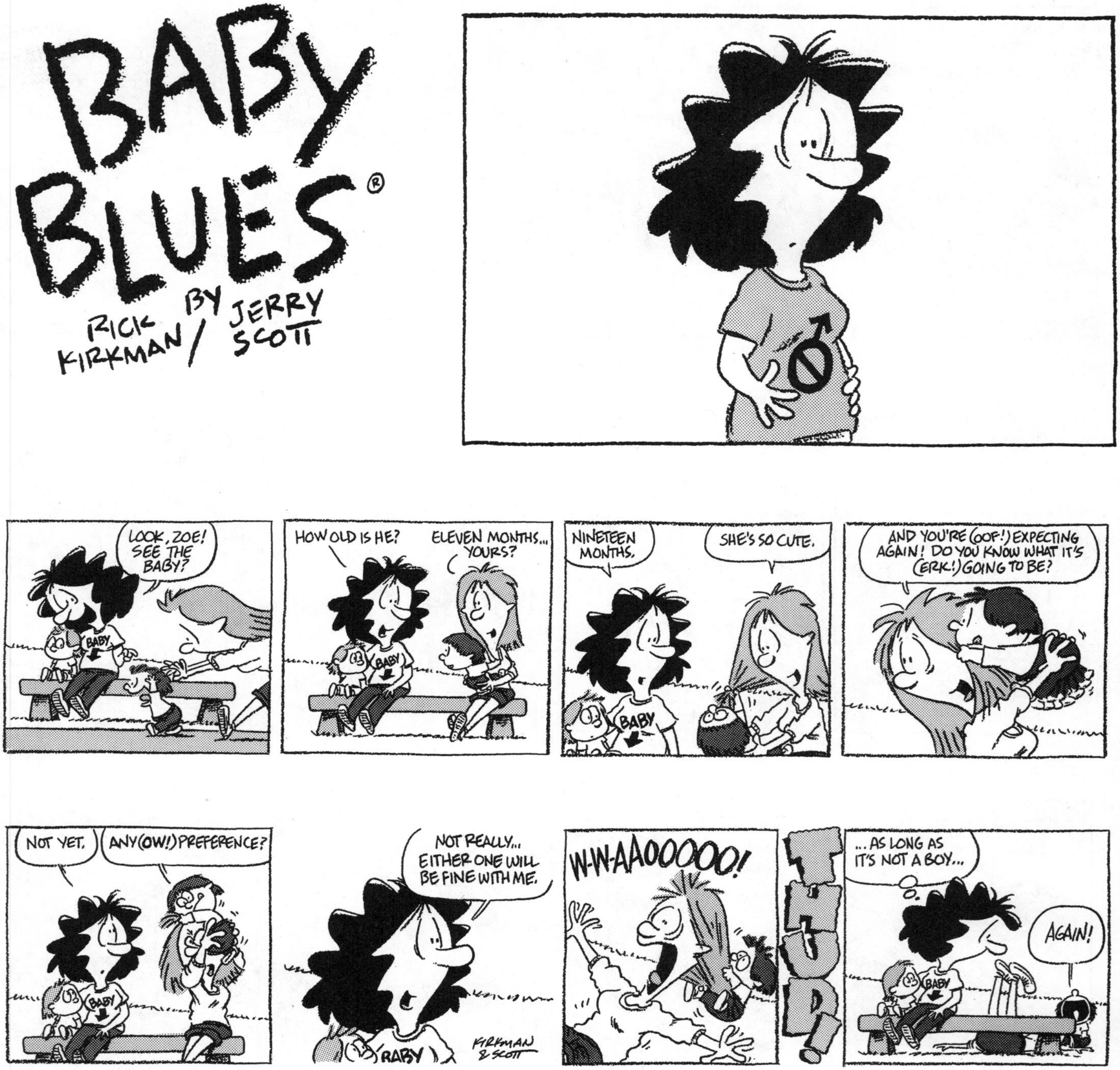

BABY BLUES®
BY RICK KIRKMAN / JERRY SCOTT
LOOK, ZOE! SEE THE BABY?
BABY
HOW OLD IS HE?
ELEVEN MONTHS... YOURS?
NINETEEN MONTHS.
SHE'S SO CUTE.
AND YOU'RE (OOF!) EXPECTING AGAIN! DO YOU KNOW WHAT IT'S (ERK!) GOING TO BE?
NOT YET.
ANY (OW!) PREFERENCE?
NOT REALLY... EITHER ONE WILL BE FINE WITH ME.
KIRKMAN & SCOTT
W-W-AAOOOOO!
THUD!
... AS LONG AS IT'S NOT A BOY...
AGAIN!

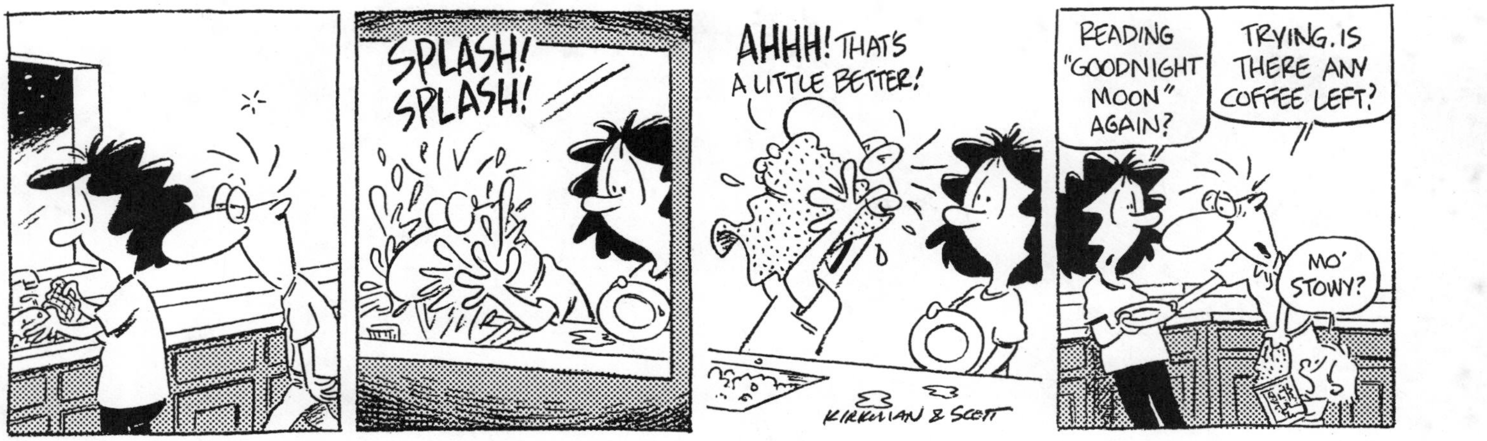
SPLASH!
SPLASH!
AHHH! THAT'S A LITTLE BETTER!
KIRKMAN & SCOTT
READING "GOODNIGHT MOON" AGAIN?
TRYING. IS THERE ANY COFFEE LEFT?
MO' STOWY?

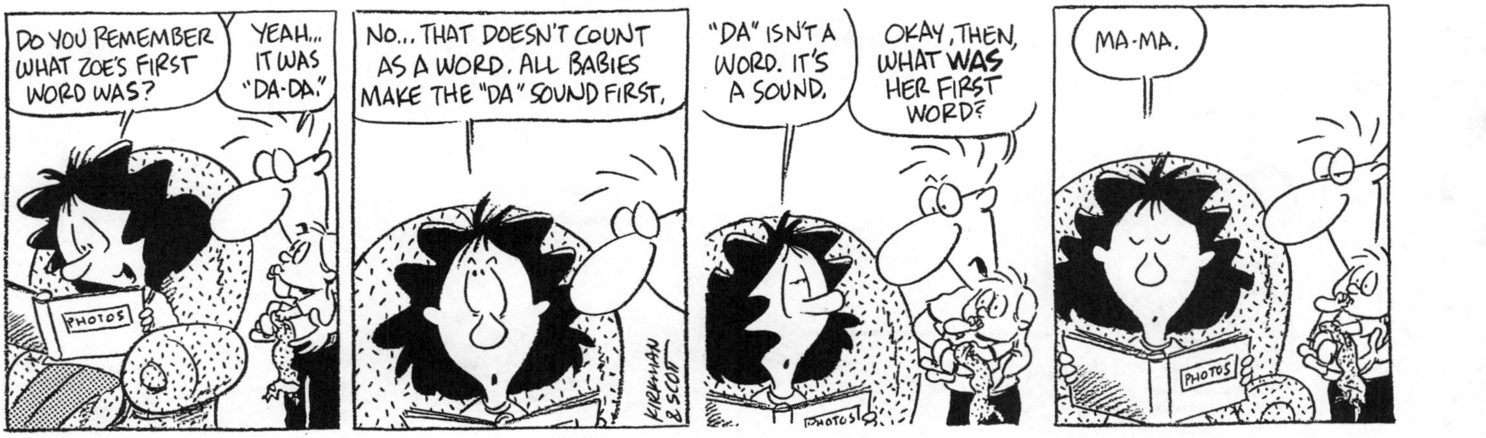
DO YOU REMEMBER WHAT ZOE'S FIRST WORD WAS?
YEAH... IT WAS "DA-DA."
PHOTOS
NO... THAT DOESN'T COUNT AS A WORD. ALL BABIES MAKE THE "DA" SOUND FIRST.
KIRKMAN & SCOTT
"DA" ISN'T A WORD. IT'S A SOUND.
OKAY, THEN, WHAT **WAS** HER FIRST WORD?
MA-MA.
PHOTOS

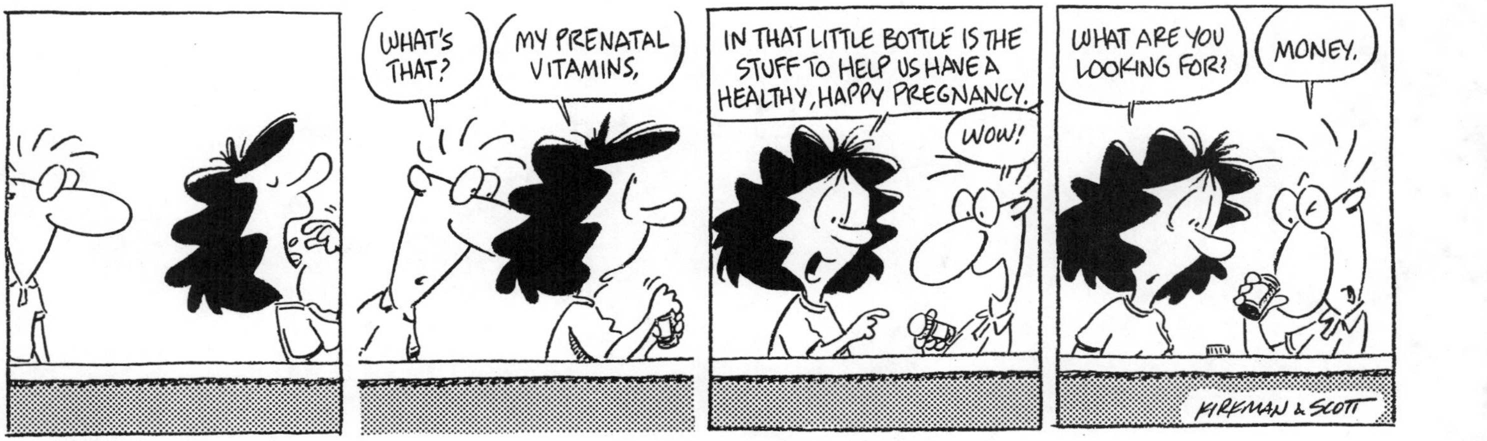
WHAT'S THAT?
MY PRENATAL VITAMINS.
IN THAT LITTLE BOTTLE IS THE STUFF TO HELP US HAVE A HEALTHY, HAPPY PREGNANCY.
WOW!
WHAT ARE YOU LOOKING FOR?
MONEY.
KIRKMAN & SCOTT

The End